Designing Federalism

A Theory of Self-Sustainable Federal Institutions

Because of the redistributive nature of institutions and the availability of implementable alternatives with different distributive consequences, the desire of federation members to change institutional specifics in their favor is a permanent feature of the federal political process. This is so for two reasons. First, states or their equivalents in democratic federations usually can succeed in renegotiating the rules if they feel sufficiently motivated to do so, albeit sometimes at the cost of secession and civil war. Second, in the case of a federation it is more or less clear who stands to benefit from any change in institutions, and coalitions in favor of renegotiation can be easily formed depending on the content of the proposal. Thus, the existence of an equilibrium of constitutional legitimacy at the popular and elite levels cannot be taken for granted. The authors show that the presence in the political process of agents who are "naturally committed" to the status quo institutional arrangement can suffice to coordinate voters to act as if they support existing constitutional arrangements, even if this is not the best option.

Mikhail Filippov received his Ph.D. from the California Institute of Technology in 1998 and is Assistant Professor of Political Science and a Research Fellow at the Center in Political Economy at Washington University in St. Louis, Missouri. He has published articles in *Public Choice*, *Soviet and Post-Soviet Studies*, *Constitutional Political Economy*, and other journals.

Peter C. Ordeshook earned his Ph.D. from the University of Rochester in 1969 and is currently Professor of Political Science at the California Institute of Technology. He has authored and coauthored many books including *Game Theory and Political Theory* (Cambridge, 1986), *The Balance of Power* (Cambridge, 1989), *An Introduction to Positive Political Theory*, *Lessons for Citizens of a New Democracy*, and *A Political Theory Primer*. He is a member of the Academy of Arts and Sciences.

Olga Shvetsova received her Ph.D. from the California Institute of Technology in 1995 and is a Fellow at the Micro Incentives Research Center at Duke University. She has published articles in *American Journal of Political Science*, *Law and Society Review*, *Legislative Studies Quarterly*, *Journal of Theoretical Politics*, and other journals and edited volumes.

Designing Federalism

A Theory of Self-Sustainable Federal Institutions

MIKHAIL FILIPPOV
Washington University, St. Louis

PETER C. ORDESHOOK
California Institute of Technology

OLGA SHVETSOVA
Duke University

CAMBRIDGE
UNIVERSITY PRESS

PUBLISHED BY THE PRESS SYNDICATE OF THE UNIVERSITY OF CAMBRIDGE
The Pitt Building, Trumpington Street, Cambridge, United Kingdom

CAMBRIDGE UNIVERSITY PRESS
The Edinburgh Building, Cambridge CB2 2RU, UK
40 West 20th Street, New York, NY 10011-4211, USA
477 Williamstown Road, Port Melbourne, VIC 3207, Australia
Ruiz de Alarcón 13, 28014 Madrid, Spain
Dock House, The Waterfront, Cape Town 8001, South Africa

http://www.cambridge.org

First published 2004

Printed in the United States of America

Typeface Sabon 10/12 pt. *System* LaTeX 2ε [TB]

A catalog record for this book is available from the British Library.

Library of Congress Cataloging in Publication data

Filippov, Mikhail.
Designing federalism : a theory of self-sustainable federal institutions / Mikhail Filippov, Peter C. Ordeshook, Olga Shvetsova.
p. cm.
Includes bibliographical references and index.
ISBN 0-521-81618-1 (hard) – ISBN 0-521-01648-7 (pbk.)
1. Federal government. 2. Comparative government. 3. World politics – 1989–
I. Ordeshook, Peter C., 1942– II. Shvetsova, Olga (Olga Vitalievna) III. Title.

JC355.F55 2003
321.02′3 – dc21 2003043938

ISBN 0 521 81618 1 hardback
ISBN 0 521 01648 7 paperback

Contents

Figures

Tables

Preface

It is natural, when thinking of democratic federalism, to begin with the classic and most successful examples – the United States, Germany, Australia, Switzerland, Canada, India, and even the more economically underachieving ones of Brazil and Argentina – and to assume that designing a federal state is a well-understood exercise of finding a suitable balance between regional autonomy and federal authority. But focusing on such examples obscures the fact that of seven European federations of the last decade of the twentieth century (Germany, Switzerland, Belgium, Czechoslovakia, Russia, the USSR, and Yugoslavia), three (Czechoslovakia, the USSR, and Yugoslavia) no longer exist, one is hardly guaranteed to remain democratic or federal except in name only (Russia), and another (Belgium) is arguably surviving as a linguistically divided state largely by virtue of its position as the bureaucratic "capital" of a nascent federation, the European Union. Add to this the fact of the American Civil War, Canada's struggle with Quebec separatism, the bloody conflicts that plagued the Swiss Confederation in the first half of the nineteenth century, India's descent to virtual despotic rule under Indira Gandhi, the earlier near disappearance of meaningful Australian federalism, wholly dissolved or disrupted federations (e.g., Mali, Uganda, Cameroon, British West India, Nigeria, Pakistan, Ethiopia), and Europe's often bumpy road to integration, and we can only conclude that the requirements of a successful design are neither trivial nor well understood.

This volume, in fact, is prefaced on the assumption (belief) that successful design, and specifically democratic design, requires something more than the mere negotiation of regional versus central authority or the establishment of a "fair" system of regional representation in the national legislature – the common foci of federal constitutional craftsmanship. Indeed, a second premise of this volume is that the institutional parameters most commonly assumed to be critical to federal success are not sufficient to implement a successful design and may not even be the ones that are of primary importance. We hasten to add that we are not about to argue that success or failure rests with socioeconomic circumstances. We would not deny the importance of such things as ethnic, linguistic, religious, or racial divisions; experience with democratic governance; and the maturity and efficiency of domestic markets. But if, in attempting to implement a stable federal state, we assume that only directly manipulable institutional parameters are at our disposal, then, in addition to the usual variables of federal design, we must consider seemingly tangential matters such as the authority of the federal center's chief executive; the timing of local, regional, and national elections; the bicameral character of the national legislature or appropriately designed substitutes for bicameralism; and the content of regional charters and constitutions.

Our rationale for reaching beyond even constitutional parameters lies in the fact that the essential difficulty with political design generally is that political institutions are, by their very nature, redistributive – different institutions imply different winners and losers so that in the long and short run different people will prefer different institutional arrangements. And the particular difficulty with federal design is that, in addition to those social cleavages with which a designer must often deal, by definition it establishes, coordinates, and legitimizes specific competing interests – notably those of federal subjects as well as the federal center. Add to this the requirement of citizen sovereignty in a democratic state whereby politicians are required to somehow accommodate the potentially myopic self-interest of their constituents, and federalism becomes especially problematic in terms of sustaining a stable institutional structure. Addressing the redistributive nature of design directly, by manipulating only a limited subset of institutional parameters artificially labeled "federal" is unlikely to yield an adequate result. Instead, we argue, the *uniquely* theoretically justifiable approach is to induce a principal-agent relationship between citizens and their elected representatives that is imperfect but nevertheless satisfies the requirements of democratic governance, that redirects political elite motives away from divisive bargaining even if such bargaining serves the myopic interests of those who elect them, and that encourages society generally to reward such imperfect agency. We are led then to those institutional variables that impact the entity that serves as the primary intermediary between citizens acting as voters and political elites acting as election candidates, the political party. Although various scholars note the importance of parties to the operation of federalism, we argue that a properly designed party system encourages the imperfect agency essential to federal success. Put simply, implementing a federal system that is self-sustaining requires that we cast our institutional net widely so as to address those things which impact politicians' strategies as they strive to win and maintain office in a democracy.

Acknowledgments

The ideas for this volume began germinating among us soon after the Soviet Union's collapse in the early 1990s, when academics and politicians within its constituent parts and in the West alike began wrestling with the problems of design and implementability of new democratic orders. The task at hand concerned more than the general and abstract issues of constitutional stability and design; the goal, with Russia especially in mind, was to identify if not the exact parameters of design, then the key substantive mechanism by which choice of such parameters could influence the survival of a federal democratic regime. In the progress that we made since then, we are greatly indebted to the vast literature on the subjects of both federalism and institutional design, historical as well as contemporary. Any study of the subject begins, of course, with *The Federalist Papers*. But what other guideposts to federal design could we identify, what propositions about the sources of constitutional stability, and what additions to the practical discipline of political institutional design (political engineering) had been erected in the two hundred plus years since their authorship? Gems of insight could be found scattered throughout the literature we surveyed, but doubtlessly the most influential contemporary piece of scholarship in our thinking was William H. Riker's *Federalism*, whose words had lingered only half appreciated in the consciousness of one of us for most of an academic career but whose full meaning materialized as our collaboration proceeded.

Among the colleagues who were with us throughout the project, we want to thank Thomas Schwartz first. Much of our thinking about constitutions, constitutional stability, and dimensions of constitutional design was influenced by his suggestions, arguments, and some might even say intellectual badgering. Russian scholars Vyacheslav Nikonov and Leonid Smyrniagin in Moscow challenged us to make our theoretical models consistent with the practical concerns encountered by nascent federations.

We owe intellectual debts to a great many others: to Russell Hardin's essay on constitutions as mechanisms of political coordination, which provided the fundamental insight for us into the perplexing matter of constitutional stability; to George Breslauer, Carol Leonard, Thomas Remington, Phil Roeder, Brian Silver, and Steve Solnick, who shared freely their ideas, insights, and depth of expertise; to William Keech, Thomas Koenig, and Simon Hug for their detailed comments on this volume; to Randal Calvert, James Endersby, Jack Knight, Krishna Ladha, Gary Miller, and Sunita Parikh for their input into its earlier versions; to Viktor Vanberg, Leonid Polishchuk, Itai Sened, Melvin Hinich, and Stephan Voigt, who encouraged the enterprise and cheered us on. We also owe a special debt of gratitude to Norman Schofield for his continued encouragement and support and for the many discussions we have held with him both about the book's material and more generally in the context of constitutional design.

Of the various conferences that proved especially valuable wherein some of the ideas offered here were set before colleagues in preliminary form, we would like especially to note Washington University Center in Political Economy's "Constitutions, Voting and Democracy" (St. Louis, 2001) and Leonid Smyrnagin's workshop on regional constitutional design (Moscow, 1995). Our work was in part supported by the National Science Foundation (Shvetsova) and the National Council for East European and Eurasian Research (Ordeshook).

Of course, the faults of the volume are of our own making, our only excuse being that the subjects of federalism and constitutional design are of such scope and complexity that no single contribution can do all things. We ask only that readers proceed with the idea that this volume merely offers a hypothesis about parties, democracy, and federalism that, like any other in the practical science of political institutional design, can only be "tested" to the extent that it raises the salience of certain matters in the minds of those who would actually design and implement a democratic federal state.

1

Federations and the Theoretical Problem

> Federalism is the main alternative to empire as a technique of aggregating large areas under one government.
>
> Riker 1964: 5

> Federalism is commonly understood as a theory of government that uses power to check power amid opposite and rival interests. Authority is limited, and no single body exercises supreme control nor has a monopoly over the use of force in society. But the idea of federalism is rendered trivial when applied only to the coexistence of state and national governments. Rather, federalism offers no less than an enabling basis for the development of self-organizing and self-governing capabilities under conditions of equal liberty and justice.
>
> Ostrom 1991: xi

1.1 Why Federalism

Before we can develop the preceding argument, we should first consider the reasons why federalism is often deemed a desirable governmental form, along with some definitions and the classic explanations for federal political stability and instability. We can begin by noting that, at a more detailed level than the assertion by Riker with which we introduce this chapter, federalism has two general justifications, one economic and the other political.[1]

The economic justification should be well known. Government (i.e., coercive) action may be required to resolve those market failures associated with informational asymmetries, externalities, and wholly decentralized decision making over public goods. However, public goods in particular vary in their

[1] For a survey of the classical justifications of federalism, see Kenyon and Kincaid (1991); Inman and Rubinfeld (1996); Qian and Weingast (1997); Breton (2000); Kincaid (2001).

characteristics, which, in turn, may require different treatments by different levels of government. For example, if the demand for such a particular government service varies with geographic location, if some public good is more efficiently produced locally, if the externalities associated with its provision and consumption have a limited geographic domain, if there are reasons for believing that information about the demand and supply of public services is necessarily more evident to local and regional polities than to national ones, or if economies of scale in the production of such goods can be realized adequately at subnational governmental levels, then the decentralized decision making that is assumed to characterize federalism – decision making that encourages competition among political subunits and the monitoring of public officials by those directly affected by their actions – allows for a more appropriate treatment of public policy. On the other hand, if there are significant externalities in consumption and production that cross political geographic boundaries, or if there are extensive economies of scale, then the treatment of "market failures" by a more unitary government can, in principle at least, better resolve market failures. The ideal federalism, then, is one that allocates the responsibilities of the state across levels of government according to rational criteria. Moreover, because technology, taste, and our understanding of things are never static, the decentralization and political competition that federalism allows offer the possibility of designing a state that can, in principle at least, move back and forth between acting in a centralized versus a decentralized way, and that makes such adjustments over time and across issues according to fixed democratic rules, especially those safeguarding individual rights.

The political justifications for federalism are somewhat more varied. They include allowing minorities – ethnic, religious, linguistic, or otherwise – the autonomy they often demand as "payment" for their acquiescence to the coercive powers of the national government, allowing for the protection of the rights of those minorities as well as the rights of all others in the federation, and allowing for local and regional control of purely local and regional matters so as to discourage the alienation that people might feel from a more distant and seemingly less controllable central government. In theory at least federalism allows individuals to join those with whom they share similar tastes for government services, thus opening the door to a general level of welfare – and, presumably, a degree of satisfaction with political institutions – unavailable to a unitary state. Federalism also is intended to allow for the decentralization of conflict, a mechanism whereby political barriers are established so as to preclude purely regional conflicts from disrupting national politics. Finally, those political entities who would form or join a federation may not be willing to abrogate their political authority wholly, and a degree of regional autonomy is often the only compromise that allows the establishment of a viable state in lieu of uncoordinated action.

Our purpose here, however, is not to survey in detail the purported benefits of federalism, the presumed advantages of federal versus unitary forms, or even the extent to which those benefits have in fact been realized in one federation or another.[2] We assume simply that such benefits exist and are theoretically attainable, and we assume as well that a federal state of some type either exists or that the decision to create one has been made. Our goal is not to justify federalism per se. We are not specifically concerned with such matters as whether Britain should be federal, whether the dismemberment of Yugoslavia is a good or bad thing, or whether Quebec should be allowed to secede from Canada. Rather, *after a decision to be federal is made*, our goal is to identify the structure of a federal state's political institutions – constitutional and statutory – that best encourage survival and its ability to meet those economic and political objectives that otherwise justify its existence.

The reason for the institutional focus implied by the preceding sentence is twofold. First, historically at least, federalism, sometimes seemingly independent of how well it has accomplished its economic or political objectives, has not been a notably successful governmental form. The ultimate character of American federalism, including the basic feature of the supremacy of federal over state law, was determined only through a civil war, even though the country at that time could not be said to have been experiencing any great economic or (intrawhite) ethnic crisis. Canada's federal stability remains precarious despite that country's relative prosperity, while Nigerian democracy has failed repeatedly.[3] Federalism in Mexico has, at least in the past, been more cosmetic than real. Democratic federalism in Argentina has only recently reappeared after a fifty-three-year hiatus. The Czechoslovak federation was dissolved even though its economic and ethnic conflicts arguably paled in comparison to other states, including some surviving federations. The dissolution of the Soviet Union seems only to have intensified the economic difficulties of its component parts and opened some of those parts to the rise of communal conflict. And few people argue that the survival of Russia as a *democratic* federation, regardless of how much money the International Monetary Fund (IMF) sinks into it, is assured.

[2] For one study that raises questions about the value of decentralized federal decision making in emerging democracies and developing economies, see Wibbels (2000), who argues that in a federal state "the coordination of national fiscal and monetary policies as adjustment tools is complicated, posing a challenge to national economic stability" (p. 688), and that "the price of ongoing decentralization in the federal systems of the developing world can be quite high" (p. 699).

[3] The First Nigerian Federal Republic started with Nigeria's independence in October 1960. The military overthrew the government in January 1966 and ruled until September 1979. The Second Republic lasted from October 1979 to December 1983, when the military resumed the control (Diamond 1988). Nonmilitary democratic rule was restored in May 1999. Yet in the first three years since military rule ended, more than 10,000 people are believed to have been killed in ethnic and religious clashes (*New York Times*, February 24, 2002).

The second justification for our focus on institutional design is our argument that the institutional variables commonly attended to in federal design – constitutional clauses pertaining to federal subject representation in a national legislature, the identities of federal subjects, the right or prohibition of secession, the supremacy of federal law, comity, the rights of federal subjects in amending a national constitution, and statements prescribing the policy jurisdictions of federal subjects versus the national government including the authority to tax – are not the uniquely critical parameters that need to be attended to. First, such clauses cannot guarantee their own enforcement, and unless they are somehow fortified by direct incentives for political participants to uphold them – unless, in the jargon of political science, they are deemed legitimate by the population generally, or, in the jargon of economics, unless they are made a part of an incentive-compatible system in which political actors find it in their self-interest to abide by them – they become mere "parchment barriers" and irrelevant to actual political processes. This is not to say that such clauses and constraints are unimportant, and it is essential that some of them be assigned specific values (e.g., prohibiting secession). But they are not sufficient for the smooth operation of a federation, democratic or otherwise. We must also attend to a second level of design that structures political processes generally, with a clear understanding of how constraints of one type interact with institutions that might otherwise seem tangential to federal matters. Thus, the things that are often omitted from the list of a constitution's explicitly "federal provisions" – the authority of a chief executive, the organization of the judiciary, and the structure of a separation of powers – are, as we argue subsequently, also critical institutional dimensions of design.

A central argument of this volume, however, is that federal design cannot stop even here, since doing so fails to address the issue of enforcement – in this case, the enforcement of the constitution as a whole. Designing a federation, then, requires that we attend to a level of institutional structure that deals specifically with individual political incentives. Some parts of this third level are formally stated and, therefore, subject to an explicit blueprint. Other parts are informally defined and, thereby, serve more as constraints on our architectural enterprise. Still other parts correspond to what we might term spontaneously generated institutions – institutional structures that arise in response to the other components of a political system but which, once formed, exert an influence that needs to be understood if we are to understand the requirements of federal design generally. The formal (and, in some instances, the spontaneous) components of this third level, which consists of such things as the political institutional structure of federal subjects and the local, regional, and national laws that shape party systems, typically receive scant attention when federal design is discussed but are crucial to the issue of self-enforcement as well as federal stability and performance.

Of course, at this point there is little reason to suppose that the logic of our argument about the scope of federal design is clear or persuasive. Nevertheless, our focus on institutions is dictated as well by the simple fact that formally defined institutions are the *only* things at our disposal when designing a federal state. Although we can assume that society's culture and traditions are critical determinants of the likelihood that constitutional democracy can flourish within it, we cannot assume that we can mold the human psyche, political culture, or even the structure of an economy. Although certainly influenced by institutions in the long run, the purposeful manipulation of such things, even if possible, lies in uncharted territory. Thus, if a democratic state, federal or otherwise, can be implemented, this inevitably requires the judicious selection of political institutions based on a comprehensive understanding of how alternative institutions interact with each other and with the prevailing political environment, and how they shape and are shaped by people's motives and actions.

1.2 Definitions

Federalism

Before we can even outline our argument, we should state some of the ground rules of analysis. First, we do not want to debate alternative definitions of federalism. We can, if necessary, adopt a definition such as Riker's (1964: 11), which identifies a federalism as a state in which "(1) two levels of government rule the same land and people, (2) each level has at least one area of action in which it is autonomous, and (3) there is some [constitutional] guarantee . . . of the autonomy of each government in its own sphere." With this definition or any other, however, we cannot envision a classification of states into discrete federal and unitary categories that would not be subject to criticism or require any number of footnotes. Does the autonomy allowed some of Spain's and Ukraine's regions render those states "federal" despite the fact that their constitutions make no mention of federalism per se? Is the United States "less federal" today than in say the nineteenth century when state and local revenues dwarfed those of the national government? If our answer to this question is yes, then do we need to offer a definition of federalism that allows for a continuous concept rather than discrete categories? The fact is that every government affords local authorities some degree of autonomy, and every ostensibly federal state exhibits (of necessity) a degree of central control. Thus, regardless of what definition we apply, it is apparent that federalism is not a concept amenable to an unambiguous descriptive definition.

The problem of definition is perhaps most readily understood by considering some of the substantive differences within these cases. To begin, Table 1.1 shows the considerable variability among federations as to the fiscal autonomy of federal subjects relative to the national government.

TABLE 1.1. *Subnational Governments' Revenues as a Percentage of Total Government Revenue*

	1997	1995	1990	1985	1980	1975
Argentina	39.8	37.3	37.7	16.5	25.0	–
Australia	32.7	33.0	28.3	25.8	24.3	24.1
Austria	24.4	27.3	26.9	28.5	26.3	28.1
Belgium	6.0	6.3	5.4	6.0	5.2	–
Brazil	33.8		25.0	21.8	24.3	–
Canada	52.3	53.8	52.7	52.6	52.6	47.8
Former Czechoslovakia	–	–	20.3	–	–	–
Former Yugoslavia	–	–	78.1	72.9	73.1	20.0
Germany	32.9	33.9	35.2	35.5	36.7	37.2
India	33.0	34.2	32.7	32.1	33.4	32.7
Malaysia	15.2	15.6	17.7	13.6	15.3	13.8
Mexico	22.9	20.9	20.7	19.9	18.5	19.3
Pakistan	–	–	–	–	–	22.8
Russian Federation	40.7	38.2	–	–	–	–
Spain	19.3	16.1	16.1	14.8	11.1	4.9
Switzerland	43.2	43.8	50.3	52.1	47.3	48.3
United States	41.7	41.5	41.7	39.9	36.6	39.6

Source: The data are selected from the *Fiscal Decentralization Indicators*, International Monetary Fund, available at <http://www1.worldbank.org/publicsector/decentralization/fiscalindicators.htm>.

Thus, even though all countries listed are (or were) federations, this measure of the fiscal autonomy of federal subjects suggests that Germany and Australia are "twice as centralized" as the United States and Canada, and three times as much as Switzerland. McKay (2000: table 3), however, offers an even more interesting table on the data from which we base our Table 1.2 that augments his findings with additional data and countries. As he summarizes his data, "[i]n the USA, Switzerland and Canada, borrowing is effectively controlled by market discipline alone or, in the case of the USA and Switzerland, by state constitutional and other limitations. In Germany, rules require borrowing to be confined to investment needs, while in Australia borrowing rules are agreed on jointly by the states and the federal government" (McKay 2000: 33). Again, even if we ignore the European Union (EU), which is the purpose of his comparisons, the important point is that there is considerable variation in the character of fiscal relations across states that are universally taken to be classic examples of the species.

Tables 1.1 and 1.2 reveal but a small fraction of the differences we can document across federations. In addition, we could consider, for example, differences in the allocation of policy jurisdictions (such as the administration of social security), the earmarking of specific tax sources to specific

TABLE 1.2. *Fiscal Arrangements and the State Role in National Tax Decisions in the Late 1990s*

	Australia	United States	Canada	Germany	Switzerland	India	Russia	European Union
State tax conformity[a]	Yes	Very little	Yes	Yes	None	Yes	Yes	None
State tax uniformity	Yes	No	Little	Yes	No	Little	Yes	No (except min. VAT rate)
Single tax administration and collection	Yes	No	Yes	Yes	No	No	Yes	No
Central authorities account for most taxes	Yes	Yes	Yes	Yes	No	Yes	Yes	No
Transfers to subnational governments from other governments, 1995[b]	39	30	24	24	23	40	15	–
Central government controls state-level borrowing	Yes	No	No	Yes	No	Yes	Yes	Yes

[a] State tax conformity and state tax uniformity refer to the extent to which constitutions and federal governments require federal units to standardize tax types and rates (McKay 2000).

[b] Percentage of total subnational revenues and grants.

Sources: McKay (2000); *Fiscal Decentralization Indicators*, International Monetary Fund, available at <www1.worldbank.org/publicsector/decentralization/fiscalindicators.htm>.

levels of government, the structure of federal subject representation in the national government, and the role of federal subjects in determining national policy generally. We should also be cognizant of the fact that the character of a federation itself may undergo fundamental change so as to belie the adequacy of any definition. For example, we might suppose that the locus of control of defense and monetary policy is a sure way to differentiate between federations and confederations. But even here we must confront the fact that the United States relied largely on state militias through the mid-nineteenth century and did not possess a central bank between 1832 and 1913. An alternative way, then, of defining the subject of this volume is to examine answers to a series of more specific and restrictive questions. For example, we can ask whether a state, to be deemed federal, must be explicitly identified as such in its constitution. Are all self-proclaimed federations, including democratic ones, necessarily federations in substance? Must the national government in a federation take a particular form – must it have, for instance, an upper legislative chamber with "meaningful" authority and explicit regional representation? What role does the word "sovereignty" play in a definition of federalism vis-à-vis a federation's constituent parts, its federal subjects? Is there anything necessarily hierarchical in a federation's intergovernmental relations, or is its structure best described as a matrix with no ranking applicable to its cells? Is there anything mystical about the number two, or can we imagine federations with three or even four or more autonomous levels of governmental structure?[4] Are we necessarily limited to a geographically defined conceptualization of federal subjects – why not subjects defined in terms of occupation, ethnicity, or the language one uses in the home?[5]

4 Any meaningful description of the Swiss institutional system, for example, would necessarily emphasize its three-tiered system of government: (1) the communes, at the local level, (2) the cantons, at the intermediate level, and (3) the Confederation, at the national level. In particular, the Swiss system is based on the sovereignty of both the cantons and local communities. The federal government cannot bypass cantonal governments to address local governments, either to impose or to negotiate fiscal or financial matters or the regulation and provision of public goods. Conversely, local governments lack formal direct access to the national government (Dafflon 1999).

5 One can speculate about the feasibility of a nongeographically defined federal system. Why not a system, for instance, in which as in the former Soviet Union, interests are given representation and some degree of autonomous governance? Renner and Bauer (cited in Linder 1998) suggest that nonterritorial federal forms may be an important means of resolving ethnic issues (see also Ra'anan 1990). Geography assumes its importance largely for exogenous reasons such as the historically difficult matter of efficiently organizing governance among a geographically dispersed population, which is a reason that may fade into obsolescence with new technologies of communication. Equivalently, there is the simple fact that many of the goods and services that concern collective action possess an important geographic component to their descriptions. For an analysis of a *functional* federalism that is based on nongeographically defined identities, see Casella and Frey (1992) and Laponce (1995).

That satisfactory answers to such questions, universally acknowledged as such (see Scharpf 1997), elude us despite decades of research suggests that wrangling over definitions and classifications is not a productive way to proceed toward a general theory of federal design. The consequence of such wrangling, in fact, is the absence of any consensus over what would constitute a general theory or even an overall conceptual scheme for thinking about it. Unsurprisingly, then, a fluidity and vagueness of ideas commonly substitutes for theory, and scholars seem compelled to speak of a "spectrum of federal societies" (Livingston 1952), a "continuum" of federal regimes, and "varieties of federal arrangements" (Elazar 1995). The fact of the matter is that federalism is not a primitive theoretical construct, and it can be identified, if it can be identified at all, only after we possess a theory of democratic decentralization that offers a clear specification of theoretical primitives and their logical relations that allow for fluid and sometimes ambiguous definitions of subsidiary concepts and constructs.[6]

Thus, rather than contribute to any conceptual or definitional wrangling, for purposes of this volume we shall say simply (and no less vaguely than our predecessors) that a state is federal if its governmental structure can be characterized by multiple layers (generally national, regional, and local) such that at each level the chief policy makers – governors, presidents, prime ministers, legislatures, parliaments, judges – are elected directly by the people they ostensibly serve or (as with judges) appointed by public officials thus directly elected at that level. To this we will, as a matter of convention, suppose that the subgovernments within a federation are geographic in nature. If a reader wishes to substitute a different definition, we are open to suggestions; we offer this one merely to outline, however imprecisely, the domain of our subject. The reference to elections in our definition, however, makes it clear that we also want to limit our subject matter to *democratic* federations, although, as with the concept of "federation," we do not want to contend fully with the definition of democracy. For example, although allegations of corruption along with undue governmental influence in the mass media permeate Russia's electoral processes, the entry of politicians and parties seems sufficiently open, even following the political "reforms" of 2000–1, to allow us to categorize Russia as a democratic federation, albeit an imperfect one. In contrast, the Soviet Union, although ostensibly federal, was not democratic,

[6] In this respect we recall the wrangling that occurred over the concept of power in political science through much of the 1950s, 1960s, and, 1970s. No satisfactory and generally accepted definition was ever, to our knowledge, achieved, and, indeed, once the individualistic rational choice paradigm gained acceptance in the profession, such wrangling ended with the understanding that theorizing about politics could proceed without a formal definition of power. Once a more comprehensive and logically structured paradigm appeared, power was seen to be little more than a convenient linguistic shorthand and certainly not a theoretical primitive.

and we have little interest in identifying institutions that would facilitate the stability of such an entity.[7]

Our subject matter, then, encompasses the usual suspects – Canada, the United States, Germany, India, Switzerland, Australia, and Russia.[8] But even though states such as Spain, Italy, and Ukraine do not call themselves federations (indeed, the meaning and content of federalism are hotly debated in these countries),[9] the combination there of democratic process and regional autonomy makes them susceptible to similar challenges as confronted by the formally federal states. In fact, our study becomes especially relevant there if they eventually choose to become more explicitly federal and if we want to understand the debates surrounding the choice of alternatives. Similarly, although monetary union does not by itself make the European Union a fully formed federation,[10] the lessons we develop here can be applied to this entity as well. We hope to show, in fact, that the EU, absent a significant overhaul of its basic structure and a reformulation of its theoretical underpinnings, is unlikely to function with the efficiency of, say, the U.S. or German models.

There is one final reason for preferring a relaxed attitude toward the definition and delineation of the object of our study. As will hopefully become clear as we proceed, a federal state is not, in our scheme, one that necessarily corresponds to some specific institutional description. Although the subject matter of this volume is institutional design, defining federalism in strictly institutional terms – in terms of, say, the allocation of jurisdictional responsibilities and notions of state sovereignty – places too great a constraint on design. Echoing the words of Ostrom (1991) that introduce this chapter, for us, ultimately, democratic federalism corresponds more to a process in which there is a continuous ebb and flow of authority among levels of government in accord with the preferences of its citizens and subject to the constraints of individual rights. Put differently, our concern here is that of describing institutions of self-governance that are self-sustaining, that ensure individual rights and the adaptation of those rights to varying circumstances, and that encourage those policy outcomes we ideally associate with a "well-functioning" federal state. Whether the institutions that are best suited to achieve these ends satisfy one definition of federalism or

[7] Later we argue that the mechanisms that encouraged the USSR's seventy-plus years of survival paralleled those that encourage stability in any democratic federation, although they were not based on any system of formal constitutional incentives.

[8] For a full list of contemporary federal regimes, see Elazar (1994). Lemco (1991) provides a list of federal regimes that existed between 1579 and 1983.

[9] On the Spanish debates, see Hennessy (1989), Agranoff (1996), Solozabal (1996); the Italian debates are reviewed in Woods (1992); Newell (1998); Amoretti (2002). For an introduction to the issue of federalism in Ukraine, see Solchanyk (1994); Wolczuk (2002).

[10] For the discussion of the federal characteristics of the European Community/European Union, see Scharpf (1988); Brown-John (1995); Hesse and Wright (1996); Wincott (1996); Sbragia (1993); McKay (1996); Warleigh (1998); Abromeit (2002).

another is not our concern. Indeed, it may be the case that the theoretical prerequisites for achieving these ends will correspond to one person's definition only after we add to it some substantive constraints that apply to one polity but not another.

It is also possible, of course, that in the end, no definitive demarcation of our subject is possible and that we must instead accept the proposition that every unitary state has federal features and that every federal state can be described as a unitary whole along one or more descriptive dimensions. If this is the case – if, for instance, the local elections allowed in, say, Sweden open the door to the problems of federal design we describe here – the theory of democratic federalism we offer is simply more general than we otherwise suggest and applies to some degree to democracies universally. Indeed, given that the concept of federalism is not a theoretical primitive, we would be surprised if it were otherwise. For example, then, when we speak of a federal state "reverting" to a unitary form, we are not asserting that it has somehow been transformed into an entity about which we can say nothing, but only that it is now something that in some ways no longer meets the design criteria of those who sought to establish a state with certain minimal features of political decentralization and regional and local government autonomy.

Stability

This volume also makes extensive use of the word "stable." But as with "democracy" and "federation," we suspect that no definition can be wholly satisfactory, nor can we assume that there exists a definition that allows for an unambiguous classification of states. For example, is Canada stable today, is Ethiopia stable despite Eritrea's secession, and is Britain stable despite Scotland's relatively successful push for greater autonomy? Should we deem Italy stable only as long as the Lega Lombardy fails to surpass some predefined threshold of electoral support? At what point between 1787 and 1860 did the United States become unstable, or is the fact of its civil war evidence that it was always unstable? Would we have labeled the USSR stable even as late as 1990? We cannot even say, then, that stability is akin to pornography – something we recognize when we see it. Stability for the Framers of the U.S. Constitution (or at least for Hamilton and Madison) required some permanence both to the law and in a state's "fundamental" institutions (Miller and Hammond 1989), and clearly by stability we mean continuity of those political processes we deem democratic.

But which institutions are "fundamental" and how much change can we admit in them and the law and still apply the label "stable"? The United States, for example, has undergone significant modification of its institutions, both formally and informally. Comparing the United States in 1800 (or even along some dimensions, 1865) with the country today, we find, among other institutional changes, at least the following: (1) direct election rather than appointment of senators; (2) the authority of the Supreme Court to rule on the constitutionality of federal law and the consistency of state and local laws with the federal constitution and federal statutes; (3) uniform direct election rather than state legislative selection of presidential electors; (4) uniform application of single-mandate election districts for the U.S. Congress; (5) uniform application of the requirement of one man, one vote; (6) universal suffrage; (7) the establishment of a quasi-constitutional national bank explicitly entrusted with monetary stability; and (8) a national income tax. And to these changes we can add the emergence of a stable two-party system as well as an extensive list of federal and state regulatory incursions into the private sector. Although most of these changes occurred incrementally so that other components of the system were allowed to adjust to them, they nevertheless represent important modifications of the original federal design set forth in 1787. Despite this and with the sole exception of its Civil War (which, incidentally, was a period in which few of these changes occurred), it is hardly unreasonable to classify the United States as anything but a stable federation.

Nor can we define stability in terms of the relations between levels of government. In the United States, for example, how would we reconcile the attribution stable with the fact that in 1902 the ratio of national to state and local revenues was .6 and today stands at approximately 1.0, or that the ratio of local to national revenues stood at 1.3 in 1902 and today at .4? If money is the "mother's milk of politics," then mom's identity has undergone significant change in this century. Although this change, like others, has occurred largely in an evolutionary way, few persons could object even today to Woodrow Wilson's (1911: 173) conclusion that "the question of the relation of the States to the federal government is the cardinal question of our constitutional system. At every turn of our national development we have been brought face to face with it and no definition either of statesmen or judges has ever quieted or decided it. It cannot, indeed, be settled by one generation because it is a question of growth, and every successive stage of our political and economic development gives it a new aspect, makes it a new question."

The notion of stability, then, along with that of an institutional equilibrium, must be treated cautiously and with the understanding that both allow for ongoing modifications in institutions and intergovernmental relations. Instead, to be judged stable a state must meet the minimal requirement of allowing change under preestablished rules – generally, constitutionally prescribed rules. But because even constitutions can be amended or supplanted according to established procedures, because secession may be constitutional, and because even a military junta can claim legitimacy as defender of a constitutional order, stability must, like federalism itself, remain an ill-defined and poorly measured concept. Somewhat vaguely, then, stability here will be taken to require a "relatively" peaceful, constitutional, and democratic adaptation of a political system to changing circumstances.

A state with an active and viable secessionist movement within it will not be deemed stable, nor will one that is subject to military usurpation of civil authority. But a state in which there is no sharp disruption of democratic process, in which politics is largely of secondary concern to most citizens, in which intergovernmental relations proceed and evolve according to constitutional rules, and in which the military remains subservient to civil authority will be deemed stable.[11] Stability, then, is an empirical dual of an institutional equilibrium whereby formal rules and individual motives generally and over time remain in agreement.

Institution

The preceding definition requires at least one point of clarification – namely, what we mean by institution. Briefly, for purposes of this volume we will interpret institutions as "a set of rules that structure interactions among actors" (Knight 1992: 3). They may influence behavior by changing people's expectations about the consequences of their actions, by changing their preferences over outcomes in some fundamental way, or by limiting or expanding their choices. Institutions, then, can correspond to a complex nexus of rules that we call a constitution, to a single rule we label a norm or law, or to the formalized framework of some organizational entity that defines a complete context of individual choice such as a legislature, a ministry, or bureaucracy.

To this definition we add one additional requirement: to be labeled an institution, the object must be directly manipulable, subject to conscious design, creation, modification, and even elimination. Thus, although a social norm such as those taught us by our parents may also be described as a "rule" that shapes preferences and action, and although both institutions and norms undergo evolutionary development, the things we label social norms generally fall outside of the scope of political institutional design. They, as part of the abstract thing we might call society's culture and traditions, are best viewed as inputs to political design and constraints with which, if prudence is to dictate our choices, our institutions should not seek to violate.

Regardless of which definition or set of labels we employ, we cannot discuss and understand institutions without at the same time understanding the incentives they engender for individual action. To see what we mean,

[11] One can argue that no country fits this definition. Even if we ignore its civil war, we should not forget the discussion among radical Federalists in the early years of the American republic of the possibility of leading New England out of the Union in opposition to Jefferson's Republicans, the Mormon Wars later in that century, bloody Kansas, the turmoil of third parties, and virtual military rule in the West. But we should not also lose sight of the extension of democratic institutions as territories moved to statehood. Our notion of stability, then, is more an ideal type – a design goal against which we judge the success of one design against another, even if it is not a goal that is ever wholly attained.

note that the political analysis of institutions typically proceeds by taking them as fixed constraints on people's actions, so that, for example, when studying elections we might take as fixed the requirements for being a voter or a candidate as well as the rules for aggregating votes that define winning. In this way, with specific assumptions about the preferences of the primary decision makers (e.g., the policy preferences of the electorate in combination with the assumption that participants labeled "candidates" prefer to "win"), we can try to deduce the strategies or choices of all participants and assess, for instance, the consequences of a plurality rule contest versus one that is held under majority rule with a runoff. However, this level of analysis, though necessary, is not sufficient for an understanding of the sources of such things as federal stability. The study of federalism is, of necessity, a macroanalysis of political systems, and as such we must also consider institutions that arise spontaneously as a product of other institutions and which, subsequently, either modify the impact of those prior institutional forms or supplant them altogether.[12] Indeed, as any student of politics and constitutionalism knows, few if any institutions are wholly immutable. Most, even under favorable and relatively unchanging circumstances, are difficult to treat as fixed and commanding universal compliance.

Given our earlier definition, these possibilities might lead us to ask whether something ought to be labeled an institution if it is mutable and a product of the choices it encourages. One can, of course, respond to such questions with the answer that any system of formalized rules can be labeled an institution even if it does not structure interaction in the intended way, structures interactions only weakly, or allows for its own evolutionary development. Nevertheless, such questions emphasize the practical fact that to understand an institution's full meaning we need to learn the incentives of people to abide by the rules and procedures that describe it, including their incentive to keep those rules and procedures in place. Suppose we learn in some specific context that, ceteris paribus, institution X is better suited to ensuring federal stability than institution Y. A mere description of X and Y, though, is of little practical value if there is nothing among the ceteris paribus conditions or among the motives X establishes that would keep relevant decision makers from subverting those rules or substituting a different set altogether. Thus, although it is tempting to attribute Switzerland's highly decentralized form of federalism to its system of referenda and the multiple opportunities for different sets of political actors to veto change, we cannot, without further argument, give such "explanations" the status of fundamental (necessary and sufficient) cause until we also understand how and why these institutional constraints are sustained.

[12] For an elaboration of the idea of the spontaneously generated institution set in the context of constitutional choice and endogenous enforcement, see Voigt (1999).

Self-Enforcement

This treatment of institutions returns us to the notion of stability and our final definition – that of the *self-enforcing institution*. An institution is said to be self-enforcing if the motives it engenders among the individual decision makers empowered to change or otherwise subvert its rules and procedures leave them with an interest in maintaining the institutional status quo. For example, election rules are often self-enforcing whenever they can be changed only by those who are elected under them, for the simple reason that people are unlikely to want to change the rules of a game in which they are the winners.[13] Federative institutions, on the other hand, are particularly problematic from the point of view of enforcement. Consider the European fascination with the notion of *subsidiarity*, or, in everyday language, with provisions that specify the legitimate prerogatives of the national government versus those of federal subjects. If we were so bold as to assume that such rules dictated the policies that different governments pursued or did not pursue, we might contemplate a study of the comparative treatments of different issues based on such prescriptions. However, anyone familiar with the interpretations that have been given in the course of two hundred years to those few clauses in the U.S. Constitution that differentiate between federal and state prerogatives or that empower the national government to act in matters of public policy knows the inherent political flexibility of language and how that language will either be contorted or ignored to serve individual interests. Thus, to understand the implications, if any, of constitutional allocations of authority, we also need to know the incentives of people to keep or change them. Put differently, the meaning of institutions cannot be discerned without understanding the incentives of people to abide by them or to interpret them one way or another.

We need to be especially careful, however, when attempting to infer or deduce motives from an institutional description. Consider, for instance, the common election requirement that unless a candidate receives at least half of the votes cast, there will be a runoff contest between the two strongest candidates. Generally, this requirement is imposed to ensure that the eventual winner commands majority support of at least half of the participating electorate. Suppose, on the other hand, that we require a runoff only if no one receives, say, 40 percent or more of the vote. It might seem, then, that we have diminished the likelihood of majority winners. But notice that if

[13] This is not to say that election rules are never changed, but only that if they are, this will most likely be done in a way to add to the advantages of incumbents, as when suffrage is extended in the attempt to bolster the electoral coalition of those in power. Nor should we ignore wholly exogenous events that dictate institutional change. Keyssar (2000: xxi), for example, in his comprehensive history of suffrage in the United States notes the fact that "nearly all of the major expansions of the franchise that have occurred in American history took place either during or in the wake of war... the demands of both war itself and preparedness for war created powerful pressures to enlarge the right to vote."

we raise the bar from 40 to 50 percent, we may be doing little more that increasing the likelihood that otherwise noncompetitive candidates will sustain their campaigns through the first round in the hopes of forestalling a determinate outcome in order to bargain for advantage between rounds. That is, the likelihood of a first-round majority winner might, in fact, be greater if we do not insist upon it as a precondition to avoiding a second round of balloting. We cannot say whether such perversity is commonplace or rare with respect to other institutions, but the researcher needs to be alert to the possibility that the consequences of an institution and the (strategic) choices it encourages may not be conveyed by its formal description.[14]

1.3 The Long Search for Stability

Regardless of which definition of federalism we choose, it is evident that Ukraine, the EU, and even China can be viewed as nascent federations. One motivation for this volume, however, derives from the belief that it is unlikely they will evolve into stable *democratic* federations without a redesign of their political institutions that proceeds in accordance with theoretically justifiable principles. A second motivation is the belief that such guidance is unlikely to be found in the existing literature, especially literature that focuses almost exclusively on representation and jurisdictions. Indeed, as we assert earlier, only some of the institutional variables critical to federal design are the ones commonly associated with that design. Many of the variables we deem most important are not even treated in federal constitutions and, rather than being the product of conscious design, are instead relegated to the often unpredictable realm of spontaneous development; or, when they are treated, it is done with considerations that have little or nothing to do with federalism per se.

The prevalence of a "federative," constraints-based bias in federal design derives, in part, from the absence of any theory of federalism directed explicitly at the components of a comprehensive institutional design. Although prior to the 1960s we saw seminal efforts at generating a theory by such scholars as Proudhon and Vernon (1979), Sharma (1953), Wheare (1964), Riker (1964), and Friedrich (1968), since then and until very recently most of what has been written about federal matters focuses on more specific policy-based questions. Interest in federalism appears to have shifted from the analysis of a concept in general to a study of the practices and policies of

[14] Indeed, paradoxes of this sort are common in game theory, and include such things as the chairman's paradox (in which the chair of a committee prefers less authority than more), various voting paradoxes, various paradoxes of representation (Schwartz 1999), and the paradox of omniscience (see Brams 1994). To the extent that game theory is a purely abstract representation of strategic interaction, the suggestion here then is that such paradoxes are a pervasive feature of formal institutions.

specific federal systems (Verney 1995), so that there is little to distinguish between studying the specific practices of federations and "the theory of federalism" (Kenyon and Kincaid 1991).[15] At least one scholar questions whether the development of a general theory has any practical relevance (Friedrich 1968: 8). Earle and Carey's (1968) title, "Federalism: Infinite Variety in Theory and Practice," tells us much about the contemporary state of research on the subject. Unsurprisingly, Davis (1978) argues that because the concept of federalism is more than merely poorly defined – owing to the variety and fluidity of the concept in practice, it is meaningless – a concrete and comprehensive theory is a virtual impossibility.

Here, however, we take issue with such views. Despite definitional difficulties, we believe that a theory of federalism – its proper design and operation – is attainable and that the great variety we see in federal forms, practices, and policies are merely the trees of a densely packed forest that for too long has either been studied too closely or without the benefit of a paradigm that can organize our ideas and experiences. Our argument is that a paradigm employing such concepts as self-interest, strategy, equilibrium, coordination, and the incentive compatibility of institutions can organize our observations and experiences to yield a theory of federal design that is universal and complete. But before we can develop that theory, we should first examine the perspectives and insights of earlier researchers, including the ways in which most prescriptions for federal success have thus far been brought into question or simply refuted by experience.

Federalism as Nuisance

Perhaps the earliest academic theme in the quest for a theory of federalism was to view the federal state as a cooperative system that, if "properly" structured, allows participants to achieve desirable common ends more effectively. Federal relations in this scheme represent a partnership among individuals, groups, and governments that relies on a commonality of interests to make all participants better off (Elazar 1991). Hence, we should not be surprised to find that those operating in this tradition, when searching for the prerequisites for stability, emphasize things that encourage this commonality. Maddox (1941), for example, identifies military and economic insecurity as the essential preconditions for federal stability. Wheare (1964: 37) identifies a "half-dozen factors, all [of which] operated in the United States, Switzerland, Canada, and Australia, to produce a desire for union among the communities concerned,"[16] and the first three items on Deutsch's (1957: 58)

[15] An important exception is King (1982).

[16] Wheare's (1964) factors are: (1) sense of military insecurity, (2) a desire to be independent of foreign powers, (3) economic advantages of union, (4) prior political association of the communities involved in union, (5) geographic proximity, and (6) similarity of political institutions.

nine-item list of things that encourage stable democratic federalism are "mutual compatibility of main values, a distinctive way of life, and expectations of stronger economic ties and gains."

Regardless of details, most researchers here agree that the distinguishing characteristic of the thing we call a federal state – the characteristic that must be preserved – is a diversity of interests among its constituent parts. Otherwise there is little justification for anything other than a unitary state. Adherents to this school of thought, then, would be anything but surprised to learn that "every single longstanding democracy in a territorially based multilingual and multinational polity is a federal state" or that "the six longstanding democracies that score highest on the index of linguistic or ethnic diversity – India, Canada, Belgium, Switzerland, Spain and the United States – are all federal states" (Stepan 1999: 19–20). The nature of the "federal compromise" is one in which participants "desire union... [but not] unity" (Dicey 1889: 137), in which the polity sustains both "integration and diversification" (Watts 1966: 21), and in which there is "a tendency [that] is neither unitary nor separatist" (Franck 1968: x). Based on such compromise, a properly designed federation is a governmental form that achieves some degree of political integration based on a combination of self-rule and shared rule (Elazar 1979), while avoiding a fusion in which members lose their identities as states (Forsyth 1981). The quest for stability, then, focuses on two things: the socioeconomic preconditions that make federation a mutually desirable governmental form and the constitutional provisions that seem best suited to protecting both harmony and diversity.

Although some scholars in this tradition view federalism as an ideal form, others see it merely as a necessary evil – an intermediate governmental system implemented primarily to accommodate the provincial self-interest of its constituent members. Perhaps reflecting the view of some of the Framers of the U.S. Constitution – that "the federal government, centralized and removed from the people, was a necessary evil" (Nardulli 1992: 17) – scholars see federalism as a halfway measure for states unwilling to relinquish full power, yet desirous of the benefits of belonging to a larger entity, a governmental form that is inherently disadvantaged in contests with unitary states (Dicey 1889) but that is nevertheless better than no central government at all (McWhinney 1962).

Whether ideal type or nuisance, the common supposition among proponents of this view is that a federation is a compact or a contract. It is not a contract among individual decision makers as in a unitary state, however, but among otherwise sovereign governments or even groups within a government. This difference marks perhaps the primary contribution of the cooperative school to the development of a theory of federalism, since in this instance we must view that contract not simply as some theoretical abstraction but as a real thing that requires explicit negotiation and design.

In 1863, Proudhon was among the first to emphasize that the Latin *foedus* means a pact, contract, treaty, agreement, or alliance between equals to perform one or more specific tasks, and for him the federal contract had the purpose "of guaranteeing to the federated states their sovereignty" while it provided the means for achieving mutual objectives (Proudhon and Vernon 1979: 39; see also Simon's 1973 review of Proudhon's federal theory). Thus, the consciously designed and written constitutional foundation of a federation is crucially important: "[T]he social contract is more than a fiction; it is a positive and effective compact, which has actually been proposed, discussed, voted upon, and adopted, and which can properly be amended at the contracting parties' will" (Proudhon and Vernon 1979: 39). Writing more than a century later, Elazar (1991) emphasizes the negotiated cooperative aspects of federalism, reiterating a conceptualization in which federalism provides for a voluntary yet contractual association of otherwise independent states for the achievement of a common purpose. And it is but a small step from here to applying the same emphasis on constitutional provisions as the essential components of a federation's design – a constitutional distribution of powers that maintains coordinate, semiautonomous governments that can perform both exclusive and concurrent functions: "[F]ederalism is predominantly a division of powers between general and regional authorities, each of which, in its own sphere, is co-ordinate with others yet independent of them" (Wheare 1953: 32–3).

The lesson to be learned from the cooperative approach is that because a federal constitution must be an explicitly written document, with the parties to it clearly identified, we must seriously and not metaphorically worry about its design and the reasons for supposing that it will not be breached through amendment, neglect, or outright subvention, or that we can rely on evolutionary developments alone to yield a viable institutional foundation. At the same time, however, we should not take this to mean that the mere act of drafting an appropriate constitutional contract is sufficient for viable federalism. We argue later, in fact, that this approach gives too much weight to federal constitutional provisions, at least as they are commonly understood, and too little weight to those ancillary institutions that help shape a state's party system.

Federalism as Engine of Prosperity

Regardless of whether federalism is seen as a nuisance or as an effective way to implement democracy in a diverse polity, a view that emphasizes federalism's cooperative nature and presents its design goals in terms of constitutional provisions contrasts with a second school of thought – one that either implicitly or explicitly sees federalism as a mechanism for accommodating asymmetries in information and for facilitating competition in order to infuse public policy with economic efficiency (Hayek 1945; Tiebout 1956; Musgrave 1959; Oates 1972; Buchanan and Faith 1987; Barro 1991; Persson and Tabellini 1996a, b; Bolton and Roland 1997). Just as perfectly competitive markets can yield something less than efficient outcomes, governments are prone to inefficiencies as well. And if one believes, as is the case with this school of thought, that the viability of a federation – indeed, of any government – depends primarily on its ability to provide public services efficiently, then design needs to give priority to those things that ostensibly facilitate that efficiency.

When looking for the potential sources of public-sector efficiency, a strictly economic instrumentalist perspective does not dispute that the citizens of a state, formed as a democratic monopolist, rely principally on competitive elections for the regulation of public policy. Competitive elections alone, however, are too blunt an instrument for ensuring that public officials act optimally or that they innovate in policy with the same enthusiasm as do firms in competitive markets. Moreover, with their authority to coerce, any such monopolist also has the ability to distort or wholly undermine the efficiencies that even competitive elections might engender (see, e.g., Rowley, Tollison, and Tullock 1988; McChesney 1997). Thus, efficient public policy requires a mechanism for augmenting the competitive pressure on political elites, and that mechanism is federalism as embodied by the rules and actions of a new entity, the federal (national) government.

In this view, then, markets and the competitive forces that are brought to bear on the original set of sovereign monopolists is a collective benefit, and the primary obligation of a federation's national government is to ensure the provision of this benefit by ensuring that federal subjects – states, provinces, oblasts, regions, Länder, cantons – coexist within a common and well-functioning market. This role thus defines the specific authority that must be ceded to the national government – the exclusive right to regulate the market's *numéraire*, the power to preclude any member state from erecting "unreasonable" barriers to trade within the federation, the authority to enforce contracts across federal subjects, and whatever instruments are needed to ensure private property and property rights generally. There are, of course, other associated powers for a national government (e.g., the power to mobilize an effective defense or to redistribute income), but the core idea is to encourage or even to compel federal subjects to coordinate and compete in the provision of public services without disrupting those parts of the national market that function well without governmental intervention. That is, federal subjects are to be made like firms and voters like stockholders who can fire a board of directors or sell their shares and invest in another firm (move to another federal subject) when, in their view, the firm is inefficient or yields a product not to their liking: "The genius of the [U.S.] Constitution is that it created a network of providers, whose role in the marketplace would rise and fall with the needs and demands of the nation. These market principles made possible political development that minimized political discord, thereby promoting cohesiveness. This cohesiveness enhanced the economic capacity of the emerging nation, unleashing its burgeoning potential and channeling its energies and resources toward productive ends. The ensuing prosperity fostered the relative stability the nation enjoyed and reenforced in people's minds the benefits of Union" (Nardulli 1992: 13).

The product of this competition is not merely efficiency within each federal subject's domain as it seeks to compete for investment and labor. It is also a global efficiency in the form of diversity in the provision of public services. This efficiency has two sources. First, it affords people the opportunity to vote with their feet (Tiebout 1956) and to realize a diversity of taste that a unitary government is unlikely to accommodate. Second, it allows for experimentation: "It is one of the happy incidents of the federal system that a single courageous State may, if its citizens choose, serve as a laboratory; and try novel social and economic experiments without risk to the rest of the country" (Brandeis 1932, 285 US 262, 311, in dissent). Federalism here, then, is not mere nuisance but rather a way to make government more efficient, responsive, and, presumably, democratic.

The arguments set forth in defense of this view, however, are largely theoretical and draw more from analogies with neoclassical economics than from empirical observation (Wibbels 2000). As a consequence, this competitive approach suffers from a singular deficiency. Specifically, markets – at least efficient ones – function within an implicit or explicit legal context that allows for the efficient enforcement of contracts and protection of property rights. The competitive theory of federalism, on the other hand, leaves unanswered the question as to how competition is stabilized so that (1) competition among federal subjects does not become so severe as to undermine all potential economic gains and (2) the coercive authority of the national government is kept in check so that the "property rights" of federal subjects are not abrogated. Qian and Weingast (1997: 83) succinctly identify the problem that confounds this economic approach; namely, it "ignore[s] the problem of why government officials have an incentive to behave in a manner prescribed... [it] take[s] for granted that political officials provide public goods and preserve markets."[17]

The "solutions" offered by the federalism-as-nuisance school are not much help in this matter, because they offer no mechanism for enforcing the federal contract beyond vague references to the self-interest occasioned

[17] After focusing on the government's role in preserving efficient markets, Qian and Weingast (see also Weingast 1995) attempt their own solution within the economist's paradigm by arguing that "thriving markets... require that governments solve this problem through credible commitment... [and] the features of federalism – decentralization of information and authority and inter-jurisdictional competition – can provide credible commitment to secure economic rights and preserve markets" (1997: 84–5). Unfortunately, what is not offered is any comprehensive or satisfactory account for why these particular features of federalism are themselves sustained, which, of course, is the central question.

by the desire to achieve a cooperative end. For rationalists in the competitive school accustomed to the apparent precision of economics, this mechanism is too ambiguous. Indeed, it is not a mechanism at all. Thus, absent practical or even theoretical solutions for maintaining a balance between national and federal subject authority, we often see an appeal to radical "solutions," such as James Buchanan's arguments for the right to secession (1995; see also Buchanan and Faith 1987; Allan Buchanan 1991, 1998). Briefly, Buchanan notes that there is one distinctive difference between markets for normal goods and services and the political markets federal states create. Normal market exchanges are noncoercive, and even if there is only one good available, a consumer has the exit option of not buying and consuming it. But in the political sphere, there are no practical exit options (aside from emigration), and political relationships are inherently coercive. Enforceable constitutional restrictions may narrow the domain of coercion, but within that domain they cannot provide adequate protection against exploitation by an overgrown central government. To correct this, in what can be described as an amplification of Jefferson's call for continuous peaceful revolution and periodic constitutional revision, Buchanan argues that the market analogy needs to be extended to federal subjects in their relationship with the center. Individually or in groups, they must be given an exit option with a constitutional right to secede from a federation and the authority to form new units or political unions. Thus, Buchanan's competitive prescription (as opposed to description) is to hold the central government roughly to its assigned constitutional limits with the threat of secession, while federal subjects are left to compete among themselves to meet the demands of their citizens.

Riker as Intermediary

With some oversimplification, we can say that the cooperative ("federalism as nuisance") and competitive ("federalism as an engine of prosperity") schools can be distinguished by the number of players participating in the federal game. Although both schools aspire to explain success and failure by comparing the "benefits" of federation – the efficiency and desirability of a federal union – with its economic, cultural, ethnic, and political "costs," the cooperative school emphasizes the opportunities for amicable agreements among federal subjects whereas the competitive school emphasizes the costs that can be applied in the event of noncompliance. Thus, in the cooperative story, the critical players are the *N* federal subjects, whereas in the competitive one, the model is an *N+1* person game, where the *N+1st* player – the federal center – is required to coordinate and enforce cooperation among federal subjects, sanctioning defectors when necessary.

Riker (1964) accepts this *N+1* person conceptualization but offers yet a third approach to solving the puzzle of stability that contains elements of the preceding two schools. Although the ostensible benefits of federation might encourage a predisposition to unite among the population in general and political elites in particular, he argues that the preceding two schools omit other fundamentally political considerations that transform predispositions into decisions. Thus, a theory of federal formation and survival requires a theory of bargaining among political elites: Riker interprets "federalism as a bargain between prospective national leaders and officials of constituent governments for the purpose of aggregating territory, the better to collect taxes and raise armies" (1964: 11).[18] He emphasizes that bargaining is no trivial matter: even if union is economically and socially desirable, there is no guarantee it will succeed in achieving sustainable results. As Haimanko, LeBreton, and Weber (2001) note, "even when economic efficiency unambiguously favors unity, the existence of compensation mechanisms seems to indicate that unity cannot always be sustained without transfers." And transfers, of course, entail bargaining.

Insofar as the incentive to form a federation in the first place is concerned, Riker's well-known hypothesis is that the danger of an external military threat is, historically at least, the universal incentive compelling politicians to participate in and compromise on this bargaining. There is, though, nothing in his argument to suppose that these incentives necessarily derive from military considerations, and, as Riker himself admits, military incentives receive such strong emphasis simply because his initial analysis applies to federations created before the rise of "welfare states" that could exert a preeminent influence on national economies – to an era when federalism was commonly a limited-purpose alliance formed for mutual military security in the face of common danger (Dikshit 1975: 224; also McKay 1996).[19] Nevertheless, Riker's assessment stands insofar as the critical component of his argument is the idea that political elites must agree to implement the outcomes of a federal bargain whenever they expect the political benefits of doing so would exceed the political costs of failing to reach or sustain such an agreement.

However, if we accept Wilson's seemingly self-evident argument that federal issues are never set in concrete in even a "stable" example such as the United States, then not only must political elites have an incentive to fashion a federal bargain, they must have incentives to keep it after the original motives for negotiation and compromise are long past. The United States, for example, no longer relies on military threats from Britain, France, and Spain for its existence, just as Canada no longer relies on the threat of an imperialist America, or Germany on France and Central Europe, or Switzerland

[18] Riker (and we in this volume) followed Lasswell's (1950: 3) conception of elites as politically influential actors.

[19] The credit for the first statement relating military incentives and federal formation apparently belongs to the anonymous author of the *Edinburgh Review* that declared in 1863 that "foreign aggression and foreign wars have created all federal governments" (vol. 118, p. 148).

on the historical nastiness of its neighbors. And indeed as Riker (1964: 49) himself admits, "although a willingness to compromise and a recognized need for military unity are two necessary predisposing conditions for the federal bargain, they cannot have much to do with its survival. If they were the conditions for keeping the bargain as well as making it, then remarkably few bargains would be kept."

On turning to the matter of sustaining a federation, we find Riker less an intermediate point between the two preceding schools of thought or mere adjunct to those schools and more a radical departure. Stability and enforcement of the federal bargain, to the extent that it is addressed at all by either of those schools, derives from the same logic that justifies the formation of a federation. In the case of federalism as nuisance, it derives from the fact that participants in the federal game can find no better alternative, whereas in its economic rationale a federation is presumed to survive because of the self-evident inefficiency of a disruption in federal relations. Riker, in contrast, focuses on institutions and especially the constitutional foundations of federalism: "[T]he operation of political institutions, both those in the formal Constitution and those which have grown up outside of it, is what immediately maintains the bargain" (Riker 1964: 111).

To contrast Riker more fully with the preceding two schools, it is useful to compare Dahl's *Preface to Democratic Theory* (1956) and Riker's *Liberalism against Populism* (1982). The two works posit diametrically opposite preconditions for a stable political system generally and reach different conclusions about a constitution's role in facilitating its own stability. Whereas Dahl's arguments can be made wholly compatible with either the federalism as nuisance and federalism as engine of prosperity school, Riker's analysis relies heavily on social choice theory and two facts revealed by that theory. The first is that coherence in majority-governed processes in the form of a well-defined (i.e., complete and transitive) social preference order over alternative public outcomes requires a nearly-impossible-to-achieve balance of citizen preferences on all salient issues or a uniformity of evaluative criteria such that all public preferences map onto a single "ideological" dimension.[20] The second fact is that, in the absence of such coherence, realized outcomes, along with the identities of winners and losers, depend critically on procedural details and the comparative skills of political elites at manipulating those

[20] The literature on this subject is substantial, but the critical contribution is McKelvey (1976; see also McKelvey and Schofield 1986), whereby we learn that under reasonably general assumptions about the typology of individual preferences, if there does not exist an outcome that is undominated by any other under simple majority rule, then the social preference order is wholly intransitive – from any two outcomes, A and X, we can find a sequence of other outcomes (B, C, D . . . etc.) such that B defeats A, C defeats B, and so on until we arrive at X, even though A defeats X. For a wholly substantive discussion of the consequences of this and all subsidiary theoretical results in the context ideologies and issues, see Hinich and Munger (1994).

details to their own advantage.[21] Riker uses these results to argue that populist institutions, which are defined as those which allow citizens direct access to and control of policy, exacerbate democracy's inherent instabilities and, rather than encourage democracy, facilitate the rise of demagogues. Thus, constitutions should not themselves or through the institutions they erect allow the direct translation of individual preferences to social policy. Instead, their fundamental if not unique purpose is the avoidance of tyranny, which they can meet only by giving political elites countervailing motives, by guaranteeing citizens the right to replace one set of leaders with another, and by recognizing that the relationship between individual preferences and public policy will ultimately be mediated by institutions and the political skills of those who occupy the positions those institutions establish. In Riker's analysis, then, constitutions – which define or regulate all other political institutions – play a critical role in facilitating or impairing democratic political stability.

In contrast, pluralists such as Dahl evaluate differently the preferences that occasion political instability, the role of constitutions, and, ultimately, the relevance (or irrelevance) of the Western constitutional experience elsewhere. In this view, stability, defined again in terms of the avoidance of tyranny, requires the instability that social choice theory describes or implies, because it ostensibly ensures against permanent winners and permanent losers. Here, the fundamental source of instability that social choice theory identifies – a complex nexus of individual preferences that do not admit of wholly determinate outcomes – is a necessary and perhaps even sufficient condition for democratic stability. Thus, whereas Riker seeks to control the consequences of an "incoherent" public preference, pluralists prefer even to encourage those consequences.

Dahl's words ring of Madison's defense of the extended republic and the equilibrating role of factions. In fact, his arguments can be taken as support for the preceding two schools of thought to the extent that in the search for stability they too emphasize society's underlying political-economic structure – the great variety of preferences, needs, talents, and interests. Unfortunately, the problem in choosing between Riker and either of these schools, or Dahl's in particular, is that no side offers a complete argument. Riker, when speaking of democracy generally, advocates familiar constitutional limits on direct citizen control of policy: a multicameral legislature, a separation of powers, and an independent judiciary. But he fails to address satisfactorily the ultimate source of stability of constitutionally mandated institutions – the mechanisms whereby these institutions do not themselves inherit the instability that adheres to the policies to which they apply. If there is no policy or outcome that can be said to stand highest on society's preference order

[21] It is this fact that Riker (1996) elaborates on when he offers his seminal assessment of the political strategies employed to secure ratification of the U.S. Constitution.

and if that order is not an order at all but can cycle endlessly to encompass inefficient as well as efficient outcomes, then why should we suppose that institutional arrangements, to the extent that they hold a bias for one outcome over others, can be ordered coherently or are any more stable than the outcomes they engender? Pluralists and their allies, on the other hand, give too little attention to the role of constitutional structure, and institutions generally. Although stability may require that there not be any permanent losers, denying a critical role for institutions also denies the fact that the political strategies chosen in pursuing policy preferences – as well as the very definition of winners and losers – depend on the institutional structures that help define the games people play among themselves. If institutions are ephemeral or merely the reflection of interests derived from other sources, then why is it not the case that anarchy is the permanent state of mankind?

1.4 The Fundamental Problem of Stability

Although what is theoretically general in his analysis focuses on the question of why federations form, Riker (1964: 136) suggests an intriguing, albeit incomplete, hypothesis about the conditions for their ongoing success: "Whatever the general social conditions, if any, that sustain the federal bargain, there is one institutional condition that controls the nature of the bargain.... This is the structure of the party system, which may be regarded as the main variable intervening between the background social conditions and the specific nature of the federal bargain." Before pursuing any suggestions we might infer from this statement, it is important to keep in mind that what sets Riker's approach apart from earlier ideas is its focus on the institutionally derived motives of political elites and the specifics of their self-interest. In contrast, what unites the cooperative and competitive schools is the assumption that a federation's "goodness" somehow ensures its survival. So to preclude false leads and to give full theoretical credit to Riker's suggestion, in this section we attempt to dispense more fully with this latter idea.

We can begin by observing that regardless of whose ideas about federalism we consider, they are uniformly laced with words such as "autonomy," "supremacy," "secession," "representation," and "sovereignty." We are led almost automatically to think of federations and federal relations in terms of some potentially conflictual interaction between and among subnational governmental units and the national government. As Qian and Weingast (1997) state the issue, "the two fundamental dilemmas of federalism [are]: first, what prevents the central government from destroying federalism by overwhelming the lower governments? Second, what prevents the constituent units from undermining federalism by free-riding and otherwise failing to cooperate?" From here it is only a small step to suppose we should model federal issues in terms of an $N+1$ player game in which the N federal subjects, in pursuit of their goals, separately or together oppose the *N+1st*, the federal center. As we note earlier, most economic (competitive)-based theories of federalism begin with this conceptualization in some form, with reference to the inefficiencies that arise if the *N* federal subjects play the game as sovereign entities as compared with the efficiencies that can be realized by letting an *N+1st* player compel cooperation. Similarly, the cooperative school emphasizes the advantages of a common state even though geographically based conflicts pressure against unity. In both instances, however, there is a tendency to at least begin theorizing about federalism, despite the warnings issued by social choice theory, by treating federal subjects and the federal center as unitary actors with well-defined interests and preferences.

There is little doubt that modeling federal relations this way is simplistic. But doing so initially compels us to confront directly several core issues of federal design. Modeling federalism, whether as an *N* or *N+1* person game, requires that, in addition to specifying the identities of "players," we also model the actions we want to make available to them. In practical terms, then, one issue that either view compels us to address is jurisdictions. Who should oversee public services such as education and public transportation, the authority to impose income, sales, and corporate taxes? Who will be responsible for regulating local and regional elections, as well as the regulation of capital markets, and the overall structure of the national and regional judiciaries. In short, a conceptualization of federalism in which the central players are the *N* federal subjects and, perhaps, a center that is created to coordinate and coerce requires that we address the allocation of power between and among levels of government. This in turn leads us to ask how in a federal state one can preclude the possibility that one government or another will overstep its bounds, and how one can ensure that any renegotiation of the allocation of responsibilities occurs only through "natural" democratic and constitutional means and in response to those social or economic imperatives that dictated the state's federal form in the first place.

The salience of such questions derives from a conceptualization that posits a relationship among states in a federation that entails, even without disruptive ethnic, religious, or linguistic divisions, those instruments presumed to impact economic activity – competition for revenues, control of natural resources, the regulation of banking and the incorporation of firms, and a demand for regional investment. Unfortunately, any theory that begins here raises more questions about stability than it answers. The reason is simple: in any purely *N+1* player model in which the costs and benefits of federation along with its structure are subject to renegotiation and in which the primary motives of the *N+1* players is expressed in terms of the outcomes of this renegotiation, the players in this game must be concerned that the only mechanism whereby they can defend their interests involves some form of potentially divisive or destabilizing process of coalition formation.

Here the core difficulty of federal design manifests itself clearly and immediately. The national government of any state must be empowered to regulate interregional relations and to ensure the efficient provision of those public services "normally" assigned to it. But the authority to do so threatens the sovereignty or autonomy of federal subjects. On the other hand, if the primary protection of these subjects against the center is a "winning" coalition against the center, there is nothing in our analysis yet to say that the center cannot form a coalition that works to the disadvantage of some subset of subjects not allied with it – that is, as a restatement of Qian and Weingast's (1997) statement of the fundamental problem of federal design, that "durable federal arrangements are possible only if two conditions hold. First, national forces must be structurally restrained from infringing on the federal bargain. Second, provincial temptations to renege on federal arrangements must be checked as well" (Bednar, Eskridge, and Ferejohn 2001: 226). Here, in the search for the sources of political stability, the competitive school in particular relies most heavily on the proposition that stability prevails because its absence implies a loss of efficiency among a federation's constituent parts. That is, if the benefits of competitive cooperation are sufficiently great and the disruption of the federation too costly, then stability is ensured or at least made more likely; conversely, "many federal arrangements ... have collapsed in the face of centrifugal forces when provincial entities decided that the benefits of membership in the federation were not worth the cost" (Bednar et al. 2001: 224).[22]

There are, though, problems with the premise that all there is to federal stability is a cost-benefit calculation for participants (unless we render the calculation a tautology: federations survive if the benefits of maintaining them, whatever they might be, exceed those of any alternative). The most apparent problem is the incompleteness of the premise that the greater the promise of cooperative gain or the threat of noncooperative loss, the greater is the likelihood of cooperation. The USSR's collapse illustrates matters where dissolution arguably derived as much from the political calculations of its chief instigators as from the union's failing (in Russia, Yeltsin's desire to remove Gorbachev from power by dissolving the state he "ruled"; and in Ukraine, Kravchuk's desire to secure his domestic position by taking advantage of nationalist sentiment) – failings that the USSR's dismemberment hardly

22 See also Le Breton and Weber (2000) for a clear theoretical statement of this argument in the context of the subsidiary argument that stability requires sufficient resources to ensure fiscal transfers that buy out potential secessionist movements. And for an example of the explicit adherence to this view in the context of offering policy prescriptions for Russia, see the collection of essays in Wallich (1994). On the other hand, Alesina et al. (2000: 1277) argue that "[world] trade openness and political separatism go hand in hand: economic integration leads to political 'disintegration.'" In particular, the economic benefits of preserving a large-size country are lower when the world is open to trade (see also Alesina and Spolaore 1997).

	Cooperate	Don't Cooperate
Cooperate	B-T, B-T	B/2-T, B/2-P
Don't cooperate	B/2-P, B/2-T	-P, -P

FIGURE 1.1. Cooperation problem without redistribution.

resolved and in many ways magnified in terms of the subsequent economic performance of its constituent parts. However, Gorbachev's early plea to the Balts to place their demands for secession on hold until they began to realize the benefits of a reformed Soviet Union revealed his acceptance of the hypothesis that a profitable federation is a stable federation.

To see the problems with this premise in abstract terms, suppose a federation consists of two subjects, and suppose that if both cooperate by paying their full share of taxes, T, each receives a benefit, B. But if one subject unilaterally defects so as to avoid paying, the benefit afforded by the federation to each subject declines to $B/2$.[23] Finally, suppose that defections are punished in the fixed amount P. Figure 1.1 portrays this situation and shows that absent any punishment ($P = 0$), as long as $T < B < 2T$ the situation is a prisoner's dilemma in which the dominant choice for both subjects is not to comply even though both prefer the outcome [comply, comply] to [don't comply, don't comply]. On the other hand, if punishment is sufficiently severe ($P > T - B/2$), then compliance is the dominant choice.

Employing the prisoner's dilemma as a justification for coerced collective action is, of course, commonplace, but now suppose that the efficiency of the system increases. There are several ways this change can be modeled within our scenario. The first is to let B increase while holding all other parameters constant, in which case, if the increase is sufficiently great ($B > 2T$), the prisoner's dilemma disappears even with zero punishment so that compliance is no longer an issue. Doubtlessly, this is the transformation of the game that Gorbachev and others had in mind when arguing that the incentives of the Baltic republics to secede would diminish if reforms were given the opportunity to work. There is, however, another possibility in which any increase in benefits is accompanied by a proportional increase in expenditures, so that it is only net benefits that increase. But now notice that if we, say, double the *net* benefits portrayed in Figure 1.1 so as to yield the game in Figure 1.2, then compliance is assured only if $P > 2T - B$.

[23] There are, of course, a great many types of public goods, such as those which if supplied to or by one person, can be consumed in equal measure by everyone else. This is the character of the good considered in our example, except that like the clean air "produced" by the installation of automobile pollution control devices, incremental contributions by each person add to the overall level of consumption. For a general classification of the varied types of public goods and the externalities associated with them, see Riker and Ordeshook (1973: 261).

	Cooperate	Don't cooperate
Cooperate	$2(B\text{-}T), 2(B\text{-}T)$	$2(B/2\text{-}T), 2(B/2)\text{-}P$
Don't Cooperate	$2(B/2)\text{-}P, 2(B/2\text{-}T)$	$-P, -P$

FIGURE 1.2. Cooperation problem without redistribution, with increased net benefits.

	Don't Cooperate	Cooperate
Don't Cooperate	X_1 X_2	$X_1+(1-\alpha)btX_2$ $X_2-(1-\alpha)tX_2(1-b)$
Cooperate	$X_1(1-t)+t(1-\alpha)bX_1$ $X_2+t\alpha X_1+t(1-\alpha)bX_1$	$X_1(1-t)+(1-\alpha)bt(X_1+X_2)$ $X_2(1-t)+[t\alpha+(1-\alpha)bt][X_1\ X_2]$

FIGURE 1.3. Cooperation problem with redistribution.

That is, if net benefits alone change, then the magnitude of punishments required to sustain cooperation must be increased by a corresponding amount.

Additional problems of compliance arise when we attempt to incorporate the redistributive possibilities into this analysis. For example, suppose a federal subject, i ($i = 1$ and 2), can generate X_i units of benefit from its own resources and suppose that if neither subject cooperates, their respective payoffs correspond to this benefit. Second, suppose subject 1 is more richly endowed than the other (i.e., $X_1 \geq X_2$). Next, let the national government as a third (unmodeled) player be empowered to tax compliant regions at the rate t so it can divide, in the ratio α and $1 - \alpha$ respectively, the resulting budget between subsidizing the poorer state and the production of a public good that benefits both players. Finally, suppose the national government's investment in the public good has a multiplier associated with it so that one unit of spending produces b units of benefit to each region (in which case, b need only exceed one-half for provision of the good to be "socially efficient"). The corresponding two-person game, then, is the one shown in Figure 1.3.

Algebra now establishes that not cooperating dominates cooperating for player 1 (row chooser) whenever $b < 1/(1 - \alpha)$. However, if 1 fails to cooperate, then player 2 (column chooser) should not cooperate either when $b < 1$, whereas if 1 cooperates, 2 cooperates as well (not cooperating is better than cooperating if $\alpha + b(1 - \alpha) < 1$, which is never the case because 1's cooperative strategy is conditioned on $b(1 - \alpha) > 1$, and $\alpha > 0$). Several conclusions follow:

1. Compliance cannot be bought. The conditional preference of the recipient of the transfer (column chooser) is unchanged by its relative magnitude. Therefore, satisfaction with the federal arrangement can

never be bought in such a way that it cannot be successfully challenged in a local campaign. The recipient's sole concern is that its marginal benefit through the public good outweighs its marginal contribution, as if no transfer took place.

2. At the same time, the incentives of the better-endowed player (row chooser) to cooperate are lowered compared with the case without redistribution. Row chooser, who without redistribution ($\alpha = 1$) strictly prefers to cooperate only if $b > 1$, now must also take the loss from redistributive policies into account and thereby fails to contribute whenever $b < 1/(1 - \alpha)$, even though it might be that the national government's productivity, b, exceeds 1.
3. Even if a subsidy is withdrawn as a punishment for noncompliance (with the central government pocketing the unredistributed resources) – that is, column chooser's payoff in the lower left cell of Figure 1.3 is $X_2 + t(1 - \alpha)bX_1$ – whether cooperation occurs depends on the constraints row chooser faces. Even if row chooser cooperates, column chooser prefers to cooperate only if $X_2 < \alpha(X_1 + X_2) + b(1 - \alpha)X_2$. But recall that row chooser cooperates only if $b(1 - \alpha) > 1$, and thus the condition always holds. The binding constraint for full cooperation remains $b > 1/(1 - \alpha)$, so nothing is changed if the poorer region is threatened with a withdrawal of the subsidy designed to encourage its cooperation.

The general conclusion we infer from such examples is that, although a drastic increase in productivity that raises individual marginal benefits above corresponding marginal costs can facilitate cooperation, efficiency in the form of increased net benefits need not do so. Absent a system of selective rewards or punishments, a federal government that is "merely efficient" will continue to confront the general problem of compliance and cooperation – a problem made only worse when it is also concerned with redistributive policies, which, as we argue shortly, are at the heart of federal public policy generally. The problems of cooperation and compliance, moreover, do not end with these examples. Even if we take an especially narrow economic view of the parameters in such models, their values will be heavily dependent on political things. For example, the parameter b, which corresponds to the "technology" of federal public good production, is a function not only of "economic" policy – regulating the right industries and providing for a budget balanced optimally between various categories of spending (all of which is determined by politics) – but also "political things" such as the degree of corruption that pervades the public sector and the incentives of political elites to make use of the latest technological innovations.

There is, though, one last potential resolution of the problem of compliance available to those who argue for the centrality of collective benefits as a source of federal stability: infinite repetition of the game. It is well known that infinite repetition in prisoner's dilemma–type scenarios introduces a new class of strategies – namely threats, or, more specifically, the threat of not cooperating in the future if one's partner fails to cooperate in the present. This expansion of each player's strategic alternatives yields a corresponding expansion of achievable equilibria, including that of full cooperation whenever each player gives the future sufficient weight.[24] But if one can argue that repetition renders cooperation and stability more likely, we can also argue that stability ensures repetition: the collective rewards of a stable federation give federal subjects confidence the game will be repeated and increase the weight given to the future, in which case stability becomes a self-fulfilling prophesy. Now, however, we have three subsidiary conceptual problems. The first concerns simultaneity. Without denying the self-sustaining features of stability, we need to learn how to encourage the economic prosperity required by stability. Conversely, how do we at the same time encourage the stability that ostensibly engenders prosperity? If the more important causal relation is the impact of stability (repetition) on prosperity, then mere attempts to ensure stability by focusing on economic policies can yield unanticipated and unsatisfactory results. But if prosperity is the more important precondition, then extraordinary (e.g., undemocratic) measures to ensure stability may not yield the prosperity required to render stability self-sustaining and democratic. Arguably, this is the dilemma that confronted those giving advice to countries of the former Soviet Union who had to balance political reform versus economic reform: which should be the first step?

An appeal to theorems about the consequences of repetition in the search for sources of federal stability encounters a second problem. If the players come to believe there is a good chance the game will not be repeated indefinitely, cooperation ends and their belief becomes a self-fulfilling prophesy. In other words, basing stability on the premise that federalism ensures economic prosperity does little more than make a federation vulnerable to the vagaries of economic policy and undermines one of the primary reasons for erecting the federal state in the first place – ensuring political and social stability in unforeseen and potentially turbulent economic circumstances. Finally, there is the matter of equilibrium selection, where even if somehow ensured, repetition can yield equilibria at widely varying levels of efficiency. This matter applies not only to the school of thought that sees federalism as an engine of prosperity but also to the first school, the cooperative school, that allows for the possibility that mere confederation and repetitive play, rather than efficient policy, make those benefits realizable.

Briefly, in addition to ensuring the existence of a cooperative equilibrium (and thereby an endogenously enforceable outcome), nearly any relatively

[24] See, for instance, Taylor (1976) and Friedman (1977), or virtually any text on game theory for the precise mathematical formulation of this discussion.

complex and interesting repeated game is characterized by a multitude of equilibria, including multiple efficient as well as multiple inefficient ones. The difficulty, however, is that even without any consideration of the pure redistributive possibilities under federalism, different players will prefer different equilibria since in them different players will be asked to assume the burden of punishing defections from cooperation. Thus, even if repetition rendered cooperation endogenously sustainable, it would not remove the incentives to bargain and, thereby, it cannot close the door to political disruption. We hasten to add, moreover, that the incentive to bargain is no less if the collective benefits of union are economic and derive from the competitive market a federation is presumed to encourage. In fact, we can give arguments for supposing that bargaining is even more pervasive and disruptive there.

Neither the cooperative nor the competitive school, then, is convincing in its arguments about the necessary or sufficient conditions for federal stability regardless of how we might choose to define terms. Largely because of this, both schools (and Riker) are generally devoid of specific, theoretically prescribed guidelines for federal institutional design, aside from the usual palliatives of a separation of powers, enumerated jurisdictions, independent courts, and "fair" representation, or detailed descriptions about how one institutional arrangement or another works in one society versus somewhere else. Thus, in the chapters that follow, we offer a description and assessment of the fundamentally problematic interaction that characterizes federal relations generally and which must be explicitly resolved and/or contained by institutional means, including specifics about those means. Here, however, we conclude with a discussion of the basic premises upon which our analysis is built, along with a brief survey of our principal hypotheses and arguments.

1.5 Basic Premises and Conclusions

If, when searching for the mechanisms whereby a smoothly functioning and stable federal state is ensured, we choose not to rely on "federalism as the efficient provider of public goods" or even on "federalism as nuisance," then it is incumbent upon us to identify a theoretically sound alternative. And even if we grant that the collective benefits of federalism play a critical role in a federal state's character and likelihood of survival, a specification of such benefits still does not constitute an analysis of the incentives of political elites to keep their bargain and the institutions that are designed ostensibly to help sustain it. In fact, the core argument of the next two chapters is that because the ongoing processes of negotiation and renegotiation in a federation pose an ever present danger to federal stability and effectiveness, regardless of its economic value otherwise, the primary purpose of federal design must be to keep those processes in check.

If Wilson's observations are general, the bargaining in federal states that dominate politics is bargaining over things in limited supply – authority, revenues, jurisdiction, power, and so on. Even those disputes that originate in a society described by salient ethnic or religious cleavages, such as the choice of an official language or the explicit recognition of the rights of some minority, can be formulated as limited-resource bargaining. But regardless of whether bargaining is negative- or even positive-sum, the normative justifications for federalism do not preclude the possibility – even the likelihood – that no outcome is stable and that there always exist other outcomes that advantage critical subsets of actors. Moreover, however self-evident might be the benefits of federalism and the losses incurred by any disruption of federal relations, we cannot assume that society in general and political elites in particular will successfully safeguard the basis of their mutual prosperity. Unless the specific arrangement yields greater benefits to any and all subsets of players empowered to disrupt federal relations than what each such subset might think is feasible by choosing otherwise, there is at least a hypothetical danger that confounds federal relations. Experience with scenarios such as the prisoner's dilemma warns us not to suppose that such dangers are always or often averted and that the collective benefits of a stable bargaining environment are necessarily realized.

There is, in fact, an inherent tension in all federal states that is a critical manifestation of this bargaining. Federalism, by its very nature, institutionalizes interests and can even align them in the form of federal subjects so as to negate the consequences of the pluralism that Dahl deems the basis of political stability. That tension is the one we note earlier; namely, preservation of a balance between the autonomy of federal subjects and the "legitimate" authority of the federal center. In most newly formed federations the main concern is avoiding federal disintegration, and thus the temptation is to award the national government special powers. Thus, Russia's concern in the early 1990s was that its ethnic republics would follow its own example when in the USSR and call for the dismemberment of the country (Solnick 2002). Equally difficult is understanding how to prevent excessive centralization, if only as a reaction to excessive decentralization and threats of secession. Some degree of centralization is essential for federal stability. Extreme centralization, though, creates a danger of transforming a federal union into a unitary state, which in turn may not only thwart the realization of the economic benefits of federalism but can produce precisely the outcome that excessive decentralization threatens, namely secession.

The dangers federal bargaining poses can perhaps be best understood if we engage in the thought experiment of imagining what a "renegotiated" American federalism might look like, or whether there would be any agreement at all. Imagine how many old and new issues would be endlessly discussed by politicians, pundits, and lawyers if people foresaw the opportunity to establish a new federal constitution and a formally revised web of relationships among today's complex nexus of governmental entities.[25] It is, doubtlessly, visions of this or some equivalent scenario that account for those attempts to limit the domain of federal bargaining either with long constitutional lists of policies that fall under the purview of the national government versus those that are the exclusive domain of federal subjects (see, for instance, the German Basic Law or Articles 71 and 72 in Russia's constitution) or with otherwise vague admonitions that promise to limit the federal center's prerogatives (as with article 3b, title II of the EU's Maastricht Treaty, which reads in part "In areas which do not fall within its exclusive competence, the Community shall take action, in accordance with the principle of subsidiarity, only if and insofar as the objectives of the proposed actions cannot be sufficiently achieved by the member states and can, therefore, by reason of the scale or effects of the proposed action, be better achieved by the Community").[26] Such lists and admonitions, which we term a part of those Level 1 constraints that seek to constrain federal bargaining, more often than not fail to serve their purpose. First, as experience has taught us, constitutionally specified jurisdictional boundaries, with but few exceptions, are inherently ambiguous, since the meaning of the very words used to state them are themselves subjects to negotiation and renegotiation. Thus, however well crafted, arguments can be made for nearly any allocation of responsibility, and all levels of government can lay claim to the right to oversee nearly any specific public (or private) activity. Independent courts as interpreters of words can alleviate some of the conflict here, but it is unlikely that they can address all of it without themselves becoming a full party to the bargaining.

Even explicitly stated bargains at this level are vulnerable. Compared with what we might find today, for instance, the Framers of the U.S. Constitution confronted preciously few issues that required explicit interregional negotiation. There was, of course, the issue of representation and the interests of large states versus small, but perhaps the most evident bargain struck in Philadelphia was between southern slave states and New England, where it was agreed that the slave trade would not be interfered with until 1808 in exchange for allowing the new federal government to regulate commerce at sea with a simple majority vote in Congress (as opposed to the initially proposed two-thirds vote). However, almost immediately following ratification, in February 1790, delegates from New York and Pennsylvania introduced resolutions in Congress calling for a prohibition of the slave trade. Encouraged by Benjamin Franklin, there ensued a debate that ended, though not

25 A narrative history of hundreds of the proposals to change the U.S. Constitution is provided by Vile (1991).

26 And one can only speculate about the feeding frenzy that will ensue among lawyers once the debate over the meaning of such words and phrases as "exclusive competence," "principle of subsidiarity," "sufficiently," and "better achieved" moves from the halls of academia and parliaments to the courts.

fully resolved, only when no agreement could be reached on what to do with emancipated slaves (the assumption being that black and white could not be integrated). Thus, with schemes on the table for compensating slave owners for the loss of their "property," had a solution to this matter been found, it seems evident that a compromise enshrined and seemingly clearly enunciated in a document drafted only a few years earlier would have been overturned (Ellis 2000).

Other constitutional provisions that we might want to include in the category of Level 1 constraints are federal supremacy and comity clauses, and rules for the admission of new federal subjects. But, of course, regardless of how broadly we define Level 1, constitutions are more than a collection of constraints on intergovernmental relations and negotiated agreements among federal subjects. More fundamentally, they establish a second level of constraint, what we call Level 2, that defines the national state, its relation to federal subjects, and its relation to the ultimate sovereign, the people. Included there are provisions for different branches of government, their obligations and authority, their relations to each other, the manner of filling federal offices, and rules for amending the document itself. There is, naturally, ambiguity sometimes as to whether a specific provision ought to be classified as Level 1 or Level 2 (e.g., rules of amendment), but a critical purpose that must be served by a federal constitution is the establishment of an institutional structure such that the machinery of the state manages successfully to direct individual self-interest so that Level 1 constraints are sustained or undergo only a gradual refinement and adaptation. Put differently, if federal stability prevails, it does so in part because institutions – usually constitutional ones – direct the actions of political elites so that their welfares are not promoted in any critical way by encouraging divisive and destabilizing federal bargaining.

To this point, then, we can summarize our argument as follows: a federation will be successful if and only if federal bargaining is restricted by Level 1 constraints – constraints that correspond in part to explicit bargains among federal subjects over the allocation of authority between them and the federal center, and other limits on their and the center's actions. We cannot assume, however, that we can merely posit constraints on the allowable domain of renegotiation. Compliance with any restriction on what can and cannot be subject to renegotiation depends on whether it is compatible with people's self-interest. Thus, a successful federal arrangement must provide not only the rules that yield stability in federal bargaining; it must also establish a second level, Level 2, that defines the core institutional structure of the federal center and its relationship to federal subjects in such a way to ensure the maintenance of these rules as a product of people's self-interest.

This view is hardly original and takes any number of historical forms, including the prescription that "ambition must be made to counter ambition."

It is, moreover, merely a reformulation of Riker's perspective on federalism, extended now from federal formation to ongoing political processes. Nevertheless, this argument and the ways in which Level 2 rules sustain Level 1 warrants closer examination because together they pose a logical conundrum. Note that it is tempting here to draw a parallel between the institution of marriage and a federation. Both are unions and both are subject to ongoing renegotiation of the terms of contract. In the case of a successful marriage, those negotiations commonly concern only "minor" matters such as what color to paint the house, who will drive the children to school, who will take out the garbage, where to go for dinner, where to take a vacation, and who will be responsible for balancing the checkbook. Descriptions of successful marriages, moreover, are likely to parallel descriptions of successful federations – compatibility of interests and tastes, mutual affection, absence of interference from in-laws, and so on. There is, though, an important difference between a marriage and a federation. Some marriages survive or at least endure for as long as they do simply because the costs of separation or divorce are too high to one or both parties. Dissolution of the union may be contemplated, but serious disputes are resolved (if they are resolved at all) because the costs of not doing so exceed whatever might be the anticipated gains. And we are referring here not merely to psychological costs but also to the costs imposed by a *preexisting exogenously defined and empowered* legal system that stands ready to punish those who defect (e.g., via abuse or infidelity) from the initial bargain. In this way the institution of marriage corresponds closely to the model of federalism offered by the federalism-as-engine-of-prosperity school.

In contrast, even if we grant Riker his argument about the importance of a well-designed constitution in maintaining federal relations, there is still the question of how a national constitution, whether taken as a whole or its separate parts, is sustained, since the law, unlike marriage, enjoys no external source of enforcement. That is, if the Level 2 rules and institutions a constitution establishes are to direct people's actions so that Level 1 constraints are not violated in any wholesale or disruptive way, and if they do so only to the extent that people have an incentive to abide by them and not stretch their meaning into meaninglessness or to abandon them altogether, then we must ask, What is the source of these incentives? If we view constitutions in the traditional way – as contracts between the state and the sovereign (the people), then who enforces the terms of the contract? Alternatively, if, as we argue later, constitutions ought to be viewed as an elaborate social norm – a mechanism that coordinates society to a particular political equilibrium of rules and procedures (Hardin 1989; Ordeshook 1993) – then we must ask, What is the game in which this equilibrium is embedded, what are the alternative equilibria that might otherwise prevail, and what aspects of this game are, like the constitution itself, subject to conscious design?

Many answers have been offered to these questions, ranging from appeals to the role of specific institutions as mechanisms of enforcement (e.g., the courts) to the consociationalist view that constitutions are sustained by an elite's consensus that failure of the constitutional order endangers its existence as an elite. Our answer is different. Briefly, we conceptualize federal design as a two-dimensional problem. The first is the constitutional one that encompasses Level 1 constraints and Level 2 institutional rules. These constraints and rules are the ones traditionally associated with both federal and constitutional design, and here we do not dispute the argument that a poor, incomplete, or inconsistent specification of them can doom a federation to failure. But at the same time, we also argue that a good constitutional design need not ensure success – witness the fact that the constitution directing the fate of the United States in 1865 was essentially the same document that governed the country in 1860. Put simply, although a properly designed constitution can establish a framework for realizing a solution to dysfunctional federal bargaining, rarely if ever are the problems of stability *wholly* solved by a good constitutional design.

This assertion might seem like heresy to those who have expended so much energy and effort at advising on the content of the many constitutions written in the most recent wave of democratization. Our argument, though, is simply that constitutions are not always the appropriate vehicle for all that is essential to federal success. If, in fact, a stable federal system is to be "a machine that goes of itself" (Kammen 1986), then when designing a federal state we must also attend to other factors – other institutions – that are also subject to human manipulation and which serve, in part, to define the game in which a constitution is embedded and which render the maintenance of Level 1 and Level 2 constraints an equilibrium from which no critical subset of players prefers to defect.

Our second dimension, then, is the part of institutional design aimed at ensuring the incentive compatibility of institutions and rules at the constitutional level and the more specific provisions that implement those rules or otherwise derive from them. The goal here is to integrate the entrepreneurial incentives of political elites at different levels of government so that compromise in federal bargaining, the avoidance of overly disruptive bargaining, and the maintenance of Level 2 rules are in everyone's self-interest. Because we cannot suppose that a constitution alone is sufficient to engender the motives we need, however, we require yet an additional layer, a third level, of rules and institutions. Indeed, it would be surprising if things were otherwise, since a constitution alone merely defines the rules of a game that is imbedded in some larger game – the game of democracy itself and the political-economic processes that describe a society.

Unlike the consociationalist view, then, elites in this scheme act to sustain the constitutional order not because of a consensus arrived at in some vague or mystical way, but rather because they respond to a set of institutions that are themselves intended to be incentive-compatible.[27] Unlike Riker's emphasis on a constitutional order, this scheme emphasizes those auxiliary institutions that implement that order, and unlike Dahl's appeal to the stabilizing influence of a pluralist social structure, it sees the necessity for directing the interests and motives in such structures in a way that they engender a subsidiary set of motives and interests that render a constitutional order an equilibrium within the larger, more inclusive game. This third level of institutional structure, then, must consist in part of rules that political elites sustain because they yield outcomes that serve their self-interest, which we assume in a democracy is winning and maintaining elected public office. Our argument, though, is more general and more institutionally specific than the consociationalist view and extends beyond merely citing the importance of the reelection motive for political elites. If, as Schattschneider (1942: 1) says, "political parties created democracy and... modern democracy is unthinkable save in terms of parties," it must also be true that political parties created federal democracies and... modern federalisms are unthinkable save in terms of parties. Our argument, then, is that the incentives we need to engender in order to secure a stable federal state are primarily the product of a "properly developed" political party system.

We are, of course, hardly the first to note the importance of parties in democracy or in a federal state. Riker (1964) points to parties, and in particular, to the extent to which they are centralized or peripheralized as key to understanding the extent to which a federation itself is similarly centralized or peripheralized. Following this lead, McKay (2000: 29) observes, with respect to the European Union's commonly cited "democratic deficit," that "[f]or Brussels to play an important part in such distributional issues as income security would require Union-wide citizen support mediated by Union-wide political parties operating through a genuinely representative European legislature much as parties operate in the United States and Britain." Similarly, Iarycrower, Saiegh, and Tommasi (2002: 5) note that "the extent to which the federal government pursues a 'national' agenda depends very much on the degree of unification and national orientation of the ruling political parties." And as Kramer (1998: 136) asserts with respect to the United States in particular, "By Washington's second term in office a more complex process had begun to emerge to protect state interests in the national political arena. The critical feature of this process was a unique system of political parties

[27] Lustick (1979: 334–5), for example, stresses that, while "all consociational models contain *the assumption* [emphasis added] that sub-unit elites share an overarching commitment to the perpetuation of the political arena within which they operated," as one moves away from "a pure type of consociational system where sub-unit elites and officials of the regime act vigorously and systematically to 'regulate' conflict, one encounters partly open [democratic] regimes in which the political behavior of sub-unit elites is much more likely to be determined by the competitive interests of their sub-units than by desires for system maintenance or the achievement of a conflict-regulating outcome."

that linked the fortunes of state and federal office holders, and in this way, assured respect for state officers and state sovereignty."

We do anything but dispute these assertions. But in contrast to the literature's tendency to view parties either as an important *intermediary* between citizens and the state or to see them, as in Riker's treatment, as *indicative* of a federal state's structure, we assign parties a more central and causal role.[28] It is generally assumed that the great trick of democratic design, federal or otherwise, is in finding ways to ensure that political elites, acting as agents of those who elect them, the principals, are perfect agents – that they refrain from excessive "rent seeking" and the expropriation of resources for their private benefit at the expense of their constituents (see, for instance, Qian and Weingast 1997). As we describe in Chapter 5, however, the great difficulty of federal design is in doing something different – namely, motivating political elites to be *imperfect* agents of those they represent and to motivate citizens to reward such imperfection. What precisely we mean by this should become clearer later, along with our argument that parties are the means for engendering and sustaining this imperfection. Parties may not be the unique tool, but the operating hypothesis of this volume is that they are, insofar as we can see, the most durable and manipulable one. Parties and party systems, then, are not merely intermediaries or indicators – they are an integral part of a federal system, and as such the institutional parameters that impact them are critical to federal design.

This argument, as much as our views on the nature of bargaining and conflict within federations, guides our prescriptions. It explains, for example, our earlier assertion that federal problems are rarely solved by constitutional provisions alone. Although party systems may be influenced by such provisions, those systems are also a consequence of a host of other institutional variables such as the frequency and simultaneity of elections; the timing of local and regional elections; the character and number of local, regional, and national offices filled by election; and so on. Thus, federal design is not some straightforward enterprise. Nor do we think that the requisite institutional structure is something that can be found by accident or "born" in some organic way. We understand, of course, that federations are not the only form of government that require conscious design. Selecting fundamental rules and procedures in a consistent way is a minimal precondition for launching any successful democracy. But federal design is made more difficult by

[28] McKay (1999b: 475) parallels Riker's treatment when he asserts that "the structure of the party system is an effective surrogate measure for the strength of the central or federal government." But to be fair, we should also note his assertion (2001: 5–6) that "[i]n democratic societies political parties are the main agents responsible for articulating interests including those based on regional or provincial distinctiveness.... Parties can play the major role in constitutional adaptation or in exploiting institutional rules in order to serve the interests of their supporters." Here, then, McKay sees parties as more than mere indicators, but as active participants in determining federal relations.

the fact that it is arguably less robust in terms of its proposed solutions. Because of the multiple conflicting goals that must be satisfied simultaneously, because of the interests it institutionalizes by definition, and because of the continuous bargaining that is inherent within them, federations are less likely to be able to compensate for design imperfections. Thus, as Bunce (1999) pointedly notes in her review of the post-Soviet experience, only the explicitly federal components of the Soviet empire dissolved after the empire itself unraveled – the USSR, Yugoslavia, and Czechoslovakia (see also Stepan 1999). The suggestion here, then, is that the precision of a federation's design must be greater than what we require for a unitary state.

Finally, we hasten to add that there are many types of institutional solutions for democracy, just as there are many different types of democratic constitutions, written and unwritten. We do not reject the possibility that quite distinct institutional alternatives would suffice in any one country. If a constitution's fundamental purpose is to coordinate society to a specific and clearly understood equilibrium of rules and procedures, it may matter less which equilibrium is selected than that some equilibrium is realized (provided that the institutions we establish at Level 3 define a game in which each alternative constitutional equilibrium is a desirable one). Nevertheless, the final premise of this book is that the critical components of a successful federal design are subject to less discretion than we might like, since all successful federations must possess institutions that satisfy certain basic universal theoretically prescribed characteristics. It is that theory and those characteristics which this volume seeks to uncover.

2

Federal Bargaining

> In framing a government which is to be administered by men over men, the great difficulty lies in this: You must first enable the government to control the governed; and in the next place, oblige it to control itself.
>
> Madison, *Federalist* 51

> The essential characteristic of a federal system is a division of powers between two levels of government, each supreme in some areas of policy making... [and] what a federal system does need for successful operation is some means of resolving conflict between the two levels.
>
> Lutz 1988: 64–5

> [A]mbitious encroachments of the federal government on the authority of the State governments would not excite the opposition of a single State, or of a few States only. They would be signals of general alarm. Every government would espouse a common cause. A correspondence would be opened. Plans of resistance would be concerted.
>
> Madison, *Federalist* 46

> In the Russian case, a bargaining model is not just analytically powerful, but also descriptively accurate.
>
> Solnick 1995: 55

The decision to form or reform a federation is an explicit attempt to confront two problems commonly associated with collective action – free-riding and reaching agreements on the allocation of the benefits and costs of public-goods provision and the regulation of externalities. If we turn to the general literature on collective action, however, it is the first of these problems that seems to receive the most attention. In addition to detailing the circumstances in which free-riding occurs, we find there a number of potential remedies and theoretical approaches. These include laying out the role of a leader and a leader's motives in directing people's actions through systems of selective sanctions and rewards (Frohlich and Oppenheimer 1970; Bianco and Bates 1990); detailing the ways in which a repetition of circumstances allows people to enforce cooperation by erecting an endogenous system of rewards, threats, and punishments that depends on the weight they give to the future (Axelrod 1984; Taylor 1987); and assessing the role of monitoring and the "spontaneous" invention and evolution of mechanisms that involve something less than the abrogation of autonomy to a governmental authority (Ostrom 1991). Insofar as these approaches have been applied to federalism, the focus has largely been on ways to ensure that there does not emerge a single player (the federal center) with motives that are inimical to the interests of the federal subjects it oversees or that some subset of subjects does not capture the coercive authority of the center and use it strictly for its own ends or otherwise succeed in avoiding punishment when it free-rides.

Clearly, we need to address the ways in which free-riding can be averted since public-goods provision, whether in the form of securing a unified defense, a common market, or the regulation of shared externalities, provides the central motive for inaugurating and maintaining a federal state. But a federal design entails more than the establishment of a mechanism for the efficient provision of public goods. A federal design can be wholly undermined if we fail to consider also the precise nature of the private benefits and costs associated with public goods and how those costs and benefits might be allocated as a function of alternative designs. Indeed, following Riker's lead, we see a grave danger for federations in the disjuncture between the general motivation to form them and the conflicts that emerge thereafter. Regardless of whether we are concerned with a limited state and a restricted set of public goods or an expansive one, and regardless of whether that state attempts to allocate revenues and costs via fixed formulas (Argentina), by independent commissions (Australia), through bilateral executive-to-executive negotiations between the center and each federal subject (Russia), by a maintained consensus on equalization (Germany), or on a case-by-case and generally ad hoc basis (United States), bargaining is a central feature of federal relations.

But bargaining is necessarily structured by rules, which may or may not be explicitly stated and which need not correspond to the institutions we erect to ensure efficient public-goods provision. Those rules may correspond to formal parliamentary procedure and an acceptance of majoritarian criteria, they may be the product of an evolved consensus, or they may consist of little more than the exercise of physical coercion. Regardless of how we conceptualize bargaining and the rules under which it proceeds, however, more than a half century of formal research in social choice from Hoag and Hallett (1926) to Black (1958) to Arrow (1963) to Gibbard (1973) and Satterthwaite (1975) to McKelvey and Schofield (1986) to Shepsle (1979) to Baron and Ferejohn (1989) to Riker (1982, 1986, 1996) teaches us that rules and procedures are not neutral in the selection of outcomes and the allocation of benefits and costs, so that one set of actors prefers one selection of rules while another set prefers a different selection. Put simply, "individuals have preferences over outcomes, they anticipate the effects of institutional rules on policy choice-making and then they support those institutional rules (at both the state and national level) that they perceive will advance their policy preferences" (Eavey and Miller 1989: 219).[1] Indeed, not only are rules and procedures rarely content-free; in extreme cases we may even see a one-to-one mapping between outcomes and rules so that preferences over rules are inherited directly from preferences over outcomes.[2]

This, then, identifies what we here consider the fundamental problem of federal design – ensuring against the possibility that federal institutions become strictly equated with outcomes, since in that case the choice of rules under which federal bargaining occurs will be subject to the same conflicts that describe disputes over outcomes and which, in certain circumstances, can threaten the stability of the federal system itself. If, as we argue in the next section, federations are, absent their institutional structure, unstable alliances, then a federal state's institutional structure is the critical determinant of how closely it matches its intended design. As a consequence, we view the principal challenge of federal design as being the need to "institutionalize" bargaining somehow so that relevant decision makers, competing in pursuit of their self-interest, do so in such a way as to minimize the extent to which conflict over outcomes infects the choice of rules under which bargaining and outcome selection occurs.

2.1 Alliances versus Federations

Before we consider the pervasive character of bargaining with which we must deal, it is useful to distinguish first between two forms of interstate

[1] Equivalently, as Riker (1980: 432) states the matter, "What prevents purely random embodiments of taste is the fact that decisions are customarily made within the framework of known rules, which are what we commonly call institutions.... And institutions may have systematic biases in them so that they regularly produce one kind of outcome rather than another."

[2] As an illustration of this inheritance, Eavey and Miller (1989: 218) offer the following explanation for why the frontiersmen of Pennsylvania and urban elite of Maryland, despite their apparent conflicting economic interests, both opposed ratification of the proposed American constitution: "In each case [this opposition] stemmed from the recognition that the new order was a threat to their economic and political position within [their respective states]. In... Pennsylvania... the fear was that the Constitution would undermine the authority of the existing state constitution, while in Maryland [it was the concern]... that the federal Constitution would reenforce the state constitution and concomitantly the dominant position of the planter aristocracy."

political cooperation – that of a federation and that of an alliance.[3] Although, as we state in Chapter 1, we do not want to be mired in confusing and ambiguous definitions, wrestling with these two ideas illuminates the potential for political instability in federal relations and the need to fashion institutions of a particular sort. Briefly, then, we begin by noting that although the public good that motivates the creation and maintenance of a federation is, in some accounts, an efficient common market, for others an effective military, and for still others specific programs such as transportation, a coherent banking system, and so on, as with most things in life, a price must be paid to secure such things. The most obvious component of this price is the economic cost of the good itself. But there is a second component – the "political" price federal subjects pay when relinquishing some of their autonomy to a central authority that is then authorized to punish and coerce. The abrogation of autonomy is, after all, an essential part of federal state formation: "If a number of political societies enter into a larger political society, the laws which the latter may enact... must necessarily be supreme over those societies and the individuals of whom they are composed. It would otherwise be a mere treaty, dependent on the good faith of the parties, and not a government" (Hamilton, *Federalist* 33).

Why states – or, more properly, citizens and political elites within them – would abrogate their autonomy rather than proceed with other arrangements is best understood by differentiating between alliances and federations. Of course, as with nearly everything else, it is difficult to draw sharp distinctions. Although we can reasonably assume that federations serve a larger purpose than alliances – that alliances are commonly limited to military ends or trade relations, whereas federations are implemented to coordinate states on a wider range of issues – such an assumption runs afoul of Riker's (1964) admittedly contested conclusions as to the historical motivation for federal state formation: the external military threat. But even if we grant Riker his argument, the one question he leaves unanswered is why the parties to the federal bargain do not prefer an alliance over the more encompassing and ostensibly more coercive federal form.

One way to fill this gap is to observe that, regardless of how we define the treaties that normally define the terms of alliance, those documents are something less than the constitutional compacts of federations. A treaty is an agreement to cooperate and coordinate on a particular issue without a ready mechanism for reaching similar agreements in the future on other issues. The members of an alliance abrogate their sovereignty only to the extent that

[3] We appreciate that only in relatively rare cases do wholly sovereign entities join to form a federation *de novo*. However, if we assume that secession, however costly, is at least theoretically possible, then we can think of a federation as an ongoing decision among otherwise sovereign entities to "join."

they signal their apparent willingness to abide by a specific set of obligations while retaining their sovereignty on all other matters. An alliance rarely if ever establishes an entity that can appeal directly to the populations that fall within its domain: an alliance is an agreement among the representatives of states and not the citizens those states serve. In contrast, entering the more costly federal agreement allows the constituent states to generate, at least in principle, benefits that can be realized presumably only through a more complex system of separate, formalized, and ongoing relations. Moreover, the entity such an agreement erects – the federal center – is one that, like the governments of its constituent parts, can appeal directly to the people for the authority to act and even to override the decisions of those parts. From this view, then, we might infer that the decision to form a federation in lieu of an alliance requires something more than a perceived common threat; it requires an appreciation of the benefits of federation that accrue across a range of issues.[4]

Even if we chose, however, to augment Riker's analysis in this way, which is little more than an acceptance of the hypothesis offered by the "federalism as nuisance" and "federalism as engine of prosperity" schools, we must still ask when these benefits are likely to outweigh the costs associated with an abrogation of federal subject sovereignty? That is, when will nations prefer to form an alliance and when will they choose to form a federation? Following Hamilton's suggestion, the hypothesis we offer here in answer to this question is that a necessary condition for forming a federation in lieu of an alliance is the realization that a federation organized as an alliance is unstable. That is, federations and the institutions that describe them arise in precisely those circumstances in which the mutual self-interest of the member states does not provide a sufficient guarantee that their coalition will survive without additional aids: "An alliance is simply some collection of agreements [and] a stable alliance is an alliance in which all states share a common-knowledge understanding that it is in all member's self-interest to abide by those agreements. A federation . . . seeks to serve the same ends as an alliance, but unlike a stable alliance . . . it is not in and of itself self-enforcing. In short, a federation is an otherwise unstable alliance" (Niou and Ordeshook 1998: 273).

This is not to say that all alliances are stable – a fact well documented by the history of European alliance formation in the later half of the nineteenth century.[5] But if we consider the two notable alliances of the twentieth

[4] For a more formalized treatment of this matter, see Schofield (2000, 2002).

[5] That history also demonstrates the power of ideas and the fact that the impossibility of a stable alliance is not a sufficient basis for federal state formation. If we appreciate that the utopians and early socialists were little more than small cadres of seemingly irrelevant intellectuals, then given the mentality and motives of political elites up until 1945, it is difficult to suppose that any part of them could foresee a circumstance in which they would willingly

century – NATO and the Warsaw Pact – we see that they can survive for long periods of time (or longer at least than most federations that formed in the same time frame) if there is a single dominant state within them that bears much of the cost of public-goods provision and that acts as the primary agent of enforcement (Olson and Zeckhauser 1966). Thus, the mechanism of *enforcement* in these two examples is the existence of a hegemon or privileged player who is willing to provide privately whatever benefits accrue to collective action and a degree of self-interest that compels member states to allow that player to rule on the issues assigned to it. In contrast, federations, we can suppose, arise when no member state is capable of playing this role or when the self-interest of member states encompasses a wider domain than pure military considerations but when that self-interest fails to engender a consensus on the necessity for a more comprehensive abrogation of autonomy to a potential hegemon.

The advantage federations have over alliances was well understood by the Framers of the U.S. Constitution, not only in light of their experiences, but also on the basis of their understanding of the Swiss Confederation of 1291–1798. It is useful, then, to digress a bit and consider the origins of this confederation, which is commonly taken as the most celebrated example of a military alliance in the guise of a "federation." Indeed, even critics of Riker's "military condition" for federal formation agree that military incentives were crucially important for the initial success of the Swiss union. Since the end of thirteenth century the area that is now Switzerland was a tangle of military alliances, treaties, and dependencies: "In modern terms we could define this as a system of small independent states united by an international treaty" (Linder 1998). The Swiss Confederation began when in 1291 three alpine communities (Schwyz, Uri, and Unterwald) formed a military alliance that by the mid-fourteenth century was extended to a loose military coalition of eight cantons, linked by six separate pacts. By the middle of the sixteenth century, it grew to thirteen cantons and a number of associated and "dependent" territories. What kept these different components together was a common military interest based on a desire to control the borders of the Swiss Alps and to exploit the dependent territories. Narrow mountain corridors conveniently connected France, Italy, Austria, and Germany, and although individual cantons could not control the passes, a military union enabled them to expropriate rents in the form of tariffs. There was, however, always the danger that the adjacent European powers would take advantage of any conflict or war among the cantons. Indeed, this was a time when the fate of

and permanently abrogate their autonomy in the form of a European Union so that they could no longer play the twin games of Empire and Cultural Arrogance (although pockets of resistance can be found in France). Forty or so million deaths and the physical devastation of the continent were required before elites there could be led (by the United States) to act under more cooperative arrangements.

small "independent" states was predictable, as when, in the middle of the nineteenth century, Swiss cantons witnessed the small neighboring kingdoms of Sardina-Piermont, Lombardy-Venetia, Baden, Württemberg, and Bavaria being absorbed by Italy and Germany. The Swiss alliance's policy of diplomatic neutrality, which had as its ostensible goal that of preventing members from participating in external military conflicts, performed an important integrating function: it restrained confederation members from being divided by conflicts among its neighbors. However, the alliance remained what it was – an alliance and not a federation. Its Federal Diet, the Swiss Confederation's sole formal institution, was little more than a venue for conferences of canton ambassadors (reminiscent of the successor to the USSR, the Commonwealth of Independent States), whereas the alliance itself was managed largely by "the infinitely complex structure" of subjection, dominance, jurisdiction, and feudal personal relationships (Hughes 1962: 8). The problematical feature of the Swiss Confederation, however, was the dominance of two cantons, Bern and Zurich, and between the sixteenth and eighteenth centuries there were at least four internal wars in which Bern and Zurich fought against small Catholic cantons and in which Bern's troops conducted punishing expeditions against individual cantons and cities. The Swiss Confederation, however, was effectively dissolved in 1798 when French troops marched into Bern, and, to reduce the dominance of Bern and Zurich, Napoleon divided the territory of the old thirteen cantons and their "Dependent Territories" into twenty-three cantons. However, absent the old system of political dominance and dependence, but, perhaps as a prototype of modern dissolutions such as Czechoslovakia and the USSR, the confederation collapsed. In fact, the next fifty years proved to be exceptionally unstable: between 1798 and 1848 (the year the modern Swiss federation was formed), the Swiss experienced five different constitutions, the federal Mediation Act by Napoleon (1803), the Federal Treaty of the Vienna Congress (1815), a number of secessions, intercantonal military conflicts, and a civil war.

Although the Framers of the U.S. Constitution acted before the Swiss Confederation's period of nineteenth-century instability, its limitations were evident:

> The connection among the Swiss cantons scarcely amounts to a confederacy; though it is sometimes cited as an instance of the stability of such institutions. They have no common treasury; no common troops even in war; no common coin; no common judicatory; nor any other common mark of sovereignty. They are kept together by the peculiarity of their topographical position; by their individual weakness and insignificancy; by the fear of powerful neighbors, to one of which they were formerly subject; by the few sources of contention among a people of such simple and homogeneous manners; by their joint interest in their dependent possessions; by the mutual aid they stand in need of, for suppressing insurrections and rebellions, an aid expressly stipulated and often required and afforded; and by the necessity of some

regular and permanent provision for accommodating disputes among the cantons. (*Federalist* 19)[6]

Madison and Hamilton then correctly predict the confederation's soon to be apparent instability: "So far as the peculiarity of their case will admit of comparison with that of the United States, it serves to confirm the principle intended to be established. Whatever efficacy the union may have had in ordinary cases, it appears that the moment a cause of difference sprang up, capable of trying its strength, it failed."

Madison, Hamilton, and their compatriots in Philadelphia acted on the belief that the American union under the Articles of Confederation was similarly unstable and could not survive as an "alliance." They not only foresaw the possibility that New England, because of commercial interests, might seek rapprochement with England or that the newly emerging western territories might find their self-interest more in tune with whatever power controlled the Mississippi; they also feared each other and the possibility that the Articles were too weak to keep the states from eventually coalescing into three or four separate antagonistic entities: "[P]oliticians now appear who insist that... instead of looking for safety and happiness in union, we ought to seek it in a division of the States into distinct confederacies or sovereignties" (Jay, *Federalist* 2), in which case, "like most other bordering nations, they would always be either involved in disputes and war, or live in the constant apprehension of them" (Jay, *Federalist* 5; see also Hamilton's *Federalist* 6 through 9).

Although much of what was written at the time in defense of the proposed Constitution was for the purpose of political persuasion, the distinction between an alliance and a federation shaped the *Federalist*'s vision of what was required in the new Constitution. And in particular, its authors understood the functional similarities between the federal center and an alliance's hegemon. They understood that they were fundamentally transforming an *N* person game of bargaining and coalition formation to a game of a different sort by creating a new "player" whose authority would be supreme in a vast array of policy domains, who would be authorized to punish any member who defected from the cooperative agreements made by the founding members of the "alliance," and who would in part gain its authority to act by being directly answerable to the people. They also understood that the powers required by this *N+1st* player for it to perform its function are themselves dangerous and subject to misuse. Thus, the game had to be designed

[6] Similarly, as James Wilson (1993: 793–4) noted in his opening address to the Pennsylvania Ratifying Convention, "[t]he Swiss Cantons... cannot properly be deemed a Foederal republic, but merely a system of united states. The United Netherlands are also an assemblage of states; yet as their proceedings are not the result of their combined decisions, but of the decisions of each state individually, their association is evidently wanting in that quality which is essential to constitute a Foederal Republic."

in such a way that, while arming this new player with the authority to tax, coerce, coordinate, raise armies, borrow and coin money, and so on, it did not give it the means or incentive to overwhelm the legitimate authority of the original players. Unlike the terms and structure of an alliance, a carefully crafted balance had to be established between the authority of the center and the now limited sovereignty of the federation's constituent parts so that the efficiencies of coordinated action were not gained at the expense of the efficiencies associated with decentralization.

2.2 The Private Character of Public Goods

Although the Framers fully appreciated the collective benefits of union, they also understood the often unavoidable inequalities in the distribution of those benefits and the economic and political costs of achieving them. The delegates in Philadelphia who debated representation, slavery, and federal regulation of commerce were hardly unaware of the redistributive consequences of their decisions – witness the specific provisions they supplied that concerned each of these issues. Moreover, the issues that dominated political discourse soon after the implementation of the new federal system – federal assumption of state debts, the establishment of a national bank, and the location of the new national capital – could only serve to underscore the redistributive nature of federal politics. Thus, regardless of the rhetoric and appeals to the imperatives of efficient public-goods provision that might precede the formation of a federal state, it is foolhardy to assume that the things motivating people's actions within a federation once it is formed correspond to whatever ideals might have motivated a willingness to abrogate autonomy in the first place.

Of course, at a fundamental level, apparent motives will change when federal institutions are established. Even if federal rules are only weakly binding, the political game people play and the strategies they must consider are necessarily altered. Even if the original motive for federal formation concerns some nexus of public goods in addition to the ones normally associated with alliance formation, we should not assume that the motives dictating policy thereafter will correspond to the simple desire of avoiding the inefficiencies of free-riding or that conflicts will concern only differing conceptualizations and assessments of those inefficiencies. There is also the conflict over the allocation of benefits and costs associated with the production and regulation of public goods – a conflict we suggest that takes center stage in the subsequent attempt to operate within and maintain federal arrangements.

That governments necessarily concern themselves with redistribution is self-evident. Public goods must be paid for and governments must levy taxes and assign costs. In addition, governments engage in redistribution as a matter of conscious choice, with the rationalization that a maldistribution of income is itself a "public bad" that needs to be eliminated.[7] What we want to argue here, however, is that redistribution is more an inherent part of public-goods production than we might otherwise suppose. Recall that public goods are commonly characterized by two things: "publicness of consumption" and "privateness of production." Publicness of consumption refers to the idea that a public good, when consumed by one person, player, or decision-making entity, can be consumed or otherwise enjoyed by all other "relevant" persons, players, or decision-making entities at zero or low marginal cost. The financial costs of production, though, are private; if they are borne by one person, they need not be borne by anyone else. But public goods, especially those that concern governments, can be seen to be private in an additional sense if we look at the *instruments* of their production. For example, although everyone may share equally in the security that national defense provides, even a rigorously "fair" tax system is unlikely to avoid the fact that federal subjects and their citizens will not share equally in the costs and benefits associated with the production of those things that contribute to defense. If one firm is awarded the contract to build a military system, then another cannot be given the same contract; if one worker is paid to sew buttons on a uniform, that wage cannot be given to someone else; and if one federal subject enjoys the benefit of having a military base on its territory, some other subject cannot enjoy the benefit of that same base. Similarly, although the consumption-side benefits of a transportation system are presumed to be public, that good in production is decidedly private: awarding a highway construction contract to one firm can be done only if that contract is not awarded to some other firm, and the decision to build a highway near one city must mean that it is built further from some other.

The political consequences of the private character of public goods are certainly well understood by politicians. There was, for example, nearly universal agreement in the first half of the nineteenth century that the United States required a transcontinental railroad in order to tie the West, especially California, to the East. The public benefits were clear. But the production of that "good" held enormous redistributive consequences, depending on whether a southern or northern route was to be selected, and this issue, perhaps second only to slavery, set North against South as a prelude to the American Civil War. In more contemporary terms, we suspect that America's interstate highway system was strategically called the National Defense Highway System in order to make the expense of building it more palatable to the general public, to obscure its private-goods features, and

[7] The most direct form of such redistribution is through federal grants. Predictably, grant allocation formulas are the subject of fierce bargaining. According to Zimmerman (1996: 13), the American "process of congressional enactment of formulas for the distribution of funds to states commonly generates lobbying by regional groupings of states with one region opposed to a specific proposed formula and another region in favor of the proposal."

to deemphasize its redistributive consequences. Similarly, few proponents of increased spending on education prefer to emphasize the financial beneficiaries of any newly proposed expenditures (teachers and those who would build new schools), only infrequently will advocates of increased defense appropriations frame their arguments in terms of sustaining employment in particular congressional constituencies, and we are hardly surprised to see the justification for some new governmental regulation framed in terms of the ostensible benefits that will accrue to, say, consumers generally rather than in terms of the benefits realized by firms who might see such regulation as a way to exclude competition (Stigler 1971; Posner 1971).[8]

Because public goods in production look very much like the private goods of the marketplace, and because this dichotomy is a universal characteristic of the goods and services that concern governments, it is an error to suppose that the public properties of the things will dictate people's actions or that people will care more about those public properties opposed to private ones (Aranson and Ordeshook 1985). That is, it is an error to suppose that citizens or politicians are motivated primarily by some "rational" economic calculation of the public benefits of a military procurement program or highway transportation system and that they pay scant attention to private benefits that accrue to people in the physical production of such things. Thus, whenever a democratic state, federal or otherwise, is established ostensibly to provide a menu of public benefits, design must take special cognizance of the fact that the state's members will engage in and perhaps even be primarily preoccupied with the differential benefits of alternative policies of production.

2.3 Equilibrium Selection and Redistribution

Because it corresponds precisely to the problem of redistribution, the task of benefit and cost assignment when treating the private character of public goods normally entails all of the corresponding instabilities and indeterminacies of bargaining over limited resources. To see how that instability frames the problem of federal design, consider a scenario in which three players (e.g., three federal subjects) must each contribute to the funding of a public good and suppose the benefit associated with that good is valued by each of them at \$7. If it costs \$6 to generate that benefit (in which case each player would, if necessary, unilaterally provide the good) and if the good is efficiently provided, then society enjoys a "surplus" of \$15 (\$7 times

[8] We are reminded of the political cartoon (whose authorship is now forgotten to us) portraying a group of generals huddled around a table, inspecting plans for a new defense system. One general speaks: "[T]he most challenging technical problem we confronted in designing this system, gentlemen, was, of course, finding 435 subcontractors . . . one in each Congressional district."

three, minus the $6 cost). Next, suppose that if the sum of promised contributions is less than $6, the benefit fails to materialize (e.g., we cannot build half a bridge or half an aircraft carrier), whereas if the players inadvertently contribute more than $6 total, the surplus "disappears" into some administrative bureaucracy (we want our examples, after all, to be realistic), and whatever externalities bureaucratic consumption might generate for the original players we assume to be negligible or evenly distributed. Finally, suppose the "game" of public-goods provision must be played strictly noncooperatively in a game-theoretic sense. That is, suppose each player must announce his contribution – a number between 0 and $6 – in ignorance of what choices the other two players make. This game, now, has an infinity of equilibria – all strategy triples in which the sum of contributions announced is precisely $6. That only such a precise sum corresponds to an equilibrium is confirmed by noting that if the sum exceeds $6, any player announcing a number greater than zero has the incentive, if given the unilateral opportunity, to reduce his proposed contribution; but if the numbers sum to less than $6, then each player has the opposite incentive – to announce a greater number, because each is willing to unilaterally fund the good if required to do so.

Of course, the players here will each prefer different equilibria – each will prefer to pay as little as possible and let others bear as great a burden as necessary. One consequence, then, of fully noncooperative play is the absence of any guarantee that an equilibrium will prevail since there is no guarantee the players can implicitly coordinate to a vector of contributions that sum to precisely $6. If each player mistakenly believes that the others are willing to bear a greater burden than himself, then each may announce too small a contribution. And if each believes that the others are not willing to pay their "fair" share, then the good may be provided but only inefficiently. Suppose, then, that the players change the game to allow face-to-face bargaining. Bargaining, however, minimally requires a rule for ending the game. There are any number of possibilities, but if we were to use our scenario as the beginnings of a model of democratic federalism, it seems reasonable to expect (require?) that the procedure they choose will be based on some form of majority rule.[9] But now there are two potential new problems. First, if no player can bribe another with side payments, then there are three unique equilibrium outcomes that cannot be upset by a majority coalition: (7,7,1), (7,1,7), and (1,7,7). In this instance, though, we would expect that the player saddled with the burden of paying the full cost of the good would try to initiate a side payment. For example, if the outcome (7,7,1) is about to prevail, the third person might propose (4,8,3), which corresponds to proposing that

[9] Some persons might argue for a rule of unanimity, but this rule makes sense only if there is a discernible status quo. And even then, there must be a rule for choosing the alternative(s) that will be put to a vote against that status quo.

the cost of provision be divided equally between himself and the first person, and that as an inducement to accept the offer, he gives the second person a side payment of 1. Clearly, though, if such side payments are allowed, the set of all feasible efficient outcomes (all outcomes in which the sum of payments is precisely $6) cycle: regardless of which cost assignment and set of side payments are proposed, we can find others that are preferred by at least two players.

There is no guarantee, then, that, as in the initial noncooperative model, simple face-to-face bargaining yields a determinate outcome. So suppose the players impose additional structure on their negotiations by, say, implementing some type of finite voting agenda. For example, we could order the players alphabetically: let the first player, A, propose a cost assignment, which is then put to a vote against the proposal of the second player, B, and the winner of this vote paired against the proposal of the third player, C. In this instance the final outcome will have player C and one other paying nothing, with the third, either A or B, bearing the full cost of production depending on who C chooses as a coalition partner for the final vote. Alternatively, we could let the first player announce what he is willing to pay, then the second, and then the third, letting the sum of their announcements dictate whether the good is produced. In this instance, C will bear the full cost. For a third alternative, we could choose one player at random and let him impose a cost assignment, in which case the final outcome is, in effect, a lottery over the set of possibilities that allows one player to pay nothing. Clearly, now, the different players will have varied preferences over these methods, as well as any other method we might propose. Why, for instance, should we choose to order the players alphabetically? Why not in reverse alphabetical order; or why not by age, weight, or height; or, recalling the substantive context of this discussion, by their population, literacy levels, median incomes, or the order with which they ratified the terms of their federation? And why limit ourselves to a simple two- or three-stage agenda? Why not allow straw votes, a reconsideration of prior votes, and bargaining within the limits of formal parliamentary rules?

It is not difficult, then, to imagine a choice over a set of feasible rules that is subject to the same conflict of preferences as the distributive outcomes to which those rules are applied, so that different players prefer different rules with the same passion as the preferences they hold over outcomes. And once the stage is reached in which players understand the implications of rules, then if bargaining is allowed to continue, the players will no longer be bargaining over outcomes but over the rules for choosing outcomes. This regress, moreover, threatens to be unending: if the players are to disagree over rules, under what rules will these disagreements be resolved? And if there are rules for regulating the process of choosing rules, what inoculates them against becoming an object of the same disagreements that apply to the rules under discussion? Put simply, because each rule implies specific outcomes in favor of some and not other participants, people will derive their preferences over rules from their preferences over outcomes. With the bargaining problem merely moving up one or a few institutional levels, what guarantee is there that the only thing that will be "produced" is not endless discussion as opposed to the public good that was the original source of disagreement? It might be that mere exhaustion or simple impatience would result in a compromise, but that is hardly a foundation upon which to erect a state.

2.4 The Federal Problem

Summarizing the preceding argument, we have:

1. Regardless of whether the goods and services that concern a government are public or private, redistributive issues cannot be avoided – redistribution is an inherent feature of the state's choice set.
2. For a wide range of preference relations (rules, such as majority rule, for transforming individual preferences between pairs of outcomes to social preferences over those pairs), redistributive issues imply cyclic social preferences over the set O of feasible outcomes.
3. For every outcome in O, there exists an institution – a method of *selecting* one outcome from O – that, ceteris paribus, yields that outcome as the social choice.
4. If the same relation applies as was used to define the social preference order over O, the social preference order over the set of all institutions, *I*, inherits the preference cycle over O.

This framework warrants two caveats. The first is to note that a description of the elements of *I* can be simple (e.g., a finite agenda, face-to-face bargaining under majority rule) or, as in the case of federal design, complex (e.g., a constitutional order or even perhaps the set of conventions that describe a society), depending on the substantive context of discussion. Our examples in the preceding section concerned things in which decisive coalitions are but simple majorities, but the lessons we draw from them apply to more complex methods of aggregating individual preferences and more complex notions of decisiveness. The outcomes that concerned Americans prior to the Civil War may have been framed in terms of tariffs, the maintenance and extension of slavery, and the route of a transcontinental railroad, but conflict over these issues ultimately manifested itself as a conflict over basic institutions and rules – over federal supremacy, nullification, and the constitutional right to secede. Our second caveat is to note that regardless of the substantive content of *I* – regardless of how we fill in the substantive details of the preceding framework – statements 1 through 4 imply only that there is the *possibility* of institutional instability. That is, the necessity of selecting an element of *I* in order to render a social decision over O can, under the shadow or redistributive politics, threaten a constant reshuffling of institutions that make even constitutions inherently vulnerable to disruption. But statements 2 and 4 concern only immediate *preferences*, and those preferences alone imply nothing about the eventual choice of an institution. We can talk about choice and move from discussing possibilities to probabilities only after we supply some description of the game people play with respect to these preferences – with respect to the rules for choosing a rule.

At this point, then, it is useful to introduce the notion of a social choice function that operates over I as opposed to O – a game form that dictates the eventual choice of an element of I. Before we do so, however, notice the generality of our formulation of the problem. Although we state matters in terms of outcomes (e.g., specific policies) and institutions (e.g., voting methods), we can contemplate a multitiered problem in which the outcome set of the second tier, O', is simply the set I, and I' are those alternative game forms (institutions, rules, and procedures) that might be employed to choose an element from I. We cannot say yet how many tiers we might need to describe a polity, but at some point, in order to ensure against an infinite regress of levels, we need to identify an institution – a social choice mechanism or game form – that is unlike those beneath it in that it is self-enforcing and not the consequence, once implemented, of any higher-order social decision process.

This is not to say that identifying such a mechanism is trivial or even that one universally exists. There is also some debate as to whether such an institution can be the product of conscious design (Buchanan and Tullock 1962) or whether it corresponds to those social conventions and norms that spontaneously arise only over time in an evolutionary and unconscious way (Hayek 1973, 1976, 1979; Voigt 1999) to "complete" a government's structure (Iarycrower et al. 2002). The argument we set forth later is that such an institution is, in fact, a combination of these two processes. Nevertheless, here we can identify the fundamental problem of federal design: finding a "method" for choosing institutions such that, despite individual preferences that fail to yield a dominant or undominated element over the things ultimately being evaluated – the redistributive consequences of government policy – this method consistently and over time yields an institutional outcome identical to or "nearly identical to" the status quo.

It should be evident, of course, that the substantive relevance of redistribution and the corresponding preference cycles they imply are not limited to federations. The likelihood that preferences over rules will derive directly from preferences over outcomes so that if social preferences cycle over outcomes, social preferences cycle over rules as well, serves as the basis of Riker's (1982) general treatise on populist versus liberal democracy. We can, then, take it as axiomatic that governmental policy in all democracies has redistributional consequences and that the instabilities or conflicts associated with these consequences determine people's preferences for institutions and rules of collective decision making, including people's desire to change those rules and institutions.

Redistributional consequences, however, pose special dangers in a federation. Because federations must maintain a balance between the authority of a center and the autonomy of federal subjects, federations are vulnerable to disruptions of a type that unitary states need not confront. First, virtually by definition, federalism institutionalizes interests by formally identifying federal subjects, each perhaps with their own political-economic character and needs. Thus, it is often more or less clear who will stand to benefit or lose from an institutional change – big states or small states, urban states or rural ones, rich states or poor ones, coastal states versus interior ones, and industrial states or agricultural states. This institutionalization of interests means that it is difficult, even impossible, to design rules "behind a veil of ignorance" – to design rules that are seen as wholly impartial before they are applied.[10] Second, federalism coordinates critical players (the polities within federal subjects) – those who are positioned to change the rules – by giving them explicit representation in the national legislature, a formal claim to the revenues of the center, and legal standing in such matters as amending the national constitution or, as in Germany, the authority to administer federal law. Thus a federation, unlike a unitary state in which the only parallel to the coalitions that federalism encourages are those to be found within the citizenry itself, necessarily provides the instruments of its own potential institutional instability. Finally, because federal subjects share state sovereignty with the federal center, the political elites who control each state's instruments of governance can usually succeed in renegotiating the rules if they are sufficiently motivated to do so – through secession, constitutional amendment, or simply by the statutes passed by state representatives in the national legislature.

Designing the Center

Federal design must contend with one additional problem that at times subsumes all others – the design of the center and its relation to federal subjects. Here, in fact, we find a practical difference between a federation and an alliance. If there is to be a hegemon when an alliance is formed – a player that will enforce the terms of agreement – the identity of that player, the nature of its self-interest, and its ability to sanction defections from the alliance will be readily apparent before any treaty is signed. For a federation, in contrast, each of these things must be the product of conscious design, and

[10] Brennan and Buchanan (1985: 30) argue that the existence of such a veil at the constitutional stage makes a potential institutional agreement more likely: "Faced with genuine uncertainty about how his position will be affected by the operation of a particular rule, the individual is led by his self-interest calculus to concentrate on choice options that eliminate or minimize the prospects for potentially disastrous results."

not always with the consequences intended. Madison, for instance, foresaw, as our initial quotation from *Federalist* 47 suggests, a general uprising among state governments for the protection of their interests in the event that the authority of the federal center became too oppressive. Yet that solution was not the one states chose in reaction to the Alien and Sedition Acts. Rather than follow Madison's and Jefferson's lead by supporting the Virginia and Kentucky resolutions in opposition to these acts, the solution they reached instead was to be found in the election of 1800 and the choice of Jefferson as president over the incumbent, Adams. Nor is the attempt to control the center via a balanced division of powers always satisfactory. Governments are complex entities, and few of the Framers would have predicted the role the court ultimately came to play in adjudicating conflict between the other two branches, or the power that would accrue to the presidency by rendering it the sole nationally elected office. To the extent that a federal state requires a more complex institutional structure than a unitary state, the consequences of federal design are less predictable than are those of a unitary design.

Thus, regardless of the solution preferred or envisioned by those who would create or reform a federation, it is evident that even if we ignore the theoretically debatable act of modeling federal subjects as unitary decision makers, simple N person models such as the one offered in the previous section expose only the tip of the iceberg of the many problems with which we must contend. If a federal state is to be something more than a mere alliance, its design necessarily entails the creation of an additional "player" with potentially complex (and even incoherent) motives. There are many ways to conceptualize the role of this new player, even in the abstract and stripped of practical difficulties – for example, as one that merely tries to coordinate federal subjects to an equilibrium, that is empowered to choose the rules of bargaining among those subjects, or that can dictate outcomes directly. But regardless of the role we might assign it, we cannot conceptualize the center simply as an entity with a life of its own, motivated by those things assigned to it by a constitution. A simple abstract $N+1$ person model of federalism in which the federal center is some disembodied creature with well-defined preferences separate from those of federal subjects is inadequate to describe or predict federal relations or the consequences of alternative institutional designs. Through representation in the national legislature as well as the role state-based political parties play in the election of national politicians, the federal center shares a genetic, if not a full biological connection to those subjects and their polities. Because that connection can be difficult to describe and the path of its evolutionary development anything but self-evident, it is reasonable to conjecture that the ultimate performance of a federal state is especially difficult to predict.

We hasten to add that even if we were able to dictate the motives of a federal center, it is not entirely clear what motives are best. Naturally, if the center "chooses" outcomes that benefit only a majority, and if it benefits that majority consistently over time, then disadvantaged players have an incentive to upset not only the outcomes the center imposes but the game itself. But even if the center is somehow motivated to choose outcomes that are "equitable," a majority may seek to overturn the result and the rules for bargaining that are part of the center's design. In other words, even if a "perfect" center is established – one that derives its authority from, say, a constitution that carefully enumerates its authority and the standards of fairness to which it must adhere – some federal subjects will, in general, have an incentive to pervert that design and transform the center's motives to serve their ends.

The problems associated with designing and motivating the federal center are well illustrated by the United States, which, upon its founding, possessed one extraordinary advantage and one evident disadvantage. The advantage was that nearly every one of the original thirteen states had both a mercantile seaboard and an agricultural interior. Thus, nearly every one confronted an identical internal political division, between urban and rural, creditor and debtor. In this environment, an event such as Shays's Rebellion was not a mere sectional concern but a threat that could be understood by the political elite of nearly every state – a threat that would motivate those elites to concerted action in the form of "forming a more perfect Union." At the same time, however, the United States also possessed one great disadvantage – the divide between slave and free. Unable to resolve this issue constitutionally (aside from an agreement to postpone any attempted resolution until 1808, Article 5, which was almost immediately ignored following the Constitution's ratification), a largely extraconstitutional and wholly artificial device was used prior to the outbreak of its civil war to avert wholly disruptive bargaining. That device was to maintain a balance in the federal Senate by admitting new states in pairs, one slave and one free. Such a balance, however, could not be sustained indefinitely. First, given new technologies, the accession of California, and the desire to render the United States a continental power, there was no apparent compromise between the North and the South in the important decision about how to best supply the public good of national transportation by choosing the route of the first intercontinental railroad.[11] Second, and perhaps more important, westward migration soon made it apparent that this balance could be but a temporary measure in the face of two related and unalterable economic facts: the unprofitability of slavery outside the regions in which it already existed, and the potential for economic growth in an industrialized North versus an agricultural South. Even the admission of Texas under the proviso that it be allowed to divide

[11] As Ambrose (2000: 31) correspondingly notes, "no free-state politician was ready to provide a charter of funds for a railroad that would help extend slavery. The Free-Soilers wanted Chicago or St. Louis or Minneapolis as the eastern terminus, but no slave state politician was willing to give it to them."

itself into as many as five distinct states could not be a solution, since slavery was profitable only in its eastern cotton regions; the economic demand for slaves in the western ranching regions was minimal if not nonexistent. Thus, devices such as the Kansas-Nebraska Act and Missouri Compromise could only postpone the day of reckoning – the day in which the South would become a permanent minority upon which a majority could impose its will.

In this context Calhoun of South Carolina became the champion of a new concept in federal design – the concurrent majority. But this concept, reduced to its bare essentials, was a proposal to eliminate bargaining altogether in the Congress by requiring unanimity – equivalently, a proposal to freeze the system at the status quo with respect to the legitimacy and legality of slavery. That restriction, though, could not be sustained any more than could the agreement to maintain a Senate artificially balanced. The attempts at compromise and extraconstitutional resolution were extensive. But Lincoln's election, which displayed the South's permanent minority status not merely in the halls of Congress but nationally as well, revealed the extent to which the free states could dictate the role and motives of the federal center so that it would no longer be a neutral arbitrator of disputes or a potential member of a southern coalition when bargaining with the North. The result, of course, was the complete disruption of the Union.

An attempt to reach federal balance by building consensus similarly failed in the case of the post-Napoleonic Swiss Confederation (1815–48), where constitutional gridlock also resulted in civil war. After Napoleon's downfall, the so-called Mediation Constitution imposed by France in 1803 was formally abolished, and between 1813 and 1815 there was no effective federal center. Finally, in August 1815, the Vienna Congress brokered a compromise whereby twenty-two cantons signed a new Federal Treaty. The new confederation (league) did not have direct authority over anything except military matters, with all other federal powers exercised through the cantons. With the exception of record keeping and certain military organizations, there were no federal agencies that were not primarily cantonal, with the treaty resting upon the principle of unanimous consent. All cantons, large and small, had one vote in the Diet, the Swiss Confederation's highest decision-making body,[12] but the Diet itself was not quite a parliament since deputies were limited to implementing the instructions of canton governments (Huber 1909: 77).

This highly decentralized organization, however, quickly collided with commercial interests (Linder 1998). The proliferation of cantonal currencies, customs barriers, weights, and measures stood in the way of a developing common market, and soon a growing middle class began to advocate a new, unifying constitution, with Liberals acting as the national political force behind these demands. There was no national Liberal Party, but, throughout

[12] The half cantons, which had been formed by division, had but one vote that they could exercise only in common.

the 1830s, cantonal Liberal groups managed to secure political power in most non-Catholic cantons, installing democratic institutions they viewed "as the best guarantee against unwanted state interference in the private, above all commercial affairs of the individual citizen" (Gruner and Piterle 1983: 36). The problem was that the 1815 Federal Treaty could only be amended by unanimous agreement of the cantons, and the bloc of small Conservative and Catholic cantons stood in opposition to reform, fearing dominance of the Liberal and mostly Protestant cantons.

The Liberals' attempts at compromise failed and they were soon outflanked by "Radicals" who rejected a federal solution exclusively within the legal framework of the 1815 Federal Pact. Their leadership, arguing that "no legal document should stand in the way of the people's desire for national unification," advocated the use of force if necessary to implement change (Gruner and Piterle 1983: 36). A frontal attack on Catholic rights began in 1841, when in direct violation of the Federal Treaty, the Radical government decreed the dissolution of all local Catholic monasteries. By 1845, gangs of Radical volunteers invaded Catholic cantons to 'liberate' them from Catholic governments. In response, seven such governments signed a separate treaty (the Sonderbund) in 1845. After Catholic deputies left the Diet in 1847, however, the Radicals there demanded the dissolution of the Sonderbund and, upon refusal, declared a military intervention. A brief civil war led to the defeat of the Catholic cantons so that without their opposition, the Radicals in the Diet could prepare a new constitution. A majority of cantons accepted it, while the Catholic cantons were forced to submit (Hughes 1962; Linder 1998). Thus, as in the United States in 1860, there was no solution to the problem of federal reform within the consensual framework of 1815–48, and the modern Swiss federation was created by less than consensual, democratic, or peaceful means.

2.5 Bargaining for Control of the Center

The destructive conflict that characterized the early American federation and the Swiss Confederation finds its parallel in nearly all failed federations – and, more often than not, without any underlying moral cause. In most cases the corresponding political instability derived from attempts by a subset of federal subjects to improve the terms of their membership within the existing union – attempts that were described by their initiators as rendering a federation "more fair." Indeed, the words Dent (1989: 179) uses to describe conflict within the Nigerian federation can be applied nearly universally: "[I]t is a sad fact of history that many of the worst quarrels are not between good and bad but between two different sorts of good." The case of the Federation of the West Indies is a useful illustration. When that federation was negotiated in 1947–57, Trinidad agreed to the terms put forth by Jamaica – a weak federation modeled largely on the idea of a customs union that awarded limited powers to the central government. Fearing it could not compete economically, however, Jamaica insisted on exceptions for a significant number of its own products, although it agreed in principle to develop incrementally a more-encompassing and authoritative union. Although the other key member of the federation, Trinidad and Tobago, preferred a strong center, a full-scale customs union, and a guarantee of freedom of movement for labor and capital, the belief that "any federation is better that no federation" led its prime minister, Dr. Eric Williams, in 1956 to accept a compromise that promised a formal review of the terms of federation after five years. Nevertheless, soon thereafter, Williams could not resist initiating a process that called for an immediate review and revision, especially of provisions designed to facilitate Trinidad's trading potential (Flanz 1968: 93–94, 111). At the same time, Jamaica demanded that seats in the federal House of Representatives be reallocated strictly by population, which would increase its vote share to about one-half (Proctor 1963: 80; see also Springer 1962). Three years of constitutional-level renegotiation resulted in a proposal for a new federal arrangement, which would have moved the federation toward an even weaker central government than was originally accepted by Jamaica. The proposal, though, was never implemented. Although the Jamaican government initially supported the idea of union under the new terms, it was forced by its domestic opposition to put the issue before its electorate. On September 19, 1961, with 60 percent of the electorate participating, 53.8 percent voted to secede. And once Jamaica withdrew, Trinidad and Tobago announced their own withdrawal, after which the remaining eight members of the federation dissolved what remained of the union (Proctor 1963).

This case illustrates what we find generally if we look at bargaining in failed federations – namely, negotiations for a compromise seemingly never collapse because the parties fail to reach agreement on some specific issue. Substantive issues, of course, underlie debate since they are the fundamental source of preferences, but collapse manifests itself in the form of a failure to agree on some core structural principle. For example, there were no specific material issues involved in the most recent instances of federal failure – those involving the USSR, Czechoslovakia, and Yugoslavia. Similarly, it is impossible to identify any particular issue, that, if resolved, might have preserved the postcolonial federations that failed in the 1960s (e.g., the Mali Federation in 1960, British West India in 1962, the Central African Federation in 1963, the Federation of Malaysia with Singapore in 1965). Instead, in all cases there was a clear disagreement among the constituent units about the alternative principles of organization and, in particular, about the scope of powers to be allocated to the federal center.

The bargaining these cases illustrate is readily misinterpreted and distorts the resulting theory that various researchers offer. It is commonly assumed that national leaders and subnational units bargain with each other for more authority – that bargaining is an *N+1* player affair and that federal design should concern itself primarily with finding ways to maintain a balance between the authority of the *N+1st* player and the autonomy of federal subjects. We might speculate that this view originates with the initial concerns of the Framers of the U.S. Constitution and the Anti-Federalists whose opposition proceeded from the argument that the proposed federal center possessed too much authority. The United States was, after all, the first centralized constitutional federation. However, the bargaining that immediately emerged there and which we see today in contemporary federal systems is more commonly a manifestation of competition *among federal subjects* (or, more properly, among those whose fates are directly tied to the welfare of federal subjects), in which case design should not necessarily limit itself or even focus on how to maintain a balance between the center and those subjects but rather should focus on finding ways to ensure that no subject or subset of them can "capture" the center to the disadvantage of the rest.[13]

Thus understood, bargaining over the allocation of federal powers is more commonly a case of some subset of subjects preferring that more power be allocated to the center while others prefer the status quo or seek a diminution of the center's power. The 1848 Swiss Federal Constitution, for instance, was a difficult compromise between the two extreme views of a unitary centralism (supported by Protestants) and a traditional loose confederation (supported by the Catholic cantons). In Belgium, federalization originally was popular only among the Flemish, whereas Wallons prefered rather limited decentralization. The governors of Russia's "nonethnic" oblasts have been among the strongest supporters of the central government's attempt to encroach on the prerogatives of the ethnic republics (Roeder 2000). The long-lasting debate in India prior to independence over the structure of its federalism is largely a conflict between Hindus, who wish to centralize governmental prerogatives, and Muslims, who advocate maximal regional autonomy in order to ensure independent decision making within the regions they control (McWhinney 1966: 30). The failure of the West Indian federation is directly related to the fact that Trinidad supported a stronger central government, whereas Jamaica opposed it (Flanz 1968). And the collapse of Czechoslovakia was the result of a disagreement between Czech and Slovak elites over the acceptable degree of federal centralization: Slovaks insisted on a looser union than the Czech majority perceived as being in its interest (Stein 1997).[14]

[13] In the United States, as Grodzins (1966: 330–1) observes: "Most great national conflicts that take on a 'federal-state' dimension find the states divided against each other, some aligned with the federal government and others in opposition to what are enumerated as national policies. The segregation conflict is a case in point. The struggle is not simply between the federal government and the states but between the segregationist states (comprising no more than a quarter of all the states) and the rest of the nation, including the federal government and over 35 states."

[14] Perhaps the unique example of postwar federal collapse that involved a dispute between the center and regional governments was the dissolution of the USSR in 1991. There, however, the dispute was not so much over the autonomy of federal subjects relative to the center, as it was a dispute of political egos and personalities and the desire on the part of those who instigated dissolution to rid themselves of any central authority whatsoever.

TABLE 2.1. *Control of the Center at the Time of Regime Failure (federations founded after 1945)*

	State(s) or Group(s) in Control of the Center	Number of Units	(Main) Federal Units
United States of Indonesia, 1949–50	Republic of Indonesia (Negara)	17	Republic of Indonesia (Negara), East Indonesia, East Java, Madura, West Java, South Sumatra, East Sumatra
Iraq and Jordan Federation, 1958	Jordan	2	Iraq and Jordan
Mali Federation with Senegal, 1959–60	Senegal	2	The Sudanese Republic (Mali) and Senegal
United Arab Republic, 1958–61	Egypt	2	Egypt and Syria
Ethiopia, 1952–62	Ethiopia (proper)	13	Ethiopia (proper), formally divided into 12 provinces, and Eritrea
British West India, 1958–62	Trinidad	10	Jamaica, Trinidad and Tobago, Barbados, Antigua, Montserrat, St. Christopher-Nevis-Anguilla, Dominica, Grenada, St. Lucia, and St. Vincent
Union of Burma, 1948–62	Burma (proper)	5	Burma proper, Shan, Karenni (Kayah), Kachin, and Karen
West and East Pakistan, 1947–62	West Pakistan	5 (1947)[a]	West Punjab, Sind, North-West Frontier, Baluchistan, and East Bengal
		2 (1955)	East Bengal
Central African Federation, 1953–63	South Rhodesia (supported with white settlers elsewhere)	3	South Rhodesia, Northern Rhodesia, and Nyasaland

	State(s) or Group(s) in Control of the Center	Number of Units	(Main) Federal Units
Libya, 1951–63	Cyrenaica	3	Cyrenaica, Tripolitaica, Fezzan
Malaysia (with Singapore), 1963–5	Malaya (11 original Malay states)	14	States of Malaya (11 states), Singapore, Sarawak, and Sabah (North Borneo)
Nigeria (The First Republic), 1960–6	Northern region	3 (1960)	Northern, Western, Eastern regions
		4 (1963)	Western region was split into two parts
Uganda, 1962–7	Ethnic groups of the North	4	Buganda, Ankole, Toro, and Bunyoro
Congo (Zaire), 1960–9	Kasai (Baluba ethnic group)	6 (1960) 21 (1962–3+) 12 (1966+)	Leopoldville, Equateur, East (Orientale), Kivu, Katanga, and Kasai
Cameroon, 1961–72	French Cameroun	2	French Cameroun, Southern (British) Cameroons
USSR, 1922(1989)–91	Russia	15	Russia, Ukraine, Kazakhstan, Belorussia, Moldova, Georgia, Armenia, Azerbaijan, Estonia, Latvia, Lithuania, Uzbekistan, Tajikistan, Kirgizia, Turkmenia
Yugoslavia, 1946(1990)–91	Serbia	6	Slovenia, Bosnia, Croatia, Macedonia
Czechoslovakia, 1969(1990)–92	Czech Republic	2	Czech Republic, Slovakia

[a] Plus 10 princely states.

It is also important to note that in nearly all cases of federal failure we can find one group or another that succeeds ultimately in capturing control of the center, leaving the losers in this contest to wield the only "institutional" sword left – the federation's dissolution. Table 2.1 lists all eighteen federal regimes that dissolved (or became unitary states at the instigation of those who gained control of the center) since 1945 and identifies the major subnational units or ethnic groups that assumed a dominant position in the federation. Rather than show that federal failure entails a takeover of federal subjects by a too-powerful center – an elimination of federal subject autonomy and the creation of a unitary state – we find instead that the center is first taken over by one or a subset of subjects and that, if a state does not become unitary, federal failure follows largely from the defensive reaction of those excluded from this takeover.

The circumstances that allow for a takeover of the center are varied, but one stands out, because careful (although not necessarily feasible) design could, in most instances, avoid it. That circumstance is the one in which one federal subject is, by virtue of its population or resources, equipped to exert a significantly greater impact on the center than the rest. This was the case in the USSR with respect to Russia, and one can reasonably argue that the USSR's other republics were as concerned with control by Russia as by some central authority.[15] Given the disproportionate advantages of population and relative economic prosperity, this was also the problem felt by Slovaks in Czechoslovakia; it was an important consideration in Napoleon's initial design of Swiss federal cantons;[16] and it was seen eventually to be an important imperfection in Nigeria's initial design (Horowitz 1985).

Interestingly, this problem was avoided in the United States not by virtue of anything contained in its Constitution, but earlier and by design under the Articles of Confederation and subsequently by a provision passed in 1787 by the soon to be defunct Continental Congress – the Northwest Ordinance. Briefly, owing to various land grants awarded by England, many of the original thirteen states could lay claim to territory far to the west. These claims overlapped in several instances, but Virginia held the most geographically extensive claim, encompassing a territory that today includes the states of Kentucky, West Virginia, Ohio, Michigan, Illinois, Indiana, and Wisconsin. Already the most prosperous state in 1780, it is evident that had Virginia been allowed to extend itself to include this vast territory, westward

[15] See d'Encausse (1993), especially chaps. 9 and 11, and although the event occurred only shortly before the USSR's dissolution, in spring 1991, certainly the leaders of its separate parts were fully aware throughout the period of the sentiment, as implied by an event recounted by Yeltsin and Fitzpatrick (1994: 37), that Russia was first among equals: "[O]ne evening my automobile ended up at the end of a line of [Soviet republic] limousines. My security people sprang forward in alarm, made an incredible U-turn, digging up the Novo-Ogaryovo lawn in the process, and finally put the car back at the head of the line – Russia first!"

[16] It is argued that the real foundation of the modern Swiss federation was laid when Napoleon, on April 12, 1798, ended the old Confederation and divided territories controlled by the largest cantons into ten new cantons. Until this division, Bern and Zurich in particular possessed extensive dependent territories and large populations and economic resources: "[T]here was a distinct tendency towards an asymmetrical development since, the more powerful cantons were often tempted towards actions and alliances independent of the rest of the Confederation" (Dikshit 1975: no. 1, p. 35). In other words, for years Bern and Zurich struggled to dominate the old Confederation, including four internal religious wars against the Catholic cantons (Linder 1998).

migration would render it dominant in a few decades. However, it was also clear at the time that none of the states had the resources to control this territory, and so in 1780 and 1781 the states ceded their claims to the Congress. Subsequently, Kentucky was split off and made an early candidate for admission, largely to secure the fidelity of its population against Spain, which controlled the mouth of the Mississippi and the region's economic lifeblood. But in what must be deemed one of the most fortuitous and farsighted acts of the Congress, the Northwest Ordinance – an act that acquired near constitutional status – required that the United States not hold the territory it had acquired north of the Ohio River and west of the Allegheny mountain ridge as colonies, but instead provided for the admission of new states on the principle of strict equality with the old. And rather than allow the Northwest Territory to enter as a single state, which itself might eventually dominate Union affairs, it required democratic governance within it and set the boundaries for not less than three and not more than five new states – ultimately, Ohio, Michigan, Illinois, Indiana, and Wisconsin. In this way the United States, in an act of conscious design, avoided the kind of asymmetry that plagued the USSR and Czechoslovakia two hundred years hence and that threatens any new federation that fails to accommodate a profoundly important parameter of design – the geographic definition of federal subjects.

Geographic definition is, in fact, a frequently overlooked aspect of design (Dikshit 1975). The United States, of course, benefited from the fact that the territories west of the Mississippi with which it had to deal were essentially blank slates where geographic boundaries could be drawn freely (since the Indian population was given no voice). But even there we have seen manipulations in the quest for stability, the most notable one being the splitting off of Maine from Massachusetts in order to maintain a balance between slave and free. In contrast, when contemplating alternative postcommunist designs for Czechoslovakia, it was assumed that if sustained as a federal state, there would be two and at most three federal subjects defined by history and ethnic composition. No thought was given as far as we know to alternatives, such as dividing the country into federal subjects that mixed the ethnic composition of each subject. This is not to say that any specific division could have been sustained, for there would have remained the issue of gerrymandering and the likelihood that one side or the other would see its interests endangered by any proposed geographic division. Few minorities or majorities are oblivious to the fact, when establishing a federation, that "a group that may or may not be a majority in a country's total population [can be] dominant within a particular region and [can use] its institutional position within a federal system to discriminate systematically against other groups in that region" (Gunther and Mughan 1993: 298). Similarly, although Gorbachev considered a wide range of reforms and compromises in his attempt to keep the USSR whole, to our knowledge no serious effort was made to implement the idea of dividing Russia itself into five or seven separate republics (but see Dunlop 1993: 17–18).

2.6 Allocating Jurisdictions

Both because of its justification as a facilitator of public-goods provision and because of the preceding political realities, a clear division of powers between levels of government (including the authority to use one tax or another to raise revenues) is commonly deemed the most direct way to short-circuit undesirable federal bargaining both among federal subjects and between those subjects and the federal center. If political elites within a federal subject fear that the center can be captured by those whose interests are inimical to their own on some set of issues (e.g., language policy, slavery, control of natural resources), then the surest safeguard might seem to be a constitutional provision that removes the corresponding issues from the purview of the center. Thus, a constitutionally mandated allocation of jurisdictional responsibilities, including long lists of exclusive and joint jurisdictions, is commonly seen as an essential part of federal design. Moreover, because any such initial allocation is assumed to have a direct impact on the identities of future winners and losers, we should not be surprised to see disagreements over a particular allocation resulting not only in the dismemberment of a union, but in the failure to erect such an entity in the first place.

Interestingly, however, the literature offers little specific yet theoretically prescribed guidance in this respect to those who would design or reform a federal state. For example, although Watts (1966, 1970) offers an excellent comparative assessment of the allocation of powers, he does little more than emphasize that a wide variety of arrangements are feasible and that there does not appear to be any apparent rule for identifying appropriate allocations. The sole advice he offers is "each federation should adopt those administrative arrangements which are most suitable to its particular circumstances rather than attempt to follow a single or theoretical model" (Watts 1970: 135). Wheare (1953: 83–4) chooses not to discuss the problem in detail and somewhat arbitrarily suggests that "what is likely to work best is a short exclusive list and a rather longer concurrent list" of jurisdictions, in which the aim must be to "get an exclusive list for the general government which contains as many as possible of the important subjects of general concern, leaving perhaps residual power to the sub-national governments, and to hope that if any new subject of general importance arises, the need for general control will ensure that it will be handed over to the general government." Of course, we then have the example of Germany – arguably one of the world's more successful democratic federations – operating under a constitution with a quite detailed list of jurisdictions given exclusively to the central government, of jurisdictional responsibilities to be shared by the center and state governments, and policy domains that require review by the upper legislative chamber, the Bundesrat. And perhaps as a precursor to the European fascination with the word "subsidiarity," Sharma (1953: 153) attempts a more practical approach – arguing that economic and functional properties of government goods and services and the problems they occasion ought to be the basis for a federal division of powers – but because no two countries are identical in their internal problems, "no rules can possibly be prescribed to guide the distribution of powers between the federal government and the state governments." Thus, "the division of powers between the federal government and the various state governments in federation is dictated by the special circumstances of the country. But the broad fact remains that naturally those powers are assigned to the state governments which vitally affect the life of the inhabitants and allow the development of the country in accordance with local conditions of the states, while matters of national importance concerning the country as a whole are assigned to the central government" (p. 145).[17]

Of course, what Sharma (along with the Europeans today who wrestle with translating the notion of subsidiarity into practical policy guidance) ignores in his admittedly qualified and ambiguous prescription is that even if a good or service is strictly and wholly public in consumption, it remains private in production and thereby entails bargaining in the determination of its supply. But if there is bargaining and redistributional consequences, then there can be no clean theoretical division between, say, purely local and purely national public goods. Even if a good is deemed purely national in consumption, there will be differential local consequences in its production, in which case there cannot be a simple economic criteria for allocating responsibilities across governments. What we have in whatever advice we can find, then, amounts to little more than convoluted restatements of the fact that, absent any compelling theoretical basis for doing things one way or another, jurisdictional boundaries and allocations of power between the center and federal subjects are determined as much by politics as anything else.

This conclusion will not come as a surprise to students of politics well versed in the classic writings of such scholars as Pendleton Herring, V. O. Key, William Riker, E. E. Schattschneider, and Robert Dahl, who see in the sweep of two hundred years of American history the constant ebb and flow of state responsibilities. In the view of the inherent redistributive nature of

[17] Credit for the first attempt to justify the separation of federal and state powers based on the characteristics of the public goods involved belongs to Madison, who in *Federalist* 45 predicted that federal powers "will be exercised principally on external objects, as war, peace, negotiation, and foreign commerce; with which last the power of taxation will for the most part be connected." In contrast, state power would "extend to all the objects, which, in the ordinary course of affairs, concern the lives, liberties and properties of the people; and the internal order, improvement, and prosperity of the State."

democratic politics, federal constraints cannot be applied rigidly. Ongoing intergovernmental bargaining is a necessary and uniformly healthy characteristic of democratic federalism, and only needs to be prevented from taking destructive forms. The notion of a constitution as a "living document" bespeaks of the idea that federal constraints must of necessity undergo continuous adjustment. Furthermore, such constraints need to be imposed prudently. Not only is it impossible to mandate every detail of decision making in a federation since federal subjects will retain a sufficient measure of sovereignty to recall issues to the table for renegotiation; it may be neither practical for reasons of enforcement nor desirable for reasons of efficiency to try to allocate much of anything in the way of policy responsibilities except for the usual and noncontroversial list of suspects (e.g., control of the currency, military, weights and measures).

One implication of this discussion, then, is that the search for federal stability should not focus on constitutional jurisdictional allocations of responsibilities, or even necessarily assume that such allocations alone can do much in the way of guaranteeing stability. Although they may have symbolic value, it also follows that, although some federal constraints need to be well protected when others are changed, we should not assume that an institutional status quo has necessarily been altered in any fundamental and dangerous way when one constraint or another is changed. In an otherwise stable federation changes in a specific jurisdictional allocation can be a part of an incremental process of adjustment and refinement in the federal structure. Certain institutional matters, moreover, may defy a permanent resolution even in the short run so that, with or without cycling, the status quo is dynamic rather than static.

To illustrate, consider the Canadian experience with natural resources. Section 109 of its constitution grants the provinces ownership of the lands and resources within their territories (the United States does the same with respect to offshore rights along the Texas coast, but not otherwise). At the same time, though, the national government, as in all other federations, manages trade and foreign policy and is empowered to protect the free flow of goods throughout Canada. The problem is that it is impossible to separate definitively these two policy domains. For example, the desire of the western provinces to maximize oil revenues during the energy crises of the 1970s contradicted the national government's purpose of ensuring adequate energy supplies throughout the federation, and Ontario's attempt to protect its log and pulpwood processing industry from competitors ran afoul of the government's international trade policies (Leslie 1987; Howlett 1991; Brown 1994). Exacerbating internal tensions over the resolution of such jurisdictional overlaps is the fact that Canada's provinces have vastly different capabilities: resource-poor maritime provinces, an industrially developed center, and resource-exporting western provinces. Formal attempts at accommodation cannot foreclose the necessity for ongoing negotiation. Although Section 92A of the Canadian Constitution (added as an amendment in 1982) expands provincial power in areas that were previously under exclusive federal control, its grant of concurrent powers requires that resolution of disputes be reached through political accommodation (Howlett 1991).

What we see here with respect to the fluidity of jurisdictional particulars we see as well with respect to explicitly redistributional ones: "[T]here can be no final solution to the allocation of financial resources in a federal system. There can only be adjustments and reallocations in light of changing conditions" (Wheare 1953: 117). In practice, the center in all modern federations controls major revenue sources and, therefore, there is always a significant political demand for vertical fiscal redistribution from and to subnational governments. Naturally, it is foolhardy to propose a federal design in which the allocation of these revenues is not subject to some political wrangling. Correspondingly, we should not be surprised to see the magnitude and importance of such transfers constantly changing across time and across units. In the United States, for example, between only 1966 and 1990, states received as little as 14.5 and as much as 47.5 percent of their revenues from the federal government, with the average shifting from 27.7 percent in 1966, 29.3 percent in 1976, and 23.8 percent in 1990.

These data and the bargaining we see from one federation to the next over jurisdictional rules are, to be said once again, a healthy feature of a vital federation. There is, in fact, a critical difference between these things and what we observe in failed federations. Renegotiation in the Canadian case, for instance, is only partial – along one or a few specific allocation dimensions, if you want – whereas in the West Indian and other cases described earlier (including the United States prior to its Civil War, where bargaining concerned not only the economic issues of slavery and the route of a continental railroad but also the more general constitutional-level issue of states' rights and the authority of states to nullify federal law) it concerned the overall structure of federalism. Bargaining in the Canadian case, then, is *institutionalized* – constrained by other components of its federal structure. More specifically, it is constrained by the politics engendered by those other components.

2.7 Three Levels of Institutional Design

In the next chapter we examine in greater detail two specific instances of noninstitutionalized bargaining, but to conclude this one we want to outline a rough conceptual scheme as an initial guide to what we want to accomplish with respect to federal institutional design. To begin, we can think of a federal system as consisting of three levels of institutional structure. At the first level, Level 1, we find restrictions on bargaining of two sorts. The first are those agreements that one may ideally want to have carved in stone or at least made especially difficult to subvert – provisions that prohibit federal subjects from engaging in certain actions (e.g., negotiating treaties with foreign powers), that require them to abide by certain constraints (e.g., the comity clause, Article 4, of the U.S. Constitution, which requires that "Full faith and credit shall be given in each state to the public acts, records, and judicial proceedings of every other state"), that prohibit federal subjects from levying taxes of a certain type, and that limit their governments to specific democratic forms. Level 1 also includes those federal constraints that, although also intended to regulate bargaining, are understood to be ultimately renegotiable – constraints such as substantively formulated jurisdictional boundaries between levels of government. These constraints may be constitutionally specified lists of exclusive and concurrent policy jurisdictions as in the German or Russian case; they may be precise constraints such as those that empower only the federal government to raise armies, coin money, and declare war; they can be imprecise authorizations such as the U.S. Constitution's provision that "the Congress shall have the power to . . . provide for the general welfare of the United States . . . [and] to regulate commerce among the several states" (Article 1, Section 8); or they may consist of jurisdictional divisions that are the product of convention, statutory legislation, or court interpretation.

Insofar as any advice we might offer here with respect to the preferred content of Level 1 is concerned, if anything we are prejudiced toward a minimum of provisions. Even under the best of circumstances, jurisdictional allocations, as we note earlier, are barriers inherently built on sand – the sand of legislative enactment, judicial interpretation, and executive order, which are themselves ongoing political decisions and the essence of political negotiation and renegotiation. Such allocations are, in fact, the essence of Madison's "parchment barriers." On the other hand, constitutional comity and residual powers clauses, clauses that limit the state's (federal and regional) ability to restrict the free flow of goods, people, and capital within its domain (thereby providing some minimal guarantee of a common market), and clauses that require democratic governance in all federal subjects – clauses, in other words, that empower the judiciary to negate capricious policy by the legislative and executive branches of all governments within the federation – are almost certainly essential.

We are less certain of what advice we might usefully offer with respect to revenue-sharing formulas, which dictate the allocation of federal tax revenues across federal subjects when the national government is primarily responsible for tax collection. However, this much is clear: locating such formulas in a constitution is an admission of their inherent instability, which, in turn, poses a paradox. First, if the redistribution of tax revenues is believed to be so unstable that constitutional provisions are deemed necessary, we cannot discount the possibility that the pressure to renegotiate any agreement will undermine the constitution as a whole through amendment and reamendment. But if that instability is, for one reason or another (e.g., a social consensus over its main character), deemed to be not so great and is believed to be relatively impervious to political assault, then in all likelihood no constitutional provision is necessary. Our prejudice, then, is to relegate such provisions not to a constitution but either to ordinary statute or, as in the case of Argentina and Australia, to special politically insulated commissions and legislation that can be changed only with extraordinary legislative majorities.

Whether such formulae are desirable or not, no Level 1 clause or provision can be of much consequence unless fortified by a second level of rules and procedures – provisions that institutionalize procedures for interpreting, executing, and changing any Level 1 constraint, as well as for making policy decisions that are not limited by those constraints. Here, in Level 2, we find those things commonly identified with the core of even a minimalist democratic constitution and, in a federal state, intended to regulate bargaining over the first level. Level 2, then, encompasses procedures for amending a constitution, the structure of the national legislature and corresponding rules of representation, and the overall structure of the separation of powers within the national government – the choice of presidential versus parliamentary government, veto rules, no-confidence votes, procedures for the passage of legislation, and so on. We should also include under this heading things we might not prefer to see included in an "ideal" federal constitution, such as any authority given to the federal government to negotiate "treaties" between itself and federal subjects (as in Russia between 1992 and 1998; see Chapter 9). Finally, this level includes rules and procedures for an evolutionary transition from a unitary to a federal state (as in Spain) or from a loose alliance to a federation (as in the European Union); a statement as to the supremacy of federal law; the process whereby new members can be admitted to the federation; prohibitions of secession; and, of course, a listing of rights intended to constrain the actions of both federal subjects and the federal center with respect to the ultimate sovereign, the people.

We would not argue that there is necessarily a clean separation between Level 1 and Level 2. Indeed, this boundary is especially obscure in those ethnically, religiously, linguistically, or racially divided societies in which it is assumed that special provision must be made in even "normal" constitutional provisions for power sharing, equalization of access to the state, and special protection of federal subjects. We might prefer to argue against the conscious design of an asymmetric federation, but, as we see in the next chapter, asymmetry beyond counterbalances of representation in the national legislature may be required to negotiate successfully the formation of a federation in the first place. And although we appreciate the view of scholars such as Rabushka and Shepsle (1972) who argue that, short of limiting democracy itself, stability is an unattainable goal in divided societies, we are not yet prepared to throw in the towel and prefer instead to look for solutions using the standard catalog of institutional parameters. But for reasons that hopefully will become clear later, we believe that if there are solutions to be found (which is not always the case), we can do so only by considering an additional level of institutions – a Level 3 – that need not explicitly address federal institutional forms.

The necessity for this third level derives from the fact that in order to be able endogenously to implement constitutional provisions corresponding to Level 2, regardless of whether we are speaking of a homogeneous or heterogeneous state, our scheme must supply appropriate motivation to individual participants in the political process. That is, as far as the overall institutional structure is concerned, we still must ask and answer the question, What enforces a constitution? and, equivalently, What keeps bargaining and renegotiation over the first level from bubbling up to encourage a renegotiation of the second? Or put in the context of our earlier abstract framework, What is the method for terminating an infinite regress of levels of institutional control? The answer to such questions lies in the character of a third level of rules that bear an integral connection to the second as well as the overall political structure of society. But here, lest we proceed to the infinite regress of adding a fourth, then a fifth, then a sixth level to enforce the one beneath it, we encounter a conceptually distinct category of institutional structure – a structure that needs to be immediately self-enforcing, by which we mean a level of constraints such that, regardless of the issues that arise to occasion incentives to renegotiate specific items found at the first two levels, those issues cannot generate motives to renegotiate the structure of the third. In other words, we want this third level to comprise, along with the first two, an endogenously enforced incentive compatible mechanism. That is, taking all levels together, we want our rules to function so that all relevant decision makers, when acting in their own self-interest, have no incentive to upset the constitutional rules at Level 2, and a positive incentive to sustain the full nexus of rules, especially those at Level 3, or, in the case of Level 1, to change them only incrementally.

Levels 1 through 3 in their entirety, then, need to occasion what Ferejohn, Rakov, and Riley (2001: 10) describe as a *Constitutional Culture*: "a web of interpretative norms, canons, and practices." However, because it encompasses all of the traditions and customs of a society in addition to its political institutions, a constitutional culture cannot be designed and implemented in the same way we build a bridge. It can, at best, merely be encouraged through the judicious selection of the institutional parameters at our disposal. Thus, although we appreciate the wide net that needs to be cast in order to describe fully the incentive-compatible federal system we seek, we will, of necessity, limit ourselves to a small subset of relevant variables. But even here, that subset will include more than "mere" constitutional provisions. Indeed, Ferejohn et al. (2001: 15–16) relay the spirit of what must be made a part of Level 3 when they observe that if a political scientist were asked "to identify the distinctive characteristic elements of contemporary American government . . . that provide the best explanation of its structure and functioning, she would probably point to single-member districts, plurality rule elections, the structure of the political parties and the party system, the administrative-regulatory state, the interest group system, the president's role as chief legislator, and perhaps the development of an extensive civil liberties jurisprudence by the courts. What these governmental features have in common . . . is that they are not fixed or specified in the text of the Constitution." The institutional variables of Level 3 that we discuss in later chapters will serve to emphasize the importance of extraconstitutional institutions and the necessity, when designing a federal state and attempting to implement an incentive compatible political system, of considering those "nonfederal" variables that impact individual choice.

Admittedly, at this point the requirement of incentive compatibility may sound utopian (which it may be for many societies) and, given the sweeping nature of "constitutional culture," vague. Complicating things further, we also admit that at times there will be only a vague separation between the institutions we assign to either Level 3 or Level 2, since much of the structure of the second will also guide people's motives and definitions of self-interest with respect to the third. In addition, the content of Level 3 will not consist exclusively of rules subject to conscious design or short-term manipulation. Nevertheless, we want to emphasize that federal design – if not the design of democracy generally – consists of rules legitimately subject to renegotiation (a part of Level 1), rules that constrain the state and any such renegotiation (Level 2), and rules (Level 3) that, by the very motives they establish, keep themselves as well as those at the constitutional levels in place.

3

Two Cases of Uninstitutionalized Bargaining

> The perilous moment for a bad government is when that government tries to mend its ways.
>
> Tocqueville 1955: 177

> All of the socialist regimes in Europe depended for their survival on maximizing economic growth and maintaining the party's economic and political monopoly.
>
> Bunce 1999: 56

> It is a fact of current life that secession movements are under way, with more to come. It is also a fact that there is growing support for including some sort of right to secede in a number of constitutions.
>
> Allen Buchanan 1991: 148

Because the fundamental problem of federal design is to supply a stabilizing institutional context for bargaining over inherently redistributive policy, and because these institutions, many of which are constitutional, are themselves subject to negotiation and reinterpretation, the idea of a constitution as a living document reflects the conventional wisdom that such things as the division of prerogatives and jurisdictions between federal subjects and the federal center should not be impervious to adjustment and redefinition as society evolves and circumstances change. If these adjustments are to remain incremental and evolutionary, however, then bargaining and renegotiation must be set in some larger and stable institutional context – a layer of institutional structure that is somehow further removed from the pressures of bargaining but which nevertheless directly impacts and regulates it. And if, for convenience, we label such institutions "constitutions" in a broad sense, then an essential part of federal design, as we outline matters in the previous chapter, is to create a constitutional supergame that encompasses federal bargaining and restrains it so that Level 1 provisions are more than mere words on paper. How these Level 1 provisions fail once Level 2 rules themselves become negotiable is the subject of this chapter.

This supergame can be thought of as a complex combination of rules, from general to specific, that work together to form an institutional equilibrium (see, e.g., Schofield 2002). Some of these rules will bear directly on a state's design (e.g., the structure of representation in the national legislature, the supremacy of federal law), whereas others may at first appear tangential to it (e.g., provisions that treat the circumstances under which a prime minister must or can call for new elections; the frequency and timing of elections; the composition of national courts; the relationship of the chief executive to the national legislature; and the appointment, legislative, and discretionary powers of the chief executive). Each of these things, though, affects bargaining within the national government and, therefore, bargaining over federal constraints. Of necessity, moreover, the institutional equilibrium we seek must be one in which we can alter one of its working parts – as when we alter a Level 1 constraint by statute or a Level 2 constraint by constitutional amendment – without destroying the operation of what remains, with the understanding that there is added potential for institutional stability in Level 2 as when constitutional devices such as a separation of powers make changes in Level 2 more difficult to effect than at Level 1.

In this context we introduce the notion of institutionalized versus uninstitutionalized bargaining. Institutionalized bargaining typically concerns details about the allocation of the costs and benefits of specific policies and programs and the determination of jurisdictional boundaries. In institutionalized bargaining, then, the character of Level 2 is not at issue, which is to say that the potentially infinite regress of cycling of rules that choose rules is terminated (here at a point we term the constitutional level). For example, the legal wrangling over who won Florida's electoral votes in the 2000 U.S. presidential election is an instance of institutionalized bargaining. Although state law may have been unclear, inconsistent, or subject to alternative interpretations, there existed, via well-defined procedures and processes, an institutional structure to which one side of the dispute or the other could appeal for a resolution, and which all sides deemed legitimate. Neither Gore nor Bush argued against the legitimacy of the courts or of the method (the Electoral College) by which votes were aggregated across the country to determine a winner. Although a few of Gore's supporters voiced dissatisfaction with the fact that their candidate had lost the Electoral College vote despite "winning" the popular vote, only his most intemperate ideological partisans suggested that Republican electors abandon their pledge to vote for Bush (none did); the majority simply called upon Congress to later consider alternative "reforms." Indeed, the one imperative about which there was essentially unanimous agreement was that the rules of the game, no matter how trivial, should not be changed until after a winner had been announced. One specific practical consequence of those rules and that agreement was that they successfully limited a potentially explosive dispute to a specific subpart of the electorate (Florida) and to specific issues (the validity of ballots). The circumstance may have been a political crisis from the perspective of the primary antagonists, but it was never a constitutional crisis – or, as one commentator noted in the midst of the legal wrangling before a winner had been formally announced, "those are TV cameras in front of the courthouse, not tanks." And as further indicator of the binding properties of those rules, once Bush was safely ensconced in the White House, proposals for reform focused on minute and some might even say boring details such as the physical structure of ballots and the opportunities to take advantage of new technologies (the internet) for counting ballots.

In contrast, uninstitutionalized bargaining corresponds to a situation in which there is no such sustainable system of constraints, and in the limit, when nearly every rule and institution becomes subject to negotiation and change, the propensity of conflict to escalate makes it difficult or even impossible to distinguish between "details" and the critical strategic components of a federation. Such a situation might have easily arisen in the 2000 U.S. presidential contest if, for example, there was no consensus about the supremacy of federal law, about the U.S. Supreme Court's authority to review the decisions of state courts, or about the procedures to be followed in the event that no candidate receive a majority of electoral college votes from among those appointed. Arguing that Article 2, Section 1 of the U.S. Constitution legitimized such action, the Florida legislature did threaten to place some institutional issues on the table when it appeared to be prepared to name its own slate of electors in the event that the Florida courts awarded that state's electors to Gore. But even then, there existed a well-defined constitutionally prescribed procedure for deciding which electoral votes should be considered. If there had not existed a consensus that Article 2, Section 1, in combination with the Twelfth Amendment, should dictate events, we could easily imagine a scenario in which a true constitutional crisis would have arisen.

However, before we turn in subsequent chapters to a discussion of ways to encourage such an appropriate Level 2 institutional equilibrium, including a general discussion of how constitutions are enforced, here we focus on things one wants to avoid – on what happens in those instances when a sustainable set of rules to constrain bargaining does not exist – when there is no equilibrium constitutional context for bargaining, and negotiation concerns nearly all dimensions of federal design. Thus, we are speaking here, for instance, of those times when the secession of one subset of federal subjects requires the renegotiation of the terms of federation among the remaining members, when military defeat or internal revolution requires the creation of wholly new regimes, or when a set of otherwise sovereign states chooses to form a new federation without the benefit of a shared historical precedent for union and the rules that accompany such a precedent.

3.1 The Czechoslovak Dissolution

Although selecting a system of federal institutions is a process with clear redistributive consequences that in even the most advantageous circumstances renders consensus difficult, it is reasonable to suppose that upsetting institutions in an ongoing federation is less easy than when new arrangements must be put in place. Institutions possess an inertia born of people's expectations (beliefs) that others will abide by the rules and procedures that describe those institutions. If each individual operates under the assumption that everyone else will act in accordance with those rules and procedures – including the "appropriate" application of sanctions and rewards for defections and compliance – then the corresponding system of beliefs becomes a self-fulfilling prophecy. On the other hand, those times in which there is no agreed-upon institutional superstructure and participants must either reach or rebuild a consensus on the key principles of union (e.g., who is to be a member, the rights of each member relative to the rest, the allocation of authority across levels of government, the rules of entry and exit, the authority of federal subjects to form their own governments and to regulate the rules for selecting their representatives to the national legislature) are especially dangerous with respect to political stability. These times of heightened societal uncertainty, which Schofield (2000) labels constitutional quandries, correspond to situations in which common-knowledge beliefs are no longer universally shared – or, if shared, cascade into a system of new beliefs that no longer support the existing institutional arrangement.[1]

The data in Figure 3.1, which include all federations formed explicitly or via some regime change since 1945 and that, in principle, could have survived at least twenty-one years (thus excluding states such as Bosnia or Russia), illustrate this argument. Figure 3.1 charts the distribution of longevity of these federations and reveals that a newly formed federation either dissolves soon after it is formed (in less than, say, ten years) or it survives (at least twenty-one years). The suggestion here, then, is that unless a federation survives long enough for the rooting of a system of beliefs that will allow the state's institutional structure to constrain actions, bargaining over those core institutions yields the quick dismemberment of the federation. But if a federation is in place long enough, then the requisite beliefs establish an "institutional inertia" that renders change more difficult. The qualitative aspects of this argument do not depend, moreover, on the post–World War II time period selected. Figure 3.2 graphs the longevity of all states, beginning with the Dutch federation of 1579, that Riker and Lemco (1987) and Lemco (1991) classify as federal. Again we see the same bimodal pattern: federal states tend to be either short-lived or long-lived, and only infrequently something in between.

[1] Ackerman (1992: 3) calls such periods "constitutional moments."

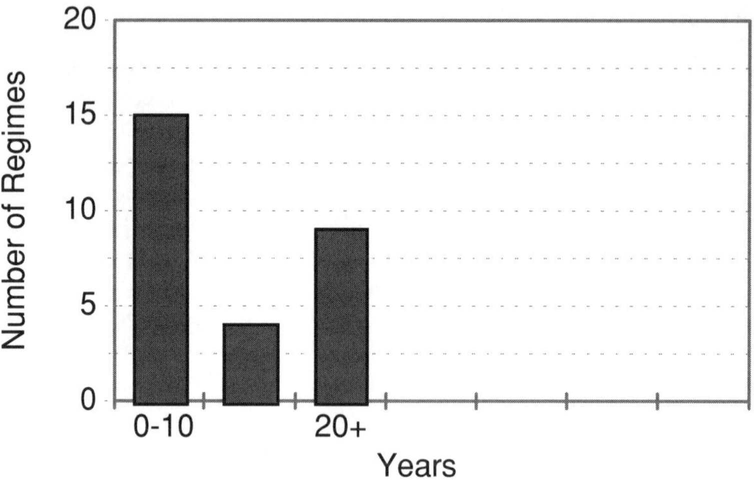

FIGURE 3.1. Durability of federal regimes created after 1945.

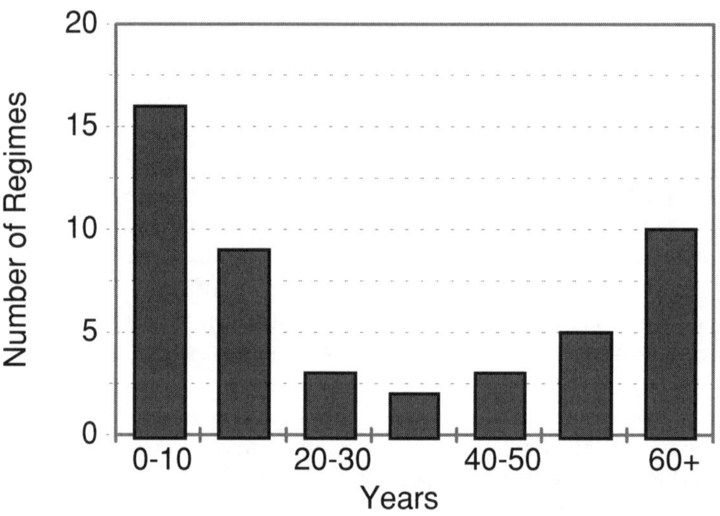

FIGURE 3.2. Durability of all federal regimes.

In terms of what undermines or blocks the beliefs required to sustain federal institutional arrangements, if we examine the processes by which the federations in Table 2.1 failed, we would find that in virtually every case the process was triggered by an explicit redistributive conflict. For example, the politics of federalization in Libya can be retold as a rivalry between the provinces of Cyrenaica and Tripolitaica, so that even after the federation's collapse, events akin to federal bargaining over rules continued until Qaddafi (whose supporters came primarily from the backward Fezzan region) led a successful coup against King Idris (whose base was Cyrenaica); the United Arab Republic dissolved because of the opposition to it by Syrian army officers whose influence would be greatly reduced in the enlarged federation (Khadduri 1963); the military coup that ended the Burmese federation was preceded by a conflict between Burmans and Karens; and the Indonesian federation ended when ethnic Ambonese split from Javanese and Sunatran nationalists in 1950. It is, admittedly, difficult to imagine a federation dissolving without some type of ethnic or interregional conflict. But is such conflict the cause of dissolution or is it merely a precipitating agent that allows some more fundamental (necessary and sufficient) cause to operate?

The case of Czechoslovakia offers several valuable lessons. First, despite its demise, it would appear to satisfy perfectly the socioeconomic preconditions for a successful federal state. There were no overt and long-standing ethnic conflicts, no history of separatism and related violence, and the political, economic, and cultural differences between Czechs and Slovaks seemed inconsequential when compared with those of other European states (Goldman 1999: 21). Indeed, as Elster (1995) argues, it would be as easy to list the dissimilarities of culture, economy, and political tradition between Yankees and Southerners as between Czechs and Slovaks. The two populations shared similar languages, a comparable set of social norms and traditions, a common education system, and an integrated economy. Although Czechoslovakia was a relatively new state, formed in 1918, the fact that Czechs and Slovaks had lived in a common state from 1526 to 1918 seemed a great advantage in terms of cementing cultural and linguistic ties. Following World War II, the two republics rapidly converged in economic and social spheres (Dedek 1996) so that by the time of their breakup "the two societies... had substantially more in common than they had at the time of Czechoslovakia's formation" (Musil 1995: 76). And in the years prior to its dissolution, there was no history of separatism or ethnic tension (Leff 1988, 1999), a significant majority of Czechs and Slovaks shared positive attitudes about each other (Krejci 1996: 171), and opinion polls consistently recorded that significant majorities of both Czechs and Slovaks favored some form of union (Wolchik 1994). Indeed, even after the union ceased to exist, a majority regretted the separation.

Thus, if we were to search for a situation in which to form or maintain a multicultural and multiethnic federation, one might reasonably believe that Czechoslovakia offered an especially favorable set of social, economic, and political conditions. The fact that the federation nonetheless dissolved raises a series of questions. Could dissolution have been averted by a more judicious choice of political institutions? Were institutional solutions available that, for one reason or another, were not considered? Does this case hold any useful lessons for future attempts at federal institutional design? And, aside from a historical account of key events, can we point to any fundamental proximate *cause* of dissolution that holds lessons for federalism universally?

In seeking an answer to this last question, it is always dangerous, of course, to scan the historical record in search of a "cause." True causation lies within the theories we construct to understand and predict events, and the theory we require is unlikely to be inferred from a single case study.[2] Instead, we want to use the Czechoslovak case to illustrate what we hypothesize is the fundamental cause – bargaining over core institutions, or equivalently uninstitutionalized bargaining. We begin, then, by noting the near consensus that it was the Slovak political leadership's insistence on a radical revision of federal principles that initially provoked events: "[O]ne might argue, perhaps, that the Czechs took the last step towards separation, [but] the first nine steps had been taken by the Slovaks" (Elster 1995: 134). This view, if correct, is all the more surprising in light of the fact that, prior to the breakup, the Czech Republic would gain economically from separation, since it would no longer be required to pay fiscal transfers to Slovakia and could free itself from the noncompetitive Slovak industries established under the Soviet regime. Indeed, the Czech Republic subsequently quickly integrated itself into the community of European states, becoming one of the first postcommunist NATO members and a top candidate for European Union enlargement, whereas Slovakia remained relatively isolated and was initially treated as a second-rank pseudodemocracy with little immediate prospect of EU or NATO membership.

In retrospect it appears that the Slovak push toward dissolution was economically irrational. Throughout Czechoslovakia's postwar history, Slovakia was the beneficiary of net federal tax revenue transfers, with estimates of the size of those transfers in 1992 ranging from 4 to 8 percent of Slovakia's GDP. Other calculations suggest that by the end of the communist period, the Czech Republic contributed 93 percent and the Slovak Republic only 7 percent to total federal expenditures (Elster 1995), and estimates for the 1990s show a significant increase in the magnitude of those transfers as partial compensation for the losses incurred by Slovakia's uncompetitive

[2] We would be bold enough to argue, in fact, that we cannot infer cause by examining even a multitude of cases, however carefully we select those cases. This is not a denial of the importance of observation and inference; comparative case studies are an important means of revealing the empirical regularities to which our theoretical constructs must be directed. Rather, it is merely a statement of the fact that the *cause* of the general tendency of things to fall to earth, for instance, is not likely to be inferred from multiple observation of leaves falling from trees, or even from a concerted effort at expanding our horizons to include rain, rocks, and whatever object a child might launch toward the sky. True cause in terms of necessity and sufficiency lies in deductive theoretical constructs. The cases examined here are not designed to reveal cause but simply to illustrate (as opposed to "prove") the operation of the fundamental theoretical forces we believe dictate the fates of federations. Thus, our recounting of events ignores a great many details but hopefully not ones that are most germane to our understanding of cause.

industries.[3] Federal integrity also seemed assured by the economic interdependence of the two states. In 1991 the Czech Republic accounted for 50 percent of Slovakia's exports and imports while Slovakia accounted for about a third of Czech trade. Fidrmuc, Horvath, and Fidrmuc (1999) offer as a point of contrast the fact that, despite their similarities in size, language, and political-economic structures, as well as geographic proximity, Norway accounts for only 6 percent of Sweden's exports. Czechoslovakia's internal interdependence, then, should have created the reasonable expectation that upon dissolution, the Czech and Slovak republics would witness a substantial decline in trade, with a corresponding negative impact on both economies. Indeed, in recognition of the economic impact of separation, the two sides did agree subsequently to retain a common currency, a customs union, and a common labor market.

Unable, then, to rationalize separation by economic factors (Batt 1993; Wolchik 1995; Stranger 1996), some observers hypothesize that the foundation of separation rested on the fact that large parts of the Slovak population attributed "a significant intrinsic value to independence as such" (Fidrmuc et al. 1999: 780) and that Slovak nationalists considered political independence "an absolute value in itself for which no economic prosperity could compensate" (Rychlik 1995: 104). However, this idea runs afoul of some facts. First, prior to the democratic revolution of 1989 there was almost no history of secessionist nationalism in Slovakia, either among intellectuals or the general population. Although the "Slovak question" resurfaced whenever there was a crisis or at moments of political change during the communist regime (i.e., 1948 and 1968), advocacy of secession was not to be found either within the Slovak Communist Party or among various dissident groups.[4] Public opinion polls mirrored these facts and consistently recorded that the call for independence lacked support, with a majority of Slovaks favoring some form of union. Between 1990 and 1992 less than one-fifth of the Slovak population supported separation and an equal or greater share supported a unitary Czechoslovak state. Nor did the major Slovak political parties promote independence in their platforms. The Slovak National

[3] Although Slovakia lagged behind the Czechs in economic development, the gap was decreasing under the predissolution regime. Between 1948 and 1989, Slovakian industrial output increased thirty-three times, compared to twelve times for that of the Czech Republic; and although Slovak per capita national product was only 64 percent of the Czech level in 1950, it reached 88 percent in 1989. Thus, it seemed that Slovakia had every reason to believe that had the federation survived, economic parity would be realized.

[4] It also seems evident that the potential for disruption was underestimated by democratic reformers. For example, when in 1990 the newly elected Federal Assembly considered deleting the word "socialist" from the official state title – the "Czechoslovak Socialist Republic" – President Havel, believing the proposal was merely a technical matter, suggested a vote on the change without consulting parliament. It apparently came as a surprise when the Slovak delegation used the occasion to challenge the accuracy of the remaining words in the state title (Stein 1997).

Party was the only major party to advocate independence unambiguously in 1990 and 1992, and its share of the vote never exceeded 11 percent. Other major parties appealed to their electorates by advocating variations on the theme of a reformed union, from a loose confederation to a new treaty-based federation. And although some Slovak politicians, especially Meciar, may have had an incentive to provoke the breakup, publicly at least all prominent members of the political elite followed the lead of these polls, with Meciar clearly stating that an independent Slovak state was not his party's goal. Thus, when in early 1992 (the year of the breakup), a nationalist pro-independence group emerged within the ruling Christian Democratic Movement (KDH), the party's leadership encouraged the group to leave. And on its own, operating as the Slovak Christian Democratic Movement, this group failed to survive the 1992 elections.

At first glance, then, the Czechoslovak dissolution is a puzzle – or at least an event that is inexplicable in terms of economic interests, ethnic divisions, or mass ideology. The puzzle persists, however, only if we ignore the bargaining among political elites and party leaders that arose over specific institutional arrangements and that, in all fairness, seems to have been unavoidable following the dissolution of the Soviet empire.

Czechoslovakia had, in fact, survived one prior instance of federal renegotiation but at a time when the Soviet presence was critical. Briefly, the 1948 Czechoslovak Constitution (modified in 1960) established an "asymmetric" semifederalism that, following the pattern of Russia's treatment within the USSR, offered specific provisions dealing with Slovakia but failed to distinguish the central government from Czech authorities. The constitution listed specific areas of Slovak competence (e.g., education, culture, and language), but provided no areas of competence for the Czech republic. There was a National Czechoslovak Council and a Slovak National Council but no corresponding Czech governing body.[5] Although these measures sought to assuage any potential Slovak dissatisfaction within the federation, they had the opposite effect by effectively equating the Czech Republic with Czechoslovakia and denoting the Slovak Republic as merely a part. At that time, however, an open discussion of federal reform did not begin until Antonin Novotny was replaced as first secretary of the Communist Party in January 1968 by a Slovak, Alexander Dubček. On March 10, an editorial in the Slovak communist daily *Pravda* demanded reform, and a month later the Slovak Communist Party created a commission to frame specific proposals. In practical terms, reform was viewed as requiring three things: greater autonomy for Slovakia, a move toward federal symmetry in the form of the creation of Czech state bodies, and the separation of these bodies from the central government. Because

[5] Also following the Soviet model, there were only two communist parties – a national party (CPCS) and the Communist Party of Slovakia, a nominally separate but subordinate organization whose control was limited to Slovakia.

these proposals seemed ideologically neutral, opposition was rare, and when expressed, the central government sharply condemned it (Skilling 1976: 488).

The issue of federal reform, then, was initiated largely by Slovakia, or more precisely, by Slovak Communist Party leaders, whereas the Czech side, while accepting the need for change, seemed relatively uninvolved in the ensuing discourse. Indeed, some observers note that Czechs exhibited a general lack of interest in and understanding of the issues (Skilling 1976: 489), which they attribute to the absence of Czech nationalism, to the fact that Czechs had little to gain from reform, and to the fact that Czechs lacked those political institutions enjoyed by Slovaks that could formulate and defend a Czech position (Leff 1988: 125).[6] Nevertheless, the National Assembly voted in July to create a Czech National Council to institutionalize Czech representation, although it was unclear as to whether the members of the new body had any incentive to distinguish themselves from strictly Czechoslovak national interests because most were incumbent deputies of the National Council. Also, the Czech National Council simply had little time to grapple with the constitutional details of federal reform, and, in fact, it took a stand only on one issue when it rejected the Moravian proposal to create a tripartite federation (Skilling 1976: 487). Thus, the general principles of a future explicitly symmetric federal constitution were accepted by both sides: the federation would consist of two equal republics represented in a bicameral parliament. Representation in the lower chamber would be by population, with Czechs and Slovaks enjoying equal representation in the upper chamber, the House of Nationalities. Ordinary legislation would require a simple majority in each chamber, but the most important issues, including constitutional changes, would, in addition to a simple majority in the lower house (House of the People), require majority approval in both halves of the upper house. Thus, Slovaks secured the right to a substantial veto in which any group of thirty Slovak deputies (approximately one-fifth of the chamber) could block constitutional change.

Both sides agreed to finalize a new constitutional text before October 28, 1968 – the fiftieth anniversary of Czechoslovakia – and discussion of specific details was left to a commission of experts (Kirschbaum 1995: 244). Although the work was interrupted by the Soviet intervention on August 20, the final draft was published in September to allow public debate.[7] The

[6] If there were defenders of Czech interests, they were not politicians or government officials but legal professors, historians, and economists. Not surprisingly, such people approached matters in abstract theoretical terms and were reluctant to "bargain" on an equal footing with active political elites who could operate within existing institutional arrangements.

[7] The main principles of the federal reform were agreed to before the Soviet invasion, and there is no evidence of Soviet intervention in the federal debate (Skilling 1976: 868). To the contrary, the character and topics of the final discussion and disagreements suggest that federal negotiators discounted the effect of the Soviet invasion, with the final constitutional provisions being the product of a compromise between Czech and Slovak views.

new constitution was ratified on October 27 and a reformed federation proclaimed on October 28, 1968. Bargaining then turned to the allocation of power between the federal and republican governments. The record indicates that the proposals of the Slovak side ranged from some form of economic policy decentralization to limiting the federal government's exclusive jurisdictions to foreign affairs and defense (Skilling 1976). A compromise was reached in which most economic activities were to be managed jointly, while each republic was awarded responsibility for education and cultural affairs.

Overall, then, it appears that most Czechoslovak leaders were willing to accommodate Slovak demands, with but one important exception: they rejected all attempts to form a parallel structure for the Czechoslovak Communist Party. In fact, although we cannot be certain of the extent to which there was a conscious understanding of the theoretical role of the party, we now know that any proposal to radically alter the Communist Party's structure was, in effect, a global renegotiation, since the party, as in the USSR, was the key "constitutional" constraint. As long as the party maintained its original form, the impact of reforming anything else remained, if not symbolic, then at least minimally distributive (Leff 1999: 210). The 1968 reforms, then, illustrate a successful *limited* renegotiation, owing to the institutionalization of bargaining within the party (and reenforced, no doubt, by pressure from its Soviet "ally," which required political stability).

Circumstances were different in 1989. Immediately upon Czechoslovakia's formal move to democratic governance (November 1989), a series of constitutional amendments authorized a modification of the communist-era charter, and in June 1990 a new parliament was elected to a two-year term with a self-imposed mandate to complete the draft of a new constitution. Repeated failures followed, however, with the nature of federal relations being one of two critical points of contention (the other being the division of power between President Havel and parliament). Insofar as federal reform was concerned, although the call for a separate Slovak state was not universally popular, the demand for a revision of the terms of union had strong public support in Slovakia. In particular, many Slovaks believed that the gains from federation were not fairly distributed (Elster 1995). Consequently, as Slovak politicians discovered that the most successful strategy was to support the idea of a common state in which Slovakia gained increased autonomy and policy-making authority, in the first democratic elections of June 1990 all Slovak political parties advocated federal reform. And since there was little to be gained from a revision of the terms of representation in federal institutions, those campaign demands focused on a redistribution of power between federal and Slovak governmental authorities.

Following the election, the first round of tripartite talks between the federal government and the governments of the two republics took place in August 1990 and resulted in the Federal Assembly adopting (December 1990) a constitutional amendment on power sharing. The amendment largely met Slovak demands since it devolved much of the federal government's powers (e.g., control of the economy) to the two republics. Although the amendment was unanimously approved by the Slovak National Council, a new round of federal negotiations was initiated in February and March 1991 by President Havel with the intent, once again, of drafting a new constitution. The Slovak side used the occasion to demand that a federal treaty precede the adoption of a new national charter in order, it argued, to formalize the sovereignty of each republic and to ensure the establishment of a federation based on the idea of a federal state being a voluntary union in which the center enjoyed only those powers ceded to it by the republics. Slovak politicians seemed unfamiliar with the U.S. experience under its Articles of Confederation since, in practical terms, they were proposing a confederation rather than a federation. Talks stalemated on the issue of whether a federal treaty could be legally binding, and discussions dragged on into 1992, with Slovaks blocking any compromise so that by the spring of 1992 the two sides agreed to postpone the discussion until after the approaching election.

While republic governments failed to move beyond talks on a federal treaty, the public debate between 1990 and 1992 encompassed a variety of alternatives, from a unitary state, a more centralized federation, the status quo, a more decentralized federation with additional powers vested in Czech and Slovak governments, confederation, and complete separation. The public forum also included discussion of a tripartite federation, with Moravia as a third republic. This kaleidoscope of options followed a simple dynamic – first, until the beginning of 1992, the Czech side accepted one Slovak demand after another, moving from centralized union to a confederation based on some type of federal treaty. In 1992, however, the logic of the electoral campaign forced Czech politicians to change their position and to demand a federation with a stronger central government. Of course, such a shift amounted to an ultimatum, since for Slovaks to accept the new Czech position required that they return to where they had started in 1990.

The 1992 elections were, perhaps, the critical juncture. As Bunce (1999: 97) describes the situation,

> The differences between Slovakia and the Czech-Moravian lands . . . only deepened in response to . . . the paralyzing effects of the decision to hold competitive elections first and to rewrite the constitution second. This had two implications. One was that it became hard for the president, Vaclav Havel, to intervene in Czechoslovak politics in general and in the growing crisis developing between the two halves of the country in particular. . . . it was relatively easy for Vaclav Klaus, the prime minister of Czechoslovakia, and Vladimir Meciar, the premier of Slovakia, to ignore him and arrogate for themselves in the process the power to determine the future of the state. . . . The other consequence was that those who wrote the constitution were far from being either interest- or national-blind. Thus, the constitution itself, along with parliamentary politics, functioned as the locus of a complex and interrelated struggle between Klaus and Meciar. *This struggle focused simultaneously on . . . institutional design . . . economic transformation . . . and the power of the two men.* (emphasis added)

Perhaps it is not surprising, then, that with literally all issues on the table simultaneously, Slovak and Czech politicians chose the only option that served both their needs – dissolution – and on July 21, 1992, the largest Czech and Slovak parties (ODS and HZDS) signed an agreement to disband the federation. Interestingly, both sides rejected a popular referendum on the issue, since there was no guarantee that the electorate would ratify their decision.

Absent a fuller understanding of the institutional mechanisms whereby federal bargains are sustained, we cannot yet offer any full causal explanation as to why this particular bargaining process failed to achieve a resolution that preserved the federation. Certainly, participants did not consider other "mechanical" options, such as dividing the federation into multiple smaller units, including units that mixed Czech and Slovak populations. It may have been that no solution was desired or deemed necessary by those in a position to influence events. Suffice it to say that the hospitable conditions Czechoslovakia confronted in 1991 were not sufficient to overcome the centripetal forces that were given full play when all issues – all aspects of redistribution and constitutional structure – were subject to simultaneous negotiation and fully intertwined with the political fates of political elites. But this much is certain: once the integrating and extraconstitutional structure of the Communist Party disappeared (as well as the glue of Soviet domination), little institutional structure remained to constrain bargaining and to keep institutional alternatives off the table that were more consonant with separation than with union.

3.2 The Soviet Disintegration

The Czechoslovak federation that dissolved in 1992 technically began its life when the Czechoslovak Socialist Federative Republic was established in 1969. The bargaining that occurred in the postcommunist period, however, did not solely concern the perceived inadequacies of this 1969 design but instead followed the softening of institutional constraints that accompanied the dismantling of a totalitarian communist state. As such, we can see how bargaining was very much a part of a well-defined regime change. However, there are instances in which circumstances, either internal or external, open the door to a fundamental renegotiation within an ongoing regime – a renegotiation of the sort that approximates the bargaining that accompanies initial state formation or an exogenous impact of the kind visited by Napoleon in 1798 on the Swiss Confederation immediately preceding its fifty years of instability.

That such renegotiation can be sufficiently disruptive to yield dissolution in accordance with Tocqueville's observation about the vulnerability of governments that choose to reform is vividly illustrated by the political dynamics of the last years of the once formidable USSR, where renegotiation was initiated at the highest level after "Gorbachev's reforms had weakened old Soviet political and economic institutions, but new institutional arrangements had yet to consolidate to organize either the economy or the polity" (McFaul 2001: 39). Created in 1922, the Soviet Union endured as a totalitarian state for nearly seven decades. Although it may be a matter of opinion as to whether it should be counted as one of the world's longer-lasting federations or merely labeled an empire, the mechanisms by which the union was sustained were not (at least following Stalin's death) wholly coercive and the federal aspects of its political processes were not entirely orthogonal to those of its democratic counterparts.[8] Indeed, because of the federal center's dominant role in the economy, the USSR, though hardly a democracy, experienced more than its fair share of bargaining and political maneuver throughout its existence.

Numerous explanations for the USSR's demise have been offered that focus on any number of things – economics, politics, culture, ideology, ethnic conflict, international forces. However, the more thoughtful analyses of its demise (e.g., Goldman 1991; Sharlet 1992; d'Encausse 1993; Roeder 1993; Suny 1994; Bunce 1999) present a more complex picture. That picture offers an accounting of events that center on the USSR's geographic mapping of federal subjects to its ethnic communities so as to encourage rather than discourage ethnic nationalism and the establishment of quasi-sovereign institutional entities within these subjects that allowed for a ready substitute to Communist Party rule: "At issue for all three federalized socialist systems [Czechoslovakia, Yugoslavia, the Soviet Union], then, was linking regionally defined monopolies to the larger economic and political monopoly of the Communist Party" (Bunce 1999: 46). This argument fails, however, as a fully satisfactory causal explanation if only because it is not stated in terms of theoretical primitives that together establish a necessary and sufficient condition for failure or success. Certainly the American constitutional experience in 1787 began with a replacement of a regime in the context of federal subjects with fully formed national structures, as did the Swiss constitutional reforms of the late nineteenth century. Yet dismemberment and conflict of the sort witnessed by the Soviet Union did not immediately ensue.

Moving back, then, to the circumstances that preceded the Soviet dismemberment, we should keep in mind that, even in hindsight, the full disintegration of the USSR was largely unanticipated by its population, the international community, and scholars who made Soviet politics their area of expertise.[9] Despite explanations that focus on the ready institutionalization

[8] As Friedrich (1968: 49) argues, the fact that "the formal federalism of the government structure is superseded and transcended by the integrating force of the CPSU . . . does not mean, as is often asserted, that the federal system has no significance in the Soviet Union."

[9] For example, in their classic empirical assessments of the correlates of federal stability, Riker and Lemco (1987) place the USSR and United States in the same category with respect to

of interethnic tensions within the USSR's federal framework, until 1988 there was little evidence of long-term hostilities among Soviet nationalities (Roeder 1991). In fact, although perhaps more for ideological reasons than anything else, the problems of separatism, regionalism, and regional autonomy, moreover, were almost never mentioned in the documents of the Communist Party once the essential form of the union was established after World War II, barely a mention is made of the dangers regionalism posed to the integrity of the Soviet Union in Gorbachev's treatise *Perestroika and New Thinking for Our Country and the Whole World* (1988), and the influential anthology of "progressive" writings edited by Yurii Afanasyev, *There Is No Other Way* (1988), fails to offer a single paragraph on the problems of regionalism (Smith 1990). We might attribute this relative silence to decades of propaganda that allowed Gorbachev to assert that "the nationalities problem has been solved," but we should also bear in mind then when the USSR did dissolve, it did so along formal geopolitical fault lines established by the USSR itself and not strictly in accordance with national identities.[10]

If we eschew ethnic conflict as the explanation and if the conflicts that arose in Armenia, Georgia, and the Baltic states did so for more fundamental causes, then the most widely cited culprit is the USSR's dismal economic performance and the gradual erosion of its position vis-à-vis the West, and the United States in particular. There is little doubt that the USSR was quickly finding itself unable to compete, especially with the development and implementation of new technologies. But even here, economics as a wholly satisfactory causal explanation fails us. It is difficult to argue, for example, that the USSR's performance was inferior to that of India, or that the economy of Russia today – now a seemingly stable federation (at least at the time of this writing and at least in terms of its territorial integrity) – is self-evidently superior to that of the USSR. Even if we accept the proposition that

secession potential – stable – and generally grade the USSR higher along several alternative quantitative measures of stability. One exception, of course, was Emmanuel Todd, who in 1979 published *The Final Fall: An Essay on the Decomposition of the Soviet Sphere*. Todd was neither a Sovietologist nor a political scientists, but rather a demographer who noticed the unparalleled (for a modern state, developed or otherwise) rise in infant mortality and declining life expectancy. However, aside from much wishful thinking on the part of others, the community of Soviet experts largely failed to anticipate events and the rapidity with which they unfolded.

10 It was not that Gorbachev did not see the importance of ethnicity – "Narrow nationalist views, national rivalry and arrogance emerge" (Gorbachev 1988: 119); rather, he and other Soviet leaders thought that the USSR had largely solved the problem: "If the nationality question had not been solved in principle, the Soviet Union would never have had the social, cultural, economic and defense potential as it has now. Our state would not have survived if the republics had not formed a community based on brotherhood and cooperation, respect and mutual assistance" (p. 118). In fact, adds Gorbachev, "against the background of national strife, which has not spared even the world's most advanced countries, the USSR represents a truly unique example in the history of human civilization" (p. 119).

the USSR's economic performance and prospects relative to the West, China, and Japan contributed to its demise, we are still left with having to explain why the end came in 1991 and why it came so suddenly and unexpectedly – why those of us who witnessed the event either in person or on television were awed by the sight of the Soviet flag being lowered over the Kremlin for the last time that Christmas Eve in 1991.

We can perhaps get a better insight into the primary contributing factors of the USSR's demise by examining the philosophy of federalism that prevailed there through even Gorbachev's years at the helm. That philosophy adhered to two principles. The first was that federalism was not a permanent structure but a way station on the road to some socialist-communist utopia: "According to Marxist theory, federalism could only be seen as a retrograde development. Basing federal divisions on a principle of ethnic or 'national' identity was viewed as particularly misguided" (Gleason 1990: 19). Indeed, as Lenin once uttered, "Marxists will never under any circumstances advocate . . . the federal principle" (cited in Gleason 1990: 1).[11] This is not to say that such ideological utterances served as a guide to Soviet federal design, for certainly issues of regionalism, national identity, and language could not be ignored. Nevertheless, maintaining federal structures was never a goal in itself and they were not intended to be refined or made to be anything more than administrative conveniences and a temporizing solution to the "nationalities problem."

The second principle held that a federation was, at least ideally, a voluntary association of sovereign states for the achievement of a common purpose (Kux 1990). The prevailing notion, shared by both democratic reformers and Communist Party bosses in the late 1980s (who were, in a sense, intellectual captives of their own ideology) was utopian. It conceptualized a federation as a voluntary creation in which each participant has the right to determine the terms of its association and the extent of its sovereignty. Correspondingly, the glue that would hold the federation together and thwart secession would be the public benefits of union. As strange as this view might seem to those familiar with the decades of Soviet domestic repression, it is precisely the lack of practical experience with the difficulties of sustaining an authentic federal balance that thwarted any critical examination of such unrealistic expectations. Thus, we are reminded of the fact that when facing the challenges to the

11 Elsewhere he clarified: "Federalism is an alliance of equals, an alliance which needs a general agreement. How can there be a right of one side to the consent of the other side? This is absurd. We are in principle against federalism; the latter weakens economic integration, it is a type of government irreconcilable with a unitary state." But federalism could be useful: "One may be a decided opponent of this principle [federalism], an adherent of democratic centralism, yet one may prefer federalism . . . as the only way to complete democratic centralism" (as quoted in Low 1958: iii). As Conquest (1967: 9) points out, the federation, in the form of the new Soviet Union, represented an advance from the "state of complete secession" that had prevailed after the old tzarist empire collapsed.

union in the 1980s, Gorbachev assumed that the Baltic states would prefer to be members of the USSR once they understood its potential economic value. Similarly, after a prolonged discussion of the nationalities problem within the party, the Central Committee proclaimed that "[t]he guarantee of our federation's durability is the completely voluntary nature of the association of the Soviet republics in a single union state in which each republic retains its sovereignty and autonomy" (CPSU Nationalities Platform, February 11, 1990).

Certainly some of this language should be discarded as mere propaganda, but so deeply rooted was this contractual notion of federalism that, even following the collapse of the USSR when Russia's territorial integrity faced serious challenges from its ethnic republics, Yeltsin's adviser on interethnic affairs, Galina Starovoitova, argued that he should continue the policy of granting as much autonomy to the regions as they preferred. In the long run, Starovoitova asserted, this approach would redound to Russia's benefit once the ostensible rewards of economic reform were realized (Dunlop 1993: 68).

This reliance on the presumed benefits of union and adherence to the notion of "federalism as engine of prosperity" – a theory of federalism that had never actually been tested within the USSR – led political elites to underestimate grossly the dangers of redistributive bargaining, especially in the formative stages of federal reformation. Most evidently, these dangers were not fully appreciated when the initial revision of statutory and constitutional arrangements initiated by Gorbachev upset the institutional status quo by shifting the arena of bargaining from within the Communist Party to previously unused or untested constitutional political structures. Those structures, whether good or bad as venues for bargaining, were not the institutions that either conferred legitimacy on policy or possessed legitimacy in their own right. Absent a set of common beliefs as to what institutions would coordinate or direct action within the union, the door was then open to a global renegotiation that not only encompassed the prerogatives of the union's constituent parts, but also the institutions that would link those parts to each other and to the center. That, in combination with the authority and strategic position of those given formal voice by a partially constructed federalism that had earlier been designed to render a heterogeneous empire a single state, was the fundamental cause of the USSR's dissolution.

To make this argument more fully, we can begin by noting that the process of liberalization and democratization that began in the mid-1980s fundamentally altered federal arrangements that had prevailed for seventy years, where the most evident and important change was a reduction in the political and economic monopoly of the Communist Party. As in Czechoslovakia, an "unwritten" constitution prevailed with respect to federal issues until the late 1980s that, as allowed by Article 6 of the official 1977 USSR Constitution, awarded control of political, economic, and cultural matters to the party. This is not to say that there did not exist degrees of regional independence and significant decentralization of authority. Uniformity was not the rule, with some republics managing to secure more autonomy than others. And just as it is in a "normal federation," regional success in dealing with the center depended on representation – in this case, on a region's representation in the party's Central Committee.

Interestingly, that representation did not mirror the constitutional structure of the union. The fifteen most populous ethnic groups that occupied the USSR's perimeter enjoyed the status of union republics, while other significant nationality groups held the status of autonomous republics.[12] The USSR Constitution described union republics as sovereign entities, and autonomous republics were made a part of union republics. As a rule, each union republic, autonomous republic, and oblast was represented in the Central Committee by their first party secretaries, as well as directors of the largest industrial plants. But more than a half of the total of the three hundred to four hundred members of the Central Committee represented regions with no federal status or entities without any formally acknowledged administrative status.[13] In this way the Central Committee was a unique federal institution that allowed for more or less equal representation and lobbying by a varied range of regional, political, and economic interests. The scheme, of course, gave the Kremlin its own levers of control. First, it and not the union republics determined the prerogatives and resources of autonomous republics (as well as the USSR's oblasts). Second, Moscow directly controlled both republican and regional leaders (nomenklatura) through the highly centralized institutions of the party. Because the only viable career path for regional elites was promotion by Moscow and maybe to Moscow, success could come only to politicians who found the right balance between serving local interests and pleasing their party "constituency."

For seventy years, then, the Communist Party was the essential coordinating force in the USSR, holding its diverse territories and peoples together – "the force that orients and guides Soviet society" (Article 6 of the USSR Constitution). Thus, according to accounts provided by party officials themselves, the crucial decision in weakening the party's role was the change in personnel policy under Gorbachev whereby centralized nominations from nomenklatura lists were slowly replaced by the direct election of officials within the party (Ligachev 1993). Democracy replaced the political

[12] There were twenty autonomous republics, sixteen located within Russia, two in Georgia, and one each in the Uzbek and Azerbaijan union republics. For the smaller nationality groups there were eight autonomous regions (oblasts) and ten national districts (okrugs). The Russian Federation as a part of the Soviet Union was itself a multinational federation, a home to sixteen autonomous republics, five autonomous regions, and ten autonomous areas, which all enjoyed certain claims to sovereignty.

[13] See, for example, Weeks (1989). Also Daniels (1976) shows that the Central Committee was mostly formed according to an unwritten code that allocated to each functional hierarchy and to each union republic (and often regions) a certain number of seats.

dependence on Moscow of regional party bosses and directed their attention instead to local party elites.[14] To limit political damage and safeguard their own survival, most regional bosses sought to slow Gorbachev's reforms, but at the same time, in response to the challenge of electoral competition, they began to request more independence from Moscow. Thus, by early 1989 the Latvian, Estonian, and Lithuanian republican first secretaries were advocating the federalization of the CPSU, the Communist Party of Georgia called for the transformation of the CPSU into an alliance of independent republic-level parties modeled after the League of the Communists of Yugoslavia, and the future president of Ukraine, Leonid Kravchuk, is on record admitting that his desire to secede from the USSR formed in 1989. While useful initially because it contrasted the electoral insecurity of his underlings with his own national popularity, the wave of democratization within the party ultimately became a threat to Gorbachev's own standing. Stepan (1999: 19) states such a circumstance generally: "The greatest risk is that federal arrangements can offer opportunities for ethnic nationalists to mobilize their resources. This risk is especially grave when elections are introduced in the subunits of a formally nondemocratic federal polity prior to democratic countrywide elections and in the absence of democratic countrywide parties."

Gorbachev, as secretary-general, was elected by the voting members of the All-Union Central Committee within which, with discipline weakening, factionalism became a serious threat. Perhaps the greatest threat to party unity, though, was the growing pressure in 1989 to create a Russian branch of the party. As in Czechoslovakia, where there was a national party (CPCS) and the Communist Party of Slovakia but no Czech communist party, there was no Russian communist party. There was a good reason for the "unwritten Soviet Constitution" to preclude Russia from having a separate branch

[14] Initially and in line with CPSU custom, Gorbachev began office with the replacement of regional party officials with more loyal supporters (Gill and Pitty 1997) so that by 1988, eleven of fourteen republican first secretaries and almost 60 percent of regional first secretaries were replaced, with the goal of sustaining discipline and compliance with the center. In February 1987, however, after less than two years in office, Gorbachev proposed multicandidate elections of state and party officials by secret ballot. Quite possibly, the measure initially strengthened Gorbachev's hand by making subordinates indebted to the center for electoral assistance. To start, the first secretaries of the fifteen republics were to be elected from a list of competing candidates, to be followed in June 1988 by competitive elections throughout party organizations as well as for the formerly rubber-stamp legislature, the Supreme Soviet. The first secretaries in each region, in addition to being required to compete in party elections, also had to compete in the March 1989 elections to the Congress of People's Deputies. These elections clearly revealed the electoral vulnerability of the regional communist elite. Even though more than two-thirds of the regional first secretaries maneuvered to run unopposed, thirty-three of the remaining sixty-five were defeated, including the first secretaries of Kiev, Minsk, Kishenev, Alma-Ata, and Frunze (Gill 1994). After such a poor electoral showing, Gorbachev once again replaced half of all regional first secretaries, this time with local personnel recruited from outside the traditional bureaucratic networks (Hough 1997: 276).

ever since it was abolished by Stalin. As the largest republic, Russia, even without its own organization, sent more than a half of the delegates to the party congresses, and its more than seventy regional first secretaries formed a good portion of the Central Committee. Moreover, were there a Russian branch with its own first secretary, those regional bosses might become more loyal to him than to the secretary-general (Hough 1997). Thus, Gorbachev vigorously opposed the formation of a Russian party and acquiesced to the idea only after the Central Committee agreed on February 7, 1990, to render the party redundant by modifying Article 6 of the Soviet Constitution and by establishing a strong USSR presidency, independent of the party. Indeed, Gorbachev began transferring power away from the party perhaps as early as the winter of 1989, whereas the creation of the presidency marginalized the role of Politburo and the Central Committee, as decisions were increasingly made either by presidential decrees or by resolutions of national or republican parliaments.

Combined with internal efforts to weaken the party, another crucial mark was left by competitive legislative elections in the republics in March 1990, which brought to office anticommunist elites in the Baltics, Transcaucasus, and Moldova. More important, the elections changed the political landscapes in the giants – Russia and Ukraine – with newly elected politicians soon leaving the party and demanding state sovereignty for their republics. Thus, by the summer of 1990 it became obvious that the party stood on the brink of oblivion or at least irrelevance, and at the closing of the Twenty-eighth Party Congress (July 1990), Gorbachev felt it necessary to assure the delegates that "those who were counting on this being the last party congress and on the burial of the CPSU have miscalculated." The congress was a personal success of Gorbachev, who was not only overwhelmingly re-elected party secretary-general but also succeeded in pushing through major changes in the party's institutions. Although its membership expanded by turning it into a representative body elected on a quota system, with each republic holding a guaranteed number of seats, the Central Committee no longer elected the secretary-general or the Politburo, nor was it involved in policy decision making. Thus, in essence the 4,700 congress delegates voted to complete the transfer of real power to elected offices. At the same time, Yeltsin (then the chairman of the Supreme Soviet of the republic) announced his resignation from the CPSU, with the newly elected mayors of Moscow and Leningrad following suit. In Ukraine, Vladimir Ivashko, elected first secretary of the republic's party in 1989, won a seat in the newly elected Ukrainian parliament and subsequently defeated eleven other candidates for the chairmanship of the legislature. But as a signal of the CPSU's waning fortunes, he resigned from his party post even before the party's congress.

The contradictions and shortcomings in the treatment of federalism in formal constitutional provisions could only be ignored as long as the party continued to enable federal consent within the republics by pursuing a personnel policy that kept politicians "properly" motivated. But the mechanism generating those incentives was fragile and had to be constantly reinforced on a case by case basis through party personnel management.[15] And once the party's control was undermined, Soviet federalism could not survive in the old form: "Constitutional conflict became the norm rather than the exception as one by one, republic legislatures began to assert their preemptive right to approve all federal legislation in order for it to have legal force on their territory" (Sharlet 1992: 89). What was soon called "war of laws" was little more than a proclaimed right to nullification, which if fully implemented rendered the USSR something other than a federation – a confederation, perhaps, but definitely something other than what it had been.

To see now how the undermining of that control opened the door to bargaining that quickly encompassed the federation's essential structure, notice that upon the unveiling of Gorbachev's plan in 1988 for a new 2,250-member Congress of Deputies, empowered to elect a 542-member permanent Supreme Soviet and which was itself to be elected in competitive contests, federal units now required new mechanisms of coordination and access to Moscow. At this point, though, embracing the previously dormant formal institutions moved the issue of the asymmetric constitutional status of federal entities onto center stage, whereupon each federal unit sought to defend and expand its status. Where their status had been determined informally within the party's Central Committee, now official constitutional provisions became decisive. And conflicting preferences were quickly manifest. The Soviet Constitution provided only limited regional representation in the bicameral national legislature, the Supreme Soviet. Historically its chambers – the Soviet of the Union and the Soviet of Nationalities – were rubber-stamp entities that unanimously approved the decisions of the Central Committee: "The real legislature was the presidium, or executive committee of the Supreme Soviet, which adopted five to six hundred decrees a year. And all of these had previously been approved by the Communist Party Politburo" (Murray 1995: 18). Now it was suddenly important that the Soviet of Nationalities consisted of thirty-two deputies from each union republic, eleven from each autonomous republic, five from each autonomous region, and one from each autonomous area.

[15] An example of mismanagement that arguably accelerated Ukraine's departure from the union, but which would have been of little consequence in an earlier era, was Gorbachev's offer to Ivashko of the important union-level party office of deputy secretary-general. An offer not to be refused, and in material terms a benefit for Ukraine's position in the union, it nevertheless abruptly took Ivashko, loyal to the center and influential in Ukraine politics, out of the republic, changed Ukraine's political dynamics, and upset its vulnerable "pro-union" status quo. Indeed, Ivashko's departure left the communist legislative majority leaderless and is often cited as a significant factor behind its willingness to accede, a week after his departure, to Ukraine's Declaration of State Sovereignty on July 16, 1990.

Formal representation was now an issue on the table, and constitutional amendments in 1988, increasing the role of these legislative bodies, substantially weakened the de facto representation of the smaller republics and autonomies. In order to broaden and, at the same time, control participation, Gorbachev instituted his new two-tiered legislative system – the Congress of Deputies, which consisted of 750 delegates elected on a demographic basis, 750 elected from national-territorial electoral districts (similar to that of the former Soviet of Nationalities), and 750 appointed members, and the Supreme Soviet, which would consist of 211 members elected from the Congress of Deputies and 211 from the Soviet of Nationalities. In the Soviet of Nationalities each union republic would have 7 seats, each autonomous republic 4, each autonomous region 2, and each autonomous area 1 seat. After the Baltic republics fiercely resisted this proposal, last-minute changes raised the number of deputies from each union republic from 7 to 11 in the Soviet of Nationalities and added an equal increment to the Soviet of the Union. Nevertheless, more than 45 percent of deputies of the Congress were to be from Russia: in the Soviet of Nationalities 35 percent of all seats were allocated to Russia, and in the Soviet of the Union Russia held 58 percent of all seats (156 of 271).

Given the potential for Russian dominance – indeed, given the self-evident fact that the Baltic states were doomed to minority status in *any* "fair" system of representation – the Estonian Supreme Soviet, acting doubtlessly in accord with the electoral imperatives that loomed on the horizon, declared the supremacy of Estonian laws until such time as an acceptable "Union contract" was devised. On the same day, the Estonian Supreme Soviet – almost as an echo of the states' rights debates in the United States prior to its Civil War – unanimously implemented a nullification provision by voting to amend its constitution and require that union legislation meet the approval of the republic's legislature before it could become valid on the republic's territory (*Sovetskaya Estonia*, November 19, 1988).

In view of growing dissent among elites within even the Baltic party organizations, one would have expected that the federal leadership would try to accommodate some of their demands. As is likely to be the case in such circumstances, however, once bargaining encompassed fundamental institutional structures, Moscow was pressured to expand the representation and rights of numerous ethnic autonomies, mostly within Russia. The problem, then, became that of finding a way to enlarge their rights and representation without diminishing those of the union republics. Since no such solution exists, most autonomous republics declared themselves union republics by 1991.

This attempt to wrestle advantage unilaterally from the center was not without precedent. Between 1922 and 1988, many ethnic autonomies sought to upgrade their status to that of union republic (or from an autonomous oblast to autonomous republic). Most such upgrades occurred before the adoption of the 1936 Soviet Constitution, and after 1936 a region's status was more likely to be downgraded.[16] In an authoritarian regime or even one with an otherwise stable institutional structure, such adjustments need not cause unresolvable problems. But such is not the case in a regime trying to make itself democratic with institutions and processes that are sustained by the very institutional devices being changed. Once Gorbachev had undermined the role of the party and sought to substitute formal representation in existing constitutional structures, the issue of the rights of the autonomies became extremely contentious since it had a direct bearing on the bargaining position and measure of sovereignty.

Although it is perhaps understandable in retrospect to view the recalcitrance of the Baltic republics as a critical landmark on the road to Soviet disintegration, events elsewhere in the union attracted even more attention among party leaders. Even before the Estonia Supreme Soviet acted in November of that year, in February 1988 the legislature of the Nagorny-Karabakh Autonomous Oblast (NKAO), largely populated by Armenians, voted to be independent of its "host," the Republic of Azerbaijan, claiming a constitutional right to national self-determination. Ignoring pressure from Moscow, the Armenian Republic's Supreme Soviet gave consent on June 15 for the NKAO to join it, provoking an open conflict between two union republics that subsequently resulted in thousands of casualties on both sides. In 1986 ethnic clashes occurred in Yakut ASSR between Russians and Yakuts, unrest surfaced in the Nakhichevan Autonomous Republic of Azerbaijan, and by the end of the year rallies in Georgia called for abolishing the Abkhaz Autonomous Republic and a restoration of Georgian nationalism.

When the Nagorny-Karabakh conflict began, the initial reaction of the CPSU's Central Committee was utopian – to send "very precise recommendations" to regional leaders on how to restore the status quo. But by June 1988 the scope of the problem was apparent and the Nineteenth All-Union CPSU Conference called for urgent measures to be implemented for the consolidation of the Soviet federation: "The conference recommends that, taking account of the new realities, legislation pertaining to union and autonomous republics and autonomous oblasts and okrugs should be developed and renewed, reflecting more fully their rights and duties and the principles of self-management and representation of all nationalities in organs of power in the center and locally. This will necessitate the introduction of the corresponding amendments to the USSR Constitution, and to the constitutions of union and autonomous republics" (Hazan 1990: 121). This declaration marked the beginning of a concerted effort by the center to equalize the status

[16] For example, the Volga German ASSR (Autonomous Soviet Socialist Republic) and the Crimea ASSR were abolished in the 1940s, Karelia lost its status as a union republic in 1956, and the Kabardin-Balkar, Kalmyk, and Chechen-Ingush autonomies were abolished by Stalin in the 1940s, although their status was restored in the late 1950s, though generally with revised borders.

of the union republics and autonomies in a way that resolved the bargaining among them.

Referring again to the Nagorny-Karabakh conflict, "in the two years from 1988 to 1990, a territorial dispute that for decades simmered at the stage of a complex but manageable problem, transformed ethnic relations in the Transcaucasus and the relations between the people of the region and Moscow in a way that was hard to reverse" (d'Encausse 1993: 71). In the vain search for compromise, the CPSU Central Committee Plenum declared in 1989 that, "taking into account the legal nature of the autonomous republics as Soviet Socialist states, it is necessary to broaden substantially their competence," including transforming some of them into union republics. In December 1989 the Second Congress of People Deputies asked the Supreme Soviet to prepare a new law clarifying the rights of the federal center, the union republics, and autonomous units, whereupon, in April 1990, the USSR Supreme Soviet passed the Law on the Delimitation of Powers between the USSR and the federation's constituent parts. The law specified that the autonomous republics were subjects of the federation that joined the respective union republics on the basis of self-determination. The autonomous republics thus had to have all state prerogatives and rights with the exception of those voluntarily transferred by them to the federation and union republics.

On the surface, a realignment of relative status might have seemed both reasonable and feasible. In terms of population and economic potential some autonomies (e.g., the Tatar and Bashkir ASSRs) were larger than some union republics (e.g., Estonia, Latvia, Moldavia) while several nonethnic oblasts (Moscow, Leningrad, Sverdlovsk) and krais (Krasnoiarsk, Krasnodar) were comparable with entire regions (the three Baltic republics combined). But a door open to the unilateral restructuring of a federation in the quest for regional advantage is difficult to close. In August 1990 Kareliya, a union republic until 1956, was the first among the Russian autonomies to declare itself a new union republic. A week later, the founding Congress of Gagauz in Moldova declared a sovereign Gagauz republic and asserted that its citizens were no longer Moldovian citizens. And by early 1991 virtually every autonomous republic affirmed its sovereignty and insisted on its participation in the negotiation of the Union Treaty alongside its union republic "host."[17] This process, moreover, did not end with formally recognized entities: the USSR also witnessed a variety of movements seeking to create wholly new and independent entities within the union republics themselves – in Ukraine, Georgia, Azerbaijan, Moldova, Estonia, and Lithuania.

[17] On May 12, 1991, Yeltsin, Gorbachev, and the heads of the RSFSR (Russian Soviet Federative Socialist Republic) autonomous republics reached a compromise on the status of the autonomous republics. "The sovereignty of the autonomous republics was reaffirmed, but it was also agreed that the autonomies would sign the Union Treaty both as members of the USSR and the Russian Federation" (Lapidus and Walker 1995: 84).

These developments should not cause us to forget the other changes that occurred as bargaining and unilateral maneuvering for advantage unfolded. In addition to Gorbachev's revised national scheme of representation, there was the creation of the office of USSR president, the USSR's first competitive elections, a national referendum on the preservation of the union, the political resurgence of Russia under Yeltsin's stewardship and the corresponding establishment of specifically Russian political-economic institutions, any number of proposals for economic reform including the short-lived and clearly absurd "500-day plan," and, of course, the fracturing of the Communist Party into competing reform and antireform blocks. Had events been allowed to proceed unchecked, however, only two alternatives presented themselves: a union composed of several dozens of "republics" plus a dominant Russia, or the eventual dismembering of Russia either because of a conscious plan to achieve a more equal balance in the influence of the union's component parts or simply as a consequence of the demand for regional autonomy and sovereignty. Clearly, neither alternative was acceptable to everyone, and given Moscow's failure (or inability) to guarantee the territorial integrity of union republics, once autonomies received the de facto right to secede from union republics, any republic, not only Russia, willing to stay within the Union would have faced a risk of being divided into many parts.

Of course, a critical contributing factor to the USSR's demise was, as Bunce (1999) argues was the case for Yugoslavia and Czechoslovakia, the prior existence of political entities that were legitimized and readily mobilized within their domains as a function of federalism itself. But it is also evident that the Soviet Union could not have reached this point until and unless the control and coordination exercised by the Communist Party had been fully undermined by a formal redefinition of its role and the mechanism of competitive elections within the party that reset incentives: "With the collapse of Communism and the Communist Party of the USSR, there remained neither a military nor a career reason for the politicians in the republics . . . to stay together with Russia" (Shleifer and Treisman 2000: 135). More specifically, the bargaining for advantage that unfolded following the fracturing of the party along the geopolitical lines designed to control the USSR's ethnic heterogeneity occurred in a context in which neither institutions nor the roles (and even the identities) of the players were fixed and off limits to renegotiation and redefinition: "The issues under discussion [viz. the Union Treaty] were the classical topics of constitutional concern: power-sharing, taxation powers, division of property, and ownership rights" (Sharlet 1992: 111). With essentially every issue on the table simultaneously, the USSR suffered from a brutal form of redistributive politics in which even the rules under which redistribution was to occur became chips on the bargaining table – a scenario that was about as close to a Hobbesian state of nature as we are likely to find in a country that earlier had been characterized as monolithic and stable.

The ratification of the USSR's disintegration that took place in Minsk following the abortive 1991 Moscow coup, which itself sought simply to roll back the clock to a pre-perestroika institutional status quo, merely ended a process that had begun once the role of the Communist Party had been eroded. It is not out of the realm of possibility that the fear factor could have brought politicians in republics back into line should a greater show of force been put up by the "putsch" organizers.[18] Had there been the means for a totalitarian solution to the problem of the unraveling institutional bargaining, such a solution might or might not have been decisive. What we argue here, however, is that no *democratic* or even *quasi-democratic* process of negotiating the rules could have produced a stabilizing result. In this regard, had the "putschists" succeeded in replacing Gorbachev at the helm but without installing a brutal dictatorship, the same processes of spiraling claims would have taken place under their reign, or at least so our theory tells us.[19]

3.3 The Feasibility of Success in Initial Bargaining

Naturally, once in possession of this explanation, it is tempting to ask whether Gorbachev's reforms could have been implemented without the unraveling of the USSR. And although engaging in such speculation is normally fruitless, given the impossibility of rerunning the experiment, we cannot resist that temptation here, if only because of our understanding of another global renegotiation that was successful – the one conducted in Philadelphia in 1787. The issues addressed there were no less profound and encompassing: the basis of representation among otherwise sovereign entities, the power of the new federal center relative to those entities, the definition of sovereignty (could both states and the new center be simultaneously sovereign?), the balance of powers within the federal center, the authority of the states in

[18] It is possible to interpret some of the developments in the non-Russian republics as the regime's willingness, if necessary, to resort to violence and repressions to enforce the country's territorial integrity and suppress the popular drive for independence – such as the use of terror by the Soviet security forces in Tbilisi, Baku, and Vilnius. Thus, for example, Hough concludes his detailed assessment of the feasibility of preserving the Soviet Union by force with the following: "Gorbachev refused to use enough force to ensure obedience to Soviet laws and to suppress separatism. An enormous amount has been written about the handful of deaths Soviet security forces caused in Tbilisi, Baku, and Vilnius, as if these acts somehow destroyed perestroika. But continuing such limited applications of force would surely have preserved the union" (Hough 1997: 498; but see Clemens 2000). We are grateful to an anonymous reviewer for impressing upon us the need for acknowledging this possibility.

[19] It is reasonable to argue, moreover that even if the coup had succeeded in aborting Gorbachev's Union Treaty and restoring that status quo, it nevertheless would have failed unless its leaders had the foresight to understand the role of the party. There is no evidence, however, that that role was understood or that it could be restored and, therefore, no reason to believe that the coup would have accomplished much except to postpone the USSR's day of reckoning.

electing or selecting their representatives, the authority of the center to tax and regulate commerce, the basis for admission of new territories, and so on. The seeds of intersectional and interstate rivalry and conflict were also fully in place, whether it be a dispute between Virginia and Maryland over fishing rights, the "annoying peculiarities" of German-speaking Quakers in Philadelphia, the Jews of Rhode Island, the religious zealotry of New England, states whose economies depended on exports versus those dependent on imports, and states with seemingly little interest in controlling their currencies versus those led by creditors whose wealth was directly threatened by loose money policies. Like the USSR, these interests existed within political entities with well-formed and fully mobilized political institutions. Finally, given that the proposed constitution was a full replacement of the Articles of Confederation and not a mere amendment to them, the implicit negotiation was indeed global. Despite the considerable political squabbling that ensued for the next seventy years, however, the negotiation did succeed in establishing a set of institutions that not only survived a civil war but which largely continued to function on both sides of the conflict even during the war's prosecution. What then, we might ask, was the trick? How was it that the states ratified the proposed constitution with little or no overt conflict, that intersectional rivalries seemed to play no role in that ratification process, and that no war of laws ensued to undermine the grand experiment before it was even halfway started?

In answering these questions we should not disregard the contribution to the success of such a fragile process of the strategic abilities, personal qualities, and shared beliefs of those who maneuvered the American Constitution into existence. Men such as Madison, Hamilton, Wilson, Franklin, Morris, and Rutledge (or, although they could only kibitz from afar or through proxies, Adams and Jefferson) were steeped in the history of classical democratic and republican governments, the philosophy of the Enlightenment, the political arguments of contemporary theorists from Harrington to Hume to Montesquieu, the strengths and weaknesses of the British political and legal system, and the experience of popular sovereignty in their individual states. It is also true that many of the Framers held a significant economic stake in the preservation and strengthening of the Union. What is noteworthy, however, is that the Framers' advantage in intelligence and experience manifested itself in ways other than the institutional framework they crafted – specifically, in the way they prepared their plan and pursued its implementation. With windows shuttered and precautions taken to ensure that likely opponents would at best be poorly represented at their gathering, they made every effort to remove themselves from the political passions that swirled around them so that one of their most ardent opponents, Patrick Henry, could only fume from the sidelines that he "smelt a rat." And, wholly consistent with the hypothesis that a successful institutional solution constitutes only one of many possible equilibria, the Framers not only kept the windows shuttered until after they could offer a complete plan defensible in its entirety but also included in that plan a formal institutionalized procedure for the ratification of their design.[20]

Thus, although the Framers had clearly embarked on a global redesign of the government's institutional structure, they sought to frame debate so as to avoid uninstitutionalized bargaining and global renegotiation.[21] In this, through planning and what Riker (1996) calls skillful herestetics, they largely succeeded, including capturing the label "federalist" when it rightly belonged to their opponents. Presenting society with a complete plan, as opposed to pursuing their ends in open debate through incremental change adjusted and defended on the fly, allowed the Framers to portray their scheme as a fully defined (institutional) equilibrium.[22] This, in turn, provided them with two tactical advantages. First, it allowed them the reasonable argument that a change in any one part of the document could only disrupt that equilibrium. The document was a take-it-or-leave-it proposition not simply because the Framers asserted it had to be considered that way, but because tinkering with any section, article, provision, or clause could only upset a carefully crafted equilibrium. The second advantage was that they avoided the instabilities associated with unrestricted multidimensional bargaining.

The alternatives were but two in number – a viable national government or none at all, even disunion – and it was left to the Framers to argue that most if not all members of society ought to prefer the first alternative. As Washington himself stated the matter, "is it best for the states to unite, or not to unite? If there are men who prefer the latter, then unquestionably the Constitution which is offered must... be wrong... but those who think differently and yet object to parts of it would do well to consider that it does not lye with any *one* state, or the *minority* of states to superstruct a Constitution for the whole.... Hence it is that every state has some objection

[20] Indeed, that procedure was itself radical. Not only did it arbitrarily allow for the new constitution to go into effect when nine of the thirteen states ratified the document (as opposed to the unanimity required for approval of measures under the original articles), but it simultaneously moved the process of ratification from the separate state legislatures to specially elected state constitutional conventions.

[21] The question that remains unanswered here is how bargaining *among the Framers* was resolved, behind those locked doors and shuttered windows. The general answer implied by our theoretical argument elaborated in Chapter 5 is that individuals in the convention were sufficiently otherwise motivated – and not merely by the depravity of their confinement, though that should not be discarded either – to reach an agreement within the group.

[22] One might see here a certain similarity to the method of selecting popes. Of perhaps more relevance, however, notice the functional similarity to the process whereby Germany and Japan "received" their new constitutions after World War II – with the Western powers in the first instance allowing for only minimal variation from a set pattern, and in the other a constitution imposed by an occupying force. In both cases, then, whatever bargaining occurred, occurred in a highly restrictive context, and the issues considered, if any, were severely limited.

to the present form and these objections are directed to different points, that which is most pleasing to one is obnoxious to another, and so vise versa. If then the Union as a whole is a desirable object, the component parts must yield" (Bailyn 1993: 305–6). Thus, despite the revolutionary character of their plan, the Framers succeeded in limiting efforts at revision to a bill of rights, which itself was but a guarantee of sorts that the document would work as advertised. Even then they succeeded in admitting only a proposal that a listing of rights be the first order of business of the newly formed national legislature.

3.4 Secession: The Special Road to Renegotiation

We cannot say to what extent such a strategy and accumulation of talent would have benefited the Soviet Union or whether there was a path to political-economic reform that would have averted the USSR's dissolution. But the Soviet demise does illustrate the consequences of allowing a renegotiation of federal terms in an uninstitutionalized context that the American experience at least suggests can, with skill, be avoided. Minimally, the Soviet and Czechoslovak cases together illustrate why a primary goal of federal design or redesign requires a full exploration of the opportunities, if any, of proceeding in a way that avoids the open unrestricted renegotiation of federal terms. Stable, institutionalized bargaining requires that only partial adjustments and renegotiation of particular issues be allowed and that this be done within a broader fixed institutional context. The delegates in Philadelphia may have fashioned a global reformulation of the terms of union, but they did so by artfully imposing new institutional constraints – secret deliberations, a single take-it-or-leave-it package, and explicit procedural rules for ratification. More generally, the purpose of erecting constitutional constraints and relatively immutable procedures is to reduce the dimensionality of federal bargaining. It may be useful, when debating policy, to allow bargainers to consider more than one issue at a time so that "votes" can be traded across issues in order to achieve some minimal consensus on final outcomes. But vote trading can yield outcomes that differ from those that prevail under myopic (one issue at a time) voting if and only if there is no multidimensional outcome that cannot be upset by some other in a simple majority vote (Schwartz 1977). There is an inherent instability, then, in those circumstances in which vote trading is potentially profitable for majorities. And although that instability need not be of great concern when the issues under consideration are narrowly prescribed, there are few if any restraints remaining on potential outcomes when they encompass core institutions.

It is, of course, one thing to offer this prescription as a goal, and quite another to achieve it. But aside from noting the American parallel, there is an implication of our discussion that provides some practical guidance. Specifically, despite James Buchanan's (1995) arguments to the contrary, we doubt whether a right to secede can be a part of a stable federation's institutional structure, even though we appreciate that disallowing secession may be too strong a condition for participants to accept when a federation is formed.[23] First, as our discussion in the previous two sections reveals, we concur with the assertion that "a secessionist outcome may be less the culmination of struggles over autonomy and independence that pit a secessionist region against the center than a *by-product* of a host of other struggles over money, power, and policy that are going on within the center and the regions" (Bunce 1999: 14), but we disagree somewhat with the extension of this argument: "secession can often be an offshoot of other ongoing political struggles, rather than a direct outcome of bargaining over the future contours of the state" – at least insofar as this argument tries to separate ongoing political struggles from the motive to reshape federal provisions. If preferences over institutions are not somehow insulated from preferences over outcomes, then the conceptual separation assumed here is not viable.

A formally recognized right to secede fundamentally changes the nature of federal bargaining, since secession as an option legitimizes the view that the existing union can be dissolved and recreated on new terms, with a new or reconfigured membership. Indeed, an institutionally sanctioned secession marks the beginnings of a new federation, either without some old members or on the basis of new principles intended to satisfy seceding members. To threaten secession, then, is equivalent to an ultimatum requiring a choice between existing arrangements and a comprehensive revision of the principles of federal organization. Whatever the nature of those revisions might be, from a designer's perspective a decision to include secession as a legitimate option poses a choice between the institutional status quo and all the uncertainty associated with uninstitutionalized bargaining.

Once again, we want to restate that we are not adopting the untenable proposition that all existing federations ought to be sustained at all cost or that all of the federations proposed or likely to be proposed in the future correspond to advisable ends. This volume simply takes as its initial premise the desire to erect a federation that is stable, democratic, and efficient, and from that perspective alone our concern with secession is predicated on the fact that in most historical cases the secession of one or several units has meant the disintegration of the whole federation (West India, Central African Federation, the Soviet Union, and, incrementally, Yugoslavia).[24] Rarer still is

[23] We prefer to avoid a discussion of alternative forms of secession (e.g., irredentism) but rather to focus on the primary lesson of our analysis; namely, that constitutional provisions of any type should not encourage any wholesale renegotiation of federal relations. For a discussion of alternative forms of secession and their different contexts, see Bookman (1992).

[24] However, in a number of cases, a separation or an expulsion of certain territories (groups) was the key precondition for federalization of the remaining states – for example, the ouster of Germans from post–World War II Czechoslovakia; and the separation of Burma, then Pakistan from India; East Pakistan from West Pakistan; Eritrea from Ethiopia; Singapore from Malaysia.

the peaceful secession of some units, except perhaps when in 1965 Singapore was expelled from Malaysia to reduce the political influence of the Chinese community.[25] However, such cases can at best be taken as a mere prelude to understanding how secession clauses actually affect the political process. A prohibition of secession is, in effect, a promise that defectors (seceding federal subjects) will be punished by those that remain in the federation. In this sense, we can think of a federation as a collective security agreement in which, in addition to promises of mutual assistance, there is also the promise of punishment for defection from the collective bargain. Suppose, for whatever reason, that the threat of punishment is credible – that federal subjects believe that a punishment will be implemented if required. If this belief is itself common knowledge – if everyone believes that everyone else believes that the threat of punishment is credible, and so on – and if the consequences of punishment are sufficiently unappealing for potential defectors, then the threat of secession as part of a bargaining strategy would not itself be credible and therefore would not be used. Thus, a credible commitment to punishing defectors keeps the issue of a general renegotiation of federal terms from being raised by those units which otherwise might have tried to blackmail the union – or it at least removes one of the weapons a dissatisfied subject might use to instigate a renegotiation.

Explicitly allowing secession, on the other hand, has the opposite effect. Here the promise is that secession will not be punished. But if the federation is valuable to everyone, then its collapse would be damaging to all, and it is a simple matter of comparing marginal utility to see whether the threat of secession can be used to strengthen a threatening member's position in the overall bargaining. Allowing secession gives the potentially seceding state a costless sanction it can apply in the event that its demands for a renegotiation of the terms of union are not satisfied. But since that threat is presumably available to all members, a credible promise to not punish defectors is equivalent to leaving all issues of the federation's structure on the table and subject to renegotiation.

An option of secession may be a critical issue when the terms of union are first decided. Political elites are being asked to give up something of value – autonomy – and in an uncertain world, they may not have the confidence that a newly formed federation will serve its purpose, in which case they may refuse to abrogate the autonomy of the states they represent without a guarantee that it can be won back with minimal effort and without sanction. Allowing secession, however, runs afoul of the prescription that, when writing a constitution, "we should strive for interpersonal impartiality not only among members of the present generation of constitution makers but

[25] There have been peaceful secessions – Norway from Sweden in 1905 and Belgium from the Netherlands in 1830 – but in both cases it would be difficult to classify the states involved as federal.

future generations as well. Hence a good constitution will not be too closely tied to the concrete needs and preferences of the present generation" (Allen Buchanan 1991: 130). Because federations should not be formed for transient interests, a right to secede reduces them to the status of "mere alliances" (or, as in the case of the European Union, with its apparent right of free exit, a mere customs union or confederation).

We appreciate that such advice will not always be followed, in which case we are left with the suggestion that secession be made as difficult as possible when the initial federal bargain is negotiated.[26] But regardless of whether our argument is persuasive, there remains the matter of how the threat of sanction in the form of a constitutional prohibition of secession would create expectations in any way different from what a promise to allow secession without sanction would lead people to believe. If these particular words in a constitution have no import – if a secession will be sanctioned regardless of whether a constitution allows it, or if it will not be sanctioned even if a constitution prohibits it – then why concern ourselves with secession clauses in the first place? Stalin's constitution may have allowed secession in principle, but we suspect that the half-life of anyone advocating such a policy for his region would have been short indeed.

Thus, understanding why the mere words of an antisecession clause would change anything moves us directly to a profoundly important issue – to the one that pits Riker's views of stability against those of pluralists such as Dahl – namely, the ultimate source of constitutional enforcement. Aren't secession clauses, like other federal constraints, mere "parchment barriers" and subject to renegotiation? If the decision to form a federation is based on the expectation that doing so will increase the welfare and security of its members, and if the decision to secede is based on a comparative assessment of these benefits as compared with a subject's welfare and security outside of the federation, why would mere words change people's assessments of these things. If the basis for forming and maintaining a federation rests on objectively identifiable benefits – if, aside from those nonfungible values of ethnicity, language, and religion, secession can be precluded as some suggest by the explicitly tangible things produced by economic policy and formulas for redistribution (Bookman 1992; Le Breton and Weber 2000) – why would

[26] There are, of course, other alternatives that might be considered in those negotiations, including the power of nullification and the group veto. In the first instance, a group (including a federal subject) is authorized to nullify a law within specific jurisdictional domains, whereas in the second such a group is given a veto that the national legislature may or may not be authorized to override with a special vote. But as with nearly everything else, even these stark alternatives come in varying shades. For example, Germany's Basic Law offers its states a collective veto through the Bundesrat and, in lieu of the authority to nullify the law, provides them with a significant degree of control over the administration of federal law. However, we postpone discussion of these other alternatives until later chapters.

people be any more or less likely to threaten and sanction because of one set of words on paper rather than another?

We postpone a more complete discussion of this issue – both in its specific form with respect to secession and its general form with respect to constitutional structures as a whole – until Chapter 5. Suffice it to say that the signals a constitution offers as to what a polity should expect people to do under different circumstances are not unimportant and can, under the "right" circumstance, coordinate them to one pattern of action versus another. That is, we can construct abstract scenarios – formal N person games if you want – in which, for identically the same circumstances, if there is the threat of punishing a secession, that threat will be implemented if necessary, whereas if there is the promise of no sanction, sanctions will not be applied in the event that someone unilaterally departs from the federation (Chen and Ordeshook 1994).

The argument we expand on in Chapter 5 is that constitutional words can be critical to the selection of one of these alternative equilibria. Indeed, whether secession is ultimately allowed or disallowed, the American experience here is especially instructive. Recall that rather than explicitly prohibit or sanction secession, the U.S. Constitution of 1787 was ambiguous, even silent, so that prior to 1861, the right of secession was subject to varied interpretations. This silence, however, was perhaps more damaging to stability than any other possibility, for it allowed the states of the Confederacy to believe, as their interests dictated, that they had a legitimate right to secede, and for the North to believe the opposite. Not only was there no prior agreement as to whether secession would be punished or allowed, it was not evident to everyone that the South (South Carolina in particular) had in fact seceded even after a proclamation severing its ties to the Union. Thus, as the Civil War commenced, the question remained, Had the Southern states legitimately seceded or were they merely in rebellion? The answer given in the North was not directed by any constitutional provision. Instead, the nearly unanimously accepted answer was one that fit the political exigencies of the moment (how else, for example, could Lincoln justify the legality of an Emancipation Proclamation that set slaves free within the states of the Confederacy if those states were not still a part of the Union?). We are not so bold to say that constitutional wording prohibiting secession would have precluded an American Civil War. But we do want to suggest that "it wouldn't have hurt" – at least insofar as avoiding the bloodshed of that war, although perhaps not in terms of preserving the Union.

Admittedly, things were different in the Soviet case. First, we need to keep in mind that individuals per se do not sanction against a secession; only individuals acting as groups, armies, political cadres, and the like can act to this end. Stalin may have been able to order a sanction, but his orders would have effect only if others acted as he directed – and then only if they found it in their self-interest to do so. In that era, of course, that self-interest derived from the common-knowledge belief that everyone, or nearly everyone, stood ready to act as directed, in which case the belief becomes a self-fulfilling prophecy (a part of the overall social equilibrium). Such is the nature of leadership, whether in a democracy or a tyrannical regime. More specifically in the Soviet case, sanctions, if they were to be applied, would have been directed by the party and by precisely those members who, during the Gorbachev era and as a consequence of Gorbachev's reforms, now applied their energies in a different direction. It was, in short, those party members who actively championed greater autonomy for their republics who would otherwise have been entrusted with sanctioning defectors. Thus, by 1991, with the party a mere shell of what it had been, it could only be common knowledge that the threat of sanction against secession was no longer credible (with the apparent exception of a drunken vice president and a small cadre of fellow "coup" conspirators who failed to understand how beliefs and their own credibility had fundamentally changed). Add to this the legitimacy provided by the proposed Federal Treaty of questioning the very foundations of the union, as well as Gorbachev's allowance for secession in principle, and you have a circumstance in which secession becomes but one of the tools that may be applied to wholly uninstitutionalized bargaining.

This discussion should not be interpreted to mean that we regard an antisecession clause as *the* critical component of a federal constitution, or that such clauses play a unique role in regulating federal bargaining. We suspect, for example, that Gorbachev's decision to legitimize secession was at best a precipitating agent and not the critical event in unraveling the union. And it would be silly to argue that other clauses are not equally important, such as those that treat federal supremacy and comity, and that prohibit restraint of trade across federal subjects. However, none of these provisions, including those that prohibit secession, can be of much consequence absent an adequate design of the critical venues of federal bargaining (via a federation's Level 2 provisions), since it is there that these Level 1 constraints will be either upheld, broken, or wholly ignored. As we have said before, our argument is not that Level 1 constraining clauses such as antisecession provisions or allocations of jurisdictions are wholly ephemeral and destined to be whatever the political exigencies of the day determine them to be. Our argument is the opposite since agreement on these things may be necessary to form a federation and since such clauses, for the reasons briefly outlined here with respect to credible threats and promises, can impact the outcomes likely to be realized under the operation of the institutional forms at Level 2. The fact remains, nevertheless, that federal design only begins with these constraints, including the decision of whether to allow secession. For instance, although we have not yet discussed the role of the courts, we cannot preclude the possibility that such constraints, even if only mere sentiments, are essential to the courts in their efforts to ensure that the state performs as intended.

This possibility, however, only underscores the argument that for these constraints to serve their purpose, the venues where they can be changed need to be institutionalized in ways that are conducive to reasonably efficient and minimally conflicting interactions among the bargaining agents. In the next chapter, then, we turn to a discussion of some fundamental principles of representation and the impact various constitutional alternatives have on the institution most likely to become the primary venue for federal bargaining – the national legislature.

4

Representation

> Had every Athenian citizen been a Socrates; every Athenian assembly would still have been a mob.
>
> Madison, *Federalist* 55

> The proposed Constitution, so far from implying an abolition of State Governments, makes them constituent parts of the national sovereignty by allowing them direct representation in the Senate, and leaves in their possession certain elusive and very important portions of sovereign power. This fully corresponds in every rational import of the terms, with the idea of a Foederal Government.
>
> Hamilton, *Federalist* 9

> That legislators have an abiding interest in the nature of opinion in their constituencies there can be no doubt. How their estimates of that opinion bear on their work in the assembly is not nearly so clear. At times they bow down before constituency opinion, and at times they ignore it.
>
> Key 1963: 482

> Opportunism by the national government is best constrained by fragmenting power at the national level. By making it harder for a national will to form and be sustained over time, these mechanisms will tend to disable national authorities from invading state authority, especially as to controversial issues.
>
> Bednar et al. 2001: 230

4.1 Two Alternative Models of Federalism

To avoid choices of the sort that led to the dismemberment of Czechoslovakia and the USSR, not only must federal bargaining be regulated to encourage coherent outcomes and discourage the inefficiencies that follow from a disruption of federal functions, but ways must be found to avoid a wholesale revision of the Level 1 constraints that are part of any initial agreement among federal subjects. These constraints are not, of themselves, self-enforcing. They may appear to hold well in an otherwise stable federation, but we cannot rely on them alone to engender their own stability. Indeed, their operational significance is more a consequence of stability than a cause. This is not to say that, when establishing a federation, a prior consensus regarding, say, the responsibility for exploiting natural resources, permissible sources of tax revenues, the regulatory authority of different levels of government, or rules for redistributing the federal center's fiscal resources is unimportant. The failure to achieve agreement over such matters may encourage disruptive attempts at institutional revision in the future and can even forestall federal formation in the first place. It is a mistake to suppose, however, that federal design ends once all such issues are negotiated. No issue-specific consensus is likely to be permanent and binding on all generations, nor can the future salience of issues be fully anticipated. Even a long-standing democracy such as Belgium illustrates issues that can lay dormant for generations and then suddenly bubble up to disrupt the state. But the primary lesson we draw from cases such as the USSR and Czechoslovakia is that even in the short run Level 1 constraints must be imbedded in some larger game that establishes incentives to abide by them or to renegotiate and change them only slowly. We are led, then, to the notion of a second level of constitutional design, Level 2, which in our scheme consists primarily of those constitutional provisions that define the formal institutions of the state that are charged with upholding Level 1.

Although many of the elements of Level 1 will normally be found in a national constitution (exceptions include quasi-constitutional revenue redistribution formulas or the chartering of independent regulatory agencies), the elements of Level 2 serve a broader purpose and are more commonly identified as the core of a constitution – those provisions detailing the structure and prerogatives of the separate branches of government and the relation of these branches to each other and to the ultimate sovereign, the people. In this scheme, then, constitutional design can be interpreted as the establishment of a game that, minimally, identifies the key political actors (e.g., members of a national legislature, the eligible electorate, a national chief executive, a national court), empowers those actors by specifying the legitimate actions available to them (e.g., the authority to introduce, pass or veto legislation, to fill public offices by voting or appointment, to initiate and vote on referenda, to acknowledge the legal actions of other governments within the federation), and specifies the formal relationship of these actors to each other so that we know the outcomes that follow from their joint actions (e.g., rules for the passage of legislation, for veto overrides, for ruling on the constitutionality of legislative and executive acts, for removal from office, for amending the constitution, and for filling cabinet or ministerial positions, and the general election laws that translate votes into winners). This game should be structured so that it satisfies certain properties, chief among them being that all relevant actors have an incentive to maintain its general structure as well as any Level 1 agreements that were negotiated in the process of the state's formation or thereafter. Thus, we cannot ignore the issue of enforcement with respect to these Level 2 institutions any more than we can with respect to Level 1, since, as we note earlier, preferences over Level 2 alternatives may be inherited directly from preferences over Level 1. However, before we explore that matter in the next chapter, here we focus on a few principal aspects of the design of Level 2 – especially the structure of federal subject representation in the national legislature – that seem especially relevant to the character of the bargaining likely to emerge over Level 1.

We begin our discussion of Level 2 with a review of the two abstract representations of a federal state that commonly guide the literature so that we can identify some of the things that might preclude a fully adequate design. Recall that the first model assumes in its ideal form that federal relations are best described as an *N* person game in which federal bargaining, although perhaps occurring within federal (national) institutions, is primarily a manifestation of disagreements among federal subjects, each of which is presumed to possess well-defined interests. One example of this form, then, is the United States under the Articles of Confederation and arguably is the view of federalism that predominated until America's "centralized federalism" appeared (Riker 1964). In more moderate versions of this view the entity labeled the "federal center" is not readily separable from federal subjects. Design in accordance with this model is not uniquely or even primarily concerned with empowering the center but focuses instead on rendering the center a venue of bargaining among federal subjects. If federal design poses a danger here, it is that the federal center proves too weak to encourage the cooperation required among subjects that would allow them to realize the presumed benefits of collective action. The alternative approach presumes that federal interaction is an *N+1* person game, and that design involves the creation of an *N+1st* player with preferences and motives independent of the *N* federal subjects. Although bargaining among those subjects is not theoretically precluded, the assumption is that the critical arena of bargaining will concern conflicts between the center and those subjects. Constitutional design here is primarily concerned with empowering this new player to be an independent political force able to coordinate and, if necessary, coerce federal subjects, while trying to avert the danger of allowing it to achieve full predominance so as to either render federal subjects little more than administrative arms of a unitary state or offering subjects an irresistible "prize" they compete to capture.

The Framers of the U.S. Constitution saw federal design as requiring consistency with a model that fell somewhere between these two extremes. Although the United States under its Articles of Confederation illustrated the alternative disliked by Federalists, an extreme and dangerous adherence to the second model was the one Anti-Federalists feared was imbedded in the document presented to them for ratification. For obvious reasons, Hamilton had to argue that the truth lay between these two extremes even though, given the absence of experience, no one could be certain what the new constitution would eventually yield.

Of these two conceptualizations, the second is more consonant with the contemporary literature, which portrays in high relief as the problem of federal stability the need to balance the autonomy of federal subjects against the supremacy of an autonomous national government. As a model and basis for constitutional design, however, it is no more adequate than the first when the primary actors in bargaining are not themselves unitary or separately identifiable governments. The key difficulty is revealed when we consider the problems associated with differentiating between those parts of any particular federal government speaking for federal subjects and those constituting the *N+1st* player, the center. Is a national legislature – even one explicitly designed to represent federal subjects – merely a collection of agents of the federal subjects and, thereby, a part of *N*, or, because it is primarily responsible for the passage of federal laws, an inseparable part of the *N+1st* player, the federal center? Is the chief executive (president or prime minister) more a part of that center, and how is the identity of that office determined as a function of how it is filled? For example, is a U.S. president, elected nationally but through the filter of an Electoral College that, under Article 2 of the national Constitution, is itself regulated by state legislatures, more a part of the federal center than, say, a German prime minister, who is chosen by a parliament that, supposedly, is a forum for regionally based political parties? And if we decide that both the national executive and legislative branches are part of the center, in combination with the federal bureaucracy and courts, how do we accommodate the different structures, roles, and motives of these branches into a conceptual scheme that allows for only one *N+1st* player?

The plain words of a constitution will usually not admit of simple answers to such questions. For example, if we were to ask for a list of countries with a strong president – nationally elected and essentially independent of the national legislature and federal subjects, and thereby a candidate for inclusion in any description of *N+1* – the United States would almost certainly be included in that list. Yet an examination of the constitutionally mandated prerogatives of that office offers the image of a weak presidency – a chief executive without the authority to fill even executive offices without the consent of the legislature, whose veto can be overridden, who can be impeached for seemingly vague reasons, who has no explicit authority to declare emergencies, who is commander in chief of a military the Congress may choose not to fund, who plays no role in the constitutional amendment process, and who cannot act unless authorized to do so by the national legislature.

The ambiguity associated with any attempt at specifying the identity of an *N+1st* player in any real federation suggests that an *N+1* person conceptualization threatens an unsatisfactory framework for federal design. Because it presupposes that the federal center has an identifiable and internally indivisible interest that is potentially at odds with the interests of all units, this conceptualization in effect assumes away the necessity for finding a design that can successfully address the problem of bargaining *among* federal subjects themselves and even assumes away the possibility that such bargaining occurs within the federal center. The consequence is that federal design instead focuses on ways to balance the prerogatives and bargaining positions of the different levels of government, and on such matters as constraints on the authority of one level of government or another via the allocation of jurisdictional responsibilities, either as specified in a constitution or in "treaties" between governments.[1] Thus, design focuses on what we might hope will be the *outputs* of federal relations rather than on the institutional mechanisms for achieving those ends. But, as we already know, such an approach begs the question of enforcement. The extreme version of an *N+1* conceptualization, then, leaves fundamental issues of federal stability unanswered and even unanswerable.

Recognition of the inadequacies of any preset definition of the federal game led the delegates to the Philadelphia Convention in 1787 to make a theoretical compromise. Recall that the debate there focused not on the allocation of jurisdictions but on a structure for a national legislature. Although the delegates were certainly concerned with the powers of the federal center relative to those of the states – a concern that was magnified by the subsequent Anti-Federalist attack on their document and the demand for a bill of rights that would constrain the proposed national government – the Great Compromise that allowed the convention to proceed concerned the composition of the national legislature, the venue for federal bargaining. Although the national government was to have a separable identity (via the institutional mechanisms of the direct election of the House of Representatives, and in the presidency through the filter of the Electoral College), it was not to be an independent creature with its own motives, wholly separate from those of the states. Instead, the core of the new national government was to be its legislature, which would be an extension of the states and which would serve as their primary arena for bargaining and coordination: "Its [the legislature's] constitutional powers being at once more extensive, and less susceptible of precise limits, it can, with the greater facility, mask,

[1] As one historian of the American experience writes, "In attempting to assuage the localist-oriented Antifederalist opponents of the Constitution, the Founders had divided sovereignty and power between the states and the national government. But they had not spelled out the exact nature of the relationship. And this proved a serious ambiguity" (Sharp 1993: 4). The error here is the assumption that there is a ready means of resolving that ambiguity.

under complicated and indirect measures, the encroachments which it makes on the coordinate departments" (Madison, *Federalist* 48). It was to be an arena, however, only partially answerable to state governments (the Senate); the other part (the House of Representatives) was to be answerable to the people directly.

4.2 A National Venue for Bargaining

We can attribute the fact that the American system did not evolve in precisely this way to any number of factors, including the country's expansion to continental status and the corresponding need for greater coordination, the rise of national parties, and the not-fully-appreciated constitutional authority of the presidency. Nevertheless, if we search for a place to begin in assessing the core Level 2 structure essential for a federal democracy, it is perhaps best to begin where Madison began, with the legislature. In doing so, however, we should not wholly discard either extreme conceptualization of federalism – the *N* or *N+1* person variant – if only for the simple reason that they are useful for describing and contrasting certain federations. Consider, for instance, Canada and the United States.

The U.S. system explicitly offers federal subjects at least two arenas of bargaining within the national government – the House of Representatives and the Senate – and, at least in its initial design, illustrates two principles of representation. The House is designed to represent the parochial interests of voters, whereas members of the Senate, originally appointed by state officials, were to represent federal subject governments. Thus, bargaining was to occur at two levels – among voters via their directly elected representatives and among state governments within the Senate. Canada contrasts sharply with this case. Although members of the Canadian Parliament are elected in single mandate constituencies like their American counterparts, the Canadian Parliament in combination with its prime minister and associated bureaucracy is, unlike the U.S. Congress, a close match to any notion of an *N+1st* player. To see what we mean, suppose a candidate for the Canadian Parliament and a candidate for either chamber of the U.S. Congress each proclaim that their primary concern is the well-being of their constituency and that *national* legislative party discipline is secondary. American voters, we suspect, would regard such a platform with curiosity as they try to comprehend the candidate's message: "Party discipline – what's that?" In Canada, on the other hand, such a campaign platform might attract some votes, but at the same time we can imagine voters being alarmed. The absence of party discipline in the Canadian Parliament can either prevent the formation of a cabinet or bring down an existing one, and it is not unreasonable to suppose that a voter there, by choosing one representative versus another, conceptualizes his or her choices in terms of an overall cabinet package. The cabinet, in turn, fully satisfies any reasonable definition of the center insofar as it possesses a national mandate to exert both legislative and executive powers.

Thus, although the cabinet (and the parliament of which the cabinet is a creature) is something with which federal subjects can negotiate, the representation of those subjects is not accomplished within Canada's national parliament. Its members do not speak with an unambiguous voice for federal subjects: as loyal members of their parties, they are a part of the federal center, so that representatives of subjects as well as the explicit arenas where such representatives bargain must be found elsewhere.

Within versus Without Representation

The contrast between the United States and Canada and between the *N* and *N+1* person approach to design serve as useful frameworks with which to begin a discussion of the core parameters of federal design. Specifically, we can see with these two examples that the essential difference between an *N* and *N+1* person conceptualization of the content of Level 2 is the character of the national legislature – whether it is more appropriate to think of that legislature as part of the federal center or as an arena where representatives of federal subjects meet. Hence, to further sort through the possibilities, and to begin laying out some more specific and substantive design parameters, the general character of the available alternatives can be presented by a simple two-by-two classification given in Table 4.1. The first dimension of this table is illustrated by contrasting those federations such as the United States and Germany, in which states are represented and negotiate directly *within* national governmental structures, to entities such as Canada and the European Union, in which representation is built around subjects of the federation who defend and articulate their units' interests *without* of the federal center by addressing or confronting the center as if it were some external force (Loewenstein 1965: 405–7; Gibbins 1982: 45–6). If the first type places agents representing the interests of units directly within the national government and thereby undermines the value of an *N+1* person conceptualization, the second keeps unit agents outside of national bodies and corresponds more closely to that conceptualization. Although this distinction between within and without does not appear in pure form in anywhere, one of them may be the prevailing type and offer the more accurate model.

TABLE 4.1. *Types of Representation and Venues of Bargaining*

	Direct Representation	**Delegated Representation**
Within bargaining	Both U.S. chambers German Bundestag Switzerland	Old U.S. Senate German Bundesrat Russian upper chamber USSR Central Commmittee
Without bargaining	Citizen initiatives	Canada European Union

Direct versus Delegated Representation

The second dimension (column) of Table 4.1 largely corresponds to the historical change in the U.S. Senate, which was designed initially to represent state governments via the authority given to state governors and legislatures to appoint delegates and which Madison foresaw as a brake on the potential excesses of the directly elected House of Representatives. However, in accord with evolving tradition, formal institutional change at the state level, and the Seventeenth Amendment, that chamber now represents citizens directly. Insofar as other examples are concerned, the Russian Federation's upper legislative chamber, the Federation Council, consisted initially of the executive heads of regional governments and the head of each region's legislature, although in an attempt to diminish the authority of regional governors, those governors are now authorized only to appoint members to the Federation Council. In both instances, a within format is the appropriate model. Unlike the U.S. Senate, however, the Federation Council's authority is limited by the fact that the lower legislative chamber, the State Duma, can override the Federation Council. Thus, if a Russian president can secure a working majority in the Duma, then much like a prime minister, he can control all legislation, which, in combination with the other powers of this office, moves the overall character of the Russian system to a without system. The Federation Council is weaker, then, than the model upon which it is based, Germany's Bundesrat – although the Bundesrat policy domain is limited to legislation that directly impacts the *Länder* (although that authority is expanding over time by convention and practice), a veto by the German chamber cannot be overridden. The representation given the *Länder*, then, is more meaningful than that given to Russia's regions, thereby bringing into question the extent to which Russia in fact corresponds to a within versus without format.

As we argue later, the ultimate character of Russia's structure of representation will depend on a number of institutional details. The point we wish to make here is simply that both forms of representation – citizen and federal subject – can be employed in an *N* player within form. In contrast, the only implementable form of citizen representation we can foresee in an *N+1* form is the nationwide initiative, somehow organized at the federal subject level. We know, however, of no attempt to fashion a workable version of this possibility, with the possible exception (via some liberties taken in interpretation) of the Swiss use of referenda on tax and expenditure legislation. Of course, discrete conceptual schemes such as the one Table 4.1 offers are heroic abstractions. There seems to be no limit, for example, to people's imaginations when it comes to formulating alternative and complex rules of representation that can influence the role of a national legislature in federal bargaining, while obscuring its appropriate classification. Germany and Russia, for example (as well as Italy, New Zealand, and Hungary), mix qualitatively different rules in the representative structures of their lower legislative chambers (i.e., the combination of both territorial and nonterritorial representatives), thereby making any placement in Table 4.1 somewhat arbitrary.

Just as the way an office is filled is critical in defining the loyalties of officeholders and influences the extent to which they feel accountable to a national versus a subnational constituency, the ways in which officeholders are positioned to interact with each other by formal rules is important as well. The fact that national legislators are attuned to the needs of their district or regional constituencies may not be enough to make the legislature the center stage for federal bargaining. Although a necessary condition, it does not preclude a situation in which strong regional executives adopt aggressive programs of improving their units' position and steal the show as far as federal bargaining is concerned. If, for instance, the enforcement of antifraud election provisions is weak or nonexistent, and if regional chief executives can influence voting or the tabulation of votes for national as well as regional offices, then those executives possess a powerful asset that can be used to short-circuit constitutional provisions written to direct federal bargaining elsewhere. Indeed, in virtually any federation there are a variety of alternative or competitive venues for bargaining. While a constitution cannot preclude regional executives (governors) or even the executives of local governments from bypassing the national legislature so as to bargain among themselves or with whatever institutions and offices might correspond to the federal center, a constitution can also establish such entities as a collective executive, as in Switzerland, that plays a dual role – that of regional negotiating forum and coordinating center. Thus, attempting to characterize a constitutional system by some simple discrete classification is almost certainly likely to reveal inherent ambiguities. Nevertheless, Table 4.1, as we now try to show, offers a useful way to think about constitutional alternatives.

4.3 Within versus Without

We should perhaps state at the outset that the within approach to representation appears to hold distinct advantages over the without alternative. First, by making federal subject representatives a part of the federal center, regional governors and legislatures are themselves distanced from potentially destabilizing bargaining. Just as a governor might try to short-circuit a national legislature, a national legislature, defending its prerogatives, can attempt to intervene in any bilateral negotiation between regional and national government entities. In addition, the effectiveness of a federal subject's representative in bargaining is enhanced and not undermined by a strengthening of the center, thereby removing (although in favor of the center) one source of contentiousness among bargainers. Several other things speak in favor of the within approach. First, because, by definition, it places federal subject representatives in the same governing body, it is more likely to connect their ability to act on a unit's behalf with their ability to achieve some minimal consensus. Because their effectiveness and ability to deliver to their constituents depends on their admission into broader alliances (legislative and parliamentary coalitions), representatives in a within format must position themselves to achieve some degree of compromise. Second, decision making by a representative body requires some minimal structure – some form of parliamentary procedure – which by itself constrains debate. And to the extent that rules of germaneness apply so as to require the separate consideration of issues, this structure encourages shifting coalitions as issues change, thereby lowering the likelihood of permanent polarizing divisions among federation members. The specific advantage here is that with shifting coalitions, bargaining is more likely to generate norms of reciprocity that discourage overtly redistributive and expropriatory cost assignments. Third, the transparency of rules provided by parliamentary procedure ensures definitive (though not necessarily permanent) outcomes, whether in terms of no agreement or an agreement in the form of the passage of some law. Decisions shaped as law, moreover, can achieve a degree of legitimacy that is often out of reach of informal bargaining agreements.

The without approach, in turn, has the advantage of flexibility. Negotiations between federal subjects and the center can be conducted on a case-by-case (federal subject by federal subject) basis. If compromise to the median is the essential feature of a within approach, we can imagine circumstances under which its alternative does not require that all federal subjects adhere to the same national standards. Nevertheless, this ostensible advantage can also be a shortcoming, because it leaves the door open to asymmetric proposals and bilateral negotiations. Unless the center can somehow coordinate discussion – and unless it has an incentive to do so – the representatives of one federal subject are likely to see the outcomes of negotiations to which they are not a part as conferring benefits to their disadvantage. As illustrated by the bargaining that occurred between Moscow and Russia's ethnic republics in the early 1990s, the normal sequence of events in such circumstances is a gradual escalation of demands, as each subject takes the last-best-deal negotiated with the center as the new status quo. Anyone familiar with school board and teacher union negotiations in the United States can see the dangers here, especially when it occurs sequentially: teachers from one district will point to some benefit enjoyed by teachers elsewhere and demand that the benefit be exceeded (as compensation for not having that benefit earlier). The result is a sequence of spiraling demands as the teachers in each district seek to take advantage of the outcome of negotiations elsewhere. There is, however, a difference between these negotiations and those likely to occur with respect to federal subjects. Teacher unions do not necessarily see themselves as being in competition with each other – indeed, to the extent that all seek simply to feed at a potentially expansive public trough, an excessive award in one district can benefit those in other districts via the precedent its sets. Federal subjects, on the other hand, are much more likely to see themselves in a competition for limited resources, especially if negotiations concern the sharing of tax burdens or, more vaguely, power. In this circumstance the without approach places federal subjects in opposition to each other and discourages the political-economic integration that can benefit federal relations.

Although there may be good reasons for supposing that the within approach provides a more coherent and less conflictual institutionalization of federal bargaining, Table 4.1 presents alternatives in simple discrete categories, whereas parliaments and legislatures will vary in the extent to which they are venues for bargaining, depending on specifics of design and other characteristics of the political system. Consider a parliamentary system in which the national legislature holds in its hands the survival of what is commonly taken to be the primary representative of the federal center – the federal executive and, thereby, the federal bureaucracy. This control not only contaminates the identity of the executive as "the center" but also introduces a new nexus of motives into the calculations of legislators. As our earlier comparison of the U.S. and Canadian systems suggests, placing the survival of the national executive in the hands of the legislature changes the interests of legislators if only because it changes the criteria voters might use when judging candidates. Specifically, legislators become less representative of narrow regional interests to the extent that voters look to the process of cabinet formation and vote on the basis of national issues in addition to purely regional ones.

In addition, full implementation of a within model does not merely require that legislators be elected from geographically identifiable constituencies. It also requires that the system's overall structure allow legislators to *bargain* effectively in the interests of their formally defined constituency. Although both are elected from single-mandate districts, members of the Canadian House, unlike their brethren to the south, possess limited legislative opportunities for promoting constituency interests. The primary factor here is how governments are organized. Governments in Canada are formed by a party or parties that possess the confidence of a parliamentary majority. Unlike an American-style separation of powers in which individual legislators are free to oppose a president without necessarily threatening their own tenure, the dependence of the Canadian premier on a parliamentary majority means that MPs, by provoking new elections, can terminate their own positions. Thus, territorial coalitions that cross party lines so as to advance interests that correlate with geography are unknown in the House of Commons (Gibbins 1982), and unsurprisingly, the committee system, which dominates the legislative process in the U.S. Congress, is weak in Canada and characterized by unstable membership and limited staff resources. Committee chairmen are but part of the government's team, and committees are not an independent source of criticism, expertise, and power. There are, then, few opportunities for legislators to examine governmental policy before draft legislation is presented to them, and they thereby have fewer opportunities to bargain and are less motivated and less credible when doing so.

At first glance, it might seem desirable to implement a design that discourages regionalism so that it does not come to dominate national politics. That is, in fact, one of the design objectives we elaborate on later. But we also need to appreciate that bargaining in some form and within some venue is an unavoidable feature of federal existence. And one form is to bargain by doing – by having national and regional governments adopt policies that are at cross-purposes. Consider Canada again. In 1970–1 the federal government attempted to practice a policy of fiscal restraint in order to offset inflation, with particular discretionary attention directed at the urban areas of Ontario (Leslie 1987). However, the provincial government of Ontario deemed unemployment the more serious political threat, and a deliberate effort was made, through the 1970 and 1971 budgets, to stimulate the economy. Conversely, during the 1980s, the federal government issued direct grants to municipalities at a time when Quebec's provincial government was trying to encourage municipalities to rationalize their finances (Brown 1994: 31). Of course, because Canadian provinces and municipalities control nearly two-thirds of public expenditures and 80 percent of public capital investment, a determined provincial administration, allied with its municipalities, can exert a significant counterinfluence on federal fiscal policy, and there are, in fact, few areas of policy making where federal and provincial governments can act in isolation (Leslie 1987; Brown 1994).

Thus, in the absence of parliamentary bargaining, but with the evident necessity for some venue for intergovernmental negotiation, we see the emergence of what some observers call "executive federalism" (Simeon 1972; Weaver 1992) – a specific variety of without bargaining – in the form of an ongoing interaction between federal and provincial ministers. Here federal-provincial conferences at the ministerial level are the critically important sites for "federal-provincial diplomacy." Indeed, for a system in which it is customary for the most important and contentious political decisions to be reached through negotiations among federal and provincial executives, we should not be surprised to find some observers conclude that the federal aspects of the Canadian Constitution are not so much what the Canadian Supreme Court says they are, but rather are what the federal and provincial cabinets and bureaucracies, in a series of formal and informal relations, have determined them to be (Smiley 1962): "The result has been the emergence of new interstate structures for territorial representation, an increasingly decentralized federal system and prolonged territorial strain within the body politic" (Gibbins 1982: 59).

With an eye to Canada, we can now begin to identify institutional parameters that locate a country in one row or the other of Table 4.1, as long as we appreciate the fact that because the character of representation in a federation is determined by a host of variables working in combination, we can at best only discuss tendencies when speaking of any one institutional parameter. Consider, for instance, the structure of a federation's upper legislative chamber, which is commonly designed to give federal subjects – their governments or citizens – direct representation in the center. If this chamber is, like the Canadian Senate, legislatively irrelevant, then its design is unimportant and the issue of within versus without is dictated by other things. When it is legislatively relevant – when its assent is required for the passage of law – it might seem that a within format is best encouraged whenever seats in that chamber are filled to represent explicitly federal subject governments. Doubtlessly, this was the purpose of the U.S. Senate's original design, the idea being that a relevant upper chamber independent of the other branches of the central government but dependent on federal subject governments, will become the primary venue for federal subject governments to negotiate among themselves and with the federal center. We cannot, however, assess what role the upper chamber will come to play until we consider the things that encourage federal bargaining elsewhere, especially within the national legislature's lower chamber or directly between federal subject governments and the center's chief executive (president or prime minister).

Insofar as the lower chamber is concerned, Canada illustrates the attenuation of the lower legislative chamber's role as a venue for federal bargaining whenever party discipline predominates over constituency interests. In contrast, the U.S. House of Representatives remains a viable bargaining venue because there "parties lack the strong party discipline found in parliamentary systems. As a result, congressional candidates can take any position they wish in their constituencies; 'although these guilds are organized nationally, the managers of the local branches have practically unlimited discretion in the choice of "goods" they wish to handle locally.'"[2] Both party-list proportional representation organized at the national as opposed to federal state level, then, and a parliamentary government itself would seem to encourage without bargaining by encouraging disciplined parties.

A further assessment of the role of either chamber requires that we consider the authority of the center's chief executive and that office's prerogatives. Consider Russia, which in terms of its legislative construction, would seem well suited for a within format. First, its upper chamber, the Federation Council, is filled directly by regional governors and legislatures. Second, although half of its lower legislative chamber, the State Duma, is filled using a national party-list proportional representation scheme that bears no relationship to individual federal subjects, its other half is filled by

[2] The central quotation here is from Lipset and Marks (2000: 38), whereas the interior quotation is from Perlman (1928: 167–8).

direct election in single mandate constituencies.[3] Finally, both chambers are legislatively relevant with their authority modeled largely after the United States (with the exception of the Duma's ability to override a legislative veto by the Federation Council). Nevertheless, Russia, as we argue shortly, exhibits an extreme form of without bargaining – bilateralism. And the critical factor here lies not in its legislative design but rather in the fact that its constitution and its political traditions provide for a legislatively strong chief executive. Traditions, of course, establish expectations that themselves can become self-fulfilling prophesies. But, in addition, Russia's new constitution allows the president, among other things, to promulgate decrees "insofar as the law is silent" (Article 90), which, in effect, gives the president first move in any legislative struggle. Thus, if the president can impede any contrary action by either legislative chamber, he can in effect promulgate new laws as long as there is no contradiction with existing statute. This authority extends to virtually all budgetary matters, including those of taxation and the responsibilities of regional governments for making payments to the federal treasury, all of which essentially compels regional political and economic elites – including even the governors and regional legislators seated in the Federation Council – to negotiate directly with the executive branch, if not the president himself.

Finally, in Germany we have a parliamentary system with an upper legislative chamber, the Bundesrat, that began life formally weaker than the lower chamber, the Bundestag, which itself has half its seats filled by national party-list proportional representation. Thus, if a parliamentary governmental form alone is sufficient to forestall the representation of regional interests in the national legislature, it seems that Germany's institutional configuration would encourage a type of without bargaining not unlike Canada's. Nevertheless, federal bargaining in Germany more closely resembles what we observe in the United States. As we argue in subsequent chapters, this fact can be partially accounted for by the structure of Germany's political parties, which are themselves the product of a complex structure of election laws and procedures. Suffice it to say that, among the institutional factors contributing to Germany's within format, we have each state's special role in the administration of federal policy and the Bundesrat's constitutionally mandated role of "protector" of regional interests. Both of these devices draw the state "inside" the national government and render bargaining

[3] Russia's electoral system mimics that of Germany. However, rather than separate lists for each federal subject, Russia is divided into several regions, and parties are required to offer several regional lists. Seats are then awarded, as in the German Bundestag, on the basis of how well the party performs nationally and in each region. However, and again unlike the German system, parties also must offer a "federal" list, and seats are first awarded to the party from that list. The purpose, of course, of this federal list is to guarantee seats to each party's Moscow-based oligarchs.

with some specific player in the center, like a president or prime minister, as either unnecessary or ineffectual.

Even this abbreviated discussion reveals the complex interplay of institutional parameters that minimally include the structure of representation, modes of election, and the authority of the center's chief executive relative to that of the legislature. Moreover, unlike Table 4.1's characterization of matters – a dichotomous choice between two polar opposites – reality presents a continuum of alternatives. Still, Table 4.1 does help us visualize two ideal types toward which we can direct a federation when designing its institutions. Before we can speculate as to which type is most likely to encourage stability, however, we should first discuss in greater detail the second dimension of choice portrayed there.

4.4 Direct versus Delegated Representation

The institutional choices that concern the second dimension of Table 4.1, direct versus delegated representation, are perhaps best discussed in the context of the U.S. Senate – a legislative body that began life as an attempt to provide state governments with representation in the national legislature and to check the potential excesses of the lower popularly elected legislative chamber, but which evolved to give the citizens of those states a second venue of bargaining. The process of evolution is well described by Riker (1955), and there is little reason to review it here. What is relevant is its institutional cause – the reasons why senators were able to resist state legislative control and why the states themselves ultimately favored direct election of the Senate. What we have here, in fact, is a case study of institutional evolution where an initial design is transformed as an unplanned consequence of other institutional parameters. And here we can point to two parameters in particular. The first is the failure of the U.S. Constitution to grant state legislatures the right of recall. The second is a senator's length of term (six years) relative to that (generally one or two years) of those state legislators who were originally intended to oversee the Senate's actions.

It seems reasonable to suppose that had the Constitution granted state legislators the right of recall, members of the Senate would have accepted instruction from whatever majority ruled their respective state governments. However, given the Constitution's clear specification of a fixed term for members of the Senate, this sanction was not available. Thus, the only sanction that could be applied was a refusal to reappoint. But here a senator's longer term relative to state legislators intervened to undermine even that sanction. As Riker (1955: 457) succinctly states the matter, "new majorities in state legislatures could not threaten a senator who, chosen by the old majority, knew he would not be re-elected anyway, or who, with a longer term than theirs, might hope for re-election and vindication from their successors." Thus, as Riker recounts the experience of a Whig's refusal to resign upon instruction of a New Jersey legislature controlled by the Democratic Party, "the Whig disobeyed and refused to resign; yet two years later he was re-elected by the expanded Whiggery at Trenton. So it seems that resignations were not easily forced when senators sat for six years, state legislators for one or two" (1955: 460). In fact, state legislatures abandoned attempts to control senators long before ratification of the Seventeenth Amendment, which merely formalized the Senate's removal from the ineffectual "clutches" of state governments.

The original intent of legislative appointment, of course, was to peripheralize the American federation by giving state *governments* some direct control over the federal center. With direct election or at least with ineffective state control of senators, however, the power of the center relative to that of state governments was increased. So important is this change that, referring to the form of federalism first introduced in Philadelphia in 1787, Riker (1955: 452) regards it as the key to answering such questions as "What was the secret of this new federalism? Why was it so effective, so nationalizing?" This is not to say that the representational structure to which the Senate eventually converged is appropriate for every federation, but we can use it to again underscore the point that the ultimate implications of any one institutional parameter depend on many other parameters. Specifically, although the term of office and the absence of any recall provision were critical in determining the eventual placement of the Senate in Table 4.1, the full implications of these two constitutional details cannot be understood without taking into account the structure of state governments – in this case, the different term of office of state legislators. It was, then, the combination of these things that explains the Senate's failure to provide state governments with a venue for intergovernmental bargaining and a certain means for checking the authority of the center.

It is most likely a mistake to attribute the full course of federal development in the United States to these parameters alone, or even to the design of its representative system. From perhaps the very moment of its adoption, the interpretation of the U.S. Constitution has traced a history of the gradual erosion of the role of state legislatures and executives in federal bargaining, and a corresponding reduction in the opportunities and incentives for Americans "to call upon the state governors and legislatures to interfere on their behalf against the national government" (Anderson 1955: 80). Earlier, the Articles of Confederation established a compact with a weak unicameral Congress fully controlled by state legislatures – a Congress in which delegates were appointed annually and subject to recall, and rules such that states, each with equal representation, possessed a veto with respect to any revenue proposal. The 1787 convention was largely a response to the immobility of government implied by these arrangements, and the very procedure by which the new Constitution was to be ratified – the requirement that specially elected state conventions consider the issue rather than state legislatures themselves – was aimed at diminishing the role of state governments in bargaining over the content of the document. Subsequently, although state legislatures retained some important authority in the national government, the states were left with only limited opportunities to bargain directly and instead had to rely on the loyalty and support of their representatives in the new national Congress. And with the Civil War clearly establishing the Constitution's supremacy, "once secession became both legally and physically impossible, states could never claim to nullify national laws" (Riker 1964: 13). Instead, they were compelled to cooperate with congressional lawmakers, so that "virtually all the activities of government in the nineteenth century in the United States were cooperative endeavors, shared by federal and state agencies in much the same manner as government programs are shared in the twentieth century" (Elazar 1962: 1).[4]

In this context, the history of the National Governors' Conference illustrates the inherent ineffectiveness of alternative venues for state government bargaining once intergovernmental bargaining becomes the purview of a national legislature not beholden to state governments. Beginning in the early 1900s, the conference met annually and until the 1960s maintained a largely hostile relationship with the federal government: the conference "added rhetoric to the vestiges of states' rights defenders, gained media attention for periodic recriminations against federal officialdom, [but] generally proved ineffectual as a national political interest group" (Haider 1974: 22). Thereafter the governors changed strategy, with the conference choosing to act like yet another lobby (Cammisa 1995). Even still, "when a governor goes to Washington his legitimacy as a territorial lobbyist is questioned by the congressmen and senators from his state... who also have an explicit mandate of territorial representation from the state electorate" (Gibbins 1982: 88).

4.5 Other Parameters of Design

Federations generally do not choose simply between direct versus delegated representation but instead try to mix these two forms. The United States, Australia, Brazil, Mexico, and Nigeria employ a direct format for both of their national chambers, whereas the majority – Germany, Russia, Belgium, Argentina, Austria, Ethiopia, India, Malaysia, and South Africa – allow their upper chambers to be delegated. Of course, such a summary ignores

4 Perhaps the only effective tool of direct bargaining against the federal government the states retained in the Constitution was the use of the judicial concept of states' rights in order to avoid further expansion of federal regulations. However, formal safeguards of such rights were themselves political and dependent on the will of the courts and national legislators. But perhaps no act diminished those rights as much as the Supreme Court's New Deal interpretation of the interstate commerce clause, after which "Congress could reach just about any commercial subject it might want to reach and could do to that subject just about anything it was likely to want to do" (McCloskey 1960: 185), and it was thus left to the Congress to decide the limits of federal expansion.

the complexity of alternative designs, including the details of representation in Belgium's upper chamber, the specific nominating process employed for South Africa's Senate, and the split forms of representation employed in Russia's lower chamber and the diminished role of governors there in its upper chamber. Direct and delegated representation appear in a great variety of forms and a simple dichotomous classification cannot accommodate the actual character of representation and the venues for bargaining we are likely to see emerge. Moreover, the explanation for the erosion of the role of state legislatures and governors in federal bargaining in the United States lies with parameters in addition to those pertaining to methods whereby seats are filled in the national legislature. Riker's argument, for example, about the tendency of the relationship between delegated representatives and state governments to evolve in the direction of increasing autonomy for these representatives should not be ignored. If delegated representation is to be sustained in the long run, it would appear that other provisions such as the presence or absence of the right of recall and the timing of elections need to be considered, along with allowing or even requiring representatives to hold dual national and regional office as was the case in Russia.

The list or relevant parameters does not end there. Returning again to the two dimensions of Table 4.1 and reiterating some of the things we have said earlier, even an abbreviated list of design parameters that are relevant to determining the venues of bargaining likely to emerge in a federation would include the following:

- *A separation of powers.* An effective separation, which we presume requires the selection of a chief executive independent of the national legislature, encourages a within bargaining scheme, whereas the absence of this separation, as in Canada, encourages a without scheme.[5] We say encourages rather than determines since Germany offers an example in which other design dimensions render a within format compatible with the absence of a separation of the type we normally associate with presidential systems.
- *Legislative authority of the parliament.* Is the parliament merely advisory as was the Russian Duma under czarist rule (and as its Federation Council threatens to be today), or is it more akin to the U.S. Congress or German Bundestag? Here we can include a variety of provisions such as the role of the legislature in amending the constitution, as well as its authority in providing budgetary oversight and the approval of executive-level appointments. Of course, the legislative authority of a legislature in a parliamentary system will vary, depending on the executive authority

[5] We should speak here of a "balance of powers" since full separation is neither desirable (else the state's branches cannot function as one when necessary) nor practical (since we cannot preclude the executive or courts from holding some legislative authority, or the legislature from holding some executive and judicial authority).

of the government and the ease with which parliament can dismiss ministers or vote no confidence in the government itself.

- *Legislative authority of the chief executive.* The sole formal legislative authority given by the U.S. Constitution to the president is the veto. As we note earlier, however, the Russian Federation Constitution allows the president to "issue decrees and executive orders [insofar as they do not]...contravene the Constitution of the RF and federal law" (Article 90). Thus, the U.S. Constitution encourages a within system, while the Russian Federation Constitution does the opposite insofar as it encourages direct negotiations with the president.
- *Amending the constitution.* Does the constitution give the chief executive a role in the amendment process? Granting such authority again encourages a without rather than a within bargaining format. Although the authority exists within the U.S. Constitution (Article 5) but has never been employed, granting federal subjects an independent means of amending a constitution can, in a similar way, encourage a without system.
- *Veto and veto override provisions.* To what extent can the chief executive intervene in the legislative process and threaten that process with stalemate? And can one legislative chamber override the veto of the other?
- *Term limits.* Are there constitutional constraints on the professionalism of legislators, and how durable are the electoral imperatives that otherwise compel a representative to advocate the particular interests of his or her constituency? The logic behind term limits, at least in the United States, is that voters are trapped in a prisoner's dilemma (Niou and Ordeshook 1985): although each might prefer a representative that considers global efficiency rather than parochial interests, it is nonetheless irrational to elect such representatives regardless of the choices made by other constituencies. If all others elect representatives who will work exclusively for them, regardless of global efficiency, then no individual constituency should choose differently; but if all or most vote for global efficiency, then it matters little what any other constituency chooses. In this way voting for parochial interests is a weakly dominant choice even if economically inefficient. Quite directly, then, term limits can impact the within character of a representative assembly.
- *The political structure of federal subjects.* It seems only reasonable to suppose that a legislative-centered structure would encourage within bargaining, especially if it parallels the legislature of the national government, whereas an executive-centered structure would encourage without bargaining to the extent that it empowers regional executives to negotiate directly with the center or among themselves so as to bypass the center.
- *Regional authority over national representatives.* This item alone encompasses a great many parameters, including (as in Riker's discussion of the U.S. Senate), the timing of legislative elections at the national and regional levels, the authority of regional governments over their national representatives (appointment and removal powers), and length of terms.

Clearly, this list can be nearly endlessly augmented and elaborated. It barely scratches the surface of the implications of a separation of powers or the choice between parliamentary and presidential systems. But it does serve to emphasize the fact that one should not attempt to say whether a specific choice for one parameter or another is good or bad, since, as experience teaches us, institutional parameters can interact in complex ways. Two examples in particular illustrate this fact. First, consider Germany's Bundestag. If we look at this body's representational structure and powers, it would seem even less suited for federalism than, say, Canada's system. Rather than rely exclusively on single mandate constituencies, half the seats of this chamber are filled on the basis of national party-list proportional representation, with adjustments made to ensure that the seats filled in single mandate constituencies do not lead to the overall overrepresentation of any party. Imbedded in an otherwise standard parliamentary system (e.g., a nearly powerless president and an upper legislative chamber with limits on its legislative authority), it would also appear that proportional representation in combination with the absence of a meaningful separation of powers would direct federal bargaining to a without rather than within format. This description, however, ignores one important institutional detail that appears to have escaped notice when, as in Russia, Germany's arrangements were transplanted elsewhere. Specifically, although half the Bundestag's seats are filled by a national proportional representation scheme, candidates compete on state-based lists. That is, although the total seats awarded to a party are determined by its performance nationally, those seats must be allocated by the party across its separate lists according to how well the party did in each federal subject. If, for instance, a party did twice as well in one state than another, then it must award twice as many seats to the list from the first state. Quite directly, then, those deputies elected on the basis of proportional representation see themselves as representing not only their party nationally but also the state on whose list they appeared. Thus, the character of Germany's Bundestag as a forum for federal bargaining cannot be fully appreciated until we understand the overall character of Germany's election law.

For an even more compelling example of the interaction of institutional parameters, consider (nonfederal) Costa Rica, whose parliament is characterized by at least these parameters: a one-term term limit, small size (fifty-seven members), and an electoral formula based on proportional representation in seven districts. It might seem, then, that if there is territorial representation here, it would correspond to Costa Rica's seven districts and that it would be especially weak given the draconian term limit – given the absence of any incentive to represent any constituency in order to win reelection. However, the interaction of these three parameters produces a different result. Absent any reelection incentive, a majority party must find other ways to motivate legislators to act during their brief tenure so as to facilitate the party's success in the next election (Carey 1998: 127–30). The solution is to divide each region on an ad hoc basis into subdistricts, assign one such district to each of its members, and make a small portion of the national budget available to legislators who can use these funds for projects of their own choosing within their assigned district (e.g., repair a road, bring electricity to a remote village, put a new roof on a school, construct a local flood control reservoir). The idea, of course, is for legislators to allocate these funds so as to improve their party's chances in the next election. But what is the incentive for legislators to do this, absent the opportunity to run for reelection? The answer lies in other institutional parameter settings. With the legislature's small size guaranteeing that the majority party will not be overwhelmed with claimants to executive-level positions, upon completion of their term and provided that the party remains in power, each of its ex-legislators can then be rewarded with some executive level positions (e.g., a ministership, ambassadorship) on the basis of how well the party does in the most recent election in the ad hoc district assigned to that legislator (Carey 1998).[6] In this way, Costa Rica's institutional structure, while not explicitly providing for single-mandate territorial representation in its national legislature, effectively encourages the informal evolution of such a system, and thereby reminds us of the complexities in the interaction of institutional provisions.

4.6 Bilateral Decision Making and the Case of Russia

When exploring alternative bargaining venues and forms of federal subject representation, one possibility – an extreme form of a without system – presents itself as a primary alternative: bilateral decision making. Earlier we note some objections to this form, but here we use Russia's recent experience with bilateralism to illustrate the inherent instability of that bargaining form and the difficulties associated with "institutionalizing" it within a stable federal system. We can begin by noting that the Framers of the U.S. Constitution clearly understood the dangers of bilateralism, and at least three parts of the document they drafted sought explicitly to preclude it: Article 1, Section 9, paragraph 4, which reads "No capitation, or other direct, tax shall be laid, unless in proportion to the Census or Enumeration herein before directed to be taken" and Article 1, Section 9, paragraph 6, which reads "No preference shall be given by any regulation of commerce or revenue to the ports of one state over those of another." Finally, to ensure against the possibility of states

[6] Carey (1998: 133) admits that, although "with the budgetary, electoral, and appointments data available, it has proved difficult to demonstrate any consistent relationship either between... pork and electoral support, or between electoral support and post-Assembly appointments in Costa Rica," it is nevertheless the case that "[d]eputies' comments in interviews overwhelmingly indicate that they believe all of these arguments to be accurate."

negotiating side agreements with each other outside of the federal structure, we have Article 1, Section 10, paragraph 3, "No states shall, without the consent of Congress, ... enter into any agreement or compact with another state."

The approach to federal relations taken by the Russian Federation (RF) Constitution is different. There, with perhaps deliberate ambiguity, Article 66 opens the door to the asymmetric treatment of Russia's ethnic republics: "The status of a republic shall be defined by the Constitution of the RF and the constitution of the republic in question. The status of an [oblast etc.] shall be determined by the Constitution of the RF and the Charter of the [oblast etc.] ... adopted by the legislative body of the relevant subject of the RF. ... A federal law on autonomous regions or areas may be adopted at the nomination from the legislative and executive bodies of an autonomous region or area. ... The status of a subject of the RF may be changed only with the mutual consent of the RF and the subject of the RF in accordance with the federal constitutional law." Additional room is left for differential treatment by Article 74, which states that, although "no customs frontiers, duties, levies, or any other barriers for the free movement of goods, services, or financial means may be established on the territory of the RF ... restrictions ... may be established under federal law, if this is necessary for ... the protection of the environment and cultural values." However, perhaps no part of the constitution opens the door more to bilateral bargaining than does Article 11, which states in part that the "authority and powers of the bodies of state authority of the RF and the bodies of state authority of the subjects of the RF shall be delimited under this Constitution [as well as] *federal and other Treaties of the delimitation of scopes of authority and powers*" (emphasis added). These provisions (and the absence of others: the Russian Constitution contains no explicit restriction on asymmetric treatment of the sort offered by the U.S. Constitution) are not only a prelude to the bargaining that ensued following the constitution's ratification in December 1993, but also reflect the politics of the federation prior to that date. We should not be surprised in the least, then, that one close observer of the process concludes that "[i]n the Russian case, a bargaining model [of federalism] is not just analytically powerful, but also descriptively accurate" (Solnick 1995: 55).

Briefly, recapitulating events, when, in 1991–2, political and economic reforms were in their infancy and the danger of federal disintegration seemed all too real, the attempted "solution" was, in effect, a highly asymmetric federalism achieved through a series of bilateral and multilateral negotiations between the Kremlin and Russia's federal subjects. Following the USSR's collapse in 1991, twenty-one of its autonomous republics became Russia's "ethnic" republics, joining a federal state with fifty-seven "Russian" regions and the eleven autonomous regions also ethnic in character (but geographically contained in "Russian" regions and, in practice, subordinate to them). The ethnic republics borrowed the rhetoric of the Russian government itself when, as part of the USSR, it had proclaimed that a democratic federation must be a voluntary union in which each participant has the right to decide the extent of its sovereignty. Once Russia declared its independence from the Soviet Union, its autonomous ethnic republics simply followed suit,[7] and while the Soviet government was still trying to reach an elusive consensus on a new Union Treaty, Russian politicians started negotiating a Russian federal treaty.[8] Despite Yeltsin's challenge that Russia's regions and republics take "all the sovereignty you can swallow,"[9] in January 1991, almost a year before the dissolution of the USSR, the autonomous republics had already rejected the first federal treaty produced by such negotiation. If the republics had learned anything from the negotiation process within the USSR, it was that being tough was a strategy with positive payoffs.

In 1992–3, with Yeltsin and the parliament disputing the division of power in a future constitution, the position of the republics was enhanced as each side of the debate sought the support of regional leaders. Weakened by the conflict, the central government could not or did not want to enforce federal laws in the regions, especially if it meant turning a region into a supporter of its constitutional rival (Sharlet 1992). Taking advantage of the confrontation in Moscow, more than a third of the subjects of the federation withheld their contributions to the federal budget in 1992–3 while demanding special tax regimes or new federal subsidies for themselves. Empowered by the old constitution to block constitutional change, the republics used their position to secure special privileges, and an initial federal treaty, adopted in 1992,[10] legitimized the preferred status of the republics (Hughes 1994).[11] Among other things, their overrepresentation in parliament was made a part of

[7] Most notably, these were Tatarstan, on August 1990 and Chechen-Ingush republic on November 1990. Although Chechen-Ingush's declaration proclaimed independence, it also included specific conditions on which the republic would agree to sign the Union Treaty (e.g., to join a reformed USSR). For a discussion of the declarations of independence, see Kahn (2002).

[8] The call for a Federal Treaty was a part of Yeltsin's campaign strategy in the 1990 presidential elections.

[9] *Argumenty I fakty*, no. 35, September 1–7, 1990, translated in FBIS-SOV-90-172, September 5, 1990, p. 113. In addition, Yeltsin promised "We will welcome whatever independence the Tatar ASSR chooses for itself.... I will say: if you want to govern yourselves completely, go ahead." *Pravda*, August 9, 1990, p. 2, translated in FBIS-SOV-90-155, August 10, 1990, p. 59 (as cited in Walker 1996).

[10] The 1992 treaty was a sequence of treaties, the first of which was signed between the center and eighteen republics (Tatarstan and Chechen-Ingushetiya demurred). A treaty with the krais and oblasts, and one with the autonomous districts followed, but the obvious bias in favor of the autonomies incited resistance from the "Russian" regions (Shaw 1992).

[11] For example, Solnick (1995) estimates that in 1992–3 the president issued favorable decrees (*ukazy*) and governmental resolutions (*postanovleniia*) that addressed the needs of eighteen of twenty-one republics (excluding Chechnya), but only fourteen of fifty-seven oblasts and krais.

the early presidential draft constitutions circulated in the summer of 1993, when the Kremlin's competition with parliament was most intense (Sharlet 1994).[12] Following the violent resolution of that competition in October 1993, the final draft, ratified in a national referendum in December, ostensibly equalized all federal subjects.[13] As we have seen, however, even that document stipulated, as a concession, that subjects could negotiate special treaties with the center and a special status for themselves within the federation on a bilateral basis.

In 1994 the administration began signing treaties with the ethnic republics that covered such issues as the form of their constitutions, procedures for electing governors, and special revenue allocation mechanisms. Many observers of and participants in those events argue that the first treaties, especially with Tatarstan and Bashkorstan, were necessary to calm separatist demands (Sheehy 1993; Walker 1996; Lynn and Novikov 1997; Treisman 1997, 1999).[14] Indeed, even after Yeltsin won the constitutional fight, Moscow could not assume the political risk of aborting treaties that had been in preparation since 1990 and that had become an important part of the promises made by the regional politicians to their constituents.[15] In December 1993 the Kremlin effectively lost the parliamentary election, which was followed by the renewed demands of regional "sovereignty" from the regional incumbents. However, although only seven "ethnic" republics secured treaties in 1994 and 1995,[16] an opening was created whereby the governors of even the "nonethnic" regions could demand relations with the center based on similar agreements (Dowley 1998).[17]

[12] The republics were promised 50 percent of all seats in the Federation Council, the upper chamber of the Parliament.

[13] Most importantly, Yeltsin removed the Federal Treaty from the final text of the constitution, thus breaking the promise he made to the republics in the summer of 1993 (*Segodnya*, February 16, 1993).

[14] The first treaty was signed with Tatarstan in February 1994. It was expected that the second treaty would be signed with the Chechen Republic (*Kommersant*, February 24, 1994). The negotiations of such a treaty with Chechen leaders started in January 1993, but on March 25, 1994, the State Duma effectively blocked them by setting a precondition that the Chechen Republic had to run federal elections first. Tatarstan also did not participate in the 1993 elections, insisting that federal elections there would only be possible after the treaty establishing Tatarstan's status in the federation was signed.

[15] For example, Tatarstan leadership held the referendum in March 1992, which asked: "Do you agree that the Republic of Tatarstan is a sovereign state, a subject of International Law, building its relations with the Russian Federations and other republics on the basis of the fair treaties?" With 81.6 percent turnout, 60.4 percent said yes.

[16] Much of early treaties' content, especially their appendixes and schedules, was kept secret to avoid interregional rivalries.

[17] For example, the 1996 electoral program of the governor of Saratov, Aiyatskov, had three main points; if elected, Aiyatskov would preserve social peace, negotiate a treaty with Moscow, and develop a consensus among regional political parties.

Matters escalated, and the signing of a treaty with the ethnically Russian region of Sverdlovsk in January 1996 marked the beginning of Yeltsin's reelection campaign as well a new stage in the federal bargaining process whereby bilateralism became an open exchange of political favors.[18] With Yeltsin's popularity in the polls sinking to single digits, the Kremlin saw regional governors as critical to electoral success and eagerly offered regions preferential treatment through a variety of power-sharing treaties (Tolz and Basygina 1997).[19] The most important tokens of this exchange concerned fiscal revenues and property rights whereby regional bosses sought to preserve control over large corporations operating in their territories. Sixteen power-sharing agreements were signed during the campaign, and Yeltsin, posing as builder of a new Russian state, argued that they had proved themselves to be the basis of a new federalism, which, he said, was founded on the principle of granting the regions whatever "independence they can handle... within the framework of the constitution."[20]

Unsurprisingly, the regions excluded from this process objected,[21] and shortly before the presidential election, officials from the seventeen regions that composed the so-called Siberian Accord issued a declaration asking Moscow to stop granting special privileges (May 1996). Later, in October, representatives from six "black earth" (procommunist) regions asked the State Duma to define formally the legislative and executive rights of federal subjects, complaining that "those who came first earned more rights." Those "who came first," in fact, concurred. Nizhni Novgorod governor Nemtsov, for example, argued that although there was nothing improper with regional lobbying, there should not be separate agreements granting special privileges to some regions but not others[22] – an argument he offered only *after* his region had procured its own treaty.

18 Interestingly, after signing the first in a series of the preelection power-sharing agreements (with the Komi Republic, on March 20, 1996), the government issued a warning that the signing of such treaties might be brought to a halt if the Communists won the June presidential election, since the latter supported nationalization of property and strong central control.

19 That the treaties were used to secure votes was immediately understood by observers of the presidential campaign (Nikonov 1996).

20 *OMNI Daily Digest*, May 27, 1996.

21 Of course, the treatyless principled opponents were easy enough to appease. Rostov governor Chub and legislative head Popov both argued that power-sharing agreements would lead to the eventual collapse of the federation. But once the neighboring Krasnodar Kray negotiated a deal with Moscow in January 1996, they signed their own in June. Similarly, the governor of Samara announced that in principle he was against the practice of signing bilateral treaties, but in July 1997 he concluded one of the best deals in the federation, comparable only with those of Tatarstan and Bashkortostan. Only once did a governor refuse a treaty, but the reason was his insistence on better terms matching those obtained by others (Aleksei Lebed in Khakassia).

22 *RIA*, November 11, 1996.

Following Yeltsin's reelection the balance of power shifted. The political value of regional bosses could now be discounted and the Kremlin prepared for a redress of the balance of power. Thus, by the end of 1996 Yeltsin instructed his chief of administration, Anatoliy Chubais, together with the justice minister and the prosecutor-general, to prepare proposals on the responsibility of regional officials and the unification of regional laws. Interestingly, Chubais's proposals anticipated by four years a similar set of measures implemented by Yeltsin's successor: namely, to increase the authority of presidential regional representatives, to unite the regions into several economic groups, and to centralize the collection of those taxes which could actually be collected (leaving the regions with receipts from the more difficult to collect taxes on corporate profits). This was also a period of active borrowing by the federal government, which offered an annual return of up to 200 percent through state bonds (GKO), thereby "vacuuming" cash from the regions. At the same time, Chubais proposed to use federal transfers as a tool of economic pressure on regional executives, including supporting local (mostly municipal) governments in their perpetual struggle with regional authorities. As a part of that effort, local governments were given larger shares of taxes and some political representation through the Council of Local Governments (created by the presidential decree in May 1997, with Yeltsin serving as the head of the council).

Only one treaty was signed after the presidential elections in 1996 – to help an incumbent governor's election campaign[23] – and none in the first half of 1997. Moreover, when treaty signing did resume in the summer of 1997, it was more an attempt to formalize the process and reduce the value of earlier treaties. With few exceptions, these were standardized documents.[24] Thus, Sergei Shakhrai, who was responsible for this activity in the Kremlin, claimed that the signing of new treaties was a step in the direction of equality among all regions.[25] Promises were made that soon every region would enjoy its own power-sharing agreement, but any effective move to equalization was aborted by the financial crisis of August 1998.[26] Although the preelection string of concessions to regions was replaced by the center's

[23] It was a "fast track" treaty quickly prepared by the presidential administration in a desperate attempt to save a governor facing a communist-backed challenger. Yeltsin's illness, however, compelled an over-the-phone signing – a fact that was subsequently ridiculed in the local press and that saw the incumbent defeated (interview with Vladimir Lysenko in *Novaya Gazeta*, no. 50, July 19, 2001, available at <http://2001.novayagazeta.ru/nomer/2001/50n/n50n-s00.shtml>).

[24] Among the exceptions are the treaties with regional leaders who were well known and highly active at the federal level – the governors of Moscow and Samara. Both governors headed federal-level political parties and were likely presidential candidates.

[25] *Nezavisimaia Gazeta*, no. 141, August 1, 1997.

[26] A treaty with Kemerovo was ready to be signed on August 10, 1998, but the financial default prevented the deal. No more treaties were signed after July 1998. Overall, treaties were signed with forty-six federal units.

attempt to regain the upper hand, that effort was crippled by Yeltsin's fading health and a financial crisis that was largely a consequence of the spending spree and distribution of favors to business tycoons initiated as part of the 1996 presidential campaign. Yeltsin kept his office, but at the price of being too weak politically to engage in a full-scale renegotiation of the federal terms. Most important, as a counterbalance to the communist-dominated Duma, Yeltsin's political survival required the acquiescence if not the support of the upper legislative chamber that was dominated by regional bosses (Paretskaya 1996; Remington, Smith, and Haspel 1998).[27]

The sequence of treaties signed between 1994 and 1998 on a first-come, first-serve basis thus created a self-evident imbalance in the institutional status of federation members (McAuley 1997; Lapidus 1999; Stoner-Weiss 1999; Stepan 2000), and the losers in this process eventually looked for ways to forge coalitions that would reverse the pattern. We should not be surprised that the Kremlin, with its authority eroding, would be a ready partner in any such coalition. In this way we can interpret the ascent of Vladimir Putin with the support of a majority of regional governors as the start of a new (third) bargaining cycle. Unsurprisingly, the only viable alternative to Putin – former prime minister Yevgeny Primakov – was backed primarily by a coalition of regional leaders from the most privileged federation members (e.g., Moscow, St. Petersburg, Tatarstan, and Bashkortostan). Following the election of 2000 and supported by a majority in the Duma and a coalition of regions, federal "reform" moved to the top of the new president's political agenda (Hyde 2001).[28] In his first state-of-the-nation address (summer 2000) Putin offered his plan for a highly centralized Russia,[29] arguing that competition for power between the federal and regional governments had been "destructive" and stressing that Russia was not quite a federation but a "decentralized state." Elsewhere Putin went on record calling state decentralization "regrettable."[30] Putin's reforms, then, were a clear signal that the

[27] In the spring of 1999, facing a vote of impeachment in the Duma, Yeltsin, while meeting with the presidents of the "ethnic republics," suggested that they were ready to take yet more "sovereignty."

[28] An infamous example of the regional support was an open letter of three governors proposing to extend the presidential term to seven years and asking Putin to reduce the total number of regions and reintroduce a system of appointed regional and local executives (*Nezavisimaya Gazeta*, February 25, 2000).

[29] In practice, Putin's "federal reform" became a complex multistep operation aimed to exert Kremlin authority over the regional politicians and prevent any possibility of forming political opposition in regions. As the *Economist* observed, "Step out of line, and we will end your political career. That, bluntly, is the message the Kremlin is sending to the 89 governors and presidents who run Russia's regions" (*Economist*, November 11–17, 2000, pp. 61–2); see also Orttung (2001). We return to this discussion in Chapter 9.

[30] Putin's speech at meeting with Canadian business, economic, and political leaders December 19, 2000, available at <http://president.kremlin.ru/events/124.html>. A week later, at a meeting with the recently appointed presidential representatives in the regions,

time of asymmetric bilateral federalism had ended, with the administration bluntly explaining that existing power-sharing treaties have "outlived their political usefulness."[31] Importantly, only leaders of ethnic republics and a few governors voiced any opposition,[32] while most welcomed the new policy and some even asked Moscow to terminate treaties with their regions immediately. The governor of Chabarovsk revealed the prevailing mood when he asserted that "federal reform is not against heads of Krays and Oblasts, it is against republics."[33]

In retrospect, we can say that Russian bilateralism was the manifestation of a divide-and-conquer tactic for the center: "Greater coordination among regional elites – either in selective blocs or as a united front – weakens the center's ability to consolidate its power. Conversely, the central government can exploit divisions among regional actors – by either dealing with them bilaterally or coopting key blocs – to gain more leverage over the provinces as a whole" (Solnick 2002: 8).[34] The bilateral bargaining that characterized Russian federal relations through much of the 1990s served a dual purpose from the Kremlin's perspective: "In addition to placating restive regions, the center may have also weakened the coordinating mechanism that had permitted the republics to act collectively since 1990" (Solnick 1995: 58). Unsurprisingly, then, this comprehensive strategy and the asymmetries it produced "affected the core functions of the national state in domains such as commerce, national defense, regulation of the media, and revenue collection. Concessions made to individual regions have undermined the legitimacy of federal law and the federal constitution, weakened the protection of civil rights and undercut any potential economic benefits that federalism might be expected to deliver.... The territorial bargaining that produced these institutions – and the asymmetries behind them – may have held Russia together in the short run, only to cripple its development in the long term" (Solnick 2002: 237–8).

Asymmetry, of course, is not uncommon in a federation. Fiscal allocations are biased toward certain states or groups of states almost everywhere, because the ability to cater to particular local needs is an essential characteristic and advantage of the federal form.[35] One might reasonably ask,

Putin clarified that a "decentralized state and weak government is largely the result of ignoring the law and lack of political will" (see <http://kremlin.ru/events/132.html>).

31 *Izvestia*, September 5, 2000.

32 For a record of such public statements, see *Rossia*, May 16, 2000, available at <www.public.ru>.

33 *Nega*, June 26, 2000 available at <http://scripts.online.ru/misc/newsreg/00/06/29_030.htmlenta.ru>.

34 Treisman (1999) argues that by compromising with few regional leaders, the Kremlin was able to accumulate resources needed to punish other challengers. See also Polishchuk (1998).

35 The United States, for instance, has considerable asymmetries in population, area, and wealth among states and yet stability does not seem endangered. Admittedly, the consequences

then, whether bilateralism facilitates replacing a uniform federal policy with a more flexible mix of arrangements. Our answer is that, although this may be true with respect to policy (which is where asymmetry is found in successful federations), bilateralism in the form that allows unequal access to the center raises the specter of outright capture by some subset of federal subjects and can lead ultimately to an amendment of fundamental institutional arrangements in which a coalition tomorrow arises to offset those with greater bargaining access today. Bilateralism thereby threatens institutional instability, and Russia illustrates not merely instability in policy but this more dangerous form of instability as well.[36]

In a traditional contractual conceptualization of federalism, the intent is to maintain a federal balance such that contracts are honored, including the contract to maintain fundamental institutions. In Russia, on the other had, we not only see a continual renegotiation of terms vis-à-vis policy, but now an instance of Level 2 institutions inheriting the properties of the base bargaining game. Included in the set of "reforms" implemented by Putin and his coalition of regional bosses are such institutional changes as (1) the

of this asymmetry are muted by the population's physical mobility (Tiebout 1956; Rose-Ackerman 1981). Although mobility is not costless for the persons involved, there are few ethnic or religious barriers to living in one state or another, as exist in other societies. Still, we suspect that if the current geographic configuration of the United States was suddenly subject to renegotiation, the issue of, say, setting Rhode Island's or Delaware's representation in the Senate equal to that of California would become a contentious matter. It is difficult to imagine harmonious relations prevailing today if, instead of having the current status quo arise naturally over decades so that it could be viewed as the accidental consequence of geography and history, America's asymmetries had been consciously chosen or imposed, say, in 1970 or 1980.

36 It should be noted that not all forms of bilateralism need be avoided even if a "within" bargaining format is sought. Suppose a supremacy clause is enacted and that the decision making is primarily in the hands of a national legislature in which federal subjects are represented both de jure and de facto. There remains, nevertheless, a variety of ways in which a unilateral actor can attempt a change in the federal status quo, such as passing a piece of regional legislation that contravenes federal statute or that brings into question the interpretation of such a statute. When a decision is made this way, even if it only applies to a specific federal subject, it is necessarily redistributive and "renegotiative," and it may establish a precedent for other subjects to follow. It is at this point, though, that the courts may intervene. When a federation member's action is adjudicated under the premise of federal supremacy, what we are in fact observing is a bilateral interaction between that member and the center (the High Court in the European model or any court in the common law model). The change in this case (in either direction) is typically incremental and occurs in a fully institutionalized context. This is so because, when challenged, a change can at most be a matter of the interpretation of standing rules rather than the revision of those rules. In addition, even if the court is deemed to be legislating via a new constitutional interpretation, its decision can still be neutralized through the subsequent action of the representative forum (Eskridge 1991). Interestingly, moreover, the higher courts in a common-law system perform the function of the center only in a complex appeals process that, while reminiscent of bilateral bargaining, typically gives ample opportunity for all interested parties either to intervene or at least to express opinions and influence the judiciary's rulings.

establishment of a new quasi-constitutional institution of the federal center – a new layer of federal control consisting of a seven-member council of "presidential envoys" to oversee Russia's regions;[37] (2) removal of regional governors from the Federation Council and their replacement by appointees of the governors (subject to a two-thirds veto of the regional legislature), who, along with those assigned to the Federation Council by regional legislatures, will serve terms that are coincident with those who appoint them; (3) implementation of a process involving the court, Duma, and Federation Council, that allows a Russian president to dismiss regional assemblies and requires new elections (which, in effect, would also require the recall of the representative in the Federation Council appointed by any dismissed assembly); and (4) granting the president the authority, without the consent of the national legislature, to remove a regional governor if the General Procurator asserts evidence of a crime, or, in the event that the president deems acts of the governor to be contrary to federal or constitutional law, with the concurrence (if appealed) of Russia's Supreme Court.

It is tempting to assert that such reforms mark an end to federalism and a return to a Soviet-style bureaucratic decentralization. But as we argue in Chapter 9, many of the institutional sources of the motives behind the bargaining that rationalized Putin's policies remain in place and it is difficult to say where, if anywhere, the system will come to rest. A question of a more general sort is whether institutional stability is compatible with the granting to one or more federal subjects a constitutional-level political advantage that goes beyond those afforded by the nature of legislative representation. Our earlier discussion of the Soviet Union and Czechoslovakia suggests that the answer is no, which is a conclusion supported as well by events in Canada and its attempt to keep Quebec in the federation on unique and constitutionally sanctioned terms. We also need to appreciate that the example of Russia in particular concerns not merely asymmetries in policy but also the destabilizing influence of the *process* of bilateral bargaining that, at its core, accepted the *principle* of unequal access and outcome. We cannot say with certainty that all bilateral federal forms can avoid the conflicts, instabilities, and asymmetries that emerged in Russia. We suspect, however, that those forms, if they do exist, require a precarious balance of powers that are difficult to design and implement.

What also needs to be kept in mind is that despite the somewhat subtle unequal treatment afforded Russia's regions and republics in its constitution, and despite the fact that whatever advantages of geography and natural resource endowment one set of regions enjoys over others seem on a par with those found in the United States, bilateralism characterizes federal relations in only one of these two states. Thus, while institutional asymmetry may be a component of any necessary and sufficient condition for bilateral "without"

[37] For a more detailed description of these "reforms," see Solnick (2002).

bargaining, it cannot be sufficient in its own right. It might seem that other conditions must be met, such as an initially cash-starved and weak center, an unsettled system of property rights, a weak national legislature relative to the authority of a president, and a philosophy of federalism that sees federal relations in contractual terms and the product of negotiated agreements. The argument we offer later, however, is that the solution to Russia's problems, the avoidance of institutionally disruptive bilateralism, is not all to be found in the revision of these parameters. There are other more fundamental causes, which can be understood only after we learn the fundamental source of constitutional stability generally.

5

Incentives

> The Constitution of the United States is an admirable work, nevertheless one may believe that its founders would not have succeeded, had not the previous 150 years given the different States of the Union the taste for and practice of, provincial governments, and if a high civilization had not at the same time put them in a position to maintain a strong, though limited, central government.
>
> Alexis de Tocqueville[1]

> Constitutional rules are not crucial, independent factors in maintaining democracy.... Constitutional rules are mainly significant because they help to determine what particular groups are to be given advantages or handicaps in the political struggle... [and] to assume that [the United States] remained democratic because of its Constitution seems to me an obvious reversal of the relation; it is much more plausible to suppose that the Constitution has remained because our society is essentially democratic.
>
> Dahl 1956: 134, 143

> The fundamental method to preserve liberty is to preserve ardently our traditional constitutional restraints.
>
> Riker 1982: 252

5.1 Institutional Enforcement

With its focus on representation and the selection of venues for federal bargaining, Chapter 4 discusses some of the more obvious parameters of federal constitutional design that, if set to the "correct" values, will hopefully encourage adherence to those Level 1 rules that seek to guide and constrain federal bargaining. Briefly, if a "within" rather than "without" bargaining format is preferred, then the reader can legitimately infer from our discussion

[1] As cited in Ostrom (1991: 96).

of Canada that by "correct" in the context of a parliamentary system we mean an institutional arrangement whereby we avoid letting the imperatives of party solidarity wholly overwhelm the representative role of legislators, since, in that case, bargaining will occur outside of parliament. For presidential systems, we use Russia to illustrate how the representative function of legislators can be rendered superfluous and a without format encouraged if we "incorrectly" award the office of president too much executive and legislative authority. It seems clear moreover that if those who would design a federation prefer delegated representation, then a "correct" design requires a legislative chamber with meaningful power and, if possible, legislators who can either be recalled by the appropriate authorities of each federal subject's government or whose terms of office correspond to the terms of those who appoint them. Aside from generalities, however, any advice we might offer about such things requires that we address the two vexing questions of federal design. First, how can nondisruptive intergovernmental bargaining proceed in the context of a federal system in which federal subjects are able to defend their autonomy while the federal center otherwise maintains its formal supremacy? Second, how might federal arrangements contend successfully with those disputes of race, language, religion, culture, or ethnicity that arise in states such as Canada, the United States, Russia, and Germany in relatively muted form as compared with, say, South Africa, Nigeria, Bosnia, India, and Ukraine, and that today disrupt the politics of even prosperous states such as Belgium, confound Spain's fully peaceful transition to federalism, and led to the dissolution of an otherwise promisingly stable state such as Czechoslovakia?

To formulate the requisite theory of federalism needed to answer such questions requires possession of a theory of democracy within which to embed our understanding of federalism, and this in turn requires a theoretically sound hypothesis about constitutional enforcement. It may be true that adherence to Level 1 rules, for example, is a form of cooperation that yields mutual gains to all participants. But if "in the absence of an enforcement mechanism, cooperation [is] not possible" (Posner 2000: 13), and if we require a second level, a constitutional level, of rules and institutions to ensure that enforcement, then we must identify the mechanisms whereby this second level is itself enforced. No theory of federalism can be deemed complete, no theory of democracy can be judged satisfactory, and little confidence can be placed in any specific prescription for political institutional design until this issue is addressed.

In searching for the mechanism or mechanisms whereby the totality of a constitution is enforced, we begin by first identifying in general terms what it is that a constitution must do. And here we gain some guidance by looking to one of America's founding geniuses, Benjamin Franklin, who, during the Philadelphia constitutional debate over the manner in which federal judges ought to be selected, offered this suggestion (as recorded in Madison's notes on the convention):

> Doctor Franklin observed, that the two modes of choosing Judges had been mentioned, to wit, by the Legislature and by the Executive. He wished such other modes to be suggested as might occur to other gentlemen; it being a point of great moment. He would mention one which he had understood was practised in Scotland. He then, in a brief and entertaining manner, related a Scotch mode, in which the nomination proceeded from the lawyers, who always selected the ablest of the profession, in order to get rid of him, and share his practice among themselves. It was here, he said, the interest of the electors to make the best choice, which would always be made the case if possible.

It is tempting to treat this suggestion as an attempt to infuse a weighty discussion with humor, but aside from noting the scarcity of his words, we should also take cognizance of the fact that Franklin the scientist was fully equipped to infer general principles from specific observations while restating general propositions in comprehensible parable-like form. Franklin's words, then, should be considered carefully, lest we make the mistake of assuming that aged geniuses cannot provide practical advice or theoretical insight. In fact, Franklin does both. He is reminding the delegates of the essential *theoretical* nature of their enterprise, while infusing his lesson with a practical illustration of the theory of institutional design that must guide their efforts. In more contemporary jargon, he is telling the delegates that their constitutional task requires the creation of an *incentive-compatible institution* – a political institution, broadly defined, that takes individual motives and, eschewing any attempt to modify their basic myopic and self-centered character, redirects them to yield a socially desirable outcome.

Of course, Franklin's lesson is itself "merely" a restatement of the one Adam Smith offers in his *Wealth of Nations* when explaining the operation of markets. And it is a lesson that reappears in various forms, most notably in the debate over ratification. The *Federalist* tells us that "the seeds of faction are sown in the nature of man" – a reminder that political institutions ought to be designed without the premise that basic self-interest can be transformed into something else – and instructs us that a viable political design is one in which "ambition counters ambition": "It is vain to say that enlightened statesmen will be able to adjust these clashing interests and render them subservient to the public good. Enlightened statesmen will not always be at the helm" (Madison, *Federalist* 10). Thus, political institutions must be such that the potentially socially "dysfunctional" motives of greed and the quest for power, which cannot be banished from the political landscape, are made to control themselves and redirected to contribute to (or not to impede) socially desirable ends. This, of course, is precisely what we want to accomplish with Level 2 constraints – to redirect the myopic and particular concerns of federal subjects so that federal constraints on bargaining are nonetheless honored or, when circumstances change, modified in a politically coherent way.

Franklin's lesson, then, stands as a theoretically general principle of institutional design familiar to anyone with any introduction either to the process whereby the U.S. Constitution was drafted and ratified or with the theories of governance emanating from the Enlightenment and Europe at the time. It seems, nevertheless, that that principle is too often or too easily forgotten. It is forgotten when legislation directs the state to specific policies without concerning itself with the ways in which the bureaus and agencies established to implement policy can be subverted in their purpose by the personal motives of bureaucrats. It is forgotten when constitutions are drafted with the presumption that individual rights will be protected merely by listing them or, as is the case with so many postsocialist documents, specific policies (e.g., housing for all, medical care for all) will be diligently pursued merely by stating them as lofty goals. And it is forgotten not only when limits, constitutional or otherwise, are placed on government action with the expectation that the words alone will bear the weight of enforcement, but also when those who would draft a constitution for a federal state presume that their task is complete after federal subjects are identified, representational schemes specified, and policy jurisdictions allocated across levels of government.

From the perspective of constitutional enforcement, however, Franklin's lesson is incomplete. It does not tell us why anyone would consent to giving up a profitable practice for a judgeship; and, more generally then, it does not tell us why a mechanism that favors some interests over others is not replaced by something that serves a different coalition of interests. Thus, the missing piece of Franklin's story, as well as of the rationale for believing that the parts of a constitution normally labeled "federal provisions" complete the task of design, is that not only must constitutions direct self-interest to specific ends but the operation of those institutions must also give participants an interest in maintaining the document's overall structure. Put differently, a fully described incentive-compatible institution is one in which, given the choices it allows, the mapping it establishes between choices and outcomes, and the patterns of self-interest over which it must operate: (1) there exists at least one equilibrium constellation of choices (individual strategies) that yields the socially desired outcome; (2) at least one of these equilibria is coalition proof in that there is no critical subset of decision makers that prefers to make and is decisive for different choices; and (3) owing to the pattern of outcomes it produces, there is no decisive subset of decision makers that prefers to abolish the institution itself, so that the institution is, like the outcomes it engenders, a coalition-proof equilibrium of some larger game. Franklin's example illustrates the first two conditions, whereas a common manifestation of the third is often found in those election laws in which the authority to change the law rests exclusively with those elected under it. In this instance, absent an alternative with self-evident and riskless advantages, the winners under existing arrangements, being the sole proprietors of the right to modify the status quo, are unlikely to prefer competing for reelection under a different set (except perhaps to "reform" those laws so that entry and competition are made more difficult), thereby giving the original set the stability we seek in constitutional provisions.

Constitutions, however, serve a broader purpose, and, insofar as their enforcement is concerned, it is by now commonplace to acknowledge that "a mere demarcation on parchment... is not a sufficient guard against those encroachments which lead to a tyrannical concentration of all the powers of government in the same hands" (Madison, *Federalist* 48). But if it is not the words that enforce, then we are led to a logical conundrum. First, if the mechanism of enforcement is exogenous to a constitution – if it lies in an oligarchy removed from constitutional constraint – then either we are no longer speaking of a democracy or we have only pushed the problem back a step, and must then ask, What constrains the actions of this oligarchy and how are *those* constraints enforced? If, on the other hand, we argue, as some do, that enforcement lies in the institutions a constitution establishes such as a national court and the associated judicial structure, then where are the things that enforce the provisions that define and limit judicial authority? If those things are entities that the constitution itself establishes and constrains, such as the legislature or the executive, then we have merely provided circular reasoning: the constitution is enforced by institutions that are constrained by other entities that are constrained by the constitution, in which case we must either identify the thing that enforces this entire edifice or at least give sound theoretical arguments for why and under what circumstances "institutions" can enforce each other.

It is worth recalling in this context our earlier discussion of the difference between alliances and federations wherein we speculate that federations for one reason or another, including the fact that they are intended to encompass a great many dimensions of collective action, can reasonably be interpreted by those who would establish them to be unstable alliances that require firmer mechanisms of enforcement if the state is to function in a coherent and efficient way. That is, because they are inherently unstable, they must be sustained by some institutional superstructure that, in effect, creates a hegemon (the center, armed with legal supremacy in its domain) equipped to enforce the terms of agreement. But if this instability is truly fundamental – if underlying policy preferences give people an incentive to prefer different institutional arrangements – what then sustains those things that empower and constrain the hegemon? What enforces the contract that defines the hegemon's character and admissible actions?

Insofar as the role of tradition and culture are concerned here, there is necessarily some truth in Tocqueville's observation about the special circumstances of the United States. Tradition and culture establish expectations about how people will act in particular circumstances, and those expectations can become self-fulfilling prophecies. If, as in Russia, there is no history of respect for private property because such property, with the exception of a few household things, did not exist in the past, then society can be trapped in an equilibrium in which no one respects private property because no one expects anyone else to do so – in which case, people's expectations are met, and rational cynicism prevails. Nevertheless, debates like the one we formulate between Riker and Dahl as exemplified by the quotations that open this chapter – debates that struggle between giving the nature of institutions preeminence in the explanation for their stability versus those who emphasize society's underlying character – permeate the literature on democracy and constitutionalism. Indeed, that debate has, in one form or another, preoccupied political science through much of its existence as a discipline. But because this search moves us to the very heart of any wholly general theory of politics, it is perhaps inevitable, given the absence of that theory, that we should see scholars even two hundred years after the drafting of the U.S. Constitution concluding that the "problem of the self-enforcing constitution has so far evaded solution" (Tullock 1987: 317–18).

Unfortunately, that same problem also lies at the heart of any theory of political system design. If one takes Riker's view, then design – federal or otherwise – should not focus merely on how some constellation of Level 2 institutions will ensure adherence to Level 1 constraints, but also on how precisely the entire edifice, taken as a whole, will be sustained. On the other hand, if Dahl's view predominates, then after identifying the Level 1 constraints that are presumed to be necessary, after perhaps seeking a consensus on those constraints when they are first negotiated, and after specifying an appropriate structure of federal subject representation, our attention should turn to those things that encourage social pluralism and a civic culture – things that are normally exogenous to a constitution and may or may not take a traditional institutional form.

We do not have the temerity to suppose we can offer a definitive resolution of this debate. But because this volume focuses on the institutional parameter values that might encourage federal stability and at least a modicum of the efficiency, it is incumbent upon us to at least offer a working hypothesis that pertains to the somewhat narrower issue of the enforcement of Level 2 constitutional provisions and of those Level 1 constraints that help define a federation. And here our hypothesis is that to solve the problem of constitutional enforcement to which Tullock refers, we must depart from the traditional conceptualization of constitutions as contracts – as a social contract among the polity or between the polity and the state.

The transient usefulness of the constitution-as-contract view is precisely that it highlights the question, If a constitution is a contract, then who enforces the terms of that contract? The classical (i.e., legal) theory of contracts leaves this question unanswered, or answers it only in the context of some overarching authority empowered to enforce specific provisions. But aside from the otherwise undifferentiated "will of the people" there is no such authority in a democratic state, since even that will, without political structure, need not be anything more than incoherent noise or the anarchy of the mob. The specific problem that confronts us here is perhaps best illustrated by constitutional secession clauses. The general view of such clauses (with which we on the whole agree) is that a constitutional right to secede "would increase the risks of ethnic and factional struggle; reduce the prospects for compromise and deliberation in government; raise dramatically the stakes of day-to-day political decisions; introduce irrelevant and illegitimate considerations into these decisions; create dangers of blackmail, strategic behavior, and exploitation; and, most generally, endanger the prospects for long-terms self-governance" (Sunstein 1991: 634). But if, as Sunstein argues further, a constitutional provision prohibiting secession is best interpreted as a contractual agreement whereby federal units precommit to strategies that preclude secession, what is the mechanism that sets any such precommitment in concrete? What renders such a precommitment credible? Why would anyone believe that a promise not to secede will be honored in the future or that the mere act of uttering or agreeing to the promise changes the likelihood of one's future actions? Why should we suppose that a constitutional provision threatening punishment of those who attempt secession will be honored? If a decision about secession is itself a response to beliefs about the responses of others who also act out of self-interest – a belief about the likelihood that secession will be punished or ignored – then why would a constitutional secession clause influence their self-interest and the likelihood that they will act in accordance with its terms. Finally, if, as some models of secession assume (Le Breton and Weber 2000; Haimanko, Le Breton, and Weber 2001), people choose to form, maintain, or dissolve a federation on the basis of its ability to resolve economic inefficiencies among otherwise sovereign states and to achieve a more or less equitable distribution among those states of the gains of cooperation, then how does any constitutional provision influence economic calculations or outcomes?

These are not mere rhetorical questions, for here game theory, the theory upon which the notion of the incentive compatible institution rests, illuminates the answers we seek and provides some practical guidance for constitutional design. We can avoid a digression into the mathematical foundations of that theory by noting that one of its fundamental lessons is the fact that there necessarily exists a vast multiplicity (if not an infinity) of alternative equilibria – of alternative sustainable outcomes – in essentially any reasonably complex social process. Indeed, almost any feasible outcome, including those that benefit no one over the status quo, can correspond to an equilibrium. This multiplicity generates a number of problems for the people whose actions we are attempting to understand, the most important one being that absent an initial mutually consistent set of beliefs as to what long-term strategy (a plan of action as the situation unfolds) each will choose, there is no guarantee that any equilibrium will prevail or that the equilibrium that prevails will be beneficial for any of them. Thus, to ensure a mutually advantageous outcome or even one that someone finds desirable, beliefs and strategies must be *coordinated.*

To this point there does not appear to be much of a problem. Coordination can occur in any number of ways, and when there is a unique equilibrium outcome that everyone prefers to all other outcomes, then even simple extraneous things can coordinate society so as to ensure its realization. However, coordination may be problematical when, as is likely in politics, the preferences for alternative equilibria are sharply divided or when complex signaling is required to ensure that one person or another will in fact choose the strategy initially agreed to. The particular difficulty the analyst confronts here is that understanding coordination will require an appeal to things – processes, events, beliefs, and the like – that are exogenous to any abstract description of the situation. And if these things are somehow incorporated into a description of the situation so that we can treat them formally, we have succeeded only in generating a more complex game that is likely to yield a complex array of new alternative equilibria in which as in some infinite regress the character of yet another layer of potential coordinating mechanisms must be considered if we are to understand social action.

This discussion has a direct bearing on the matter of understanding how the provisions of a constitution, federal or otherwise, are enforced. First, it gives theoretical meaning to Tocqueville's observation with which this chapter began; namely, that America's early political experience helped coordinate it to certain functionally useful values, procedures, and political institutional devices. For example, the reader will search in vain for the words "majority rule" or their equivalent in the U.S. Constitution. That document is careful to specify the circumstances when something other than a simple majority was to decide an issue, but otherwise of course the majority would rule and there was no need to coordinate to that rule. In contrast and perhaps as an indicator of the fundamental nature of the disagreements that belie the completed transition of the European Union to a fully formed federation, we notice that the constitution proposed by the *Economist* (October 26, 2000: 21) for the EU specifically requires majority rule for both a newly formed Council of Ministers and Commission.

More generally, our discussion of coordination suggests the need for a profoundly different conceptualization of a constitution than is offered by the contractual argument. To see what we mean, consider the fact that it probably matters little in the life of the American democracy whether the House of Representatives contains 435 or 345 members, whether states are represented by two or three senators, whether an executive veto override requires a two-thirds or three-fifths vote, whether budgetary legislation must originate in one legislative chamber or another, whether the admission of new states to the union requires a majority or three-fifths vote of Congress, or whether the secretary of state or defense stands highest in the order of presidential succession. We can also imagine the United States surviving with a different rule for admitting new states, different age requirements for members of Congress, a different rule for ratifying treaties, a different system of presidential impeachment and conviction, or even (within limits) a different procedure for amending the constitution itself.

This is not to say that American history would be the same had other alternatives been chosen, but it is far easier to imagine the Republic in peril if its constitution were wholly silent or explicitly ambiguous on each of these things. The early history of the United States consists of a number of critical junctures because of what the U.S. Constitution did not say (about, for instance, the Supreme Court's authority or the right of states to secede) rather than because of what it did say, or because what it did say left the door open for confusion and unintended consequences (about, for instance, electing vice presidents versus presidents). Because the ongoing political process of any nation almost certainly allows for an abundance of equally acceptable equilibria of rules, what is important is that society's members be coordinated to the same set of rules so that whenever one or the other comes into play, its precise meaning is not the subject of self-interested and self-serving debate or that when debated, discussion is otherwise limited by what the document says, including the rule for conducting and terminating that discussion.

So, to sum up, our argument here is that a theory of federal design, if not democratic design generally, needs to abandon the view of constitutions as social contracts. Admittedly, it may not be a radical conceptual departure to argue that things like voting, amendment, and succession rules are points of coordination. And it may be true that certain provisions of a constitution are best described in contractual terms – most notably, the Level 1 provisions that attempt to establish the legitimate prerogatives of the federal center and that oftentimes are the product of compromises reached among federal subjects at the inception of a constitutional order. But to treat the entire document as a contract leaves unanswered – even unanswerable – the question of enforcement. And if that is true, then we cannot address the issue of democratic stability, federal or otherwise, which by definition requires constitutional stability. Our argument here, then, is that we need to employ a conceptualization of constitutions that sees such a document as a mechanism of sociopolitical coordination – as an incentive-compatible mechanism that becomes self-sustaining when no decisive coalition's interest is served by a unilateral defection from its provisions. Put differently, "a constitution does not depend for its enforcement on external sanctions. . . . Establishing a constitution is a massive act of coordination that creates a convention that depends for its maintenance on its self-generating incentives and expectations" (Hardin 1989: 119).

5.2 The Court

Although the primary advantage of conceptualizing a constitution this way is that it promises to resolve the matter of enforcement, it is nevertheless useful to speculate on whether or to what extent the view of constitutions as coordination devices is compatible with that of the Framers of the U.S. Constitution, and Madison in particular. It seems evident that Madison's coauthor in *The Federalist Papers* and subsequent political adversary, Hamilton, with the emphasis he placed on securing the new nation's finances and ensuring a strong central government, saw the Constitution as an "unfinished work" – a document that would fail unless other auxiliary institutions were quickly erected (most notably, a national bank). It is also true that the words "contract" and "compact" can be found throughout Madison's writings, and that more than a little debate was directed at the issue of whether the new federation represented a contract or compact among the separate states or their citizens taken as a whole. Finally, it is true that we can discern the notion of a constitution as a contract in Madison's initial argument that it was redundant to include a bill of rights in the proposed document:[2] as a contract, a mere listing of rights would have been but a "parchment barrier" that served little purpose, whereas the ultimate enforcement of rights would be attainable either with the national legislature and the control citizens exercised over its members, or with individual states who were closer to and more readily controlled by the citizenry (although certainly there was considerable distrust of state governments in this respect). Madison's argument here, however (including his argument that the autonomy of states would be protected by the control their governments exercised over the Senate and their constitutionally mandated authority to choose the manner in which presidential electors would be selected), can be recast as an argument about the nature of the equilibrium this particular constitution was about to establish – an equilibrium in which the self-interest it engenders leads ambition to counter ambition and, in the process, negates any opportunity or desire to supplant constitutional rules with alternatives.

Still, even if we convince ourselves that Madison is on our side, we must move further. While granting constitutions their equilibrium selection role, Madison's *Federalist* defense is concerned primarily with the issue of saying how, *given* a constitution, it is in the self-interest of the players to follow its particulars. As with Franklin's comments on methods for selecting judges, what he does not enumerate fully is why the Constitution *in its entirety* would not be challenged and supplanted by something else. That is, although the Constitution ostensibly defies a game that is an equilibrium

[2] With the understanding that part of Madison's argument served a purely political purpose: to wit, admitting that a bill of rights was needed might be taken by those who were undecided on ratification that the proposed constitution created too powerful a center and that rights were needed as an additional constraint on its authority.

within itself – an equilibrium that dissuades any one player or subset of players from overwhelming the rest, provided that all players operate within its rules – what was to keep the entire edifice in its place? That is, if a constitution is a coordination device, then what is the game that requires coordination? And what are the political institutions that are part of that game which, as much as the constitution itself, require careful design?

Before we consider that larger game, however, it is only prudent that we examine the explicit enforcement schemes found within such a document that work to sustain its particulars – additional Level 2 tools at the designer's disposal – if only so that we don't attempt to shape the institutional components of that game in a way that is inimical to the self-equilibrating components of a constitution. Here, of course, we enter the more traditional discourse on constitutional enforcement and the role of the state's separate branches. And, despite some disagreement as to the capabilities of the legislature in this respect, the weight of opinion identifies the court (generally a supreme or constitutional court) as the most likely candidate for filling that role. Briefly, then, as Young (1999: 3) identifies them, a court can act in accordance with three alternative models when defending federalism: "(1) 'Process' federalism, which relies upon the states' representation in congress as the primary means of protecting state sovereignty, and envisions judicial intervention only to ensure that this process is functioning properly; (2) 'Power' federalism, which seeks to articulate substantive limits on federal power, particularly on Congress's power to supplant state regulatory authority...; and (3) 'Immunity' federalism, which protects state governments themselves from direct molestation at the hands of the federal government, but does little to protect the ability of the states to act as authoritative regulatory entities in their own right." The argument, then, is that even if we acknowledge that a court cannot enforce either the constitutional regime in its entirety or those Level 2 rules which pertain specifically to it, it is not precluded from enforcing those Level 1 constraints which seek to regulate bargaining across levels of government or even those Level 2 rules which describe the structure of other branches of the state and their relation to each other.

However, in questioning whether the court is critical or even relevant to constitutional enforcement of this form, Kramer (1994: 9) offers one argument as to why such bodies are ill-equipped to serve even this limited function: "[C]ourts are poorly situated to make (or second guess) the difficult judgements about where power should be settled or when it can be shifted advantageously. Judges lack resources and institutional capacity to gather and evaluate the data needed for such decisions. *They also lack the democratic pedigree to legitimize what they do if it turns out to be controversial*" (emphasis added). Put differently, in the event that a court attempts to impose a policy or allocation of jurisdictional authority that is somehow inconsistent with whatever equilibrium prevails or is inconsistent with the policies and outcomes engendered by the normal operation of the rules and institutions that flow from an otherwise consensual status quo, then the court is either ill-equipped to avoid offering "bad" policy, or, by focusing on specifics, it can only threaten its role as adjudicator of more general constitutional conflicts.[3]

Kramer's argument, though, is largely normative, pertains to what a court is best equipped to do versus what it sometimes does, and relies exclusively on the American experience as opposed to states in which courts may be authorized to intervene in the legislative process by offering opinions about the constitutionality of legislation before it is even fully formulated. And it is counterintuitive to say the least to argue that courts, regardless of constitutional language, are inconsequential when adjudicating federal disputes. In a well-functioning federation, they often hold the authority to interpret the language of a constitution. In fact, how and why they fill that role underscores the utility of conceptualizing a constitution as an equilibrium selection or coordinating device. Consider again the issue of the advisability of including a bill of rights in a constitution. If constitutions were somehow perfect equilibrium selection mechanisms and if society was otherwise static in the interpretations it gave to rights, then a supreme or constitutional court might, arguably, have little to do other than to recommend sanctions for defectors. But, whether contract or coordination device, a constitution cannot be perfect because the language it employs, however detailed, is necessarily incomplete and requires interpretation and reinterpretation. A constitution needs a dynamic dictionary that reflects the contemporary meaning of things. A *fair* trial, an *unacceptable* incursion of the state into freedom of the press, or *appropriate* compensation in the event that the state abrogates a property right may be one thing in one era but something else in another. Thus, a constitution needs an agent empowered to codify and clarify what might otherwise be only ambiguously understood and which requires further societal coordination so that disruptive bargaining and renegotiation can be averted. It is only reasonable to suppose that constitutions coordinate imperfectly in some matters and that they need to establish an institution that does something other than merely direct the normal operation of the state – an institution that fills in the gaps of its own structure and which thereby sustains an ongoing dynamic of sociopolitical coordination. And that institution commonly is the court.

In rendering its interpretations, though, a court needs to be mindful of the fact that it lacks the means of enforcement available to the state's legislative and executive branches – the power to tax, spend, and physically coerce.

[3] Also one cannot ignore a possibility of an ideological bias. Thus, Baybeck and Lowry (2000) show that in the American case the protection of federalism comes as a by-product of justices's ideological preferences, such as when, in deciding federal issues, "a justice's preferences on the federalism dimension are less important than his or her ideological priorities" (p. 96). See also Cross and Tiller (2000).

Instead, it must rely for the enforcement of its decisions on the prior existence of a political-economic equilibrium, on the perceived legitimacy of its actions. An effective court, then, is one that whenever possible, frames its decisions as politically viable interpretations of that equilibrium. Because a court cannot directly enforce anything but requires the participation of other actors via the coordination it supplies to them, it can raise the cost of defection only if there are other components of the state or society that stand ready to sanction defectors from its decisions – only if society deems its decisions legitimate.

It is, of course, too simple to argue that courts merely interpret legislation and a constitution, for one of the ongoing debates of American politics is the extent to which they ought to be allowed the legislative function of establishing new precedents and conventions (or the extent to which they have in fact assumed that role). The difficulty is that if the court is required to coordinate to one equilibrium versus another, or to reestablish an equilibrium because changing taste and technology have subverted the one that existed, then the mere act of coordination – of providing contemporary meaning to words – is itself an instance of negotiation (since otherwise equilibrium selection is unnecessary). And this, in turn, threatens to render the court less a coordinating agent than an active participant in politics, including bargaining over the Level 1 constraints that outline the terms of relations among governments in a federation. Here, then, we find a theoretically unambiguous justification for such things as a politically independent judiciary, life tenure, and all the other institutional devices that remove the judiciary from day-to-day political disputes and which may allow its members to be motivated primarily by the goal of ensuring a smoothly functioning and stable state that adheres to some general, yet potentially evolving, notions of democratic practice. And it is here as well that we find reasons for disliking constitutional language that encourages a court to intervene directly in the legislative process (as was the case with Russia's old Constitutional Court prior to Yeltsin's 1993 coup), since doing so invites other political actors to capture the court for their own ends and to undermine judicial independence.

Nevertheless, it is unreasonable to suppose that the political potential of courts can be banished by any design, since, as we have just said, if courts are a coordinating adjunct to a constitution, then they are necessarily a part of politics. But an emphasis on constitutions as coordination devices does allow us to identify some of the characteristics of good judicial and constitutional design in addition to those provisions intended to serve judicial independence. Briefly, if a court is to augment effectively the coordination role of a constitution by infusing that document with contemporary meaning, it must possess legitimacy, which in this context means that (1) within its domain there should not be competing agents of coordination and (2) the population generally must share in the belief that everyone will act in accordance with its decisions so that that belief becomes a self-fulfilling prophesy. The first condition can be satisfied in part by avoiding the Franco-Russian monarchist temptation of constitutionally anointing chief executives with a title such as "defender of the constitutional order." The second condition is more difficult to satisfy institutionally, and the extent to which it is satisfied depends on the court's own tactical skill at selecting issues for adjudication – specifically, those issues where the population deems the need for coordination more important than the specifics of the realized outcome. Any number of models in game theory pertaining to the strategic manipulation of reputation and beliefs convey the message that a court must choose its battleground carefully so as to build ammunition (i.e., credibility) for those contests that are more explicitly redistributional.

If we view the court as an adjunct to a constitution in its coordinating role, we can also infer a justification for arguing that although a constitution ought to include a reasonably unambiguous enunciation of rights, it should offer at most only an outline of the terms of the federal bargain in the form of an allocation of jurisdictions across levels of government. First, in their most basic form and as descendants of England's 1689 Declaration of Rights, rights are barriers to state action – things that limit the actions of *all* governments subject to a constitution's jurisdiction. Rights, then, seek to constrain an entity that can, when its legislative and executive parts act in concert, coerce society to its ends. Because there is no guarantee that those parts will always act in opposition to each other, we require special safeguards in those domains most likely to occasion unwarranted coercion. And as history has taught us, although a bill of rights and an otherwise independent judiciary cannot provide a perfect guarantee against such coercion and the primary danger of democracy – a tyranny of the majority (Dahl 1956) – it is nevertheless prudent to encourage whatever guarantee they do offer. The specific source of that guarantee is the court's use of a constitutional listing of rights as a basis for coordinating society against the remaining parts of the state itself. That is, absent such a list, the court must invent them in direct opposition to branches of the state that can otherwise overwhelm its authority. In this context, then, the court at best becomes a player in a political game that pits potentially transient majorities against minorities. But a listing of rights gives the court something upon which to hang its decisions – words to which it can appeal when arguing that decisions limiting the authority of the state or regulating relations within it are merely refinements of an equilibrium to which society has already been coordinated.

It is difficult, however, to apply this argument to federal matters with the same force we apply it to individual rights. Here perhaps we come closest to agreeing with Kramer (1994) that courts are imperfect coordinating agents with respect to relations among levels of government, and in agreement as well with the argument that constitutions are unlikely to provide anything other than crude coordination over the terms of a federal bargain. Rights in the form of limits on the state are not static, but there are reasoned arguments for supposing that they change or at least ought to change more slowly than do relations across levels of government and the assignment of jurisdictional responsibilities. Technology may change the economies of scale that pertain to the provision of some public service or the extent of the externalities associated with unregulated markets in ways that alter the level of government best equipped to oversee the provision of that service or the regulation of those externalities. But the rights associated with, say, a constitutional guarantee to trial by jury, freedom of the press, or the freedom of assembly change, if they change at all, only slowly. If there is change here, it is most likely to occur at the margins, as when a right is extended to include policies or state action not otherwise believed or presumed to fall under its purview. In contrast, a successful or well-functioning federation is not a static creature. It is a dynamic entity in which the authority to determine policy should, ideally, move back and forth across levels of government as a function of changing tastes, technology, and the political fortunes of competing interests. Moreover, federal subjects are not organic entities that enjoy rights of the sort possessed by people. Federal subjects are, in fact, administrative and organizational conveniences designed to allow for a more efficient, stable, and smoothly functioning public sector. While rights may be inherent and inalienable, the autonomy of federal subjects and the prerogatives of a federal government exist by human design for practical ends. Thus, although a document such as the U.S. Constitution may identify certain policies as belonging exclusively to federal versus state governments, it also allows for a wide range of concurrent domains in which state law governs unless displaced by federal legislation and thereby leaves most issues (especially those that pertain to redistribution across states) unresolved. A court, then, has little in the way of a fixed target if it seeks to fashion the details of a federal bargain, and also little upon which to hang its decisions in the event that it chooses to regulate relations across governments or the intergovernmental redistributive consequences of the political process.

This is not to say that a constitution can or ought to be silent on the nature of the federal bargain; only that what it does say is necessarily more fluid than what it might say about rights or even the basic structure of the state. In this domain, then, a court is necessarily more a follower than a leader of state action, and it can at best offer interpretations of a constitution to ensure only that the most basic of constraints are not violated. Although politics enters the domain of the definition and enforcement of rights, one hopes it does so in minimal fashion. But in the domain of federal relations, it is primarily the political process that regulates adherence to whatever constraints a constitution might establish over the outcomes that arise from federal bargaining. A court may enter the political fray, but it does so with a weak hand relative to the powers of the national legislature and executive (who are authorized to reallocate jurisdictions via the supremacy of federal law, or who can "buy out" individual federal subjects via their control of the federal purse). And it does so at its own peril in terms of its ability to facilitate constitutional coordination on other issues. We do not mean that the concept of federal subject rights needs to be banished. It is certainly proper at least to try to establish an initial set of expectations as to which level of government is responsible in one policy domain or another. It is certainly important to know beforehand whether federal subjects have an independent authority to tax, whether they are precluded from printing money, and whether the national government can regulate commerce across federal subject boundaries. But, to refer again to the unsuitability of the contractarian approach to the enterprise of design, it is an error to suppose that rights in the form of allocations of jurisdictional responsibilities, which are intended, after all, to serve the needs of citizens generally and not some set of governmental institutions filled with political elites and bureaucrats, are, along with judicial oversight, the core of such design. Such a scheme is, in fact, an attempt to render the court the ultimate enforcer of federal provisions. But in that role it is bound to fail since it makes the court less a coordinating agent and more an active participant in redistributive politics, leaving unanswered the ultimate question of constitutional enforcement as a whole.

5.3 Some Simple Rules of Constitutional Design

If we return now to the general conceptualization offered here with respect to the issue of enforcement, a view of constitutions as an equilibrium selection device solves problems pertaining to its component parts and also provides some guidance to their general design. Admittedly, this view is relatively new and the precise nature of that guidance has yet to be worked out (Ordeshook 1992, 1993). But consider Article 38 of the Russian Federation Constitution, which states, in part, that "Able-bodied children who have reached the age of eighteen years shall take care of their parents who are unable to work," or Article 44, which requires that "Each person shall be obliged to care for the preservation of the historical and cultural heritage and cherish historical and cultural monuments." Although perhaps noble sentiments, such provisions seem silly to students of Western constitutional practice and design. But why would we deem them silly, and why might we expect their enforcement to be especially problematic? For another example, we note that it is our experience that even when undergraduates wholly untrained in constitutional concepts are presented with a document of three hundred or even one hundred pages of text, there is nearly universal agreement that the document is overly long and less than satisfactory – again, even silly. And indeed, one precept of design upon which most students of constitutionalism appear to agree is "keep it simple." But what is the theoretical principle that justifies simplicity and brevity? Isn't it better to attempt to close all foreseeable loopholes and to anticipate all contingencies as best we can?

We can answer such questions and provide the requisite principles by noting that every society, by definition, possesses a great many things that facilitate social coordination in the same way we argue constitutions operate – things we identify as norms, customs, and social conventions that also must be self-enforcing (Coleman 1986; Hardin 1989; Calvert 1995; Posner 2000). However, even if we accept the view that "constitutions are codified social norms that help overcome the equilibrium selection problem" (Kolmar 2000: 373), such documents can at best be only a part of society's fabric, and to make its provisions effective, it should parallel the design of those other self-enforcing mechanisms. The first thing to appreciate, then, is that social norms and customs are effective only if they are readily understood by nearly everyone. Complex rules cannot coordinate. A rule or norm such as "give an old woman your seat on the bus if you are young and agile" may leave room for interpretation, but it is more generally effective than one which states "if you are younger than 45 and in reasonably good health as determined by a licensed physician on the basis of an exam administered no more than fourteen months earlier, and if a woman stands before you, no more than 1 meter distant from your seat with no alternative seating apparent, relinquish your seat if she gives evidence of being older than 55, walks with difficulty, or is carrying more than 15 kilograms in groceries; otherwise, relinquish your seat only if requested to do so, and then only if her request is in the form of..." It may be true that the actual application of a common norm or convention will require complex contingent decisions that parallel this legalistic contractual version. But simplicity is required if the general intent of the norm is to be effectively communicated and universally accepted. The ambiguity that accompanies simplicity can be accommodated on a case-by-case basis – by common sense and, if necessary, the development of additional conventions – in the same way a constitution is interpreted and reinterpreted over time by the various arms of the state and evolving social consensus.

This view of constitutional provisions, then, suggests a rule of constitutional design that answers most of the questions we ask earlier about length and complexity. Specifically, constitutional provisions ought to be simple and concise, unencumbered by legalistic complexity. Moreover, since a constitution in its ideal form ought to be a part of a social consensus that consists of all the norms and conventions that describe a society, if a society has a democratic tradition – even one that lies in the distant past – then any constitution ought to make as few changes in those traditions as possible and should strive to link itself to that past as much as possible, using the language and even, when practical, the institutions from that past.

The argument that a stable constitution is part of society's structure of norms and conventions rationalizes another rule of design that applies to the issue we just discussed of whether a constitution is an appropriate place to try to regulate individual behavior, such as when children are required to care for aged parents. Few Western specialists in constitutional design would be sympathetic to the inclusion of such a provision in any constitutional document. Lawyers, economists, and political scientists alike would decry its imprecision, the infeasibility of enforcement, and its invitation to unwarranted incursions into private affairs. More generally, however, if we view a constitution as a part of society's overall system of coordination, then we can infer that such a document should not try to rewrite preexisting norms and conventions that are consistent with democratic practice, since doing so jeopardizes its legitimacy and ability to coordinate. Absent a reason for believing otherwise, it is safer to assume that social norms and customs have more permanency than any newly written document, at least in the domain of everyday social life. A constitution may choose to restate some of those norms and customs, but there is always the danger that mere words open the door to a misinterpretation of things or to government meddling in matters best left to less precise social processes. One can only begin to imagine the legislation that would ensue and the incursions into everyday life that would follow from a provision that, in effect, authorized the state to regulate the structure of family relationships, the financial obligations of children with respect to their parents, and the definitions of such words and phrases as "able bodies" and "unable." Doubtlessly, some politicians will find it advantageous to try to get the state to meddle in such things, but there is little reason to offer them encouragement in a constitutional document. In any event, our argument here is merely a restatement of the idea that a constitution should be molded to the culture it serves. But rather than try to draft a document that *explicitly* satisfies this objective, a far easier approach is to minimize the document's domain. Here, then, is the rationalization for a rule of design that requires a constitution to focus on those institutions minimally necessary to ensure society's ability to coordinate to those policy goals democratically identified as socially desirable.

Our final general rule concerns the level of specificity we require in a constitution. If a constitution is essentially a coordination device, then the institutional design it offers should be based on the presumption that any need for greater specificity will be attended to by the legislative and judicial institutions it establishes and by the evolutionary development of subsidiary institutions, norms, and conventions. This rule is not an argument for wholesale ambiguity. Great skill and foresight are required when trying to assess which things require explicit provision and what can be left to evolutionary development. The most evident failure of the U.S. Constitution occurred, as we note earlier, with respect to an issue on which it was largely silent and which was not covered by a social or political-economic norm that could serve as a substitute – namely, the right of secession. A great many things can be cited as causes of the American Civil War, but certainly an important contributing factor was the fact that the Constitution neither explicitly allowed nor disallowed secession. The states of the Confederacy might have chosen a different path had the Constitution explicitly disallowed secession, and Lincoln might have been unable to rally the Union to war had it allowed it. We cannot, of course, test such a hypothesis here, but it is evident that ambiguity, absent a consensus on the legitimacy of one action or another as supplied by some other coordinating mechanism, left the Constitution and the country open to disruption.

We hasten to add that our emphasis here on rules of design should not be interpreted to mean that all dimensions of design, all institutional structures relevant to federalism in particular or democracy generally, need to be or even can be laid out in a constitutional document. Here, in fact, we defer to Voigt's (1999) argument that much of political institutional design occurs in spontaneous fashion – as the by-product of the interplay of constitutional institutions, political necessity, and history. This is not to side with the extreme form of Hayek's (1973, 1976, 1979) position that institutions are less the product of rational choice than the precursor to such choice, but rather to agree with the obvious – that a constitution's meaning is, more often than not, determined in the context of subsequent political competition, which yields not only interpretation but those institutional forms essential for implementing political decisions. This fact is well illustrated by the emerging role of the court in the initial decades of American history (Epstein, Knight, and Shvetsova 2001), by the common practice of leaving the details if not the core structure of electoral rules to subsequent legislation and a considerable amount of manipulation and experimentation, and by the evolutionary development of procedures, political norms, and traditions borne of necessity or political conflict that subsequently attain the status of constitutional provisions to the extent that they coordinate society's politics no less than a codified, carefully and consciously planned document (the most evident example of which is Britain's unwritten constitution).

Absent a theory of constitutional design on a par with the rules by which we erect bridges or design airplanes, there necessarily exists a gray area in which it is unclear what properly belongs in a constitution and how much detail that document ought to provide. This is especially true of federal constitutional design. In this case we must establish not only the relations of agencies of the state to citizens and to each other in a context in which we are willing to admit the fiction that we can approximately distinguish among legislative, judicial, and executive functions, but where we must also establish the relation of various semiautonomous parts of the state to the federal whole, each of which possesses legislative, executive, and judicial components that bear its own connection to citizens. To say that we can satisfactorily anticipate the ultimate equilibrium that will prevail or the path to some equilibrium is, of course, pure fantasy and, thus, it is impossible to say with certainty that a constitution says too much or too little. The preceding rules of design, however, do serve the purpose of emphasizing that, in trying to anticipate the consequences of a specific design, we need to keep in mind the full context in which it is placed, especially the interests, traditions, and existing institutions that also serve to coordinate society's political choices.

5.4 Voters versus Elites

The preceding rules of design pertain to constitutions generally, and rather than try to infer additional rules from abstract conceptualizations, we need to address the more specific issue of *federal* constitutional design. And for that purpose recall our argument that if a constitution is an equilibrium selection device, then it must itself be an equilibrium in some supergame, where the choice set includes sustaining or challenging it in its entirety. Two constraints, though, need to be kept in mind when we specify such a game (which itself requires the implementation of additional institutional structure that we discuss in subsequent chapters). The first is that a constitutional equilibrium must be more than one in which no *individual* prefers to defect unilaterally. It should also be coalition-proof, by which we mean that no significant *subset* of persons has an incentive to coordinate a defection to an alternative constitution (or no constitution at all in the case of the dismemberment of the state or anarchy). If constitutions coordinate political action, we must be certain that they do not do so in such a way as to coordinate, say, incumbent politicians, a military elite, or the mass public, so that they prefer to and can change the constitutional game into something else.

The second constraint requires that we take a more abstract, even philosophical, view of our design task. Briefly, if a constitution is an equilibrium selection device, and if the game in which it is imbedded requires coordination to achieve specific outcomes and consists, at least in part, of rules and institutions of conscious design, then once again we must confront the problem of enforcement – in this instance, enforcement of the rules of the supergame. It might seem, then, that like those who conceptualize constitutions as contracts, we have merely pushed the problem of enforcement back to yet another level of institutions that must somehow be enforced. However, we should keep in mind that even without imagining any additional institutional layers, a constitution is necessarily imbedded in a game that consists of society's general structure – its system of norms, conventions, and those things one might choose to call culture. Here we assume that many of the components of this supergame lie outside the realm of conscious design so that we can focus on formal rules and the question of whether choices exist that encourage federal stability regardless of culture. Nevertheless, the issue of enforcement remains, and our solution in this instance must be a bit different than before. Specifically, taking all political institutions in their totality, constitutional or otherwise, we want those institutions to be not only incentive-compatible but also *fully* self-enforcing. That is, we want the full nexus of institutions, imbedded in society's structure, to yield outcomes such that no one has an incentive to disrupt what exists – or at least not to disrupt it in ways other than what the rules endogenously allow. Thus, we want a nexus of rules such that not only will no one defect unilaterally from acting in accordance with any part of them – if we are allowed the freedom to interpret a constitution as a subset of rules – but that no subset will be changed except in a manner prescribed by the remaining rules in the system. Referring once again to Franklin's example, we not only want a system of rules such that, when acting in their self-interest, lawyers make the appropriate (social-welfare-maximizing) choice, but also a system such that no subset of lawyers will prefer a different procedure given whatever rules exist for making changes, and such that those rules of change are themselves endogenously supported.

The full meaning and requirements of such a set of rules should become clearer in the chapters that follow. Here we note simply that with these two constraints in mind our immediate task can be best specified by recalling the design requirement set forth in the previous section that constitutions need to be limited documents that address only the core structure of the state and that resist the temptation to try to direct the actions of the sovereign, the people themselves. That is, if a constitution, federal or otherwise, seeks to redirect people's actions, it should do so only insofar as those actions pertain to the roles and functions the document uniquely establishes for them. Of course, a constitution creates a great many roles, including those of legislator, president, minister, judge, and so on. But the critical ones can be sorted into two categories – voters and elected officials (although at times we might substitute "federal subject" for "citizen" and include "appointed official" in the category of "elected"). And although we appreciate the great abstraction implied by this dichotomy, it is nevertheless adequate for our purposes – which is to specify the relationship that needs to exist between these two classes of actors in a stable federal system.

With regard to the first half of this dichotomy, we can begin by supposing that voters are not concerned directly with stability or instability, or even with such grand notions as the legitimacy of a constitution or its consistency with other social norms. This is not to say that once an institutional equilibrium is established, citizens are impervious to arguments that one action or another on their part or on the part of a politician endangers the constitutional order. Nevertheless, when designing a federal state it is only prudent to proceed from the perspective of the Framers of the U.S. Constitution – from the assumption that "the seeds of faction are sown in the nature of man," which we take here to mean that voters are primarily concerned with their myopic self-interest, expressed in simple constructs such as increased services, lower taxes, greater access to the government's bureaucracy, and so on. In this scheme, then, the sole political act of voters is to express their self-interest by voting for those candidates who promise, either on the basis of campaign platforms or past performance, the greatest immediate reward.

In this scheme, then, the burden for ensuring stability falls on the shoulders of elected political elites. That is,

Principle 1. A system of individual-level incentives designed to ensure federal stability should apply not to individual citizens but to political elites since it is they, virtually by definition, who coordinate and "lead" a society to one equilibrium or another.

When proceeding in accordance with Principle 1 we are, in effect, trying to satisfy two objectives. First, and quite directly, we want to follow the Anglo-American concept of democratic constitutional design and acknowledge that such documents ought to constrain only the state and its agents, and not the sovereign. Thus, we must proceed under the assumption that the sole institutional variables at our disposal are those that apply to political elites and not to democracy's citizens. Second, we need to acknowledge that, regardless of their idiosyncratic motives, the generalized motive all politicians share in a democracy is the desire to win elections and that *absent any contrary incentive*, they would, like their constituents, readily challenge or overstep any constraint on federal bargaining if doing so serves that interest. Abiding once again by another precept of *The Federalist Papers* – namely that "if men were angels no government would be necessary" – we want to exclude the idea that we can rest the stability of the state on the fragile foundation of the good intentions of those who would lead it. The search for stability, then, requires that we design a game that motivates officeholders to resist or somehow redirect constituent pressures to overstep the rules.

Principle 1 can be divided into two more specific subprinciples. First, note that our earlier discussion of bargaining highlights the fact that the goal of providing incentives for political elites to reach accommodating solutions is especially problematic when speaking of regional elites, whose electoral support is tied to specific geographic constituencies. It is they, after all, who directly respond to narrowly construed electoral pressures. Thus, a subsequent principle is:

Principle 2. Any mechanism intended to establish a federal constitution as an effective coordination device must give local and regional political elites an incentive to uphold federative constraints even when, as is likely, their constituents prefer otherwise.

Principle 2, though, is only half of the equation. The other half concerns the incentives of national elites – those whom we might associate with the center or at least who can direct the center's authority to coerce federal subjects via the application of any constitutional supremacy clause.

Principle 3. Any mechanism intended to establish a federal constitution as an effective coordination device must create political (office-related) rewards for national elites that encourage them to acquiesce to the legitimate authority of regional governments and dissuade them from overstepping their constitutionally prescribed authority.

We appreciate that the preceding principles appear utopian or applicable only to specific cases. For example, it is sometimes argued new democracies need firm central direction and a period of benevolent authoritarian rule before a firm constitutional order is established. It is not unreasonable to assume, in fact, that often chief executives or heads of state will seek to augment their authority – or at least the authority of the federal center – on the basis of noble motives. Too often, though, such a prospect sets in motion a chain reaction of responses in which federal subjects attempt to preempt matters by augmenting their authority, which in turn makes the center's demand for firmer control seem more legitimate and imperative, which in turn ... and so on and so forth. Such is the process observers fear they see in Russia today. The result can either be a federalism that becomes a mere facade for unitary rule or the dissolution of the state itself. Principles 1–3, then, are restatements of much of what we have already said in this volume – of the necessity to maintain a balance between the center and federal subjects, to keep bargaining within the boundaries of constitutional constraint, and to have the maintenance of this balance and these boundaries in the self-interest of political elites even when their constituents might prefer otherwise. To these principles, however, we need to add a fourth:

Principle 4. Federal stability requires that regional and national political elites maintain some (possibly evolving) consensus over the definitions of "constitutionally prescribed" and "legitimate authority."

Clearly, the preceding Principles 1–4 throw the burden of maintaining federal constraints on the shoulders of political elites. They stand in sharp contrast, then, to those a pluralist would emphasize: citizen involvement, citizen values, and a civic culture. Moreover, despite their emphasis on elites, these principles also contrast sharply with those promulgated by consociationalists. A consociational view also emphasizes the need for a cooperative consensus among elites, although the net they cast is not limited to politicians but includes business and intellectual elites as well. However, because it is the state alone that possesses the authority and power to coerce, Principles 1–4 focus on political actors and their electoral incentives. Thus, rather than await a consensus based on vague and varied sources of self-interest – shared values, shared economic interests, shared ideology, or whatever – these principles identify as the target of Level 3 design the relationship of political elites to those who would maintain or preclude their official positions, their constituents.

Principles 1–4, though, pose a paradox, because an assumption implicit in them is that electorates cannot be expected to treat Level 2 constraints any differently than they do those that compose Level 1. Constitutions may possess mass legitimacy, but if a group of sufficient size can achieve its preferred revision of the rules, it is only prudent to suppose that it will do so if the opportunity presents itself. Examples of a mass-based support for the revision of even a wholesale disruption of the constitutional order are well known. For example, while Ukranian voters chose to overwhelmingly support the Soviet Union in March 1991, once Ukraine's political leadership championed independence and expressed its dissatisfaction with the USSR's economic performance, the electorate quickly fell into line, and awarded an elite-sponsored referendum on independence in December nearly the same margin of victory given to unchallenged Communist Party officials in previous decades. Similarly, following his rise to power through an internal party coup in 1986, Milošević immediately used nationalist rhetoric to argue that Serbia was discriminated against within Yugoslavia, both politically and economically. Following the boost to his rhetoric given by intellectuals within the Serbian Academy of Sciences, and aided by the rise of the anti-Serb mobilization on the part of the Croatian elites, the public was readily mobilized to take up arms against their countrymen and to abandon any pretense of civilized conduct despite years of seemingly harmonious relations. The role of elites as entrepreneurs of ethnic conflict in the pursuit of political advantage is, of course, well documented. But even in less extreme cases, we can find the same forces – those forces calling for a wholesale revision of the constitutional order – in operation, as Canada well illustrates with Quebec's on-and-off campaign for separatism.

These examples illustrate a common phenomenon – that of elites acting as political entrepreneurs, engineering support for themselves by encouraging preferences that allow them to act contrary to Principles 1–4. In the Canadian context, for example, because politicians "have a vested interest in provincial status and power which the several provincial electorates perhaps do not fully share" (Corry 1969: 53), we see those politicians attempting to move beyond the preferences of their electorates so as to make federal stability more problematic than what it might otherwise be. In perhaps one of the most divisive instances of political entrepreneurship, Riker (1986) offers the example of the issue of slavery and its role in precipitating the American Civil War. Briefly, prior to 1860, a nascent Republican Party saw itself as a permanent minority vis-à-vis the Democratic Party if competition persisted on traditional issues. The issue of slavery, however, divided Democrats between North and South, and thus afforded Republicans a wedge with which to win office. Of course, we would not argue that the Republican Party alone accounts for slavery's ultimate salience or that its strategy violated any explicit Level 1 constraint (although the states of the Confederacy did argue and truly believe that federal interference in their "unique institution" constituted a violation of states' rights and agreements implicit in the Union's founding). But, in addition to being a moral issue, slavery was a redistributive one as well, and when confronted with the opportunity to increase its electoral salience, Republicans seized the opportunity to wrestle power away from their political opponents.

Thus, when attempting to craft our institutions so that Principles 1–4 are satisfied, we must appreciate that mass preferences are not altogether set in concrete – they are, to some extent, manipulable, and political elites will, if it serves their purposes, attempt appropriate manipulations. This is not to say that political elites in all democracies will always seek to take advantage of divisive issues. In contrast to an issue like slavery in the early history of the United States, or ethnic nationalism in Yugoslavia and Czechoslovakia, we can also find examples in which divisive issues were taken off the table. Anti-Semitism is such an issue in the United States following World War II. Although few congressional constituencies contain an electorally significant Jewish population, politicians of all ideological persuasions and constituency types have, in effect, sustained a long-term collusive agreement to preclude anti-Semitism from rearing its ugly head in American politics in any serious way, even though this issue (along with its twin, anti-Catholicism) were effective in earlier eras.[4] Similarly, as we argue in Chapter 9, political party elites in the member states of the European Union, in order to advance their agenda of integration and thwart competition from the right and left, have long colluded to discourage letting the redistributive consequences of that integration become a salient electoral issue (although, as also appears to be the case, that collusion has begun to incrementally unravel).

When elite collusion occurs to preclude political competition on divisive issues as opposed to the deliberate engineering of those issues is, of course, a question that should be central to any understanding of democratic stability. The specific formulation we want to address here, then, concerns the conditions under which elected representatives can be expected to bear the burden

[4] We would not argue that such collusion always has beneficial consequences or serves the public's interest. Consider the following letter (November 16, 1989) addressed to the Speaker (Democrat) and Republican Party leader of the U.S. House of Representatives, signed by the leaders of both parties following passage of a legislative pay raise (*Congressional Quarterly*, December 2, 1989, p. 3326): "Dear Mr. Speaker and Mr. Republican Leader: The ethics reform package [*sic*] that was adopted in the U.S. House of Representatives today provides an opportunity for all federal elected officials to move away from a growing dependence on special interests. As leaders of our political committees we are all well aware of the political dangers that Members of Congress might face if this issue were to be misused in the campaign of 1990. The four of us have agreed to issue instructions to our staffs that the vote on HR 3360 is not an appropriate point of criticism in the coming campaigns. Further, we will publicly oppose the use of the issue in any campaign in the 1990 cycle. This agreement demonstrates our commitment to helping provide a positive political and ethical environment in which qualified people can serve in government. We applaud the House leadership for the work they have done in this difficult and important area and pledge our continuing support for their efforts. Sincerely, Ron Brown (Chair, Democratic National Committee), Guy Vander Jagt (Chair, National Republical Congressional Committee), Lee Atwater (Chair, Republican National Committee), Beryl Anthony (Chair, Democratic Congressional Campaign Committee)."

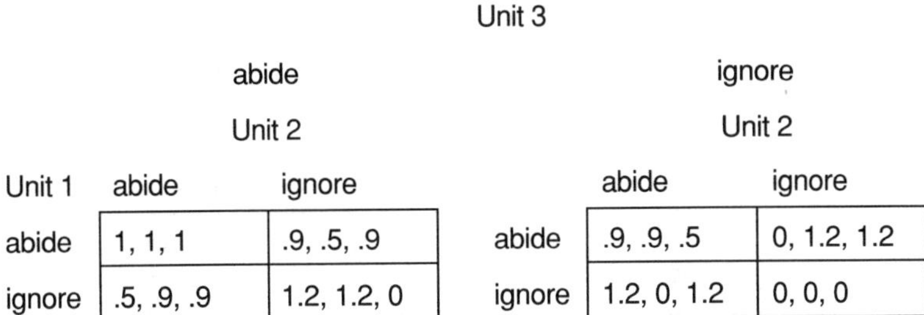

Unit 3: abide

Unit 1 \ Unit 2	abide	ignore
abide	1, 1, 1	.9, .5, .9
ignore	.5, .9, .9	1.2, 1.2, 0

Unit 3: ignore

Unit 1 \ Unit 2	abide	ignore
abide	.9, .9, .5	0, 1.2, 1.2
ignore	1.2, 0, 1.2	0, 0, 0

FIGURE 5.1. Constitutional legitimacy problem when popular mandates are received by perfect agents of the voters.

of Principles 1–4 and resist the temptation to either shape citizen preferences to their own ends or, what is an even graver challenge, to follow those preferences when it suits their purposes regardless of the implications of their actions for political stability. The problem with sustaining these principles, absent an institutional mechanism of some sort in addition to a constitution is illustrated by a simple game. Consider a polity of three voters or, equivalently, three federal subjects and assume that whatever interactions occur among constituencies on federal matters occur through their elected representatives. Referring now to the strategic form game in Figure 5.1, notice that we design the payoffs there so that abiding by the rules is an equilibrium – no player (constituency) has an incentive to defect and ignore whatever rules we might establish to preclude destructive federal bargaining. But notice also that payoffs are arranged so that this equilibrium is not what game theorists call coalition-proof. If any two players coordinate their defections, then both can move the situation to a different equilibrium in which each realizes a gain at the expense of the nondefecting player, thereby capturing the notion of a critical subset of players capable of toppling a constitution. Of course, the coordination required for such a move may be difficult or impossible to achieve in unguided mass electorates. But the coordination of political elites and, subsequently, their constituencies is precisely what a federal constitution should encourage. That is, federal institutions give constituencies, through their elected representatives, the ability to choose outcomes they might not be able to realize through unilateral action. Thus, even if we somehow render abiding by federal constraints an equilibrium in a narrow sense, it need not be an equilibrium if circumstances allow for coordinated action among elected representatives.

Fortunately, the world is not populated only by the likes of a Milošević, and elites do sometimes play a positive role in maintaining federal stability. In addition to the removal of anti-Semitism from the American political agenda, we can also cite the 1992 Constitutional Referendum in Canada, which, although ultimately unsuccessful despite the support of all provincial prime ministers and the national government, attempted to direct voters to

	Unit 3: abide		Unit 3: ignore	
	Unit 2		Unit 2	
Unit 1	abide	ignore	abide	ignore
abide	1, 1, 1	$.9+.1p$, $.5+.5p$, $.9+.1p$	$.9+.1p$, $.9+.1p$, $.5+.5p$	$1.8p-.8p^2$ $1.2-p+.8p^2$, $1.2-p+.8p^2$
ignore	$.5+.5p$, $.9+.1p$, $.9+.1p$	$1.2-p+.8p^2$, $1.2-p+.8p^2$ $1.8p-.8p^2$	$1.2-p+.8p^2$ $1.8p-.8p^2$ $1.2-p+.8p^2$	$p(2.4-2.5p+1.1p^2)$ $p(2.4-2.5p+1.1p^2)$ $p(2.4-2.5p+1.1p^2)$

FIGURE 5.2. Transformation of the constitutional legitimacy problem with the introduction of imperfect political agency.

a profederal position. The question, then, is whether we can find a source of such motives in a game like the one in Figure 5.1. Suppose, then, that we change this game as follows. If a representative is instructed to ignore federal bargaining constraints by his constituency, he does so only with probability $1 - p$, and continues to abide with probability p. Ignoring for the moment the source of such probabilities, consider the strategic form game in Figure 5.2, which is the appropriate transformation of Figure 5.1 under this probabilistic assumption. Notice now that for our transformed game, the strategy triple for voters (abide, abide, abide) remains an equilibrium. But consider the cell (ignore, ignore, abide). In Figure 5.1 this cell corresponds to an equilibrium and confers an advantage on constituencies 1 and 2. Now, however, notice that if $1.2 - p + .8p^2$ is less than 1 (if p is greater than or equal to .25), then (ignore, ignore, abide) is no longer an equilibrium and the cooperative equilibrium (abide, abide, abide) is coalition-proof – the constitution has acquired popular legitimacy. Thus, if the likelihood of abiding by federal constraints is sufficiently great for all representatives simultaneously even when their constituents indicate an opposite preference, then somewhat paradoxically, sustaining those constraints is an unavoidable equilibrium among constituents.

This is not to say that each representative will prefer unilaterally to choose a value of p greater than 0. Indeed, if all other representatives have $p = 0$, then the constituents of the defecting (imperfect) representative will, on average, fare less well than all other constituencies. Nevertheless, this game demonstrates the potential advantage of having politicians that only imperfectly represent their constituencies. Specifically, even though constituents prefer to break the rules of restrained federal bargaining, that imperfection in politicians leads constituents nevertheless to act as if the representation they receive is perfect. As simple as it is, then, our example brings to the fore two important questions. First, how do we establish rules – a supergame – so that political elites not only find it in their self-interest to act with a high enough p, but also to sustain those rules, whatever they might be? Put differently, how do we find a way to make it advantageous for elected officials to act contrary to the myopic self-interest of their constituents? Second, how do we ensure the legitimacy of those rules among the electorate – rules that lead to an apparent thwarting of their will – where by *legitimacy* we mean simply that voters are willing to issue or at least accept mandates to their elected representatives to act in accordance with constitutional constraints? In effect, then, we are asking the following question:

> *Design Question.* How, in a democracy, do we render representatives imperfect agents of their principals, their constituents? And how do we design our institutions so that those principals (voters) will nevertheless reward their agents (elected officials) for being imperfect – reward them in the long run despite the possibility (probability) that they will signal them to act contrary to these motives in the short run?

5.5 Desirable Imperfection and a Democratic *As-If* Principle

That we might not want public officials to adhere strictly to the immediate desires of their constituents is, of course, reflected elsewhere in the literature on democratic process and design. Carey (1997: 69), for example, in describing the problems of finding a suitable balance between cohesive and incohesive parties, cites the case of Brazil, whose electoral system "creates strong incentives for legislators to cultivate personalistic loyalties among voters, even when doing so means ignoring their parties' broader agenda. One result is that presidents cannot count on stable legislative coalitions or negotiate policy.... Another is that legislators' relentless pursuit of government patronage and pork-barrel spending contributes to rampant political corruption." On the other hand, if, to rein in excessive constituent attachments, we somehow gave "central party leaders... the power to impose discipline on elected politicians, responsiveness to minority groups and local interests is necessarily compromised." However, before we address such trade-offs, we should note the important difference between what our design question implicitly requires (along with Carey's concerns) and the usual approach to principal-agent problems that we find in the literature. Whether we look to the literature on rent seeking or to the more general theory of principal-agent interactions, the problem commonly considered is how to get agents (e.g., elected representatives, attorneys, employees) to act in the interest of a principal (e.g., voters, clients, management) – how to structure choice so that for the particular circumstance under consideration, an agent's self-interest corresponds to the principal's (Kiewiet and McCubbins 1991; Epstein and O'Halloran 1999; Lupia 2003; Strom 2003). Instead, our design question turns this problem on its head and seeks to render elites imperfect agents. For reasons that should become clear shortly, though, we must do this in a way that is not a simple backtracking of the problem that the design of perfect agents is intended to solve.

Briefly, the source of the problem in the more traditional principal-agent literature is that principals are assumed to be able to monitor their agents' actions or the circumstances these agents confront only imperfectly, in which case agents can take advantage of these informational shortcomings to realize private gains at the expense of their principals. The most evident political example of this problem is corruption, but it in fact has broader application, including the issues we address here. For example, in de Figueiredo and Weingast's (1999: 263) model of negotiations between Serbs and Croats over the future of Yugoslavia, citizens can only see if negotiations succeed or fail, in which case if negotiations fail (in the interest of those conducting them), the population in general can never really know why: "Perhaps it failed because genocidal Croatians sabotaged peace"; or "perhaps it failed because a treacherous Milosevic sabotaged it."

The problem we confront is different than the one the principal-agent literature tries to solve. Although we want politicians to be imperfect agents of voters, imperfection should not be based on secrecy and imperfect information. We do not want our institutions to be deliberately democratically flawed at the outset or biased in terms of who can learn what about events and processes. We still strive to secure a political structure that satisfies some admittedly idealistic notions of democracy and that provides reasonable guarantees of individual rights. Thus, we want each agent's actions to be fully observable and accountable, but at the same time we want their imperfect actions to be supported ultimately by those who judge them in the voting booth.

The difficulty here, of course, is that in searching for a mechanism to accomplish this, we cannot look to the constitutional provisions we want to protect or to moral (utopian) imperatives. As Section 5.1 suggests, in the first case we would merely end up with an infinite regress of reasoning. If provision A enforces provision B, and if provision C enforces A, then what enforces C? If enforcement is provided by provision D, then what enforces D, and so on? And in the second case, we cannot engineer moral or social imperatives – or at least we do not know how to do so. We do not want to travel down the road of Marxian theology and suppose that the human psyche can be reengineered. And even if we adopt a more limited definition of what we mean by a moral or social imperative and assert, as consociatonalists do, that stability is achievable through some elite consensus, then we have merely restated Principle 4 without offering guidance as to how that consensus is achieved – without identifying the specific institutional forms that will sustain that consensus. Our search for a way of satisfactorily answering our Design Question while simultaneously satisfying Principles 1–4, then, must lie elsewhere. And here we suggest that since we are concerned solely with *democratic* federalism, we should once again begin at the beginning – by examining more closely the fundamental motive of *elected* officials, which we assume is to win and maintain office. This, of course, is but another way of saying that we cannot escape the paradox of wanting our elected officials to function within a democratic state while being rewarded by their electorates for imperfectly representing them. However, we can begin to see our way to a resolution of this paradox if we assume, as a starting point, that politicians *act as if* they care not only for the constituency they currently represent but also about other constituencies, including, but not necessarily limited to, those they hope to represent in the future. Our appeal here to *as if* and to the admittedly ambiguous *but not necessarily limited to* is not intended to obscure the solution to federal stability we seek but is designed to leave open the possibility, elaborated in subsequent chapters, that elected elites can be led to serve the interest of a constituency different than the one they currently represent, and that voters can be induced to *act as if* they approve of such action.

Our appeal here to the notion of *as if* is somewhat different from its common use in the rational choice paradigm. There, *as if* refers primarily to a method of investigation. Because such things as motive, preference, and perception cannot be observed directly, and because we must limit testable hypotheses to what we can observe – the choices people make – theories of individual decision making must operate under the assumption that these things are, much like electrons, postulated constructs. We can attempt to infer motives from actions, but we can never know what those motives really are. Nor can we test hypotheses about these things other than in terms of the individual choices they imply in the context of specific models. If people's choices are consistent with the predictions derived from one set of postulated motives versus another, then we cannot say for certain that they in fact hold those motives; instead, it is more correct to say that they are acting *as if* they hold them. Admittedly, this linguistic twist might seem like hairsplitting, but it serves to emphasize the methodological problems associated with discovering *true* motives. Instead, those who operate within the rational choice and individualist paradigm infer any motives necessary in order to maximize the consistency between observed choices and postulated models. And just as there are no true motives to be discovered, there are no true models – only models that fit our data better than others.[5] If, for example, a model assumes

5 Admittedly, the *as-if* principle seeks to resolve an additional problem within the rational choice paradigm. Much of that paradigm relies on models that appear to assume that people are able to make complex mathematical calculations – indeed, that they know all that there is to know of advanced mathematics. If, for instance, we sought to predict the actions of the expert billiards player within the paradigm, we would most likely offer a model of someone who, regardless of education, appears to be wholly familiar with trigonometry and the physics of

that politicians maximize votes, then their responses to surveys are irrelevant insofar as the model's validity is concerned. If this assumption allows us to predict the decisions of politicians with sufficient accuracy, the *as-if* principle can be invoked to say that they are acting as if they maximize votes, without implying true motives or requiring that the objects of investigation be conscious of the motives that explain their actions.

Here, when addressing the issue of constitutional design, we want to adapt the *as-if* notion to mean that instead of concerning ourselves with whether or not politicians see themselves as representing their legally defined constituencies and regardless of whether voters see themselves as rewarding their representatives for championing their interests, politicians can be led to act as if they represent broader interests and voters can be induced to act as if they support those actions. Conscious motives and true intentions notwithstanding, we might even prefer that politicians justify their actions in terms of representing narrow constituency interests when they are in fact acting otherwise, and that voters suppose they are choosing on the basis of narrow self-interest when they are in fact sustaining more global concerns.

The full meaning of this adaptation of *as if* should become clearer as we proceed, but at least with respect to politicians, it might somehow seem strange, perhaps even utopian, to assume that representatives can be led to act as if they serve a constituency other than the one election law assigns them. We can do this in any number of ways, but, as we elaborate on later, an especially important one is to assume that elected officials act with an eye to moving up a ladder of electoral advancement from local to regional to national office – to offices of greater national visibility, prestige, and power. In this scheme, then, the objective to be realized through Level 3 design is to mute the reflection of a single constituency's particularistic demands by giving its representatives an interest in the welfare of other constituencies. Modifying a representative's motives in this way, though, has two preconditions: (1) a ladder of advancement in which the state offers multiple offices at multiple levels so that there is an adequate supply of elected offices to be filled and so that elected officials can reasonably anticipate the possibility of finding a higher rung on the ladder open to competition; and (2) elected officials who give sufficient weight to the future so that even an uncertain

friction and inelastic bodies, and who holds in his head all the values of sines, cosines, and the like for every angle and with great precision. Despite appearances, however, our model would not concern itself with whether the player actually knew these things. Instead we would state our hypotheses in the form of asserting that the player's actions were, in this circumstance only, consistent with such knowledge – that the player was acting *as if* he knew these things. Whether he actually knew them or whether his actions derived from instinct learned from years of practice would not be our concern (unless we were interested in the process of learning itself); our concern would simply be whether the model predicted his actions (and the actions of other expert players) with sufficient accuracy. For a more extensive discussion of this example and the *as-if* principle in general, see Friedman (1953).

prospect of winning higher offices can outweigh the value of focusing solely on the interests of one's current constituency.

If one of these preconditions is satisfied, but not the other, then the goal of rendering representatives imperfect agents is subverted and alternative approaches must be considered. Suppose the first condition is satisfied but not the second. For example, if political elites proceed initially with a shared belief that political instability *and* economic underperformance are inherent features of their polities, then planning horizons are correspondingly shortened and little weight is given to winning and maintaining office. Instead, the long-term goals of winning and advancement are supplanted by the short-term one of "getting what you can while the getting is good."[6]

Suppose, on the other hand, that the second condition is satisfied but not the first. Here, the representative is encouraged to secure his or her current position by whatever means possible regardless of how that representative might be viewed by a larger (e.g., national) constituency. In a state with a strong party system – a system in which a politician's regional agenda is dictated by national elites or at least must be negotiated with them – those "means" need not threaten stability. But if the party system is weak and if society is simultaneously characterized by intensely felt ethnic, linguistic, religious, or racial divisions, those "means" can be especially dangerous, as when political entrepreneurs incite their constituencies by appealing to a majority and demonizing a minority. Indeed, society can be trapped in yet another destructive equilibrium. If the imperatives of reelection give elites reason to answer the question, "Is a resolution of intense but conflicting preferences in the plural society manageable in a democratic framework?" the same as Rabushka and Shepsle (1972) – namely, "We think not" (p. 217) – then the initial presumption of democratic failure, federal or otherwise, will most likely be a self-fulfilling prophecy.

The reader should see in this discussion a reflection of the two schools of thought reviewed earlier in our initial search for the sources of federal stability – namely the notion of federalism as nuisance and as an engine of prosperity. There, however, we assert that unless augmented by additional argument, neither school provides a satisfactory explanation for stability

[6] Indeed, with Russia and Ukraine in mind (as well as most other ex-Soviet states and an extended list of Latin American and Southeast Asian countries), we can readily imagine society generally and elected officials in particular being trapped in an unsavory equilibrium in which unsettled political and economic circumstances lead people to expect everyone else to pursue immediate financial gain, in which case the only rational response is to do the same. While everyone sincerely bemoans the consequences of the corruption that precludes effective state action, pervasive corruption from the lowest to the highest levels becomes society's uniform characteristic (Klochko and Ordeshook forthcoming). The linkage between social outcomes and the weight people give to the future, then, is this: "People who care about future payoffs not only resist the temptation to cheat in a relationship; they signal their ability to resist the temptation.... The resulting [signals], which I describe as social norms, can vastly enhance or diminish social welfare" (Posner 2000: 5).

or instability or much guidance to federal design. Both schools give an incomplete accounting of how federal bargaining can be controlled, which institutions best facilitate that control in a democratic context, and how those institutions can be made self-enforcing. Our discussion here, on the other hand, can be interpreted as a generalization of those two schools so that each is an argument about the things that impact the political discount rates of elites and that subsequently coordinate them to alternative equilibria. This generalization, though, does more than merely suggest the possibility of a reinterpretation and restatement of matters. It also directs our attention once again to Riker's (1964) arguments about the relevance of politics (as opposed to simple economics) and the incentives of political elites to keep what he terms the "federal bargain." And it does so by focusing on the electoral connection between elites and the citizenry.

This focus is no mere cosmetic addition to a squabble about federalism's nature. When seeking an institutional solution to the problem of dysfunctional bargaining, our argument is that we must consider more than the jurisdictional agreements a constitution might offer in the hope that they provide an economically justifiable and politically salable allocation of responsibilities (Level 1 constraints) or those provisions that define the national government's structure and which try to provide different levels of government with ways to defend their position (Level 2 constraints). Our search for the sources of federal stability must also consider the institutions that make the otherwise incoherent voice of the people coherent for political elites and that transform the short-term concerns of the average citizen into long-term motives for those who scurry about for political advantage. This discussion, then, suggests that the provisions – constitutional or otherwise – relevant to federal design are not limited to those commonly labeled "federal." They also include electoral provisions that are commonly established with other purposes in mind, such as ensuring fair representation or simply facilitating the reelection of incumbents.

Transforming the popular will into something other than what citizens might consciously intend might seem a perversion of democracy. But, as we argue in the next chapter, that is precisely what an appropriately configured political party system ought to do. Indeed, our argument here is that the federation's party system and the institutions that help shape it are *the* critical components of sustaining a federal constitution. However, before we can argue that the preceding two conditions – a ladder of advancement and a low discount rate on the future – are critical to solving the problem of federal stability, that they are not merely the consequences of a degree of political stability achieved by other means, and that political parties hold the key to satisfying them, notice that the game in Figure 5.2 upon which our discussion is based lacks one critical element – a competing cadre of elites who promise values of $p = 0$ by promising to reflect faithfully the wishes of the electorate whenever that electorate lays claim to some particularized benefit. To ignore this possibility is to ignore the lesson taught us by our experience with federal failure. Consider, for example, the successive civil wars that accompanied the dissolution of the Socialist Federal Republic of Yugoslavia: "In the political milieu of ethno-federalism, where concessions could be attacked by political rivals as betrayal of one's own (ethnic) nation and where there was no longer any central institution authorized to decide disputed issues, escalating threats, displays of armed might and ultimately the use of force could not be avoided" (Hayden 1992: 25). Similarly, in describing the logic of ethnic conflict Horowitz (1985, 1991) emphasizes that although there are instances in which elites held more extreme positions than their followers, in country after country politicians who began as leaders inspired by ideals of panethnic nationalism, socialism, and interethnic compromise were reduced, against their wishes, by the sheer calculus of electoral competition to the more limited status of the leaders of a particular ethnic or otherwise defined group. And this same story of moderately inclined elites finding themselves outflanked by populist extremists is repeated by Rabushka and Shepsle (1972: 80–6).

It might seem then that resting the stability of a federation on the shoulders of some electoral scheme is folly, and it is not surprising that some scholars conclude that the impetus for a successful federation must come from other things such as the ideological commitment of charismatic leaders: "[W]here there is no paramount ideological commitment to the federal ideal," the mere creation of federal institutions will not resolve the conflicts that will arise within the federation (Franck 1968: 174). In this way observers of the European Union frequently cite the "pro-European idealism of heads of government" as the decisive factor of successful integration (see, e.g., Moravcsik 1991) – an idealism in which political elites overcome and perhaps even ignore their and their constituencies' short-term interests. We appreciate, of course, that behind such idealism lies strong material interests (Sandholtz and Zysman 1989; Moravcsik 1998). But as we argue in Chapter 9, despite a general acceptance of the concept of Pan-European integration, citizens at large have thus far played a marginal role in determining the scope and the pace of integration (a fact commonly given the catchy label of the EU's "democratic deficit"), with elites enjoying significant freedom to act, provided that integration remains a limited, incremental affair.[7]

The European example suggests that an appeal to parties and their promise of political advancement is not a necessary motive for political elites to act in accordance with the game portrayed in Figure 5.2. However, with its members having been ravaged by two world wars, with its basic structure

[7] The suggestion here is that although members of the European Parliament are elected in ways that leave them unconstrained by voters, if and when those members are required to be more responsive to the demands of their constituents, the Parliament may choose to slow or even derail the pace of integration (Tsebelis 1991, 2002).

initiated in the shadow of a Soviet military threat, with its economy confronting an even more permanent economic threat from the United States and Japan, and having been initially pushed in the direction of integration by the hegemonic authority of the United States, the EU's circumstances may be special and not a basis upon which to plan other federations. It remains to be seen, moreover, how far integration will proceed under current institutional arrangements before nationalism and sectional rivalries disrupt the flow of events. Thus, when considering the requirements of stability elsewhere, we are not surprised to see a sympathetic attitude toward the somewhat less-than-democratic suggestions of Rabushka and Shepsle (1972) that include (1) a denial of independence, such as through a reimposition of colonial rule; (2) extreme decentralization so that few issues are allowed to become national (as in the case of the newly imposed constitution of Bosnia); (3) restrictions on free political competition, for example, secrecy in government action (but see Sened 1995 for the value of information for the spontaneous development and enforcement of rights); (4) restrictions on the overall scope of government; (5) creation of homogeneous societies, for example, the dissolution of heterogeneous ones; and (6) the creation of permanent external enemies.

This is not to say that Rabushka and Shepsle would seriously regard any one of these proposals as feasible or even desirable. They are offered more in the spirit of emphasizing the difficulty of securing political stability in plural societies. The substantive suggestion we offer is that by restricting a politician's vulnerability to populist challenges and allowing elected officials the luxury of giving the future sufficient weight, an *appropriately configured party system* plays a critical role in encouraging federal stability. Defining "appropriately configured," identifying institutional parameters that need to be manipulated in order to achieve the configuration we deem necessary, and sorting out cause from effect so that the type of party system we deem appropriate is less the consequence of stability than its cause are the issues to which we now turn.

6

Political Parties in a Federal State

> Political parties created democracy and... modern democracy is unthinkable save in terms of parties.
>
> Schattschneider 1942: 1

> Here is a factor in the organization of federal government which is of primary importance but which cannot be ensured or provided for in a constitution – a good party system.
>
> Wheare 1953: 86

> Whatever the general social conditions, if any, that sustain the federal bargain, there is one institutional condition that controls the nature of the bargain in all instances... with which I am familiar. This is the structure of the party system, which may be regarded as the main variable intervening between the background social conditions and the specific nature of the federal bargain.
>
> Riker 1964: 136

> In a country which was always to be in need of the cohesive force of institutions, the national parties, for all their faults, were to become at an early hour primary and necessary parts of the machinery of government, essential vehicles to convey men's loyalties to the state.
>
> Hofstadter 1969: 70–1

6.1 An Extreme Hypothesis

Hofstadter's argument is drawn from his assessment of the United States, but like the views of Schattschneider, Wheare, and Riker, that argument can apply to any stable democratic state. If the primary objective of political elites in a democracy is to win and maintain office and if political parties are the primary organizational vehicle for achieving that end, then parties and their relation to the state must play a pivotal role in any understanding not only of democracy generally but of the intergovernmental relations of federations in particular: "[P]olitical parties are the main means not only whereby provincial greivances are aired but also whereby centralist and decentralist trends are legitimized" (McKay 2001: 16). As seemingly self-evident as this fact might be, however, parties and party systems are not uniformly identified as critical components of federal systems or federal design. For example, the index to Ostrom's (1991) otherwise seminal analysis of American federalism makes no mention of "party," nor does Burgess and Gagnon's (1993) or Smith's (1995) edited texts on comparative federalism; none of the essays in Elster and Slagstad's (1988) edited volume on constitutionalism pays heed to Riker or Wheare's arguments; and the chapter on federalism in Lijphart's (1984) text on democracy offers no discussion of parties whatsoever. Even when there is some awareness that parties and party systems are relevant, they often receive only superficial attention. Keohane and Hoffmann's (1991) edited text on the European Union, for instance, offers a scant one and one-half pages on parties (and there the discussion concerns parliamentary coalitions as opposed to their electoral structures), while Lemco's (1991) treatise on federal stability awards five pages to an assessment of the impact of party systems as compared to the thirty pages devoted to the usual suspects: modernization, economic development, and economic growth.

This failure to link party systems, the institutions that impact those systems, and federal design is mirrored, for instance, in Russia's 1993 constitution. Despite the salience of federal matters at the time of its drafting, the clauses contained in that document's "federal" section (Articles 65 through 79) concern only traditional provisions – those pertaining to the identities of federal subjects, procedures for amending borders, jurisdictional allocations of authority, a supremacy clause, directives for regional governmental organization, and, as a compromise with its republics, the Kremlin's authority to negotiate bilateral agreements. Although this categorization is hardly unique, the drafting of that document proceeded in a way that, with the exception of the structure of regional representation in the upper legislative chamber, the Federation Council, those issues which even at the time were assumed to impact party development most directly – presidential and legislative election laws, the authority to draft and administer those laws, the legally allowed partisan role of the president, and the timing of elections – were either addressed in a context wholly divorced from any discussion of federal matters or simply relegated to subsequent legislation. And despite the role given to the demise of the Communist Party in explaining the Soviet Union's dissolution (Sharlet 1992; Fish 1995; Bunce 1999; Solnick 1998, 2002), this treatment of parties is not mirrored in the discussion of Russia's subsequent failings in federal matters. For example, in both Wallich's (1994) edited volume for the World Bank on suggested federal reforms and Hahn's (2001) assessment of President Putin's most recent administrative changes, the role of parties is nowhere discussed, while in Shleifer and Treisman's (2000) text, subtitled "Political Tactics and Economic Reform in Russia," the words "political," "parties," and "elections" are wholly absent from the index.

This failure to appreciate the importance of parties in a federal democracy is surprising in light of the traditional importance given them in the literature. In addition to Schattschneider and Hoffstader's views, we can also cite V. O. Key (1964) and Pendelton Herring (1940), who wrote their seminal classics seemingly as if they were directly addressing the issues of contemporary federal design ("Political parties constitute a basic element of democratic institutional apparatus. They perform an essential function in the management of succession of power, as well as the process of obtaining popular consent to the course of public policy. They amass sufficient support to buttress the authority of governments; or, on the contrary, they attract or organize discontent and dissatisfaction sufficient to oust the government.... Whether the party system constitutes the only way in which succession may be arranged presents another type of question. Democratic orders seem to have discovered no other technique for the purpose..." [Key 1964: 9–10]; "With a large and heterogeneous population a working agreement among citizens can be achieved only by organization. Parties must be formed if this broader will is to be expressed" [Herring 1940: 71]).

Following in this tradition and at the opposite end of the intellectual spectrum of those who ignore the role of parties in federal relations we of course find Riker's (1964) argument about parties as the mediator between "social conditions" and the "federal bargain," McKay's (1999a,b, 2000, 2001: 5–6) views of the centrality of parties to democratic federal process ("In democratic societies political parties are the main agents for articulating interests including those based on regional or provincial distinctiveness"), and Horowitz's (1985: 293) insights into the role of parties in ethnically divided states ("the contours of the party system in an ethnically divided society have a profound effect on ethnic outcomes of party politics"). There is, however, perhaps no clearer statement as to the role of parties in a federal constitutional system than Kramer's (1994, 2000) interpretation of Wechsler's (1954) assertion that American federalism at least is protected by a political process that does not require formal defenses by, say, a supreme or constitutional court, but in which instead the electoral interests of parties are *the* key component in the protection of states' rights and the preservation of a federal balance: "[O]ver the course of American history, the principle institution in brokering state/federal relations – the one around which others developed, the one that in fact steered their development for the most part – has been the political party" (Kramer 1994: 21).[1]

[1] See also Choper (1980). For a critique of the reliance on "political safeguards" in the protection of American federalism, see Prakash and Yoo (2001) and Hamilton (2001). These

Here then we see parties as something more than mere intermediaries between citizen preferences and elite actions, or mere indicators of the overall structure of a federal system. They are the things that "convey men's loyalties to the state" and imbue the state, its definition, function, and limits, with what we might call legitimacy. They are institutional entities that are critical to shaping people's beliefs, expectations, and political strategies. In this view, then, parties sustain a level of federal centralization suitable to their electoral needs. In its most extreme form, this argument contends that parties, somehow conceptualized, determine which federal constraints will guide policy and which will be ignored; the federal constitution itself is not a constraint, at least with respect to federal matters, and the primary or only concern of those who would design a federation should be the establishment of a good party system. Thus, institutional provisions that do not affect parties and their strategies are of secondary importance, and may even be counterproductive to the development of an appropriate party system. Minimally, to the extent that those provisions do not impact the nature of the balance arrived at in partisan competition, their relevance and operation will be determined largely by the nature of that competition and the resulting willingness of politicians to abide by them or discard them altogether as a consequence of electoral incentives.

Of course, this argument, especially in this extreme form, is subject to any number of criticisms. First, the mere fact that every federation has a written constitution and every such document seeks to place some constraint on federal and federal subject jurisdictions suggests that those who have authored constitutions in the past are either uniformly uninformed (a dangerous supposition) or they perceive things not envisioned by this approach.[2] Absent a more complete theoretical treatment, coordination by convention via an endogenous political process remains a utopian proposition when the federal problem is conceptualized as distributive bargaining over things especially relevant to people's welfares and where that bargaining can infect the very rules designed to regulate conflict. But, second, this approach largely leaves unanswered the question as to the precise nature of a "good" party system – the system most conducive to federal stability – and the institutional parameters that need to be manipulated in order to encourage the development of such a system. Admittedly, the literature does attempt some guidance. Wheare (1953: 86–7), for example, argues that "A good party system is one

debates are largely normative, with limited use of empirical evidence (Epstein and King 2002). Positive analysis of the compliance of different American states with the constitutional constraints can be found in Kiewiet and Szakaly (1996) and Endersby and Towle (1997).

[2] It is plausible to argue that Great Britain can, by some definition, be classified as federal – at least, there are "many elements of federalism in the British society" (Livingston 1952: 259; see also Burgess 1995). We suspect, however, that if Britain were to become more explicitly federal, then much of its internal structure would no longer be left to unwritten convention but would instead take the form of more clearly specified constitution-like documents.

in which sectional differences of interest and opinion have their opportunity and their due weight but where also an integrated organization can be created capable of effective political action on a nation wide scale." Truman (1955: 133) argues that "the national political party is the most responsive instrument of restraint upon federalism's centrifugal tendencies." Wholly consistent with this view is Riker's (1964: 129) more substantive observation that "the federal relationship is centralized according to the degree to which parties organized to operate the central government control the parties organized to operate the constituent governments. This amounts to the assertion that the proximate cause of variations in the degree of centralization (or peripheralization) in the constitutional structure of a federalism is the variation in degree of party centralization." Of course, there are those comparative assessments that point to such Level 1 and Level 2 parameters as enumerated powers, Switzerland's system of referenda, the presidentialism and separation of powers of the United States, Germany's constitutional allocation of federal administrative functions, and Canada's politically impotent Senate as critical determinants of a state's political party system.

Unfortunately, these observations are too general. What is especially unclear in the absence of a theoretical structure that disentangles cause from effect is the precise nature of the relationship between stability, a "federal friendly" party system, and the institutional choices that encourage such parties. Does a federal-friendly party system yield a stable, balanced, and efficient federation or is that system the product of such a federation? Unfortunately, even careful comparative cross-national assessments are unlikely to yield the theoretical structure we require. Certainly such assessments will suggest hypotheses and point in the direction of key parameters and causal relations, but they cannot escape the statistical fact that fundamental cause cannot be discerned from a purely empirical approach that allows for more variables than we have observations. Thus, we cannot yet exclude the possibility that parties in a stable and well-functioning federation are, for one reason or another, merely auxiliary agents of those Level 1 and Level 2 provisions that describe and delimit the state, including those that set jurisdictional boundaries, that prohibit secession, that assert the supremacy of federal law, that seek to regulate the political structures of regional governments, and that assign oversight of the constitution to the courts. Nor can we exclude the hypothesis that the operation of these provisions is determined by other things, including the nature of party competition, which is, in turn, determined by something else. Indeed, in light of views such as Schattschneider's, Key's, Hofstadter's, and Herring's, it is perilous to assume that even an extreme hypothesis such as Kramer's is less viable than anything else offered in the literature to explain federal stability and efficiency.

Placing responsibility for federal performance on the shoulders of party systems does have the benefit, admittedly, of bypassing the issue of constitutional enforcement because in such a scheme institutions are not self-enforceable per se but instead are selectively used by parties in the pursuit of the self-interest of their members. Enforcement, if it exists, exists because political elites, operating within the shell of parties and motivated by the forces that party competition engenders, choose to enforce. This argument, though, cannot be complete. Unless there are identifiable constraints that coordinate political elite choices within party structures, and which those elites are disinclined to break, the problem of federal bargaining merely reemerges in a slightly different form – as a conflict within and between parties rather than among federal subjects and against the federal center. And our earlier discussion of the dangers of unconstrained bargaining applies to parties as much as anything else. Thus, even if Riker, Wheare, Truman, McKay, Horowitz, and Kramer are essentially correct about the importance of parties for understanding federal relations, party systems need to be encouraged by appropriate institutional choices lest parties of an inappropriate sort become the primary vehicles of political competition and federal disruption. Put simply, there is nothing inherently good and noble about parties per se that prevents them from participating in those disputes that threaten federal stability, as is well illustrated by the collapse of national parties and party systems in ethnically and regionally polarized societies and the numerous instances of the emergence of parties with the avowed purpose of upsetting the institutional status quo.

6.2 Parties in a Democracy

Despite the possibility of dysfunctional parties and the admittedly American-centric perspective of scholars such as Schattschneider, Key, Hofstatder, and Herring, it is the operating hypothesis of this volume that a properly designed political party system – or, more correctly, an institutional arrangement that has as its primary goal that of encouraging a party system of a particular type – is the most durable source of federal stability. However, to dissect the role of parties properly and to identify those institutional parameters that need to be considered when attempting to encourage federal-friendly parties, it would seem that we should first dispense with one piece of terminology – namely, that of "party" as unitary actor. Although parties are sometimes well-organized hierarchical entities with a definitive leadership, a coherent political agenda, and tangible resources, more often than not they are none of these things. Parties, as in the United States, are often Potemkin villages characterized by little more than a sharing of labels among politicians and political elites. Indeed, although the United States is generally described as a two-party system, it is more accurate to say that it is a *two-label system* in which a vast number of local and state political entities share the label Democrat or Republican and meet on a more or less regular basis to socialize, drink, and perhaps even nominate or endorse the campaigns of various candidates for public office. Herring's (1940: 217) New Deal description of

American parties is as applicable today (with the appropriate substitution of labels) as it was when he wrote: "The Republican party is better viewed not as a national phenomenon but rather as an organization containing New England Republicans, prairie Republicans, and lily-white Republicans. The varied natures of their Republicanism result from their local traditions, loyalties, and economic and social conditions. There are Democrats of the cotton states, Tammany Democrats, New Deal Democrats, and Democrats who 'take a walk.' Concern with national party principles is ill suited to the task of compounding regional differences."

We appreciate that the United States almost certainly offers a limiting case of parties in decentralized if not wholly amorphous form and that European parties commonly stand in sharp contrast to this example. But even there parties often lack a central directive except when we speak of their legislative or parliamentary manifestations, and then only for purposes of forming a governing coalition. In fact, it is not unfair to say that European parties are centralized and organizationally secure – except when they are otherwise.

A second reason for abandoning the notion of party as unitary actor is that until we do so, we cannot understand their full impact on people's motives and, in particular, on how elected elites can be encouraged to be imperfect agents of their constituencies as described previously. If Schattschneider and others are correct in their assessments of the importance of parties, and if those elected officials who bargain within a federation as representatives of federal subjects are to be imperfect agents of those they represent while voters nevertheless reward them for doing so, then parties must be understood in terms of the incentives they create within a polity, including the incentive of politicians to form and sustain parties of a particular sort. Indeed, the impact of no institution, organization, rule, constraint, law, and constitutional provision can be understood or predicted until we understand its impact on individual motives (and the impact of those motives on them). Treating a party as if it were a thinking unitary decision maker with a well-defined preference thwarts this epistemological imperative.

To uncover the special role parties might play in a federation, then, we first need to understand why parties as manifestations of a particular form of collective action exist in the first place – why politicians value them and why voters pay them any heed. Of course, the Founders of American democracy identified parties as but another faction to be controlled by constitutional constraint and the operation of the state: "There is nothing I dread so much as a division of the Republic into two great parties, each arranged under its leader and converting measures in opposition to each other" (John Adams 1780, as cited in McCullough 2001: 422). Nevertheless, following ratification of the U.S. Constitution, James Madison proceeded almost immediately to take advantage of those nascent state, county, and local political entities to organize a party in support of Jefferson's bid for the presidency upon

Washington's retirement. The question we should ask, then, is why parties, whether of the European or American sort, exist universally in a democracy – or, more properly, why most people would say a democracy is "mature" only after its politics are characterized by competition in the context of a stable, well-defined party system.

The most evident answer to this question is that they serve as an informational tool for the electorate. Political information is not costless and since even the smallest constituencies rarely offer an individual voter the opportunity to be decisive, voters can reasonably assume that it is impractical, even irrational, to gather much information about the alternatives presented to them – unless, of course, the voter regards politics much like a sporting event in which memorizing batting averages, yards gained rushing, free-throw percentages, and goals scored per game is itself an enjoyable pastime and not instrumental to any other end. At times voters may know a great deal about individual candidates as when scandal or advocacy of some especially salient policy dominates the headlines. But candidates in a mass democracy cannot rely on such detailed information to carry them successfully into office. Instead, it is prudent to associate oneself with a brand label, like one for soup, cereal, or baby food, that conveys if not the candidate's general policy predispositions, then at least the security associated with being a member of a larger entity that is itself protective of the value of that label, an entity unlikely to endorse candidates with ideas and predispositions unacceptable to the "party's" core source of support. Thus, if a candidate is endorsed or otherwise carries a label such as "Socialist Worker," and if the party in question is known by voters to act largely in the interest of "Workers," then voters who classify themselves accordingly can feel the same security in voting for that candidate as they do when buying a product from a firm that is known to be generally protective of the quality of its merchandise. Knowing that a candidate is a Democrat or a Republican in America, a member of the Conservative or Labour Party in Britain, or a member of the Christian Democrats or the SPD in Germany does not tell you how that person would act in specific instances if elected (except perhaps when parliamentary party discipline is high). But it does tell voters something about a candidate's general sympathies with respect to, say, welfare, taxes, and government spending. And because no vote is likely to be decisive, the cost of an erroneous choice – one a voter might change if provided with better information – is slight and is certainly lower than the cost of securing that information.

Of course, in some political systems and for some parties, labels do convey relatively precise information about some of the policies candidates prefer to implement (e.g., Europe's environmental parties, Israel's religious parties, or parties in Belgium that associate with one side or the other of its linguistic divide), whereas in other systems labels convey little more than a vague ideological orientation with respect to the interests of labor versus capital. But even when issue-specific informational content is minimal, labels do offer valuable signals. If the parties are long-standing and competitive, then among other things they tell voters that the candidates using their labels are unlikely to be radical revolutionaries, are prone to be defenders of the constitutional order, and most likely support a broad range of implicit long-term intra- and interparty agreements. Again with reference to the amorphous content of America's parties, "Both Democrats and Republicans have, on the whole, the same vision of the kind of society there ought to be in the United States. They differ only over whether that society is more likely to be attained by . . . much or little regulation of labor unions, by one or another form of taxation – or by Republicans or Democrats holding office" (Boorstin 1953: 137). Party labels also tell voters that candidates for state or federal legislative office who share those labels will most likely be part of the mainstream of legislative organization and will thereby be more effective representatives of constituency interests than are candidates bearing other ostensibly more obscure or ephemeral labels even if those candidates more explicitly articulate the interests of their particular constituencies during the campaign.

Despite the nearly universal importance of party labels, the preceding discussion raises the question as to why parties and the nature of party systems are presumed to be critically important to the *functioning* of a democracy. Although as consumers we might prefer to buy a brand-label soup or cereal, we do not normally believe that the number of brands (provided there is more than one) or the internal organization of the firms that hold them has much to do with our nutritional health or the satisfaction we derive from eating soup or cereal. Why would we assume otherwise with respect to parties? Why, as political scientists, would we care about the number of parties in a democracy, about their longevity, or about their internal organization? If, in fact, they are amorphous entities formed by little more than the labels their members share, how is it that they come to serve any useful systemic purpose?

We can approach the answer to this question by noting that, among other things, parties allow candidates to pool monetary and reputational resources while providing ladders of political advancement in democracy's political hierarchy. Put simply, to the extent that voters rely on party labels when choosing among candidates, a party's endorsement secured through a formal nomination process becomes an important, and even the primary, avenue to higher office. With this endorsement and its associated label comes a ready means to enhance a candidate's standing in his narrow constituency, and subsequently allows the candidate to compete in constituencies broader than the one he currently represents and in which he is otherwise unknown. Indeed, the collection of party organizations that exist in those constituencies is a resource for mobilizing voters and fiscal support that few candidates can replicate in the course of a single campaign or even a long sequence of campaigns.

Again, however, why should we care about the career opportunities of political elites any more than we care about the avenues of advancement of corporate executives in those firms whose brand labels we trust as consumers? The answer here lies in the incentives such parties – parties that promise political advancement – engender among its candidates. Among other things, party labels are important for the trade-offs they compel candidates to make. Much like a corporation with a brand name, candidates will cultivate their label so that it is uniformly attractive to voters. Indeed, we can say that a label converts the private benefit a politician might derive from good actions into a public good for all politicians who share his or her label. Good performance, then, has a multiplicative positive effect, but so does bad performance, and to this extent members of a party have an interest in not only attracting as many popular and viable candidates as possible to their flag but also in facilitating the electoral standing of their colleagues across constituencies. Thus, if the treatment of some issue is especially problematic for a party's candidates at one level of government, its candidates at all levels have an incentive to find a solution, such as moving the issue to a different level or resolving the issue internally within the party. If the label's currency is diminished by open disputes within a party, the solution is, in lieu of maintaining ideological purity and contracting one's coalition, to negotiate internal differences out of public view and, in a self-regulating way, to otherwise repress disruptive issues. For example, state governors in the United States might chafe under the weight of federal rules, regulations, and mandated programs. But such things are rarely allowed to become a dispute in which, say, Democratic governors openly challenge a Democratic president so as to make such disputes the centerpiece of their reelection campaigns. Instead, state governments choose to act much like other interest groups – lobbying members of the legislature behind the scenes for more advantageous legislation or negotiating with members of the administration for changes in policy. The incentive, then, to cultivate a party label and to expand one's electoral coalition yields the subsidiary motivation to isolate disputes from the part of the political process that can divide an electorate and inflame passions.

This review underscores what we see as the two key ingredients to understanding the importance of a party in facilitating a stable federalism – the cultivation of labels by political elites, and the ladders of advancement party systems offer those elites. To elaborate this argument and to understand its implications for federal design, the next section turns to consider precisely what it is that we want parties and a party system to accomplish for us.

6.3 The Idealized Party System

Although we earlier rejected the notion of party as unitary actor, one way to envision what we want from a party system is to imagine a party as a player who, armed with the proper incentives, can be introduced into the federal game for the explicit purpose of resolving the critical problems of stability. We hasten to add that we are not assuming that we can directly provide for such a player or that some organizational entity can, in and of itself, perform the role outlined here. Nevertheless, entertaining the thought experiment of assuming that the requisite unitary actor can somehow be willed into existence can yield a useful template for subsequent design efforts.

Briefly, if the main problem of federal institutional stability is disruptive bargaining over outcomes that can infect the institutions that seek to direct and constrain that bargaining, then we want a player who can act to isolate bargaining over substantive issues from those institutional constraints, encourage political outcomes that are profitable for society at large, moderate the temptation among political actors to overthrow status quo institutional arrangements, and, as part of the incentives it engenders, impose its will. There are, we suspect, many paths to this end, but one way to accomplish this is to bring into existence a player who does not hold preferences for some particular vector of cost assignments, aside from those that are reasonably efficient, and who can engender motives among all other political actors to abide by its decisions so that those decisions are self-enforcing and decisive. Such a player would, by design, have no incentive to move from one institutional alternative to another as long as no feasible alternative promised a greater overall level of benefits *for that player*. From its perspective, all efficient institutional alternatives are equivalent, and to the extent that the status quo facilitates its decisiveness, that player would possess a positive incentive to maintain (enforce) current arrangements.

It is no mystery that the identity of this new player in our analysis is the political party, although shortly it will be necessary to strip our discussion of its anthropomorphic character and speak of the motives and strategies of real people. Here we note simply that placing this burden on a party or party system derives, in part, from the fact that individual federal subjects or even coalitions of subjects are unlikely to fill the role outlined here, because the thing we need to control, whether based on ethnic conflicts, the struggle for control of natural resources, or simply the ongoing contest for political power, is precisely their interest in challenging the institutional status quo. Nor is the federal center, either in the guise of a chief executive or national legislature, likely to be any more satisfactory. Absent other endogenously enforceable constraints, we cannot suppose that the center will not be captured by a subset of federal subjects or achieve a life of its own to the detriment of all subjects. The courts alone cannot perform this function because they possess no independent mechanism for enforcing their decisions, and because their composition, if not the motives of their members, are subject to the manipulation of other political actors. More generally, none of the institutional constraints discussed thus far in this volume, constitutional or otherwise, offer a solution since the issue of the self-enforceability of the constraints we prefer to impose on our imaginary player's actions and motives remains unresolved until we establish the game in which the constitutional-political process is embedded. Finally, although "benevolent" dictators might seem to be an appealing alternative in some contexts, too often such a dictatorship, even if successfully implemented, cannot be sustained beyond the life of its creator.

The fragile benevolence of dictatorship also tells us that merely throwing the onus of stability on a political party does not resolve the matter of identifying the source of our imaginary player's motives and the mechanisms we might want it to employ when attempting to sustain the policies it chooses. A party in a democracy, however, is a creature of electoral competition. We know that chief among the factors determining its motives (again, pardon the anthropomorphic view) are electoral rules and the geographic distribution of the party's membership and electoral support. These things, however, are themselves endogenous. Electoral rules can be changed (and, indeed, are commonly not even a part of a constitution or the Level 1 rules that seek to regulate intergovernmental relations), whereas the nature of a party's membership and basis of electoral support is something that needs to be engineered, if it can be engineered at all, only indirectly by the choice of political institutions, including the structure of legislative representation. Nevertheless, staying with our idealized scheme, there are two extremes to be considered. At one there are those parties which derive their support primarily from a single federal subject or subset of subjects, or a readily identifiable part of the population (ethnic, religious, and so on). Such a party, owing to its evident objective of fashioning and implementing a redistribution favoring its supporters, has the same incentive to challenge the institutional status quo as its constituency (which would include federal subjects if its support correlates with geography). At the other extreme are those parties which deem the benefit of each federal subject as being of approximately equal importance (adjusted, of course, by such things as population), which cater to no identifiable group within the electorate, and which thereby prefer more equitable allocations of benefits.[3] To the extent that existing public policy yields such an allocation, a party of this type will be more likely to champion the institutional status quo owing to the electoral success it enjoys under it. Reality and feasibility lie somewhere between these extremes, since even in

[3] We need to be careful and more precise here. If, for instance, a party's support within a subject (e.g., its probability of winning that subject) is linearly and monotonically increasing with the benefits it brings to that subject, and if all subjects weigh equally in the electoral formula for winning, then the party should be indifferent among a wide range of equitable and inequitable allocations of benefits. However, suppose a party's support is monotonically increasing with benefits, but at a decreasing rate (i.e., diminishing marginal returns within a subject). Then if the same functional relationship between benefits and votes pertains in each subject and if, as before, all subjects are of equal electoral weight, then the unique optimal allocation of benefits for a party is one that divides those benefits equally across all subjects.

an idealized state we want a party capable of pursuing such redistributive goals as encouraging the economic growth of less developed regions and awarding compensating privileges to otherwise disadvantaged minorities regardless of their geographic concentration or dispersion. Nevertheless, it is clearly a party of the second type that we prefer when encouraging institutional stability or at least institutional inertia.

What we require, then, is a fictional player that possesses the motive as well as the means to increase the payoffs to more than a simple majority of federal subjects. Indeed, we do not even want a player that chooses to form and sustain a coalition of some supermajority subset of federal subjects to the permanent detriment of the minority. Doing so not only violates the ostensible purpose of federalism (i.e., the realization of mutual gains by all components of the federation), but can also threaten the state's ultimate viability. Instead, we want a player that, at least in the context of federal bargaining, violates Riker's (1962) size principle on a grand scale by including at least portions of the electorate from more federal subjects than otherwise seem necessary to ensure a redistributive outcome, and which can sustain such violations into the indefinite future.

Clearly, the parties that can emerge in a democracy need not match this description. Especially in divided societies, parties (or more properly, party elites and candidates) are more likely to prefer asymmetric allocations of benefits, with different parties emerging to represent competing allocation agendas. Here, however, we see a partial resolution of the dispute between Riker and Dahl discussed in Chapter 1, and a reemergence of the Madisonian argument for the extended republic. If a society is described by two or a few clear-cut ethnic, religious, linguistic, or racial divisions, parties, unless dissuaded somehow from doing so, will most naturally tend to form around those divisions so that compromise and negotiation can only occur outside of them. But if society is beset with innumerable crosscutting cleavages, then parties, absent any natural division of the electorate, are compelled by their competitive natures to address internally whatever disputes might arise within their electoral coalitions. To this extent Dahl is correct to note the ameliorating effects of pluralism in an extended republic. But Riker is right as well to assert that the institutions within which parties must operate must be conducive to the full expression of this pluralism. It is Riker's perspective, moreover, that is our source of leverage in design. When contemplating the institutional form that today's federal state should assume, we are unlikely to possess Madison's advantage of being able to gaze westward and see vast lands awaiting settlement and the corresponding promise of an emerging plural society. Short of redefining national boundaries, we cannot engineer society's plural or nonplural character, except, perhaps, to recommend the dismemberment of a federation or the creation of a new one from otherwise sovereign entities. But since we have defined as the perimeter of our subject the design of a federation once the decision has been made to implement a federal system, our objective must be to find institutional alternatives that would compel parties in divided societies to act *as if* they existed in a pluralistic environment. This is no mean feat and it may, in fact, often be an unachievable goal. There may not be a democratic solution to the Bosnias of the world.

Moreover, framing the requirements of our fictional player in terms of Riker's size principle does highlight an additional problem of design. Specifically, there is no guarantee that a party, oversized or otherwise, will command the actions of even its members, with the internal tensions of a party likely to grow along with its coalition. If parties are but labels that denote crude ideologies and policy preferences, it may be difficult to see how loyalties are established of a sort that ensure near consensual adherence to the party's program and, in its idealized form, adherence to nondisruptive federal bargaining. This, however, is a critical characteristic of our idealized party. It must command the loyalties of all members, regardless of the constituencies they serve, since otherwise the disruptive bargaining that can characterize federal relations would be transferred to relations within the party itself. In that case, the party would no longer act *as if* it were a unitary being and would not function in the political process as the ideal type we intend.

6.4 Integrated Parties

We have not sketched this notion of the idealized party merely to establish some utopian goal, for in fact Riker and Wheare do provide substantive guidance in identifying the party most conducive to federal stability. Specifically, they hint at the notion of the *integrated* party (or, equivalently, the integrated party system) in which politicians at one level of government bear an organizational relationship to politicians at other levels (as well as to politicians within their level). Dyck (1991: 129) states that "if a political party functions more or less successfully at both levels of government and if the relations between the two levels are generally close, it can be called an integrated party." We here can begin to clarify the meaning of such integration for elite incentives with two examples, drawn from American politics, that convey this concept's meaning. First, consider the (possibly apocryphal) story of the candidate for local judge in New York City during one of Roosevelt's presidential campaigns, who gave his campaign funds to the local Democratic Party in anticipation of professional assistance (Lubell 1952). Weeks passed as he waited for his campaign to commence, but he saw nothing – no posters, campaign buttons, flyers, or radio broadcasts that mentioned his name. Agitated and uneasy, he returned to party headquarters to complain and learn what had been done with his monies. Seeking to reassure the candidate that his funds had, in fact, been put to good use in promoting his candidacy, the local party chairman took him to the southern tip of Manhattan where the ferry from Staten Island docked and, as a ferry pulled in, pointed to the floating debris that swirled at the ferry's stern, towed by its wake, and said "the name of your ferry is Franklin Delano Roosevelt."

This story or ones similar to it are commonly offered to illustrate presidential coattails and the fact that in an election in which voters confront scores of candidates about whom they know little or nothing, the essential commodity possessed by candidates is partisan labels shared with popular candidates for national office. What we want to emphasize here, however, is the bidirectionality of this relationship. While the name Roosevelt and the label "Democrat" doubtlessly helped the local candidate for judge and countless other Democratic candidates for office that year, the organizations erected to nominate and facilitate local and state elections were and remain an essential part of any national candidate's campaign. The candidate for judge does not win unless Roosevelt wins; but Roosevelt does not win unless the candidate for judge and thousands like him integrate their campaigns with his – including, as in this example, allowing their campaign resources to be used to elect Roosevelt. Thus, in a symbiotic relationship like those found in nature, local and national parties and candidates rely on each other for their survival and success.

Our second example comes from McKitrick's (1967) assessment of the fundamental reasons for the different fortunes of Lincoln and Jefferson Davis in organizing the war efforts of the Union and Confederacy respectively.[4] It is generally accepted by historians that throughout the war Lincoln enjoyed far greater success at maintaining a united front and at ensuring the subservience of state militias to national direction than did his counterpart in the Confederacy. Especially in light of the fact that through most of that war, the Union seemed on the verge of defeat, explanations for this difference have focused on the relative political skills of the two presidential antagonists. McKitrick, however, offers an alternative hypothesis: namely, the existence of a competitive (and integrated) party system in the North and an uncompetitive system in the South. Briefly, following secession, the South was left with a single-party system that lost much if not all of its unifying focus once the issue of secession had seemingly been resolved. The Union, in contrast, retained not only the whole of the Republican Party but the northern wing of the Democratic Party. Because northern Democrats remained a viable political force, capturing several governorships and control of several state legislatures, Republican candidates for state and local office were compelled to rely on Lincoln's national leadership for political survival, just as Lincoln, mindful of the role of governors in the prosecution of the war and implementation of the draft, and equally important, uncertain of his prospects in the forthcoming 1864 presidential election, never

[4] McKitrick acknowledges that the roots of his argument derive from Porter (1960).

lost sight of the need to maintain the support of state and local Republican Party leaders and candidates. Neither Davis nor the governors of the states of the Confederacy confronted equivalent political challenges, so governors there had little to gain politically from coordinating or cooperating with Davis when doing so ran counter to the interests of their state constituencies. Thus, as with Roosevelt and the candidate for judge, Lincoln and Union governors were compelled by the forces of political competition to coordinate their electoral strategies, including, in this instance, cooperating on national matters (e.g., the draft) even when regional interests dictated otherwise.[5]

What these two examples demonstrate is that mutual dependence in the never-ending campaign for reelection is critical to the relationship between local and national politicians in an integrated party. More specifically, if we dissect these examples while keeping in mind the brief wish list offered in the previous section for an ideal federal party, we can infer the following criteria when assessing whether a party is integrated:

1. The party's organization exists at all levels – national, regional, and local – and fields candidates at all levels.
2. The party's electoral success at the national level facilitates the electoral success of its candidates at the local and regional level. Defecting from the party coalition, especially if it is successful nationally, is costly to local and regional candidates.
3. The regional and local organizations and candidates of the party retain sufficient autonomy, nevertheless, to direct their own campaigns and to defect from the national party (or a candidate of the party for national office).
4. National platforms are acceptable in local terms and are interpreted in local terms by local politicians campaigning on behalf of national parties in national elections.
5. Every component part of the party contributes to the party's overall success, so that the defection of any part diminishes the party's overall strength in its competition with other parties for other offices.
6. Winning nationally requires that the party and its candidates campaign locally.
7. The offices the party seeks to fill through election at the local and regional levels are meaningful – they control valuable resources and those who fill them can implement policy that can either aid or thwart the policies implemented at the national level.

5 While television advertising, direct mail, and changes in the campaign finance regulation contributed to the rise of candidate-centered campaign techniques undercutting parties' monopoly on campaign resources (Wattenberg 1991), American parties still play an important role by providing candidates with valuable endorsements, money, information, and activists' support (Aldrich 1995).

Although some of the prerequisites for satisfying these requirements will be contained in Level 2 rules and institutions, we are not yet prepared to detail the variety of institutional parameters we believe are critical to that development. First we must specify precisely how an integrated party encourages federal stability – how it might act as our idealized player via the incentives it creates among its members to cooperate, coordinate, and avert direct challenges to the institutional status quo. We can begin by noting that one characteristic of the party implicitly described by the preceding conditions is a "wedding cake" structure that mimics the federation and spans it both horizontally and vertically. Thus, as we noted earlier about the United States at least, it is incorrect to say that political competition occurs in the context of a 2-party system; it is a 100- or even 100,000-party system, where each of those parties is local and regional but where all of them operate under one of two labels and organize themselves in the national legislature and in national election campaigns according to those labels.[6] One consequence of this decentralization is that American parties differ ideologically as much within themselves as from each other. A subsidiary consequence is that to compete for the presidency salient issues are negotiated within party structures, lest a party be unable to organize an effective national campaign.

By its very nature, then, if the party (or, more properly, its members) is ultimately critical to the enactment of change, either in policy or institutional structure, then an integrated party inflates the size of a coalition – both the coalition of voters and the coalition of political elites – necessary to enact that change. Unsurprising, then, is Rossiter's (1960: 11) characterization of American parties as "vast, gaudy, friendly umbrellas under which all Americans, whoever and wherever and however-minded they may be, are invited to stand for the sake of being counted in the next election." Parties of this type are inherently conservative if only to avoid radical proposals that alienate any core parts of their membership, and among the consequences of this conservatism is one that is especially important in a federation; namely, in their ideal form, those who hold or seek national office as representatives of an integrated party will find it to their advantage to withdraw from state-level political discourse, while state and local level politicians will prefer to focus their campaign rhetoric and policy proposals on things other than the national-level issues. Of course, from time to time a regional candidate, as in California with respect to the issue of illegal immigration or federal energy policy, might campaign on an issue that directly pits the interests of the state against the federal government. Such conflict is normal when it occurs

6 For example, if one attempts to look up the telephone number for, say, the Republican Party in the San Gabriel Valley of California, one finds instead telephone listings for "Republican Party of Alhambra," "of Arcadia," "of Whittier," "of West Covina," "of the 59th Assembly District," and of "Los Angeles." Put simply, "American parties persist only at state and local levels" (Chandler 1987: 153).

across party lines, as when, say, the governor of a region is of a different party than the head of the national government. But otherwise jurisdictional disputes are muted in order to maintain party cohesion, and if the authority or functions of different levels of government are to change, then it is in the interest of an integrated party to ensure that that change occurs only in a slow and evolutionary manner and when sufficient consensus exists against the institutional status quo.

It might seem that we can go most of the way to establishing an unwillingness on the part of politicians from different levels of government to trespass in the jurisdictions of others by simply adjusting the constituent connections of national politicians. The argument here would be that if elected from narrow territorial constituencies, members of the national legislature are less likely to assault the autonomy of state and local governments than if their attachment to specific constituencies is weak or nonexistent (as, for instance, with Russia's national proportional representation scheme for the State Duma). This was the argument for the U.S. Senate as originally conceived, and for its House of Representatives as it has existed throughout the life of the republic. But even if we ignore the change that has occurred in the ability of state governments to control members of the Senate, representation schemes, while hardly unimportant insofar as they encourage a within versus a without form of federal bargaining, can provide only a partial solution to the alleviation of jurisdictional conflicts. There remains a creeping assault on the autonomy of regional governments, against which the constituencies of individual legislators need not provide any safeguard. Specifically, a representative of a unit in the national legislature may very well consider that body an appropriate place to make most if not all decisions regarding his own as well as all other federal units. And, as we know from experience (see, e.g., Bednar et al. 2001), such encroachment is a robust possibility. Thus, we must find ways to motivate political elites within and outside federal subjects to abide by the rules by which federal process is conducted and to campaign without resorting to attacks on the jurisdictional authority and autonomy of other levels of government. Echoing the argument of the preceding chapter, we want political elites to be imperfect agents of their constituencies.

The route to this end via the notion of an integrated party is to define such a party as one in which, for national politicians, the long-term strategy of preserving the party's overall electoral coalition takes precedence over the short-term tactic of seeking immediate gains from challenging local and regional autonomy. Even though the unit representatives at the national level might, ceteris paribus, prefer aggrandizing as much power as possible, they will not act accordingly because it is more important for local and regional party members to remain political allies. Conversely, local and regional politicians will not seek to disrupt unduly the functions of the federal government for fear of damaging the electoral standing of national politicians from their party and, thereby, their own subsequent electoral chances.

Thus, state governors during the American Civil War were willing to enforce federal law with respect to a draft despite the evident public opposition to it (including riots in New York that needed to be suppressed via the intervention of the army). As Kramer (1994: 1507) states matters, "all factions of a[n integrated] party, no matter how bitter their squabbles, are agreed at least on the preservation of the party itself. The fact that they continue to associate themselves with it sufficiently indicates that, for example, even the most disaffected Republicans would rather be Republicans than Democrats. In short, intra-party squabbles are moderated by the understood compact to preserve the party in a way that conflicts between parties are not."

Here we note that a critical feature of an integrated party that facilitates cooperation across levels of government – cooperation that often matches the efficiency and flexibility we seek from federal design – is what we might call mutual delegation. If a party draws support from many units with diverse preferences, there will typically be a variety of issues on which it would want to tailor its electoral platform and policies to the particular demands of each unit, especially if those demands are noncontradictory. The best way to accomplish this and to monitor those demands is not only to allow regional and local party autonomy but also to motivate them to that end by letting subnational governments retain a substantial measure of sovereignty. Doing so, moreover, isolates the national party and its national campaigns from local and regional conflicts, the resolution of which provides few if any benefits at the national level. Indeed, these issues, if taken to the national level, are the ones most likely to provoke an institutional renegotiation that can threaten the positions of national political elites. Conversely, just as there are issues that are problematic for a party when addressed at the national level, there are issues of the opposite sort as when locally unresolvable problems nevertheless demand attention (e.g., minority rights) and are treated as the de facto jurisdiction of the federal government. In this way a local incumbent can take credit for national policy among those who care strongly about the issue, while downplaying the issue generally – perhaps even offering the argument that "the federal government made me do it."

Ideally, of course, this exchange across levels of government will match the economic justification for federalism and the European's notion of subsidiarity – that of surrendering to local jurisdictions those policies which are most efficiently addressed by them and allowing the federal government to treat issues with a larger domain of externalities or more evident economies of scale. Here, however, our discussion deals with a special type of efficiency and a motivation that differs from that of simple economics – the political motivation of maximizing the party's overall competitiveness. If a party system satisfies this requirement, then the division of jurisdictions, even if taken out of alignment by some external shock, will be temporary for a federation whose balance of powers is self-equilibrating via its party system in the neighborhood of a constitutionally prescribed institutional configuration.

An issue that is too controversial to be resolved by consensus at the national level, for example, can drift into the jurisdiction of subnational governments so that local preferences dictate local resolutions. At the same time, issues that are salient for minorities within federal subjects but which cannot be resolved to their satisfaction owing to the presence of near indifferent majorities everywhere, could reappear at the national level, where legislators are unlikely to be penalized by the indifferent majorities in their constituencies for merely participating in (in contrast with fully controlling as a local government would) decisions they care little about but which are likely to attract the attention and votes of intensely interested minorities.

What is important to appreciate about this process is that it is self-generating and self-regulating. In the United States at least, "the parties haven't self-consciously brokered federal/state relations; no one made deliberate decisions about how to allocate power and required officials to abide by them. Rather, the parties influenced federalism by establishing a framework for politics in which officials at different levels were dependent on each other to get (and stay) elected" (Kramer 1994: 1512).[7] Of course, we need to reemphasize that we have not yet identified the institutional means to induce such electoral incentives. Integrated parties are not born of nothing, an inherent part of a federation. They, as much as anything else, are the product of design – the design of institutions that compel politicians to erect parties of a particular sort because that sort, and not some other, serves their interests.

6.5 Integration outside the United States

If the preceding argument is correct, then the trick to federal design is not only to encourage integrated parties but also parties that efficiently transfer responsibilities in such a way as to minimize the disruptive consequences of conflict and exogenous shocks to the political-economic system. Before we can assert, however, that integration as we describe it holds the key to a stable and productive federal state we must expand our discussion beyond examples drawn from the American experience. We should ask whether integrated parties are possible only in presidential systems, whether presidential systems that are federal require a specific type of party that federal parliamentary systems do not, and whether there are institutional substitutes for parties of the American sort that can be found elsewhere in stable and efficient federations. To state this differently, notice that if we look at the provisions of a federal constitution that are not explicitly labeled federal, perhaps the two most salient institutional parameters that nonetheless seem germane to the

[7] Rodden (2001) assesses the validity of this argument for federal practices in Germany, Australia, and Canada, devising comparable measures of the extent to which the vote for subunit politicians is affected by the vote for their copartisans at the federal level.

state's federal character are the choice of presidential versus parliamentary government, and the structure of representation in the national parliament, most notably the choice of single- versus multimember (proportional) district representation. Thus, we can reformulate our questions to ask whether the choice of any one of the four combinations of parameter values here impacts the likelihood of a polity developing an integrated party system.

In contrast to the American version of an integrated party system whereby electoral outcomes are defined largely in terms of two parties, parliamentary systems, especially those that employ some variant of party-list proportional representation, generally tolerate a larger number of labels and parties (Taagepera and Shugart 1989; Shugart and Carey 1992; Ordeshook and Shvetsova 1994; Jones 1995). At the same time, the imperative of controlling the government encourages stricter party discipline, at least in parliament, and therefore requires a tighter programmatic connection between organizational levels at the electoral stage. Absent competition for the presidency or equivalent motives (and possibly absent as well the strategic imperatives of a winner-take-all majoritarian format in legislative districts), it is reasonable to suppose that, ceteris paribus, members of regional, issue-specific, or ideologically similar parties would find fewer reasons to coordinate under a single label or organizational structure. Because regional, special-interest, and third parties in parliamentary systems can all hope to play a role in the formation of the national government and exert a corresponding impact on policy, they need not negotiate policy disputes prior to an election in order to win representation. Instead, resolution of disputes can be postponed, to be negotiated ultimately in parliament, while extreme positions, including those on institutional issues, can continue to characterize party electoral platforms.

Our goal in this chapter is to describe the linkage between party systems and federal institutional stability, leaving design issues to the chapters that follow. Nevertheless, it is important to note that acceptable solutions are found in different basic types of institutional arrangements. Thus, parliamentary Germany and Australia appear to have party systems that function much like the one we see in the United States, whereas parliamentary Canada does not, although it relies, as Australia and the United States do, on single-mandate districts for elections to its parliament. Adding to the mix of institutional and historical circumstances considered, we also consider India's postindependence party system, which, together with our discussion of Australia and Canada, serves perhaps to emphasize the fact that there is no unique path to party integration.

Australian Federalism and the Role of Parties

Of the four cases we consider here, Australia comes closest perhaps to the U.S. institutional configuration (although absent a president, it has a meaningful Senate intended to represent individual states, and a lower chamber

TABLE 6.1. *Labor and Liberal Party Performance in Australian State Elections, 1945–2001*

State	Number of State Elections	Two-Party Share (%)	Range	Largest Party Share (%)	Number of State Elections Won by Federal Opposition Party
New South Wales	18	80.1	67.0 (1999) 86.0 (1976)	46.7	13
Queensland	20	66.3	52.1 (1957) 76.3 (1956)	43.9	12
South Australia	18	87.7	75.6 (1997) 95.8 (1968)	49.2	13
Tasmania	17	89.3	85.4 (1982) 98.0 (1955)	49.8	11
Victoria	19	80.7	61.5 (1945) 91.9 (1985)	43.3	10
Western Australia	18	84.1	68.4 (2001) 94.3 (1986)	45.7	13

elected in single-member districts). And at a superficial level at least, the same seems true of its party system. Were we to calculate the shares of the vote in state elections won by Republicans and Democrats in the United States, that share would nearly universally exceed 90 percent. Table 6.1 gives the average vote shares of the two largest Australian federal parties – Labor and Liberals – in each of that country's six states in contests for regional parliamentary seats from 1945 to 2001, as well as the average share won by the winning party. Notice first that in all states with the exception of Queensland (where other national parties managed to occupy second place), Labor and Liberals (or Liberal coalitions at the state level) are the two largest contenders. Second, although only Tasmania and South Australia approach the level of two-party dominance witnessed in the United States, the data in Table 6.1 suggest that Australia is not a sharp contrast to the United States. Thus, although a parliamentary form opens the door to minor parties, that form need not preclude two national parties maintaining their competitiveness at the subnational level reasonably uniformly throughout the federation.

One might conclude, then, that Australia's national parties play an integrating role similar to the one played by Democrats and Republicans in the United States. Nevertheless, although Australia can be classified as one of the world's most successful federations, we need to consider that its federal character experienced dramatic changes in the period immediately following the union's formation, and, in the not-too-distant past at least, it was not at all clear that its federal character would be preserved. Created in 1901 as a decentralized and limited union of six autonomous states, Australia nevertheless became one of the world's most centralized federations so that by the late 1940s it became fashionable to foresee the imminent demise of its federal structure. The speed and scope of this transformation was striking, as revealed by its treatment in two seminal essays separated by eighteen years, Wheare's *Federal Government* (1946) and Riker's *Federalism* (1964). Whereas Wheare included Australia in his exclusive four-member group of "truly federal states" (along with the United States, Canada, and Switzerland), Riker wondered why Australia bothered with federalism at all. In light of Riker's assessment, then, we might question whether Australian parties need to serve any integrating role. As we argue shortly, however, although the governing parties were participants in a decades-long trend toward centralization, it is also true that those parties set the limits of that trend and today serve as the ultimate safeguard of the federal model.[8]

We can begin by noting that the founders of the Australian Commonwealth sought a decentralized federal union. The logic of their design followed directly from the specifics of the bargaining process, which corresponded to a classic "coming together" of six states with extensive experience in parliamentary self-government, plus the island of Tasmania (Hicks 1978).[9] Moreover, owing to the enormous size and low population density of the Australian continent, the six states prior to the federation's establishment were at best only weakly connected economically and politically.[10] As the *New York Times* observed (December 22, 1889, cited in Rector 2001), the colonies were "as if they were separate independent states... there is more jealousy between them than existed among the old American colonies. They adopt different fiscal policies, and keep up a continual tariff war; they have no common view for defense, [and] their coinage and postage stamps are different." But there were economic advantages to coordination that the colonies first attempted to secure through regular but informal meetings of colonial executives. The scheme failed and so a Federation Council was formed in 1885 as the next step toward unification. Composed of two

8 The Australian case also offers evidence with respect to an important theoretical debate – namely, whether the development of the party system defines the degree of federal centralization, or whether the degree of party system centralization is a response to the level of federal centralization. Riker argues that the degree of federal centralization is a function of party centralization, while the literature frequently looks at party centralization as the dependent variable (see, e.g., Chibber and Kollman 1998). The Australian case lends support to Riker's hypothesis. Despite the centralization of the state that occurred between the 1910s and the 1950s, the trend of party organization was the opposite, and ultimately acted as a break on trends within the state.

9 Five states – New South Wales, Queensland, South Australia, Tasmania, and Victoria – established constitutions in 1850s; Western Australia was organized as a separate colony in 1890.

10 Indeed, as evidence of their relative isolation as colonies, when railroad construction began, there was no agreement as to rail gauges and three neighboring provinces (Victoria, Queensland, and New South Wales) entered the federation with three distinct standards (Dikshit 1975).

representatives from each colony (plus New Zealand and Fiji), the Federation Council was little more than a coordinating entity and failed owing to the refusal of New South Wales, the most developed colony, to participate: New South Wales politicians were ready to accept only "either a union in which New South Wales should predominate or none at all" (Beach 1899: 666). The third and ultimately successful attempt at intercolonial cooperation began in 1890, with the proposal to draft a federal constitution. In April 1891 a conference of appointed delegates from the colonies adopted a first constitutional draft, and in March 1897 a second constitutional convention with popularly elected delegates agreed on an amended version that was submitted for consideration to state parliaments. A final draft was presented in 1898 for popular approval, but was defeated in New South Wales, and received approval there in 1899 only after a conference of colonial premiers accepted amendments that increased New South Wales's influence, including the provision that the federal capital be eventually located there.[11]

As a product of this intense interstate bargaining, the new constitution gave the federal center only a few enumerated powers, with all residual powers given to the states. The next fifty years, however, became a period of "gradual transition from the predominant power residing in the States to a centralization greater than in any other classic federation" (Hicks 1978: 145), and more than a few observers attribute this transformation to the Australian High Court. In fact, the court, rather than allowing itself to become a venue for federal bargaining, largely directed the resolution of constitutionally *unspecified* matters to the political process. Although the three justices of the first High Court, all major figures in drafting the federal constitution, consistently reasserted the principle of federal decentralization, soon enough the federal government began manipulating the court's composition,[12] and in 1920 a new majority revised the previous "profederal" decision of Australia's landmark *Engineers* case.[13] Since then, as a rule, the High Court's decisions had served to allow an expansion of the powers of the Commonwealth and Parliament.[14] What needs to be understood here,

[11] While New South Wales would not ratify unless the capital was located within its borders, Victoria demanded that the federal capital not be within one hundred miles of New South Wales's capital, Sydney.

[12] From 1903 to 1906 there were three judges; from 1906 to 1912, five judges; from 1912 to 1931, seven judges; from 1931 to 1947 six judges; and since 1947 there have been seven judges on the Court.

[13] *Amalgamated Society of Engineers v. Adelaide Steamship Co. Ltd.* (1920).

[14] Zines (1997: 8) affirms that "Since [the *Engineers* decision] all judges of the High Court have purported to follow that case. After more than 70 years, it probably remains the most important case in Australian constitutional law." But, as Justice Windeyer stated the matter, "in 1920 the Constitution was read in a new light, a light reflected from events that had, over twenty years, led to a growing realization that Australians were now one people and Australia one country and that national laws might meet national needs" (cited in Zines 1997: 15–16).

though, is that although the court's record leaves no doubt as to its historical bias, in essentially all important cases it did not *require* that the federal government implement decisions leading to greater centralization but instead simply refused to assert limits on the expansion of the Commonwealth's jurisdiction. Thus, the High Court decided that restrictions on the Commonwealth's authority to encroach on states' powers were not implied by the constitution's residual powers clause, and that it was for Parliament and electors to devise such restrictions not directly expressed in the constitution (Sawer 1967). In other words, limits on the federal government that were not clearly and unambiguously defined by the letter of the constitution should not be determined by court interpretation, but should be determined by the political process (Galligan 1987, 2001; Patapan 2000).[15] Thus, the problem in this initial period in the evolution of the Australian federalism was that the Australian political process failed to produce adequate safeguards against centralization, with neither the House nor the Senate being effective protectors of states' rights.

In truth, the framers of the constitution understood that House members, although elected in single-member districts, would not represent states effectively. It was also clear that the House and, therefore, the government would as a rule be controlled by the two most populous states, New South Wales and Victoria.[16] But they hoped that a Senate would act as a protector of states' interest, and to encourage that they opted for a powerful and directly elected Senate with equal representation for each state. Much like the American model, the powers of the Senate were equal to those of the House, including the exception that all "laws appropriating revenue or moneys, or imposing taxation" must originate in the House. But again, as in the American case, rather than develop into a "State House," the Australian Senate was soon dominated by disciplined political parties: "All elections to the Senate have been fought on a party basis and no party has ever adopted

[15] Similarly, when in 1940 states challenged legislation leading to extreme forms of fiscal centralization, the High Court ruled that such centralization was a legitimate exercise of Commonwealth powers, but whether the federal Parliament should exercise its legislative powers in such a way was, according to its chief justice, a matter of politics: "We have nothing to do with wisdom or expediency of legislation. Such questions are for Parliament and the people"; see *South Australia v. Commonwealth* [Uniform Tax Case] (no. 1) (1942). In essence the Australian High Court's approach to the constitutional balance between the federal government and the state closely approximated the "political safeguards" principles expressed by the American Court in *Garcia v. San Antonio Metropolitan Transit Authority*. There, the U.S. Supreme Court argued that judicial intervention in federal issues is unnecessary because the national political process itself could protect the interests of the states. "[T]he political process ensures that laws that unduly burden the States will not be promulgated" (U.S. Supreme Court, *Garcia v. San Antonio Metro. Transit Auth.*, 469 U.S. 528 (1985)).

[16] Indeed, almost all (all, since 1945) Australian prime ministers are either from New South Wales or Victoria.

any narrow or state programme ... the national character of each party has been evident in its election manifesto and actual working. Senators have, for this reason, owed loyalty to the party and not to the State they represent. If the same party is in majority in both houses, the Senate simply dittoes the measures that come to it from the lower House. But if the Senate contains a majority of the party which is in minority in the lower House, there is some trouble and the Senate does become conspicuous in political life. Even then the real battle is between the parties and not between different States" (Sharma 1953: 509; see also Overacker 1952).

With respect to the parties themselves, prior to federalization, state-level parties competed largely on the issue of tariffs (Free Traders versus Protectionists), but with the emergence of Labor at the national level, these antagonists were driven to ally in a common front. In response, the national Labor Party transformed itself into a centralized and disciplined entity, which in turn stimulated the opposition to develop centralized and disciplined national organizations as well so that by 1910 the primary pattern of competition in federal politics became a division between Labor and non-Labor (Overacker 1952; Reid and Forrest 1989; Jaensch 1994). This pattern is especially important to Australian federalism. It is reasonable to suppose that one condition for federal institutional stability is for all major parties to support the core elements of the federal constitution. But in this instance Labor initially did not. Before the document was adopted most state-level Labor parties campaigned against its federal character,[17] and at its 1908 national convention, the party pledged itself to constitutional amendments aimed at abrogating federalism so that when the party won a majority in both houses in 1910, it immediately initiated a program of economic and federal reforms to that end. Of course, centralism came naturally to a party espousing a socialist ideology, since federalism was perceived as a barrier to radical social change. And, in perhaps as classic an example of convergence to the median as we are likely to see in electoral politics, once Labor demonstrated the electoral appeal of its platform, the logic of electoral competition compelled its opponents to respond in kind.

Interestingly, however, when the issue of centralization was set before the electorate in the form of referenda on constitutional amendments, those proposals fared poorly. Of forty-four proposals to change the constitution between 1901 and 2000 that were accepted by parliament and set before the

[17] Those parties, however, entered politics too late to have much influence on the constitution's character (Galligan 1987). Although state-level Labor parties became important players in state politics during the late 1890s, and in Queensland Labor even formed the government for a brief period in 1899, only one Labor candidate was elected to the 1897 Federal Convention. Some Australian historians even argued that the creation of the federation was an attempt to prevent the Socialist and Labor movement from taking control in individual colonies or at least from "jumping over to extreme socialism" (Evatt 1940, as quoted in Irving 1997: 213).

electorate, half sought to enlarge the powers of the Commonwealth but only two were approved (Joyner 1958; Goldsworthy 1997; Saunders 2000).[18] This lack of success of referenda initiated by national parties' parliamentary caucuses did not imply that the parties at large were consistently more procentralization than their electorates. State-level organizations as a rule stood in opposition to the centralist tendencies of their national leadership and frequently campaigned against the procentralist constitutional referenda put forth by their own parties in Parliament. As Holmes and Sharman (1977: 103) conclude, "the failure of so many attempts to carry referenda increasing the power of the central government under the constitution is more attributable to the internal federal organization of the Labor, Liberals and National Country parties than it is to any other factor."

The source of such intraparty dissent is not difficult to find. Put simply, the procentralist stance of national parties was unlikely to be a successful electoral platform for state-level elections and, in fact, association with the incumbent federal government became somewhat of a liability at the state level. Although Labor and Liberals dominated state elections, more often than not, as the last column of Table 6.1 shows, a party in opposition to the incumbent federal government was likely to be stronger in state elections. And as the electoral fates of federal and state parties moved in opposite directions, a gap emerged between national organizations and state-level politicians so that the more their interests diverged, the more the state-level organizations perceived themselves as having a vested interest in preserving state power.

The relevance of this intraparty dynamic to federal institutional stability is most clearly illustrated by the history of tension among national and state-level Labor organizations. Already in 1908, after the national party committed itself to constitutional amendments aimed at increasing the power of the central government, the party began to face strong internal opposition from its New South Wales branch. In particular, a popular New South Wales Labor leader, W. Holman, became "an eloquent champion of state rights because he expected a Labor victory in NSW well in advance of a federal Labor victory" (Galligan 1987: 87). After the federal party won a majority in the House and Senate, the national party leadership initiated a constitutional referendum aimed at expanding central powers, but a powerful group of New South Wales Labor members, led by Holman and New South Wales Labor Premier McGowen, refused to support the referendum and it was defeated (Joyner 1958). In the 1930s the split between federal Labor leaders and their New South Wales colleagues reached such proportions that at the same mass rally Labor supporters could be asked to vote yes on a constitutional referendum

[18] These referenda were usually held the same day as a Commonwealth general election, and a party was often returned to office only to find that its request for increased central government powers has been simultaneously denied (see Vile 1957).

by national leaders and no by state leaders (Galligan 1987: 25). Most importantly, a 1944 referendum, which if passed might have ended federalism, was defeated because of the opposition of four Labor-controlled state governments. The referendum produced a clear defeat for the Labor government (54 percent of all voters and majorities in four states voted against), despite the stable electoral support for Labor at the federal and state level during the war.

As Galligan (1987: 24) summarizes matters, "the federal system divided Labor against itself." Although the national organization pushed toward an unitary model, its structure was decentralized so that the selection of both state and national Labor candidates remains the responsibility of state branches (Stevens and Weller 1976). Other parties also have only state-level selection procedures for both state and national offices. Thus, "there is no such thing as a national power base for a politician – he must preserve the support of one of the six state branches if he is to preserve his career" (Holmes and Sharman 1977: 108). And, in particular, with state-level Labor parties able to preserve their independence, possessed of a vested interest in maintaining state power, and generally more successful in gaining government control than their federal counterpart, the national organization, "with very limited financial resources, no power to endorse candidates, and largely at the mercy of the state organizations in conducting election campaigns... [was] likely to move cautiously, especially when challenged by New South Wales or Victoria, which together include two-thirds of the population of the Commonwealth" (Overacker 1949: 693). In this way Australian federalism was saved by a balance of power between national and state party organizations.

In summary, Australian parties, like their American counterparts, remain loose federations of many groups and factions: "There is a formal entity called the Australian Labor Party, but this is composite, and an unstable one, of the six state parties.... Except in a strictly formal sense, there is no such thing as the Liberal Party of Australia which, in practice, is a composite of seven parties.... The National Party, despite its name, is the most horizontally divided of all three. Its state branches are autonomous to the greatest degree, and its national organization almost non-existent" (Jaensch 1994: 120–1). The resulting factionalism often results in a lively competition for a party's endorsement, especially since endorsements can decide the outcome of many elections. Specifically, more than half of all seats for national and state parliaments are considered safe for one major party or another so that "gaining a party label virtually ensures a candidate election in a safe seat," whereas even in competitive districts "the premium that the label provides to a pre-selected candidate is considerable" (Johns 2000: 404). The balance of power, especially within Labor, depends on control of a multitude of factions, but since cleavages among the national party's major factions cut across states, no politician has been able to consolidate control either at the national or state level. Instead, to succeed electorally all groups and factions have to seek cooperation with other national and state groups (Leigh 2000). In respect to federal matters, such cooperation closely resembles what we define as "an integrated political party."

Canada

Canada, in contrast to Australia, was designed initially as a relatively centralized federation and moved in the direction of decentralization. Yet, as with Australia, the court is often seen as the decisive player in this transformation, especially since from the mid-1890s to the late 1940s the Supreme Court and Judicial Committee of the Privy Council (which until 1949 was the court of final appeal on constitutional issues) generally interpreted the British North American Act (1867) as limiting the federal Parliament's power at the expense of the provinces. Hence, as supporters of the court's role argue, it and the Privy Council resisted "the encroachments of the Federal Parliament upon the powers of the Provincial Legislatures and *vice versa*" (Stanley 1969: 142, as cited in Smiley 1972: 23). However, reducing the explanation of the centrifugal trends in Canadian politics to the court and Privy Council has two shortcomings. First, as in Australia, judicial decisions at most created opportunities for the political process to lead in certain directions and it remained for that process to implement centrifugal policies the court rendered legitimate. Second, there is the matter of enforceability: if a judicial decision contradicted prevailing political tendencies, why would the federal government abide by it? It is often argued that the Privy Council could play the role of exogenous referee because it was a British institution beyond the reach of the federal government. But this is true only to a point. Although the institution itself was out of reach, the practice of deferring to it is endogenous to Canadian politics. Indeed, this practice was abolished, but only in 1949. Why not earlier, especially since the Balfour Declaration of 1926 gave de facto recognition of Canada as a judicially independent state and the Statute of Westminster in 1931 formally allowed all dominions to claim judicial independence?[19] We can only conclude that the Privy Council's position on constitutional issues suited the government or at least that, as in Australia, that there were other political processes acting to sustain the Privy Council's role in Canadian politics.

In fact, Canada's federal decentralization paralleled that of its parties and party finances. Briefly, in the nineteenth century both Liberals and Conservatives relied heavily on patronage, railroad tariff concessions, and traditional pork barrel – all of which was controlled by national party leaders: "[I]t was to the leaders of the national party, therefore, that seekers after jobs and

[19] The Court was not established by the Constitutional Act of 1867 but by a parliamentary act in 1878 and could be changed or even abolished by an act of Parliament. In other words, it was within the power of the federal government (controlling parliamentary majority) to change the court's functions at any moment.

contracts had turned" (Mallory 1954: 42). Both parties, then, developed a highly centralized system of finance, with most funds coming from corporations based in Montreal and Toronto, so that provincial branches typically relied on the central party funds to finance provincial and even local elections (Paltiel 1970). In the beginning of the twentieth century, however, technological change stimulated economic activity at the provincial scale (e.g., paved roads, electric power stations). Thus, "provincial governments entered into direct and important relationships with a great variety of businesses to whom their policies now became a matter of paramount importance. Money contributions went to provincial party officials, and the dominant power in Canadian party organization passed into the hands of those who controlled the provincial party machines.... This change in the internal structure of the party machine is one of the most important causes of the shift in the centre of power in the federal system away from the Dominion and toward ever increasing provincial autonomy" (Mallory 1954: 43). In the 1930s and especially after World War II decentralization of party finances progressed further with the increased importance of natural resource development (the primary area of provincial jurisdiction) so that the provincial wings of the Liberal and Conservative parties became wholly self-supportive in resource-rich British Columbia and Alberta (Paltiel 1970: 13; Smiley 1972: 91).

The changing character of party finances alone and the historical-technological trends that correlate with those changes, however, seem inadequate for understanding the overall character of Canadian federalism, and in Chapter 7 we discuss more fully the institutional influences on Canada's party system. Here we want to examine more closely the nature of that system, and we begin by noting that, although Canada's two primary national parties, the Liberals and, prior to 1993, the Progressive Conservatives, look at first glance much like America's, there are profoundly important differences. First, unlike in the United States, a variety of regional or purely provincial parties compete with each other and with the federal parties for provincial offices. As Table 6.2 shows, since 1970 the provincial status of federal governing parties grew especially weak in Quebec and the western provinces. In each of these five provinces the party in power nationally commanded on average less than 30 percent of the vote in the 1971–95 provincial elections. Second, the fortunes of even the Liberals in provincial and national elections do not always go hand in hand and commonly move in opposite directions (Erikson and Filippov 2001). For example, between 1940 and 2000, in twelve of nineteen federal elections Liberals won over half of Ontario's seats in the Canadian Parliament, whereas Conservatives won fifteen out of seventeen of Ontario's provincial elections. Ontario's Conservatives won a clear majority in the 1995 and 1999 provincial elections but secured just one seat in the 1997 and no seats in the 2000 federal elections. Third, although the selection of delegates to the Democratic and Republican national party conventions in the United States is dominated by state

TABLE 6.2. *Average Vote for Liberals and Conservatives and for Federal Governing Party in Canadian Provincial Elections, 1947–1995 (%)*

	1947–1970			1971–1995		
Province	Number of Elections	Liberal and Conservatives	Federal Incumbent's Vote	Number of Elections	Liberal and Conservatives	Federal Incumbent's Vote
Newfoundland	6	95.1	53.2	8	91.8	43.7
Prince Edward	7	99.1	52.4	7	96.9	52.1
Nova Scotia	7	93.4	46.3	6	83.0	44.0
New Brunswick	7	97.4	50.3	6	84.9	38.9
Quebec	9	90.1	44.0	6	52.0	29.9
Ontario	6	78.6	34.3	6	71.3	30.4
Manitoba	7	68.3	38.3	7	61.8	26.1
Saskatchewan	6	45.5	33.4	5	53.0	28.3
Alberta	6	31.9	21.0	5	66.2	22.0
British Columbia	8	31.8	24.5	6	15.1	4.6

party organizations, which are in turn creatures of local party organizations (as is true of Australia as well), the national conventions of Canadian parties are dominated by national party organizations that are generally distinct from the party organizations bearing the same label and that serve the candidacies of provincial politicians.

Although much has been written about Quebec, its parties and secession, Table 6.2 and the preceding discussion suggest that political party history there is not altogether unique. Nevertheless, as a point of contrast, it is useful to review that history. Briefly, Quebec's provincial elections have always been largely shaped by two parties – initially between Conservatives and Liberals, then beginning in the 1930s between Union Nationale and Liberals, and finally beginning in the 1970s between Liberals and Party Quebecois. Until 1936 the Liberal Party campaigned as a pro-provincial and pro-autonomist party. Its platform changed after 1936, however, with the formation of the Union Nationale, a strictly provincial party that ultimately succeeded in establishing itself as pro-autonomist largely because Liberals had formed the federal government since 1935. Quite simply, the longer federal Liberals stayed in power in Ottawa, the easier it was for Union Nationale to present itself as the defender of provincial interests (Lemieux 1978).[20] Correspondingly, provincial Liberals, being a more or less integrated part of the national party, sought to avoid the federal-provincial issue altogether, so that the party's 1958 Quebec leadership convention failed even to mention the issues of federal-provincial relations, of Quebec's place in the federation, or the language rights of French minorities (Latouche 1986).

Following the party's federal defeat in 1957, Quebec Liberals found themselves able to modify their electoral strategy. With John Diefenbaker forming first a minority Conservative government and achieving even greater electoral success in 1958, Quebec's Liberals were now free to attack the federal government (which, in the short run, served the interests of the national Liberals, since Quebec was crucial for winning back control of the federal government). In 1960 Quebec Liberals decided, as a part of their electoral strategy, to incorporate for the first time proposals to change the workings of Canadian federalism into its official election platform (Latouche 1986: 14). The party won the closely contested 1960 provincial elections, and a month after taking office the new Liberal premier Jean Lesage demanded changes in Quebec-federal relations. He also proposed a constitutional tribunal to reformulate federal relations, fearing an absence of impartiality on the part of Canada's Supreme Court since all judges had been appointed by the central government. Lesage continued to build his reputation as a

[20] A 1959 public opinion survey confirmed the Union Nationale's advantage: a majority of respondents said it was unable to distinguish between the two parties on any issue except that of defending of provincial autonomy, where the Union Nationale emerged as the clear winner (Latouche 1986: 18).

tough negotiator on Quebec's behalf even after the Liberal Party regained control of the federal government, demanding the return of an ever increasing share of taxes collected in the province.[21] Cynics and political opponents however, reminded the public that, before his provincial premiership, Lesage was in federal politics and was known as an ardent supporter of federal intervention in provincial affairs. When Lesage served as a federal minister of northern affairs and national resources (1953–7), he never spoke on behalf of French-speaking Canadians.

Despite the strained relations between the federal government and Quebec under Lesage's premiership, in comparison to what followed, the era was called a "quiet" revolution (1960–6). After 1963 and the Liberal's success in regaining control of the federal government, the Quebec Liberal government was once again confronted with a loss of credibility in its role as the province's champion. It was then, in 1964, that a formal separation took place in Liberal Party structures – between the Quebec provincial organization and the party's national wing – whereupon the Lesage government initiated its demands for Quebec's "distinct" status. At the same time, the newly elected Liberal federal government (Pearson), owing to its minority status and dependence on Quebec voters, offered concessions including Quebec's withdrawal from a number of national programs (with full fiscal compensation) and the creation of a Royal Commission on Bilingualism and Biculturalism. The Quiet Revolution ended in 1966 when Quebec's Liberals were defeated by the Union Nationale, who offered voters the slogan "equality or independence," and by the end of 1968 Parti Québécois entered provincial politics on a platform of Quebec sovereignty "in an association with Canada." Quebec's Liberals, following perhaps the dictates of a simple spatial strategy, moved again to a profederal position, squeezing the Union Nationale between them and Parti Québécois. This shift in platforms, however, was not accompanied by any return to an integrated party model since little in the province's electoral logic had otherwise changed.

Although the substance and specifics of the issues that might be cited as catalysts to the process may differ, events in Quebec find their parallel in Canada's other provinces, with separate party systems coexisting at both federal levels. Indeed, the separation in party organizations between the national and provincial parties that technically bear the same label is so deep that, in perhaps the most evident contrast between Canada and the United States, the career paths of politicians in Canada remain strictly confined to either one of the two levels. Although approximately half of those who held elective office before succeeding to the presidency of the United States served

[21] Lesage was also the first prominent provincial official to present the provincial government as the liberator and champion of the defeated French Quebec, arguing that to fill that role, the provincial government required a larger bureaucracy, greater authority, and more money from the federal government.

as governor of a state, no prime minister of Canada has ever served as head of a provincial government. This pattern is even more pronounced in view of the fact that, although it is arguably the case that American federalism has become more centralized, especially in this century, the role of governors vis-à-vis the presidency has increased. Of the eleven presidents elected before the outbreak of the Civil War after Thomas Jefferson (excluding Zachary Taylor [1849–50], a general), only two (18 percent) held the office of governor of their state as their last elected post before becoming president whereas nine served in Congress; between 1860 and 1900, three (43 percent) of seven were governors and four were in the Congress (excluding Grant, a general, and Arthur, who held only minor state offices); but between 1900 and today, eight were governors and seven were from the Congress (excluding Taft, Hoover, and Eisenhower). In Canada, on the other hand, "there is very little movement from provincial to national office. Aspiring politicians appear to make an early choice between a provincial or a national career, and once launched on their path very few cross over. Provincial office is not a way station on the road to national office but rather an alternative" (Gibbins 1982: 141). For example, among the 301 members of the Canadian Parliament elected in 2000, only 26 had previously been elected to provincial parliaments, and only 12 of 101 senators had provincial-level political experience.[22] Canadian parties today, moreover can be summarized thus: "The Canadian party system is bifurcated. Of the three parties that compete at both the federal and provincial level, only one has an integrated party organization. Only for the New Democrats does membership in a provincial party automatically lead to membership in the federal party. . . . But the NDP is distinctly a minority federal party. It averages about 10 percent of the seats in the House of Commons" (Uslaner 2000: 5).

One consequence of Canada's failure to develop an integrated party system is that the de facto regional representation in governing coalitions is biased – a fact illustrated in Table 6.3. This table shows several things. First, notice the wide swings in regional representation from one election to the next in all regions except the Atlantic provinces. Second, notice the negative correspondence (r = –.59) between Quebec's representation and that of the West – a correspondence that underlies the conflict of interest between these two parts of the federation – as well as the overall negative correspondence with Ontario (r = –.71). Finally, notice the general decline in Quebec's representation since the 1960s (ignoring the Conservative victory in 1979).[23]

[22] Information from Official Canadian Parliamentary site, available at <http://www.parl.gc.ca>.

[23] Of course, simple correlations here are bound to be negative since numbers here must sum to one hundred. But for purposes of comparison we note that the simple correlation between Atlantic and Western representation is –.13, between Atlantic and Ontario –.07, between Atlantic and Quebec –.14, and between Ontario and the West –.07.

TABLE 6.3. *Regional Representation: Governing Party, 1896–2000 (%)*

Election	Governing Party	Atlantic	Quebec	Ontario	Western[a]
1896	Liberal	14.5	41.9	36.8	6.8
1900	Liberal	21.1	43.8	27.3	7.8
1904	Liberal	18.7	38.8	27.3	15.1
1908	Liberal	19.5	39.8	27.1	13.5
1911	Conservative	12.0	20.3	54.1	13.5
1917	Unionist	13.7	2.0	48.4	35.9
1921	Liberal	21.4	55.6	17.9	5.1
1925	Liberal	5.9	59.4	11.9	22.8
1926	Liberal	7.8	51.7	19.8	20.7
1930	Conservative	16.8	17.5	43.1	22.6
1935	Liberal	14.5	31.8	32.4	21.4
1940	Liberal	10.5	33.7	31.5	24.3
1945	Liberal	15.2	42.4	27.2	15.2
1949	Liberal	13.5	35.2	29.0	22.3
1953	Liberal	15.8	38.6	29.8	15.8
1957	Conservative	18.8	8.0	54.5	18.8
1958	Conservative	12.0	24.0	32.2	31.7
1962	Conservative	15.5	12.1	30.2	42.2
1963	Liberal	15.5	36.4	40.3	7.8
1965	Liberal	11.5	42.7	38.9	6.9
1968	Liberal	4.5	36.1	41.3	18.1
1972	Liberal	9.2	51.4	33.0	6.4
1974	Liberal	9.2	42.6	39.0	9.2
1979	Conservative	13.2	1.5	41.9	43.4
1980	Liberal	12.9	50.3	35.4	1.4
1984	Conservative	11.8	27.5	31.8	28.9
1988	Conservative	7.1	37.3	27.2	28.4
1993	Liberal	17.5	10.7	55.4	16.4
1997	Liberal	7.1	16.8	65.2	11.0
2000	Liberal	11.0	20.9	58.1	9.9
1896–1930		15.1	37.1	31.4	16.4
1935–1953		13.9	36.3	30.0	19.8
1957–1984		12.5	30.9	37.4	19.2
1988–2000		10.7	21.4	51.5	16.4

[a] The Yukon, the Northwest Territories, and Nunavut are included in the Western region.

Perhaps a fuller understanding of Canadian parties can be gained by considering Germany, which, like Canada, is parliamentary but about which it is reasonable to offer an observation that is identical to one we can apply to the United States: "[P]olitical parties in the national and regional arenas and the central and regional government administrations are the principal mechanisms for federal 'checks and balances'" (Hadley, Morass, and Nick 1989: 81–97). In fact, since Lehmbruch's (1978) classic *Party Competition in the Federal State*, there is a consensus that recognizes the decisive role of parties in maintaining Germany's federal model. For example, Renzsch (2001: 21) emphasizes that "the whole process of federal-Länder negotiations is accompanied by negotiation within the political parties" and that politicians within parties have electoral incentives to seek consensus and compromise or at least the "second best" solution instead of a gridlock of extreme demands (see also Leonardy 1991). Lehmbruch in particular describes political parties in Germany as reacting to integrating institutional incentives and therefore acting essentially as integrated parties.[24]

As integrated entities, German parties exhibit many of the characteristics of their American counterparts. On one hand, with the peculiar exception of Bavaria, and after unification, of East Germany, the party system is essentially the same at the federal and state levels.[25] As Renzsch (2001) describes it, the sixteen diets are more or less smaller copies of the Bundestag with one or the other of the two largest federal parties – the Social Democrats (SPD) and the Christian Democrats/Christian Social Union (CDU/CSU) – forming the largest caucuses. And, unlike Canada, regional party organizations follow national guidelines, with adjustments appropriate to the specifics of each state: "[W]ithin a regional party organization political positions and tendencies might gain prominence which represent only a small minority within the national organization" (Habek 1987: 32). National party conventions are dominated by state party organizations (Conradt 1999), and the candidate nomination process is wholly controlled by local and state party organizations: nominations for the Bundestag's single-member mandate districts are "the jealously guarded prerogative of the local and county party organizations and memberships.[26] The party lists, for which a second ballot is cast in German federal elections, are drawn up at state party conventions through a formal vote usually preceded by informal agreements between the county organizations and wings of the party" (Schuttemeyer 2001: 45–6). Party finances and campaigning are integrated (Heidenheimer 1963; Gunlicks 1988; Arnim 1993), and a principal preoccupation of the parties is the competition for local offices, with virtually all major and

[24] Whereas we focus on institutional motivations, however, most German scholars emphasize "cultural factors" and "behavioral norms." Lehmbruch (1976), for example, identifies "behavioral norms" of cooperation in the Bundesrat. In his view, such norms follow from German historical experience and a "tradition of compromise."

[25] The CSU is the dominant party in Bavaria but operates nationally and at the European level in coalition with the CDU. The Party of Democratic Socialism (PDS), the former East German Socialist Unity Party, is successful only in the East German diets, although it competes nationally.

[26] Membership and official position in some party, moreover, are essential for a political career at the federal level. In the late 1990s, for example, less than 10 percent of members of the Bundestag held no official position in their party organization, while almost 75 percent were chairpersons or members of the executive boards on at least one territorial level (local, county, state, and federal) of the party (Schuttemeyer 2001).

most local councillors running on party tickets (Saiz and Geser 1999; Renzsch 2001).

Perhaps the starkest contrast with Canada and similarity to the integrated federal form of the United States is provided by the fact that German national political figures have roots in local politics to nearly the same extent as their American counterparts (Golsch 1995). Previous state-level leadership is a virtual requirement for seeking federal leadership positions. Since 1949 there have been only seven federal chancellors, all of which had political experience at the regional level: Adenauer (1949–63) was mayor of Cologne; Erhard (1963–6) was economic minister of Bavaria; Kiesinger (1966–9) served as prime minister of Baden-Württemberg; Brandt (1969–74) was mayor of West Berlin; Schmidt (1974–82) began his political career in state Hamburg politics; Kohl (1982–98) was a prime minister of Rhineland-Palatinate; and most recently, Schröder won the 1998 federal election while being the prime minister of Saxony. Moreover, since the 1960s, all but one opposition candidate for the post of chancellor launched their bids from the Minister-Presidency of one of the Länder (Jeffery 1999); and mobility is bidirectional, so that former federal ministers might continue their political careers in state government (Scharpf 1995). In summary, "within the party it is the local and state branches that are most important within the federal structure. Access to a political career is clearly defined by the local level of a party. The rise within party ranks and from local mandate to state or federal legislature is parallel, and party offices and public mandates and offices are held concurrently. Strategic offices within the party such as county chairperson or on the local level such as mayor are kept even if one gets a seat in the Bundestag, as this is the way to control and preempt potential challengers" (Borchert 2000: 36).

6.6 India

The preceding discussion establishes that integrated parties can develop in both presidential and parliamentary systems and with both proportional representation and first-past-the-post electoral arrangements. Each of the cases considered thus far, however, concerns a state with a viable economy and a well-developed civic culture. The case of India provides an interesting contrast. Just as Czechoslovakia illustrates federal failure despite seemingly ideal circumstances, India seems its opposite number – a reasonably successful and democratic federation despite the odds against it. Practically all preconditions the literature traditionally deems essential for democratic success are absent, including being an artificial creation whose diversity and internal divisions were derived largely from Britain's somewhat self-serving colonial policies. Indeed, at the height of British rule, over two-fifths of its territory was a collection of principalities ruled by more than five hundred princes – a territory torn by rivalries among more than a dozen language groups, between Hindu and Moslem, and among castes and classes. Nevertheless, although both democracy and federalism suffer from numerous shortcomings,[27] the country arguably remains the most successful and stable democratic federation among postcolonial states. With the exception of an eighteen-month interval in 1975–7, India has been governed since independence in 1947 by democratic institutions and constitutionally prescribed parliamentary and state elections. Governments at both the national and state level have routinely experienced electorally mandated transfers of power, and although Wheare (1953) called India a quasi federation – something between a unitary state and a federation – most contemporary observers agree that Indian federalism is real.[28] States have well-defined legislative, executive, and fiscal jurisdictions and enjoy significant (but highly unbalanced) budget decentralization so that, similar to the provinces in Canada, their share of public expenditures exceeds 50 percent.

India's status as a democratic federation seems a puzzle: "The most astonishing thing about the Indian political system is that it works, and works democratically. The enormous forces of disunity are somehow being overcome; national integrity has been maintained; and federalism, like democracy, is operative, though doubtless unique. The explanation of these phenomena is a wide open door to the political researcher" (Leonard 1963: 141–2). Dozens of studies address this puzzle, offering explanations that include the role of traditional Hindu norms and charismatic leaders, the benefits of British rule and pre-independence federal experiences, the commitment of Indian politicians to unity and consociational principles, and even the advantage of being so extremely divided that no group can dominate politics nationally and in its states (Lijphart 1996). Nevertheless, nearly all commentators seem to agree on the importance of the integrating role of the Congress Party, which dominated Indian politics for years and remains an important and arguably the only truly national political party.

Congress's role in the development of Indian democracy is evident, but what concerns us here is the question of why the party was successful for such a long time in winning competitive elections and in presiding over order and stability. In his now classic study *Party Building in a New Nation* (1967), Weiner notes the limitations of most popular explanations

[27] The latest edition of Lijphart's *Patterns of Democracy* (1999) now includes India in the sample of thirty-six democratic regimes, even though some scholars still debate the quality of Indian democracy (for an overview, see Varshney 2000; Gupta 2000).

[28] In Wheare's words (1953: 28), the 1950 Indian Constitution was "a quasi-federal constitution. Whether, in its operations, it will provide another example of federal government remains to be seen." Current debates though center not on whether India is a federation but on the effect of its federalism on the country's economic and political development. Thus, Parikh and Weingast (1997: 1606) argue that, although India "has an authentic federal system," Indian federalism is not "market preserving" in that it does not allow for credible commitment to limiting the role of the center in economic regulation.

(e.g., great leaders, the legacy of a broad pro-independence movement, strong pre-independence organization, nationalism) by observing how common these characteristics were for parties elsewhere in the developing world, the majority of which nonetheless failed to endure. The hypothesis he offers – Congress's relative uniqueness – focuses on the prevailing goals and motivations of its leaders and rank-and-file members: "Elsewhere many governing parties are concerned with either mobilization or controlling population. In contrast, Congress is primarily concerned with recruiting members and winning support. It does not mobilize; it aggregates. Although a few Congressmen dream of transforming the countryside, in practice most Congressmen are concerned simply with winning elections. In its efforts to win, Congress adapts itself to the local power structures. It recruits from among those who have local power and influence" (Weiner 1967: 14–15). This classic assessment is seconded by Kochanek (1968: 272), who stresses the pragmatism of the Congress electoral strategy: "While the Congress leaders officially and publicly articulate many formal criteria for selecting candidates, the dominant calculations are based on the ability to win, which involves selecting candidates in accordance with the social composition of each constituency." Manor (1995: 106) goes so far as to compare the postindependence Congress with the old Democratic Party in the American South: "Congress operated as a political machine – or, more precisely, as a cluster of state-level political machines – which maintained its dominance partly as a result of history, but mainly through the distribution of resources to a broad enough array of social groups to keep winning re-election."

Congress's leaders, then, were primarily interested in winning elections. This, in combination with the party's dominance, made it beneficial for its leaders to act like an integrated party and sustain democracy and federalism. Of course, those familiar with European or American parties find such motivations natural. But in other societies, parties are ideologically constrained and the opportunities to expand and sustain one's coalition restricted by the number of voters with similar ideological or policy preferences and the number of competitors competing for the same votes (Bartolini and Mair 1990). It is not universally true that a party will put ideological differences aside and seek to win as many votes and seats as possible by building a broad nearly amorphous coalition of members and candidates who are united by the goal of winning elections. Nevertheless, India's Congress Party, like those in the United States, was such a coalition.

The question is why the party functioned in this way. Certainly it was not predicted at the time of independence, when groups within it sought to transform it into a nationalist party or ideological party as opposed to a "seat-winning machine" (Weiner 1967).[29] Gandhi, in fact, opposed pure

[29] Weiner (1956) himself failed to notice the evolution of the Congress into an election-oriented party at first. He argued that Indian politics was characterized by "the ambivalent feeling of

electoral objectives. When, in January 1948, a special commission prepared proposals to reform the party into an electoral machine, Gandhi criticized the draft and prepared a memo outlining his views. The party's general secretary formally received the memo on the afternoon of January 30, a few hours before Gandhi was assassinated, but ultimately Gandhi's lieutenants disregarded his advice for reasons that now seem evident – it failed to suit their purposes.

Leadership Incentives

It is perhaps reasonable to say that not any one reason but a combination of factors contributed to the transformation of the Congress from a nationalist movement into an electorally oriented federal party. The Indian tradition of hierarchical social relations was important, and we can only speculate as to the influence of British rule and the struggle for independence. The precursor to the party, the Indian National Congress, was founded in 1885 by an Englishman, Allan Hume, in cooperation with English-educated Indian citizens. The Congress was designed as "a loyal opposition" and its early leadership consisted of men who "endeavored to learn the British art of governing and to benefit from the blessings of the British constitution" (Krishna 1966: 413).[30] Unsurprisingly, in its early years, the party consisted of mostly Western-educated, English-speaking elites that by 1935 united a vast cadre of Indian intellectuals and industrialists – so much so that when it chose to boycott the government, the British faced a problem of being unable to find people to fill official positions (Ehrmann 1947; Krishna 1966).

While scholars continue to debate the influence of British political tradition, it is nevertheless true that following independence, India's political institutions were modeled largely after Britain's, a critical component of which was the Westminster single-member legislative district.[31] This fact alone colors the electoral competition that ensued. The Congress, though,

many Indian politicians and of the party rank and file toward political power as an objective" (p. 394). In particular, because "Hindu tradition, while it accords high status to the Kshatriya ruler, holds it important that others should not strive for positions of authority. Each man must accept his own dharma (duty) and perform his duty well. Better to perform one's own duty poorly, say the scriptures, than to perform someone else's duty well. Authority is acceptable, but to struggle for a position of authority is not" (p. 395). Thus, argued Weiner, leading Indian politicians had reputations for "sacrifice" and "political detachment."

30 The Congress first acted as a pro-Indian and pro-middle-class lobby within the framework of British rule. In the 1920s Gandhi reorganized the party into a mass movement to resist the British rule and the party became the leading champion of Indian independence. From 1935, with the introduction of provincial self-government, the Congress began the transformation toward a governing party (Brass 1994).

31 The Indian Constitution was based largely on a lengthy constitutional document prepared by the British Parliament – the British Act of 1935. That act, the longest document ever produced by the British Parliament, described all imaginable details of the proposed constitution for India and in 1950 it became the basis of the even longer constitution.

was not systematically involved in electoral campaigning until 1936. It boycotted the first legislative elections in November–December 1920, whereas in 1923, it let members to decide for themselves whether they would take part in the elections. The British Act of 1935 gave greater power to provincial governments and forced the Congress to compete for provincial offices by relying on the support of a diverse collection of local elites, which in turn diversified the party's membership (Weiner 1967: 471). Following the general elections of 1936–7, the party captured control of eight of eleven provincial governments, and participated in coalition governments in the remaining three (which were predominately Moslem). Overall, it won 711 of 1,585 seats, with the remaining 392 non-Muslim seats divided among fifteen other parties. By then the party had become skilled in electoral politics, and in the general election of 1946 it polled 91 percent of the Hindu vote, while in that year's election for the Constituent Assembly, it won 97 percent of all general seats (the Moslem League won 92 percent of those seats specifically designated as Moslem), giving it an overwhelming majority of 207 out of 296 seats (Ehrmann 1947).

From that point on, the party developed an interesting internal schism – between members with a position in the government versus those who served the party's general organization. Probably not a single study of Indian politics does not discuss the conflict between "governmental" and "organizational" factions, and although this conflict led ultimately to the decline of the Congress's electoral fortunes, the factors behind it were the same ones that contributed to its prolonged electoral success. The roots of the conflict can be found in the party's initial pro-independence coalitional nature. Because, under the British rule, the Congress sought to develop a broad coalition that united all those who supported independence, it became a highly decentralized entity with loose discipline. In most instances, its decisions were advisory and the only requirement of membership was "not to act in the name of the Congress in a way contrary to its official policy" (Krishna 1966: 428). However, even in this initial period, organizational decentralization coexisted with a significant degree of leadership autonomy. Within the party itself, democratic procedures were not applied, which served to separate rank-and-file members from the top leadership. A small group, often termed the "High Command," which included Gandhi, the Congress president, and members of the Working Committee, determined Congress policies (Kochanek 1966; Krishna 1966; Weiner 1967; Brass 1994). One consequence of this arrangement was that the rapid expansion and shifts in nature of the Congress's electoral support posed no challenge to the leadership. That leadership welcomed almost anyone willing to participate in electoral campaigns, provided there was no internal threat to their status. The postindependence Congress was characterized by the same division between the rank and file and top leadership (Brass 1994). Thus, Nehru became Congress president in 1949 largely on the basis of Gandhi's recommendation, who, after being asked by the British viceroy to form an interim government, drew his cabinet largely from the party's Working Committee. Nehru then advanced the primacy of the office of prime minister and definitively moved the party's locus of power to the government (Kochanek 1966).

One might suppose that the government's monopoly on power within the party would erode in the course of competitive elections, because one cannot win elections without maintaining the active support of local organizations and the rank-and-file members, which, if dissatisfied, could join the opposition. This, however, was not the case, at least until 1967. Here, the government was shielded from the pressures from below by the Congress's unique electoral strategy. By securing a supermajority in excess of over 70 percent of the seats in the first three general elections, party leaders ensured that no candidate or group within its coalition could claim to be pivotal to its electoral success. No local faction or group, regardless of its position with respect to the leadership, could seriously threaten the government's monopoly on power within the party. Instead, those factions worked to increase the strength of the Congress's parliamentary majority, with party MPs voting a straight party line so as to assure an automatic and easy majority for all government-sponsored legislation.

Thus insulated from its rank and file, the party's leadership could continue to run the Congress as a broad and internally diverse electoral coalition that welcomed almost everyone who might increase its vote share, especially since this strategy fed on itself and sustained the leadership's position of power. There was, however, a second reason why the party's leadership pursued a strategy of maximal inclusion. Although the party had five years in office to prepare for the first postindependence general election, both the government and the party's rank and file faced a serious challenge: universal adult suffrage. Prior to independence, the franchise was limited by restrictive property or income qualifications. For example, in the 1935 election the number of electors for the Central Legislative Assembly was about 5 million, while the number of provincial electors for all provinces was approximately 30 million out of a population of approximately 400 million (Ehrmann 1947: 667).[32] Thus, by the time of the first general election (1951–2), the Congress had to create an electoral machinery capable of bringing into the fold newly enfranchised groups in the population. Moreover, most Indian constituencies were (and still are) overwhelmingly rural. A campaign in a rural India constituency required a candidate able to deal with voters in upwards of one hundred villages in a state assembly election and at least five hundred villages in a parliamentary election (Brass 1994: 95–7). In most villages, one or two

[32] In the first two elections of 1920 and 1924 the restrictions were even stricter: the total number of Indians eligible to vote for the representatives in the Legislative Assembly was around 1 million, and for Provincial Councils, 5 million. Only about 17,000 were allowed to choose Council of State members (upper chamber).

TABLE 6.4. *India's First Four General Elections*

	Percentage of Vote				Percentage of Seats			
	1952	1957	1962	1967	1952	1957	1962	1967
Lok Sabha	45.0	47.8	44.7	40.9	74.4	75.1	73.1	54.6
State Legislative Assemblies	42.2	44.9	43.6	40.1	68.4	64.8	61.4	48.6

large elite castes controlled most of the land and other economic resources and often were able to control the votes of the low castes (Brass 1994: 6). Dealing with more than a dozen states, some of them European-sized, and generally lacking direct contact or any effective means of communication with voters, the Congress's leadership had little choice but to access the electorate through traditional, mostly informal, local organizations (Weiner 1967: 24). Thus, to win elections nationally, the Congress had to become an electoral alliance of numerous local parties and elite organizations.

The importance of sustaining electoral coalitions with local parties and groups was magnified by the use of the first-past-the-post plurality electoral system. Although such a system is associated theoretically with two-party competition, in India competition evolved between the Congress coalition and numerous smaller parties.[33] With a plethora of small parties as well as literally thousands of independent unaligned candidates, the first-past-the-post system allowed Congress to receive a disproportionate share of seats. But what was perhaps a more important consequence was the value it placed on formal and informal alliances with numerous state and local groups. The only winning strategy under the circumstances was to ally electorally with as many popular local politicians as possible, regardless of their political ideologies (Chibber 1999). While the electoral system magnified the Congress's gains as its vote increased, it also magnified its loss in the event of an electoral decline, which is precisely what happened in 1967. Then, although its vote merely declined from 44.7 to 40.9 percent, its share of seats fell from 73.1 to 54.6 percent (see Table 6.4).

Rank-and-File Incentives

Regional and local politicians often find it more advantageous to promote their own parties with local appeals rather than submit to the leadership of

[33] In the 1935 general election, over a dozen parties and groups competed against it; the Election Commission officially recognized fourteen all-India and fifty-two state parties to participate in the first general election in 1952; in the second general election of 1957, on the basis of having won at least 3 percent of the valid votes in the preceding election, the Election Commission recognized four national parties and twelve state parties, in addition to thirty-six other parties that were eligible to contest one or more states; and in 1962 the commission recognized nine all-India parties and seven state parties.

a broad and amorphous national party. Indeed, after 1967 the same trend of regionalism prevailed in India as well. But during the formative years of electoral competition, the logic of competition drove a significant share of local elites throughout the country to join the Congress and use it as a tool to prevail over other groups who, in response, joined a different faction within the Congress, a different party, or campaigned independently. Importantly, there was sufficient local factional conflict among property owners and dominant castes so that no party could unite all local elites within a region, and with the fierce competition among fragmented local elites, groups allying with the Congress secured a competitive advantage. Here again, the plurality electoral system magnified incentives.

Given its enormous advantage in patronage owing to its position as the ruling party, politicians were likely to seek power within the Congress first and join the opposition only if they failed there. As the result, there were "few prominent opposition leaders in India at the national, state, or district level who have not at one time or another been Congressmen" (Weiner 1967: 470).[34] Also, there were few prominent state and local groups that have not at one time or another formed an alliance with the Congress. Local groups joined when it promised to increase their chances to gain local control and abandoned the party if it did not. Thus, "rival groups aspiring to capture executive posts in the district forge alliances with opposition parties. Cutting across party lines they try to gain controlling positions which they can use for distributing spoils and offering patronage.... As ideologies and principles do not count for much... groups form, break and reform only to be broken again with every change in the situation" (Roy 1967: 204).

The dynamics of these ad hoc electoral alliances led to significant electoral volatility across states and districts. Although until 1967 the overall electoral support for the Congress remained stable, the geography of victory was less predictable. For example, in the 1957 state elections Congress won 2,009 seats; in 1962, the party retained only 1,280 of those seats but won seats in 637 new districts. Importantly, the party lost and gained seats in all states. In other words, there were no stable coalitions of states and districts, and in every election the Congress had to compete actively across the entire country. Using a strategy of broad coalition building, the Congress dominated elections nationally and in most states until 1967. During this period, it was a custom to characterize the Indian party system as "a dominant party system," although commentators stressed that the capacity of Congress to win adequate majorities in the states and at the center rested largely "on a judicious balancing of factions, keeping them under control and preserving the coalition character of the party" (Krishna 1967: 73).

[34] For example, up to 1998 all of India's "non-Congress" prime ministers (Morarji Desai, Charan Singh, V. P Singh, Chandra Shekar, H. D. Deve Gowda, and Inder Kumar Gujral) were formerly members of the Congress.

The Party and Federalism

The coalitional character of the party endowed it with a well-defined federal structure that was supportive of state autonomy. While formally the party's leadership had unconstrained authority, during the first twenty years of independence, state party organizations enjoyed significant autonomy, with the High Command arbitrating and mediating between competing factions. Thus, while the party's Central Electoral Committee had final authority in the selection of candidates for the state and national legislatures, the committee did not come into play until state lists were compiled locally. Normally, approval of the slate was a formality, and the committee intervened only to offer compromise candidates when state party organizations were badly split by factions. To be sure, the leadership insisted on having the final say in naming state chief ministers, because those ministers were regarded as part of the party's "governmental" wing. But, even here, Nehru and his successor let regional party leaders exercise significant discretion in making decisions in line with local sentiments. In many cases the high command named chief ministers demanded by state (Pradesh) organizations, most notably in such important states as Madras, Andhra, and Bombay. A Congress policy held that no man could be elected chief minister unless he was first elected to the legislature (Kochanek 1968: 263). When particular state leaders were especially popular, the all-India Congress leadership made them chief ministers, even if they opposed the policies of the government. Alternatively, when the central leadership refused to compromise, state party leaders did not hesitate to campaign against the candidates proposed by Delhi and frequently ensured their defeat (Franda 1962).

Some observers suggest that by the mid-1960s forces within the Congress at the state level and below exerted more influence than the national leadership (Manor 1995). Others, however, note that the high command made no attempt to squash the power of state party organizations, as did Indira Gandhi. For example, the leadership preserved the practice of simultaneous national and the state legislative assembly elections (abolished by Gandhi in 1971 in an attempt to tighten control of the states). In 1956, facing growing demands by state party organizations, the leadership agreed to reorganize states on a linguistic principle, and during the Nehru period state party organizations were allowed to become financially autonomous (Weiner 1967: 46). The strength of state organizations was further augmented by an expansion of the powers of old local government bodies and the formal transfer of control of resources from local bureaucracies to local elected officials. New elected offices were created at all levels, including villages, which served to augment the influence of state parties in village-level politics (in the Indira Gandhi period local elections became a formality and a number of states stopped holding them altogether).

One can reasonably speculate that the party's pre-Gandhi leadership did not invade the authority of state parties because it lacked the will or means but because it had strong electoral incentives not to do so. State party organizations were combinations of numerous factions and groups, competing for influence, office, and power. Factions were united only by the desire to win state seats and political control, and under this circumstance any attempt to subordinate a state party to central directive could only be implemented through the cooperation of other state and local leaders and factions. Such a strategy, however, could backfire at the polls for two reasons. First, those leaders and factions willing to be dominated by the party's central leadership were more likely than not to be relatively weak and less popular. Second, though the center could encourage and perhaps strengthen particular groups within state Congresses, that would serve only to alienate other factions that would have little reason to stay within the Congress if it interfered in their fight for the local control. Thus, the most important and difficult role of the central leadership was to preserve the balance among state-level factions and to keep any group from dominating the state governmental apparatus.

A way to preserve factional balance was to insist that minority factions be given some representation in the cabinet and a voice in candidate selection. Another way was to encourage and institutionalize competition among factions. For example, party offices and nominations were distributed among factions somewhat proportionally to the size of the faction's "primary" membership, which stimulated factions to sustain large memberships, if only on paper and for a period immediately prior to elections.[35] Perhaps the most important inducement, however, was the introduction of numerous electoral offices, down to the village level. After administrative functions were turned over to locally elected governments, the traditional struggle for administrative influence moved to the area of open electoral politics. As conflicts emerged within a village, village factions looked upon party struggles as an opportunity to further their own interests. A faction might support the Congress in one election and an opposition party in the next, while another local faction might switch to Congress in its place, driving the local Congress leadership to stay friendly with many if not all of them.

1967 and Thereafter

The balanced coexistence of the Congress central and state party organizations collapsed after the 1967 election, in which the party's seat share in the Indian parliament declined to 54 percent and it lost its majority position in eight of nineteen provincial assemblies. Although any other party might view such a result as a victory, in the Indian context the election marked the

[35] After the Congress became an electoral party in 1949 and opened enrollment to new members, within six months 30 million new "primary" members joined the party. In certain villages enrollment exceeded the adult population or equaled the total population of the village. For the whole period of 1949–67, records indicate that millions of members joined the party in and around election years.

beginning of a totally new coalitional dynamic. Absent the supermajority required to neutralize any challenge to the party's leadership, that leadership turned for support to the strongest factions and the most important states. Absent the party's ability to maintain a delicate balance within state organizations, factions that found themselves on the losing side now had less incentive to remain within the Congress, and as a consequence the party suffered massive defections and severe splits in its own leadership. In 1969, at the peak of the power struggle, then prime minister Indira Gandhi was expelled from the Congress and officially lost control over the party organization. She did, however, manage to preserve her support in parliament, which allowed her to form a new faction, the Congress (R), which stood in opposition to the old leaders of the party, Congress (O). Congress (R) was supported by 223 of the 283 incumbent Congress members of the 520 seat parliament, and unscheduled national parliamentary elections (but not state elections) were called in 1971.

Unable or unwilling to preserve the Congress as a coalition of state organizations and factions, Gandhi moved to the politics of personal popularity, so that the campaign ran largely as a populist referendum on Gandhi versus the party leadership. The strategy seemed successful, at least for Gandhi personally – Congress (R) won 44 percent of the vote and 68 percent of the seats. The old party bosses were defeated and with them the coalitional nature of the Congress. Shortly thereafter the civil war and secessionist movement in East Pakistan began, and Congress (R), with the approval of major opposition parties, tentatively decided to postpone state elections. Gandhi's personal popularity reached a record high following the defeat of the Pakistani army, at which point she strategically scheduled state assembly elections for March 1972. Again, the main issue was her personal electoral appeal ("I seek another mandate – from the States" [Palmer 1973: 542]), with the party's primary tactic being that of selecting only those candidates who would be loyal to her and supportive of the proposed radical policies: "[I]n no other election did the Prime Minister, the members of the Central Election Committee, and other central party leaders play such a decisive role in the selection of candidates" (Palmer 1973: 538). Once again the strategy succeeded: Congress (R) won 48 percent of the popular vote across states and 71 percent of all seats, which allowed it to control all state governments. Gandhi moved quickly to impose a high degree of centralization within the party, especially with respect to the nomination and replacement of party offices. Appointments of state chief ministers became subject to Gandhi's wishes, who replaced every Congress chief minister with an independent power base. The party became Gandhi's pyramid of power, and the party itself, both in organization and tactics, mirrored the USSR's Communist Party.

As often happens in a political system in which the government can no longer rely on the "democratic self-interest" of political elites for its authority, India succumbed to "emergency" authoritarian rule, which saw the jailing of tens of thousands of political opponents, press censorship, and limits on civil liberties. Ironically, however, the Congress's electoral success corresponded to a significant decline in its influence within the states. Central control came at the expense of state organizations and in some states the activities of the party virtually ceased.

Gandhi might have maintained authoritarian rule indefinitely, but in 1977 she called for new parliamentary elections and an ease in the provisions of emergency rule. The result was a surprise for everyone. Although the opposition had only a few weeks to prepare, the Congress was decisively defeated by the Janata coalition, which consisted largely of former Congress politicians whom Gandhi defeated in the intraparty competition. With only 35 percent of the popular vote, the Congress won 28 percent of seats, while Janata, in contrast, won 41 percent of the vote and 54 percent of the seats. Morarji Desai, the conservative finance minister whom Gandhi had dismissed and subsequently jailed in the initial confrontation with the old party leadership became the new prime minister. A standard textbook explanation for the Congress's defeat is miscalculation by Gandhi – the consequence of a censored press and a corresponding lack of information about her true level of popularity. However, it is also possible to view defeat as the price the party paid for the destruction of its state organizations and the failure to deal with local factions. If anything, the election did demonstrate that no party could win in India without the support of a meaningful coalition of local elites. Absent that coalition, Gandhi and her son Sanjay were not even able to keep their own parliamentary seats.

Today India no longer has a dominant national party, and competition entails three major contenders – the BJP, the Congress, and the United Front coalition. These parties are distinguishable on both a left-right and sectarian-secular dimension. Nevertheless, it is a legacy of the period of Congress's political dominance and now an ingrained trait of Indian federal political system that any party that hopes to win control of the central government must form alliances with a multitude of regional and state parties (Rudolph and Rudolph 2002). These alliances take two forms: preelection "seat adjustments," which is an agreement among parties not to compete against each other directly in selected constituencies, and postelection parliamentary coalitions (Pai 1998). Partners treat these alliances as mutually beneficial, short-term opportunistic partnerships. In a seeming replay of the pre-Gandhi era, the major players pursue regional support where they have no base, while their regional partners seek to improve their bargaining position with the center and strengthen their positions against opponents in their own states. In this more competitive environment it is not surprising to see the instability of alliances involving numerous regional parties. The coalition that unexpectedly defeated Gandhi in 1977 quickly dissolved and allowed the Congress to return to national power in 1980. The National Front coalition then successfully defeated the Congress in 1989, but as a ruling party it survived less than two years, so that in every subsequent election, an assortment of smaller parties has attempted to bring regional and state parties together and revive the National Front in order to defeat both the Congress and the Hindu nationalist Bharatiya Janata. With the Congress deinstitutionalized, its electoral fortunes are now closely linked to the popularity of its leaders. Thus, notable Congress successes in the 1984 and 1991 general elections are commonly attributed to sympathy waves following the assassinations of Indira and Rajiv Gandhi, respectively, while Sonia Gandhi's decision to assume control of the party is presumed to explain its relative success in the 1998 elections – the party finished first with 25.8 percent of the vote.

The question naturally arises now as to whether India's experience with federal democracy has thus far been merely fortuitous – the early and accidental development of an integrated party that facilitated federal harmony? Is that experience unlikely to be replicated in the current more competitive environment, where winning is no longer defined in terms of near majorities of the vote but rather simply in terms of pluralities over the closest competitor? Absent the cement of a Congress party able to resist demands from its parts for disruptive redistribution, will competition now render redistributive appeals a strategic imperative in electoral competition? And finally, to the extent that our answers to the preceding questions are yes, then we must also ask whether there are institutional fixes for the country's potential problems. Such questions, of course, cannot be answered until we understand better the institutional prerequisites for integrated party development. However, our survey of India does answer one question: namely, whether the development of an integrated party system is precluded by first-past-the-post electoral arrangements in a parliamentary system. Put simply, the institutional parameters that need to be considered when designing a federal state with an eye to encouraging integrated parties necessarily concern more than a simple choice between presidential versus parliamentary government or single-member versus proportional forms of representation. The discovery of the parameters that need to be considered is the subject of the chapter that follows.

7

Institutional Sources of Federal Stability I

The balance of social interests, the separation and balance of powers, were meant to secure liberty, but it was still uncertain, after the instrument had been framed and ratified, whether the balance would not be too precarious to come to rest anywhere; and whether the arms of government, separated in parchment, could come together in reality to cooperate in the formation and execution of policy.

Hofstadter 1969: 70

The constitution of the United States is an admirable work, nevertheless one may believe that its founders would not have succeeded, had not the previous 150 years given the different States of the Union the *taste for, and practice of, provincial governments.*

Alexis de Toqueville[1]

I confess, as I enter the Building, I stumble on the threshold. I meet with a National Government, instead of a Federal Union of Sovereign States.

Samuel Adams 1787, on the U.S. Constitution

7.1 Introduction

Adams can be forgiven his initial cynical assessment of the newly proposed Constitution since he played the critical role in ensuring its approval by the Massachusetts ratifying convention. His cousin John, on the other hand, was perhaps less enthusiastic of its possibilities, for Adams "knew full well the dependence of republicanism on the character of the people" (Wood 1969: 570) and in this respect he was more than a little apprehensive of the future. Nevertheless, Adams became one of the documents strongest defenders (see his *In Defence of the Constitution*), because he saw in it what its opponents

[1] As cited in Ostrom (1991: 96; emphasis in original).

feared – a strong and balanced national government. What is perhaps most interesting about Adam's arguments and of those labeled Federalist and Anti-Federalist, however, is that in at least one respect, all arguments were flawed – perhaps not fundamentally, but at least insofar as the implications one can draw from them. Each side of the debate wrote and spoke as if there was only one institutional form that could be federal, democratic, and stable. Either the national government had to be weak and designed as the mere agent of the states, who would remain the ultimate repositories of popular government (the Anti-Federalist view) or the national government, with its powers divided, had to be endowed with supreme authority (the Federalist view). What neither side seems to have understood fully was the possibility that there would be a great many political institutional forms compatible with their objectives.

The potentially great variety of successful federal designs derives in part from the fact that the performance of any specific design will be decided by a multiplicity of interdependent institutional choices. Thus, in choosing the tools to apply, the most one can hope for is that a given choice will move the political process in a desired direction and contribute to sustainable broad coalition building associated with integrated party systems. In arguing this, we are not departing from the conventional literature, where the commonly cited dimensions of a design are the choice of a unitary versus federal form, a presidential versus parliamentary system, the choice of an electoral system, the choice of the basis for citizenship, and whether a constitution should, in addition to constraints on government action, specify the state's distributive responsibilities with respect to citizens (Lijphart 1984; Grofman 1996; Grofman and Reynolds 2001). Instead, our argument is that although it may be tempting to examine comparatively the various instances of federal stability and instability with an eye to cataloging the institutions that seem most conducive to or compatible with stable and effective federal government, such an approach would prove fruitless for a practical design effort.

Moreover, since a federation can be judged to be stable and effective regardless of whether it is parliamentary or presidential, regardless of whether representation is based on single-mandate or multimandate districts, regardless of whether it provides for a powerful chief executive or entrusts federal subjects with the administration of national government functions, regardless of whether it must abide by a constitutionally mandated form of redistribution or allows redistribution to be the unrestrained product of politics, and regardless of whether it overrepresents specific groups in society or seeks to be wholly symmetric in all respects, then we also cannot say that stability and effectiveness are *caused* in any scientifically fundamental way by specific institutions. Rather, in terms of identifying necessary and sufficient conditions, it must be that they are caused by something that institutional configurations of a particular sort, in combination with other characteristics of society, facilitate or impart to society. What we require, then, before we can have even tentative and qualified confidence that a design might work is the identity of that cause. Only then can we properly interpret the meaning and implications for stability of one constellation of institutions versus another or proclaim that one federation is stable because of its institutions while another is unstable because it has chosen less wisely.

The preceding chapters, in fact, along with the paradigm within which this volume operates, identify that cause. It lies in the motives of the players in the political game. If we reduce that game to its essential components – elections and the passage and execution of laws – those players are voters, candidates, and candidates in the role of incumbents. From voters we want an electorate that stands ready to support candidates who espouse policies not detrimental to federal stability and an evolutionary adaptation of federal structure to changing circumstances. Naturally, voters will not be conscious of this motive except in extreme circumstances, as when the choices presented to them include radical ethnic, linguistic, racial, or religious appeals. We cannot suppose, however, that the human species can be transformed whereby an entire society defines its self-interest in terms of some abstract collective interest. Perhaps more important, we also cannot suppose that such definitions of self-interest can be manufactured directly by institutional means, if only because, virtually by definition, the interaction of voters with political institutions is minimal and consists almost exclusively of merely choosing one candidate or list of candidates over another in an election. If institutions have a direct impact on motives and strategies, that impact will apply primarily to elites. Nevertheless, as described in Chapter 5, we want voters who will act *as if* their self-interest lies in supporting candidates whose campaigns are not framed exclusively in terms of limited constituency appeals. The means to this end is an institutional structure that impacts the motives and, therefore, the actions of elites (candidates and incumbents) in such a way that voters, acting in their myopic self-interest, would nevertheless support candidates whose policies serve a greater interest than of those who formally elect them.

This is not a call for massive electoral delusion but instead for institutionally induced elite incentives such that an objective assessment of the electorate's self-interest yields choices that favor the constitutional order. We can, in fact, see the essential nature of the system we seek. In its simplest form (recall Figure 5.1), assume a voter must choose between two candidates. The first explicitly champions the voter's immediate and ostensibly "narrow" self-interest and disavows any chance of compromise with competing forces. The second candidate offers the opposite – at best an acknowledgment of the legitimacy of that self-interest, a promise to try to realize only a part of it even if doing so requires negotiating away some of the voter's secondary concerns. A candidate of the first type we might suppose, then, carries the label of a party that is indifferent to being inclusive, and which prefers instead to give its label strict ideological, territorial, or ethnic meaning within the confines of a well-defined albeit potentially narrow constituency. The second candidate, in contrast, carries the label of a party with wholly amorphous ideological content, with a constituency that can be held together as an electoral coalition only if compromise is made on nearly every issue, including the allocation of public benefits across federal subjects. Our voter's rational choice, now, requires an assessment of the likelihood of the first party's success at implementing its platform or at least in influencing government policy versus the trade-offs the second party will be willing to make in order to secure a fraction of what our voter's self-interest demands. Absent other information, we cannot say unambiguously which choice is best, since what the rest of the electorate does also enters into this calculation. But, if the argument we offer in the previous chapter about the stabilizing role of integrated parties is correct, then we want a political system in which the voter rationally chooses the second candidate. And, of course, we want something else: we want an institutional structure such that the second alternative – the inclusive candidate (or several such candidates) – is in fact a choice that will be offered.

7.2 Level 2 and *The Federalist Papers*

A theory of federal process that begins with the supposition that the critical determinant of stability and effectiveness is contained in the motives established and expressed by a state's party system is not, of course, wholly consistent with the theory of federalism propounded by Hamilton and Madison in their *Federalist Papers*. Parties there were merely another faction to be controlled by constitutional constraints. Parties – or at least national factions that bore a striking resemblance to the integrated parties we see today – nevertheless developed: "The election of 1796 was clearly a contest between Republicans and Federalists, and as each party sought to give victory to its candidate, party lines tightened, party spirit rose to new heights, and political parties became a more ineradicable part of American political life" (Sharp 1993). It is also evident, however, that parties were largely sectional and, therefore, merely representative of the very geographic interests Hamilton and Madison hoped the new constitution would constrain. Thus, even if the Level 2 institutional structure established in 1787 and analyzed in *The Federalist Papers* does not describe a sufficient condition for federal stability, because the mechanism of self-enforcement is not fully contained in that level, it is silly to reject the hypothesis that that structure is nevertheless a critical component of a sufficient condition.

Hamilton and Madison's theory of federal stability is well known, and we require here only a minimal survey of its essential parts to explore this hypothesis.[2] Without trying to distinguish between what was written merely

[2] See especially Elkins and McKitrick (1993) and Wood (1969).

as political rhetoric versus statements that are part of a coherent theory of political institutional design, Madison and Hamilton describe two cures for the instabilities that characterized earlier republics: an extended republic and a properly structured federalism: "In the extent and proper structure of the Union, therefore, we behold a Republican remedy for the diseases most incident to Republican Government" (*Federalist* 10). But while the notion of an "extended republic" seems clear, the meaning of "proper structure" is a bit of a puzzle since Madison and Hamilton's definition is vague and incomplete.[3] There are, though, several components of design that seem essential to such a structure as they saw it. The first is a tripartite, balanced separation of powers, and there is little doubt about the presumed necessity for applying this principle to state governments as well as the national one: "In the compound republic of America, the power surrendered by the people, is first divided between two distinct governments, and then the portion allotted to each, subdivided among distinct and separate departments. Hence, a double security arises to the rights of the people. The different governments will control each other; at the same time that each will be controlled by itself" (*Federalist* 51).

A balanced separation is a virtual axiom of *The Federalist Papers* for achieving a stable republican government, federal or otherwise, but much if not most of Madison and Hamilton's argument is directed at countering the criticism that the powers granted the new national government by the proposed constitution would quickly usurp the legitimate authority of states. However, there is also little doubt about their unwillingness to compromise on the issue of supremacy: "[T]he laws of the confederacy, as to the *enumerated* and *legitimate* objects of its jurisdiction, will become the SUPREME LAW of the land; to the observance of which, all officers legislative, executive, and judicial in each State, will be bound by the sanctity of an oath. Thus the Legislatures, Courts, and Magistrates of the respective members will be incorporated into the operations of the national government, as far as its just and constitutional authority extends; and will be rendered auxiliary to the enforcement of its laws" (*Federalist* 27, emphasis in the original). But to leave the matter here would have rendered ratification of the new constitution impossible. Thus, additional requirements had to be met to ensure that participant states would find it in their interest to form such a federation. Those requirements, as outlined in *The Federalist Papers*, are four in number:

1. A guarantee of state sovereignty with respect to those policies for which there is little rationale for federal involvement. To counter federal incursions into state power, states must be armed with a

[3] The emphasis on the words "proper structure" was first brought to our attention by Vincent Ostrom (1991, see especially chap. 4).

guarantee of sovereignty that Hamilton and Madison asserted was fortified by the constitution's limited assignment of powers to the federal government.

2. State representation in a meaningful upper legislative chamber of the national government.

Hamilton, in fact, virtually equates these two requirements with the definition of proper structure: "The proposed Constitution, so far from implying an abolition of the State Governments, makes them constituent parts of the national sovereignty by allowing them a direct representation in the Senate, and leaves in their possession certain elusive and very important portions of sovereign power. This fully corresponds, in every rational import of the terms, with the idea of a Federal Government" (*Federalist* 9). Representation in the Senate was, of course, the cornerstone of the Great Compromise whereby small states were empowered to protect their interests against the larger ones. But, in adhering to the demands of the more populous states, the U.S. Constitution was presumed to give states a dual protection:

3. In addition to seeing the Senate as representing states and the House as more responsive to "the people," *The Federalist Papers* identify *both* chambers as giving the states representation – small states in the case of the Senate, large ones in the case of the House.

Madison's caveat that the lower chamber be sufficiently large to ensure meaningful representation but not too large emphasizes the local character to the intended structure of representation: "[*A*]*fter securing a sufficient number for purposes of safety, of local information, and of diffuse sympathy with the whole society*, they will counteract their own view by every addition to their representatives" (*Federalist* 58, emphasis in original).

Although Hamilton and Madison's arguments here are colored by more than a little political rhetoric, the general principle they emphasize and consider a proper answer to the states' potential anxiety comes through clearly. Both chambers of the Congress (like both chambers of the German, Swiss, and Australian parliaments) give explicit representation to the states, their people or governments, and thus both chambers, at least in theory, provide states with some degree of protection. In the United States and Australia, this is accomplished in the lower chamber by single-member districts contained wholly in each state; Switzerland generally implements proportional representation at the canton level, and in Germany it is accomplished by having parties fill seats in the Bundestag by both single-member districts and by party lists generated within each state. The Swiss and German systems are, perhaps, more explicitly "federal" in the way they fill their lower legislative chambers, and although the U.S. House of Representatives is not designed to represent states per se, to the extent that state interests are an aggregation of local interests, it was assumed to perform this function. The final condition specified by Hamilton and Madison is:

4. Concurrent jurisdiction. Unlike a unitary state in which the central government is alone responsible to the people and merely assigns powers to federal subjects, and unlike a confederacy in which the federal government has no direct connection to the people, proper structure requires that both the national government and state governments have their own direct connection to the ultimate sovereign.

As Hamilton states the matter, "we must resolve to incorporate into our plans those ingredients which may be considered as forming the characteristic difference between a league and a government; we must extend the authority of the union to the persons of the citizens, – the only proper objects of government" (*Federalist* 15), and "The government of the Union, like that of each state, must be able to address itself immediately to the hopes and fears of individuals.... It must, in short, possess all the means and have a right to resort to all the methods of executing the powers, with which it is entrusted, that are possessed and exercised by the government of the particular States" (*Federalist* 16)

It is true that Madison and Hamilton argue for concurrent jurisdiction primarily as a way to empower the national government. As we note earlier, there was little need in 1787 to empower states; they existed as fully functioning entities under the Articles of Confederation. Nevertheless, if we take their argument at face value, then the following assessment by Ostrom (1991: 80) of *The Federalist Papers*'s definition of "proper structure" is an appropriate summary of their position: "Sovereignty, conceptualized as the authority to make laws, is divided so that the people of the member republics are subordinate to the authority of the Union with respect to national affairs, but are independent with respect to those prerogatives that apply to the jurisdiction of the separate states or republics. The states, in turn, serve as constituent parts of the national government by their representation in the Senate. Governments do not govern governments as such. Concurrent governments reach to the persons of individuals, including citizens and officials claiming to exercise governmental prerogatives under constitutional authority."

The question nevertheless remains as to whether this structure is sufficient for the development of those private incentives occasioned by integrated parties and which we argue are essential for the endogenous enforcement of constitutional provisions and the stability and balance described in *The Federalist Papers*. It may be true that parties do mold incentives in precisely the way Chapter 6 describes, and that constitutional enforcement requires those incentives. But it may also be true that the constitutional provisions as discussed by Madison and Hamilton are sufficient as well – that integrated parties and those institutions exogenous to the constitution that encourage them are the natural product of the constitution itself, so that the institutions that are the focus of Madison and Hamilton's treatise, though not the proximate "cause" of federal stability, nonetheless constitute the underlying basic cause. In this scheme, then, and in the case of the United States at least, parties are at most a subsidiary protection of stable federal relations. The hypothesis we offer here, however, is that not only is this not the case today, but it was not the case even in the early history of the republic and that the parties that emerged were as much the product of other institutional arrangements as anything else. This is different than saying that the Level 2 rules that correspond to constitutional provisions, as well as a thoughtful and restrained approach to erecting Level 1 constraints, were superfluous. We are hypothesizing only that those provisions needed to be fortified with a third level of institutional structure.

There is something else that needs to be added to our hypothesis. Saying that the constitution as ratified was conducive to integrated party development is different from saying that such parties would develop quickly or that the United States was not able to take advantage of a variety of fortuitous and unique circumstances. Insofar as uniqueness is concerned, consider this fact: with the exception of a few small states (Delaware and Rhode Island), the geographic configuration of the original thirteen states of the Union was essentially east-west, which is to say that each state possessed a mercantile seaboard and an agricultural interior (New Hampshire's seaboard may have been minimal, but it nevertheless existed). Thus, each such state possessed a creditor (seaboard) and a debtor (interior) class, and each, thereby, confronted an equivalent domestic political division. We know that this fact grew especially salient with Shays's Rebellion in Massachusetts, which was one of the background motivations for the Constitutional Convention itself. We can only speculate about that fact's subsequent role in facilitating the development of a party, the Jeffersonian Republicans, that could make electoral appeals when competing for the presidency or the Congress that did not necessarily pit the interests of local and state officials in one state against those in any other. Even though the first campaigns might be viewed in sectional terms owing to Federalist Party dominance in the Northeast, the rapid decline of that party following Jefferson's ascendancy to the presidency attests to the viability of more universalistic appeals.

It is unlikely that a review of the history of America's political parties would yield an exhaustive list of background conditions that facilitated their development. Nevertheless, some observations can be made. Most important, we need to appreciate the possibility, in particular, that the specific "complication" for American federal constitutional design – that states in 1787 were entities with functioning governments that possessed significant if not complete autonomy – was not in fact a complication but an advantage just as Tocqueville describes. That states were functioning entities in 1787 meant, in addition to having interests elites within them wanted to protect or promote, that they also experienced electoral competition – competition for state legislatures, city councils, the office of sheriff, and even offices of state militias. In addition to this, there were a great many structural variables to be determined at the state level that would be of intense interest to the new body politic. For example, between 1790 and the 1850s, every state held at least one state constitutional convention, which necessarily required elections for delegates to those conventions. And among the issues to be debated was the important one of suffrage.[4] Voting requirements varied widely across states and even within a state from one election to the next and from one county to the next (Keyssar 2000). In New Jersey, for instance, anyone might have been allowed to vote if it served the interests of those who controlled the administration of suffrage at the county level, in which case it was not uncommon for women to vote and to see counties reporting turnout rates in excess of 120 percent of those officially on the voting rolls. Because the United States did not begin its life with universal suffrage, this opportunity to manipulate the right to vote and the administration of election law provided local and state politicians with a strong incentive to organize to win control of state governments and the local offices (usually sheriffs) that administered those laws.

It was upon this base – the latent party systems established at the city, village, and county level to compete for these offices – that America's national parties were built. The first such national party may have been assembled to overthrow the Federalists and seat Jefferson in the White House. But the most expedient route to that end was organizing elements of this base, so regardless of whether it was intended, the first truly national party in America was an integrated one. The pressure for integration was further encouraged by the constitutional structure erected in 1787, and here we begin to see the interplay of institutions that belies any simple causal explanation for the path of America's party development. In particular, we need to keep in mind two important Level 2 background conditions. The first is the executive-legislative separation of powers. Put simply, to control the national government, one had to control both of these separately elected branches. The second condition concerns the method whereby electors to the electoral college were selected and the rules under which members of the House of Representatives were elected – to wit, by state legislators. Although some states proceeded directly to popular election of electors, others manipulated these procedures with great frequency. For example, Massachusetts chose electors by popular vote in 1788, 1792, and 1796, turned to legislative

[4] An additional issue was the method of selection of governors. Although most states allowed for direct election in their early constitutions, it is only in 1824, and only as a by-product of the agitation for reapportionment, that the selection of the governor of Georgia was moved from the legislature to the citizens of that state (Green 1930). The change in other states occurred even later: North Carolina in 1835, Maryland in 1836, New Jersey in 1844, and, last of all, Virginia in 1850.

selection in 1800, returned to the popular vote in 1804, back to legislative selection in 1808, returned once again to popular vote in 1812, back again to legislative selection in 1816, and, finally, back to popular vote in 1820. New Jersey, Georgia, and North Carolina made almost as many changes, and only Maryland and Virginia began with a popular vote and stuck with it. Similarly, when electing members of Congress, Pennsylvania began in 1788 with an at-large system (of single nontransferable vote, SNTV), changed to a district system in 1791, returned to the at-large system in 1792, and permanently changed to single-member districts in 1794 (Hoadley 1986). Maryland began with a "mixed" system but changed to the district system in 1790, whereas New Jersey began with SNTV, changed to a district system in 1798, returned to SNTV in 1800, and changed subsequently and permanently to a district system. In all cases, these changes were governed by the fortunes of different factions or protoparties within the states, and the opportunity to implement such changes, like changes in apportionment and suffrage, were part of the rewards encouraging state party formation.

Thus, to compete nationally for the presidency as well as for control of the national legislature, a party had to compete locally for control of state legislatures, which held the keys to both. And to compete locally a party had to forge those city, village, and county organizations into an effective entity. We have here, then, a forceful example of the interplay of a set of Level 2 constitutional constraints (the electoral college, state legislative selection of electors, the nature of legislative representation in the national legislature, and an executive-legislative separation of powers) and a set of preexisting features – let's say extraconstitutional or Level 3 conditions (political competition within the states, state control of suffrage, proliferation of elected local offices, and, with the exceptions noted, each state's common geographic configuration) – that encouraged state and local competition and integrated party development. Indeed, these background conditions appear to have made integrated parties the only political alternative, and the eventual disappearance of the Federalist Party is a partial confirming test of this hypothesis. We hasten to add that our discussion is not intended as confirmation of the view that the United States enjoyed a unique set of circumstances that are unlikely to be met in other instances of federal design. It may be that America benefited greatly from preexisting democratic processes at the state and local level that encouraged a national party development of a particular sort. But those processes were themselves the product of institutions of human design, including even those institutions which seemed accidents of history, such as the geographic definition of states. Nothing suggests that similar institutions, or simply institutions with equivalent consequences with respect to the motives of elites to organize in a particular way and to sustain the constitutional imperatives that must operate side by side with them, cannot be implemented elsewhere. Indeed, the core of our argument is that these extraconstitutional institutions are an essential component of any successful design.

7.3 Level 3 Institutions

We should not overstate the extent to which national parties in today's terms developed in the early years of the United States. The locus of political power of greatest concern to the average citizen continued to rest with state and local governments, and much of the early activities of "parties" in the United States focused exclusively on politics there: "For nearly fifty years popular attention in politics was absorbed in operating the local system, already 150 years old. Interest in the new federal politics developed with extreme deliberation" (Nichols 1967: 164). Certainly national issues arose almost immediately – the Jay Treaty, the Alien and Sedition Act, the debt, and the contest for the presidency in 1800 – but national parties, as compared with state organizations, remained weak, as can be seen by the fact that national party conventions were unknown until the 1840s.[5] Structural parameters and simply the technologies (or, rather, their absence) of transportation and communication made inevitable the federalized, bottoms-up development of national parties. We may tend to forget, for instance, that the theoretical upper limit on the speed of commerce and communication was, until the advent of the railroad, the speed of the horse. However, the limits of technology have been largely erased, and structural parameters, including the relevant Level 2 constraints, can be changed. Thus, we should also ask why integrated parties have, for the most part, been a permanent feature of American politics.

To answer this question it is useful to consider a few contemporary features of American politics that make national party labels especially valuable. There is, of course, some dispute over the extent to which federalism has eroded in the United States. We do not want to enter that debate, aside from noting that although the federal government's share of public expenditures after the Korean War greatly exceeded that of state and local governments, the trend since then has been a return to the more nearly even balance that prevailed in the 1930s. Thus, although there are good arguments in favor of the view that erosion has been excessive, we cannot say that long-term trends point unambiguously in any one direction. Parties, in the meantime, remain decentralized, yet integrated. Indeed, a survey of the chairs of county party organizations has revealed that during the 1980s local standing of the two main American political parties remained strong: "Though

[5] Although state conventions became firmly rooted in the Middle Atlantic states by the mid-1820s and in New England by the mid-1830s, it was not until 1844 that an organization analogous to a national committee first appeared, and it was primarily a confederation of state organizations.

TABLE 7.1. *Number of Local Governments and Elected Officials in the United States, 1992*

	Governments	Elected Officials
General purpose		
County	3,043	58,818
Municipal	19,279	135,531
Town or township	16,656	126,958
Special purpose		
School district	14,422	88,434
Special district	31,555	84,089
TOTAL	84,955	493,830

it appears that Democrats draw slightly more support from local groups than do Republicans, it is still common for both parties to receive support in terms of candidate endorsements, volunteers, and money contributions to candidates" (Gibson, Frendreis, and Vertz 1989: 83). These authors also find that "there appears to be a substantial balance between Republican and Democratic organizational strength within the counties" (p. 84), which suggests that an equilibrium local organizational presence of parties is maintained as an integrated party system matures. Their conclusion, based on the panel data for local party organizations from the late 1970s and 1984, is that in the 1980s, "the dominant pattern is one of the maintenance of [local] organizational strength, what change has occurred has been in the direction of strengthening party organizations.... State and national party organizations have taken an interest in developing strong local parties.... This may foreshadow a 'nationalization' of party politics and perhaps a significantly greater degree of intraparty coordination and integration than has been previously thought possible by observers of U.S. political parties" (p. 86).

Asking what keeps American parties both decentralized and vertically and horizontally integrated, there seems to be only one place to look: electoral systems. Perhaps the first and most striking feature of the American electoral system is the pervasive use of elections. Indeed, just as Mark Twain once wrote that a person is no more harmlessly occupied than when making money, it would seem, with upward of 600,000 offices filled by election in the United States, that Americans believe that a politician is no more harmlessly occupied than when running for public office. As indicated in Table 7.1, the overwhelming majority of these offices are local.[6] And although much of the competition to fill those offices is nonpartisan, we can be assured that many if not most of the competitors are anything but indifferent to party positions

[6] Table 7.1 offers a breakdown of the nearly half-million offices filled by direct election at the local level in the United States, as well as the considerable number of local governments themselves.

TABLE 7.2. *Number of Statewide Executive Offices, in Addition to Governor, Filled by Direct Election*

Range	Number of States
0	3
1–5	5
6–10	18
11–15	12
16–20	10
21–25	1
>25	1

Source: The Book of the States, vol. 30, 1994–5, Council of State Governments, Lexington, Ky.

and allegiances. Even if we limit our perspective to the level of states, however, we see a vast array of offices filled by direct election. As a consequence largely of the historical abuses of patronage, U.S. state constitutions require not only that the office of governor and seats in the legislature be filled by direct election but that a variety of other offices be filled in the same way – offices such as lieutenant governor, secretary of state, treasurer, attorney general, superintendent of schools, secretary of agriculture, commissioner of insurance, highway commissioner, commissioner of labor, commissioner of elections, commissioner of mines, state auditor, and so on. Table 7.2 gives the distribution of the number of executive offices that are normally filled on a statewide basis in addition to governor and reveals that the median number is between six and ten.

It might seem unproductive, even inefficient, to have a dozen or so executive offices filled in this way, not to mention the hundreds of thousands of local offices such as mayor, aldermen, city councils, county governing bodies, and school boards in addition to the state legislature and city, county, and state judiciaries.[7] After all, we cannot assume that voters will have good information about many, if any, candidates for these offices. Few voters would know much about the candidates for, say, inspector of mines (Arizona) or commissioner of the general land office (Texas). So what then are the benefits of having so many offices filled by direct election, and what is the relevance of these elections to the character of federalism?

Those benefits take three interdependent forms. First, as we indicate earlier, pervasive use of elections at the state and local level facilitates the formation of state and local party organizations that can be the building blocks for

[7] After initial appointment by the governor, state supreme court justices must secure reappointment in general elections in thirty-nine states, of which more than half (twenty-three) run with their party affiliations listed on the ballot.

integrated national parties. Just as competition for state legislative office was the basis for state party formation in the 1790s, we should not be surprised to learn that, because northern and central states subsequently made greater use of direct election for state office than did their southern counterparts, the development of political parties proceeded more quickly in the North than in the South (Formisano 1981). The second benefit of filling a multiplicity of local and state offices by direct election is that it increases the value of party labels by increasing the cost of being a "fully informed" voter. In the manner described earlier, the increased value of a party label strengthens national parties and integrates them with local and regional ones. And even if a significant share of local elections are nonpartisan, local party organizations are hardly indifferent to the partisan leanings of those who fill those offices. Finally, extensive application of direct elections gives those with political ambition a vast menu of often innocuous starting positions, a ready means of moving up the ladder of political position, and a home to those who would compete for the next rung. And as it is with the farm clubs of professional baseball, it is only natural for party elites to recruit candidates for national office from among those who demonstrate effectiveness at campaigning and governing at the local or regional level. All of this, taken together, ensures that those who achieve national office have a strong genetic connection to local and regional politics, parties, and politicians.

It is reasonable, nevertheless, to conjecture that the multiplicity of elections here would not have had the integrating impact we attribute to it had it not been for one feature of America's Level 2 institutional design – a constitutionally weak presidency. As we note earlier, an American president can make few appointments without the consent of Congress, his direction of the military can be proscribed by statute, he plays no role in amending the Constitution or even for that matter in the impeachment of federal officials, his veto of legislation can be overridden, his authority to introduce legislation that the Congress must consider derives only from convention and subsequent statute, he is not anointed "defender of the Constitution" or of the "constitutional order," and he holds no formal authority to act except in pursuit of and as authorized by the law. The apparent strength of the American presidency, then, must lie outside the Constitution or at least outside of and in combination with the Constitution. And once again the most apparent "other thing" is the political party system. Because an American president cannot lead simply by manipulating the formal (constitutional) levers of power, occupants of that office rely for their authority on the due exercise of what we might call leadership. As vague and imprecise as this concept might be, it certainly includes making full use of one's partisan connections. Indeed, a president has as much incentive to cultivate a party label as anyone else. It is, after all, the party, or more properly, the countless local and state party organizations, that nominate him for office and upon which he must rely for the conduct of his campaigns. And although his allies in passing his legislative agenda will normally include members of both parties, it is his own party that is the basis of nearly any legislative coalition he might try to form. Thus, as in 2001 when a single defection from the Republican ranks threw control of the Senate to the opposition, the defeat was regarded not merely as a defeat for the party in Congress but for the president personally.

Just as we earlier better understood Lincoln's success at prosecuting his side of the Civil War owing to an integrated party system, the integrated party today is perhaps as much a source of presidential power in the United States as is any constitutional provision. And just as a specific president is in a symbiotic relationship with others in his party, the institution of the presidency itself is in a symbiotic relationship with America's party system and the institutions that help sustain it: the presidency secures its authority because parties are integrated, and parties are integrated in part because of the institutional weakness of the presidency. The full impact of an integrated party system is felt, however, through yet another (Level 3) feature of the American electoral system – the simultaneity of elections and the corresponding simultaneity of campaigns. When handed a ballot in a presidential election, a voter more often than not confronts more than a choice for president and vice president, but also choices for both chambers of the national legislature, state executive and legislative offices, state and county judicial positions, and county and city executive and legislative offices. Typically, the ballot is more than a single sheet of paper, but a booklet that lists the names of innumerable candidates running to fill countless offices. By recalling our earlier story about the candidate for judge during one of Roosevelt's campaigns, we see that simultaneity of campaigns affords successful presidential candidates the opportunity to legitimize the claim that the fates of countless members of his party depend on him, thereby strengthening integration.[8]

What needs to be stressed here again is that this simultaneity is not constitutionally mandated or the product of any other provision we might assign to Level 2 but is instead the product of state law and an understanding among those who write such laws of the advantages to them of allowing integration full play in the political process – of allowing their electoral fates to be linked via the party labels they share. These are things we categorize as Level 3 institutional choices. Therefore, the combination once again of institutional provisions across institutional levels – in this instance, the

[8] Deschouwer (2001: 15) provides in essence a similar example from the Belgian experience: "In Belgium, both in 1995 and 1999 the regional and the federal elections were organized on the same day (in 1999 even coinciding with the European elections).... The simultaneity of the elections allowed them [parties] to put all their candidates together and select carefully who could be put on the list at what level. The parties also put their bigger names on the lists of more than one level, not to have them elected at different levels – that is not possible – but just to attract votes."

constitutional weakness of the presidency, state-mandated simultaneity, and the multitude of offices filled by election – contributes to integration.

We should resist here any attempt to assign weights that allocate importance across these institutional parameters. They do not function as with some simple linear separable model. Even if we were to possess the data necessary for such an exercise, it would not merely be silly but theoretically irresponsible to formulate some simple linear regression model that attempted to estimate the relative importance for party integration of one institutional parameter versus another. Institutions operate and interact in complex nonlinear ways and any such regression commits the first error of statistics – specification error. There is, however, one additional implication of our discussion. If parties hold the key to a stable and effective federalism, and if "federal friendly" parties are the product of motives induced by a complex interplay of institutions across levels of government, then simple institutional solutions for a failed or failing federalism are unlikely to be successful. Although we can only hypothesize that it is true, we suspect that America's parties would not have developed as they did had only direct election to the national legislature been provided for, if only a constitutionally weak president had been established, if only the geographic definition of the individual states had been defined so as to give every state a common set of economic interests, or if presidents, senators, and members of congress were appointed and direct elections occurred only at the state level. Had the American political system in its totality been other that what it was, then unless a different set of happy circumstances prevailed, the adjustment of any one of these design parameters would have been insufficient to achieve an integrated party system or a smoothly functioning federation.

Thus, as part of an argument that we expand on in our final chapter, Russian federalism is unlikely to be made more efficient by simply removing regional governors from its upper legislative chamber or by a diminution of the power of the presidency. Similarly, the European Union is unlikely to transform itself from confederation to federation by simply adjusting the relative authority of its Council of Ministers versus the European Parliament or by removing the authority of its member states to withdraw from the union. It may be the case that the adjustment of such design parameters is essential to achieve specific objectives of federal integration, but no single change is likely to be decisive unless all other parameters are properly set as well.

7.4 Australia, Canada, Germany, and India Revisited

Germany

The reader should not infer from the preceding discussion that there is a unique path to the development of "federal friendly" parties. Indeed, even a brief comparison of Germany and the United States should convince anyone that there is no unique constellation of institutions that engenders integrated parties or stable and efficient federal relations. The United States is presidential and Germany parliamentary; the United States relies almost exclusively on single-member district representation at both the federal and state level, whereas Germany uses proportional representation at the state level and a combination of proportional representation and single-member districts at the federal level; although a great many executive-level state offices are filled by direct election in the United States, in Germany equivalent offices are ministerial and filled by appointment; since all offices filled in the United States by direct election are for fixed terms, American elections occur on a schedule that allows for simultaneity, whereas German elections are only accidentally simultaneous; and although American states have a direct role in amending the U.S. Constitution, German states have no role except through their representatives in the national parliament. In addition to these differences we can also cite the unequal representation of German states in its upper federal chamber as compared with the equal representation in the U.S. Senate; a far greater reliance in the United States than in Germany on own source of revenues for state and local governments; and central control of state borrowing in Germany but not in the United States. Nevertheless, German parties more closely resemble those found in the United States than they do in, say, Canada, which shares Germany's parliamentary structure. It may be true that party discipline in Germany at the national level mimics what we see in Canada, but German national parties share the same strong local and regional roots as their American counterparts (Schuttemeyer 2001). Clearly, the motives facilitating political party integration, insofar as they have an institutional source, have a different source in Germany than they do in the United States.

To identify that source, we note that during the Weimar era (1919–33), regional parties were dominated by their central headquarters in Berlin – a dominance that was at least encouraged by a switch from single-member district elections to a high district magnitude system of proportional representation that moved a party's recruitment from local committees to executive offices in Berlin. The Western powers reinstituted political parties following World War II, but first at the local and state levels and only later at the national level. Thus, when Adenauer became chancellor in 1949, the federal organization of the Christian Democrats (CDU) did not yet exist, and it was not until 1950 that the party established itself nationally. This postwar sequence impacted overall party structures: "State and local organizations used the political vacuum on the federal level in the early days of the Federal Republic to gain a firm hold that they were not willing to cease afterwards" (Borchert 2000: 35).[9] In particular, the Christian Democrats (CDU/CSU)

[9] Postwar political parties were first formed at the municipal level, and local elections were held in 1946, three years before the first federal election. The restoration of democracy first

and Liberals (FDP) emerged as loose federations of regional party organizations, with regional leaders playing key roles in federal party organization (Lehmbruch 2000).

History, however, was not a uniquely decisive factor, as witnessed by the fact that the Social Democrats (SPD) began with a highly centralized organization, but then subsequently decentralized during the 1960s until its structure matched that of the Christian Democrats (CDU/CSU), the Liberals (FDP), and, later, the Greens (Jeffery 1999). There were in fact advantages given to local and state organizations by the electoral system. Although half of the Bundestag seats are filled by proportional representation on the basis of national vote totals, parties do not compete via national lists.[10] Instead they compete via state lists, drawn up by state party organizations in accordance with state law. Roughly, if a party wins, say, 30 percent of the vote, and if 10 percent of its vote comes from state X, then state X's list is afforded 3 percent of the seats – .30 times .10 – that are to be filled by proportional representation. Correspondingly, while nominations for the single-member district mandates in Bundestag elections are "the jealously guarded prerogative of the local and county party organizations," the party lists, for which a second ballot is cast in German federal elections, are drawn up at state party conventions through informal agreements among county organization (Schüttemeyer 2001: 45–6).

Alongside the mechanisms protecting the autonomy of subnational parties, the German system (unlike in Canadian) offers strong incentives for maintaining cooperative relations within parties. One is the 5 percent electoral threshold requirement that punishes a regional party that fails also to compete in other Länder. For example, the East German Party of Democratic Socialism (PDS) has been forced to campaign in the West despite its dismal electoral strength there, because the 1 or 2 percent of the vote it gathers there is vital for the party's chances of clearing the threshold. A second incentive for parties to compete in all states is that the results of state elections can trigger changes in federal coalition politics. In a highly proportional system with low electoral volatility the shares of seats controlled by the major

at the local level was a part of the Potsdam Agreement: "The administration of affairs in Germany should be directed toward the decentralization of the political structure and the development of local responsibility... (i) local self-government shall be restored throughout Germany on democratic principles and in particular through elective councils as rapidly as consistent with military security and the purposes of military occupation; (ii) all democratic political parties with rights of assembly and of public discussions shall be allowed and encouraged throughout Germany; (iii) representative and elective principles shall be introduced into regional, provincial, and state (Land) administration as rapidly as may be justified by the successful application of these principles in local self-government" (as quoted in Dolive 1976: 9).

10 The precise form of representation and the operation of Germany's electoral law is dictated by statute (in accordance with Article 38 of the Basic Law) and, thus, can be classified as a Level 3 institutional parameter.

parties in the Bundestag are quite stable, and, until 1998, changes in federal governments came not as direct consequences of election outcomes but from shifting coalitions among parties (Klingemann and Wessels 2001).[11] Thus, "[p]arties and media alike . . . treat state elections . . . as if they were very important by-elections for the *federal* parliament" (Scharpf 1995: 33).

Additional incentives for interparty integration follow from the role of Germany's upper legislative chamber, the Bundesrat, which perhaps better fulfills the role Madison and Hamilton envisioned for the U.S. Senate – that of the federal voice of states. Not only are state governments authorized to appoint their representatives, but they are also authorized to recall them (Article 58.1). Moreover, the votes of each state may be cast only as a block vote (Article 51.3) under direction from its government.[12] The Bundesrat has absolute veto on all legislation affecting the Länder, which in practice is more than a half of all federal legislation since it includes all legislation affecting policy areas for which the German Basic Law (constitution) grants the Länder concurrent powers and which the Länder must administer (Article 74a.2). Moreover, since 1949, there has been a clear trend toward expanding the Bundesrat's role, and as a result "the Bundesrat increasingly became a 'prize' of federal party competition. This applied both to the federal government, whose interest was to have an equivalent party majority in the Bundesrat in order to ease the process of passing its legislative program, and to the federal opposition, whose interest was to gain a majority in the Bundesrat and with it the potential to co-determine the federal government's legislative program" (Jeffery 1999: 135). Finally, there are the integration-inducing mechanisms that derive from the fact that the Länder, as opposed to the national executive, administer federal law (Section VIII). State offices are critically important for any party that seeks to control the national government. Indeed, owing to the fact that German states are, in effect, the executive arm of the national government, control of the state requires some minimal vertical control of Länder governments.

Thus, although proximate institutional causes differ, the German system is one in which, like the United States, it is difficult to imagine national parties divorced from regional ones. This is not to say that the federal government and German Länder march in lockstep on all issues. In particular there are recurrent tensions among large states, small states, and the federal government over the fiscal distribution. Disagreements arise especially if a state government is controlled by a party other than the one that controls the Bundestag, or, most recently, the national government is committed to

[11] In 1998 the CDU/CSU was voted out after experiencing the biggest loss ever (6.2 percentage points), while the winner, the SPD, enjoyed its largest increase ever (4.5 percentage points).

[12] Members of the Bundesrat are appointed by their respective Land governments. The number of seats for each Land (from 3 to 6) depends upon population. Among the members are state's minister presidents and key ministers. Their mandates usually end whenever they cease their governmental functions.

equalization across the former East-West divide and can pursue this policy only at the expense of the more economically developed West. But a smoothly functioning democratic federalism does not promise unanimity on all issues, and it is remarkable how much stress an integrated party system can sustain. Indeed, Germany uses explicit direct fiscal transfers from rich to poor states ("horizontal redistribution") in addition to the redistribution that occurs through normal federal policy: "[F]rom an American perspective, continued unquestioning support for financial equalization is puzzling if not bizarre. It would be as if Connecticut each year transferred millions of dollars of tax surplus to Mississippi and never once questioned the arrangement, only requested adjustments at the margin" (Adelberger 1999: 14).[13]

Canada

Regardless of the issues that might arise to make politics less than harmonious across levels of government, Germany's institutional structure yields a political system in which, as in the United States and in accordance with what we ask of an integrated party system, individual-level incentives are such that regional and local politicians are compelled to act as if they represent the interests of more than a narrow constituency. Germany and the United States, then, demonstrate clearly that the institutional configurations encouraging party integration need not be unique. But the case for focusing on institutional parameters grows stronger if we add Australian and Indian designs to our discussion and draw a contrast with Canada.

[13] Länder politicians do sometimes challenge federal redistributive policy, although they usually cannot overcome resistence within their own parties. Recently, the cost of financing the poor eastern states following reunification fell heavily on several wealthy western states, including Bavaria. The largest and one of the most populous states, Bavaria is the only one dominated by a regional party (the CSU). As expected, when Bavaria's status changed to that of financial donor, the party felt pressured to demand a renegotiation of federal terms. Facing a decline in support for the federal CDU/CSU coalition, a group of CSU politicians led by Bavaria's premier (Stroiber) called in 1998 for a reform of financial and legislative relations that would reduce the state's burden. Most observers agreed, however, that the proposal was primarily an attempt to burnish the CSU's image as a party willing to put the regional interests above those of other Länder and the federal government. As Stoiber put it, "the CSU is a Bavarian party, whose first priority is of course to secure Bavarian interests" (Jeffery and Mackenstein 1999: 170). While "CSU officials in the federal government were outraged at the explicit displays of regionalism" (Ziblatt 2001: 19), their federal partners from the CDU effectively ignored the call for reform. For non-Bavarian politicians of the CDU/CSU any redistributional reform could only spell electoral trouble. The CDU leadership feared recriminations in the East, especially accusations from the PDS that it had "sold out" eastern interests to the rich Bavarians (Ziblatt 2001). Consequently, the call for reform resulted in nothing more than an agreement that the federal government pay a larger share on behalf of all state governments. As a nice finishing touch, once Stoiber himself became the candidate of the CDU/CSU for federal chancellorship in 2002, the proposed reform ceased to be one of his priorities. In general, state politicians who hold positions in national parties advocate policies attractive to voters nationally, "moderating what might otherwise be more pronounced regional self-interest" (Adelberger 1999: 5).

As we note in Chapter 6, it is tempting to begin and end an account of Canadian federalism with only one item – that, unlike Australia, Germany, or the United States, Canada possesses a sharp linguistic divide that correlates with the geography of its provinces – and to give primacy to this fact when discussing either the relative fragility of Canada's federal system or the character of its political parties. But doing this ignores another fact; namely that the absence of vertical integration predates the Quebec separatist sentiment that bubbled to the surface in the 1950s and that it fails to explain as well the fact that national and provincial parties are no better integrated in provinces outside of Quebec. As if to emphasize this, we note that neither Mallory's (1954: 57) description of "the near disintegration of the Canadian federation under the impact of the depression" nor Brady's (1938: 957) observation some sixteen years earlier that "Canadian federalism in recent years has been passing through the sharpest crisis in its history" refers to anything resembling the crisis in federal-Quebec relations. Instead, they focus on the severe pre–World War II institutional conflict between a dominant Ontario and Quebec on the one hand and the western provinces on the other.

We need not downplay the importance of its linguistic divide to note that the specifics of its federal design and attempts to change it in the 1930s ensured a "without" rather than "within" structure of provincial representation, which in turn encouraged the vertical and horizontal disintegration of Canadian parties. Canada's "first" party system (up to the1920s) looked no less integrated than the U.S. system of the same era. Its two primary parties (Liberals and Conservatives) relied heavily on patronage (Carty 1988; Thorburn and Whitehorn 2001), where both could be described as "vote gathering machines held together by the incentives to gain or to maintain office. Little distinction was made within the parties between federal and provincial politics. On the contrary, the fusion of federal and provincial politics made patronage work even for the party which was in opposition" (Renzsch 2001: 5). Still this early party system was ill-equipped to handle shocks to the political system. Because the British Northern American Act (BNAA) of 1867 made no provision for amendments other than by acts of the British Parliament, when, in the late 1920s, Britain prepared to withdraw from playing an active role in its dominions, Canada was forced to open constitutional debates. This is by itself a dangerous juncture for any federation. But the Canadian federation confronted a special problem: the deepening asymmetry in the status of its western members. Historically, the West was annexed to the Canadian federation as a subordinate region. The prairie provinces of Alberta, British Columbia, Manitoba, and Saskatchewan did not exist as distinct territories but were late creations of the federal government (Manitoba in 1870, British Columbia in 1871, Alberta and Saskatchewan in 1905) and entered Canada on unequal terms. Most important, until 1930 they were denied control over their natural resources, despite the fact that such control fell to Canada's originating provinces under the BNAA. The western provinces also were the focus of the so-called National Policy – a protectionist policy of high tariffs on manufactured goods and controlled grain prices – which the West viewed as a redistributive mechanism favoring industrial Ontario and Quebec. Institutionally, the asymmetric status of the West was maintained by its marginal electoral importance – in all federal elections it was populous Ontario and Quebec that decided the outcome – while at the same time no federal decision-making body existed that provided for any overrepresentation of small or sparsely populated provinces. Once elections concluded, the "responsible government" model in Parliament required strict party discipline and precluded effective provincial representation.

It was only in the late 1920s, when their assent was necessary for a constitutional adjustment, that the western provinces gained the chance to demand equal status. In 1927 Prime Minister Mackenzie King called a federal-provincial conference to discuss the Statute of Westminster, which was soon to make Canada legally independent of Britain. In fact, the 1927 conference marked the beginning of five decades of bargaining over *how* to amend the BNAA, where all proposed schemes (or at least all proposals acceptable to Ontario and Quebec) provided provinces with the power to veto future constitutional revisions either individually or in groups.[14] Thus, the need for fundamental constitutional reform gave the provinces and, in particular the West, leverage against the federal government and each other.[15] Once the door to federal-provincial bargaining opened, politicians found themselves in a new strategic situation,[16] whereby new provincial parties campaigned successfully in opposition to the federal government. Both federal parties – Conservatives and Liberals – were viewed as being primarily interested in winning the support of Ontario and Quebec, although their western provincial branches repeatedly sought to dissociate themselves from their federal counterparts.

Although it would be an overstatement to say that all new parties emerged as a response to federal-provincial conflict, the fact is that these parties advocated various economic and social policies as a part of federal-provincial

[14] The 1982 Constitution Act adopted the "seven-and-fifty" formula – constitutional amendments require the ratification of any seven provinces that contained at least half the Canadian population.

[15] For example, the 1927 federal-provincial conference resulted in the transfer of control over natural resources to the western provinces, but in return Ontario and Quebec were given provincial control over hydropower and the Atlantic provinces increased federal subsidies. Likewise, in the 1960s, when a new round of constitutional debates was initiated by Quebec, the western provinces insisted on further enhancing their control of natural resources as the price for their assent to constitutional revisions (Gibbins 1980; Romanow, Whyte, and Russell 1984; Braid and Sharpe 1990; White 1990).

[16] Thus, "the 1930s brought strong and able provincial leaders devoted to provincial autonomy – Duplessis in Quebec, Hepburn in Ontario, Macdonald in Nova Scotia, Aberhart in Alberta, Pattulo in British Columbia" (Smiley 1972: 24).

bargaining. Thus, the Social Credit Party successfully entered Alberta's provincial politics on the platform of a populist monetary policy, but "an examination of developments in Alberta from 1935 to 1942 indicates very clearly that Alberta's attempts to introduce Social Credit were directed primarily towards the object of strengthening the political position of the province in its relations with the federal government. Monetary reform thus was a means to an end" (Clark 1954: viii). Parallel developments occurred in Quebec. In the mid-1930s a splinter group from the Liberal Party allied with the provincial Conservatives to form the Union Nationale, which won the 1936 provincial election by campaigning against the federal government. Interestingly, while the Union Nationale successfully defeated the provincial Liberals by campaigning against Ottawa Liberals, Quebec voters gave overwhelming support to the incumbent Liberals in the federal elections of 1945, 1949, 1953, and 1957. Thus, the apparent pattern of the Quebec electorate was to vote for the strongest federal party as a way to protect provincial interests, so that during the Liberal incumbency it remained "overrepresented" in the governing party caucus.[17]

Overall, electoral outcomes were consistent with the strategy of supporting a nongovernment party in provincial elections – a regional or provincial party in Quebec and the West, the Conservatives in Ontario. Thus, in 1979 the victory of the Conservatives at the federal level spelled trouble for provincial Conservatives: "The election ... posed the Lougheed administration with a very new situation in federal-provincial relations. Previously, with the Liberals in Ottawa, Premier Lougheed could afford an adversary relationship with the federal government.... But now the Tories are in power and he must tread more carefully. The situation is equally precarious for Prime Minister Clark. If he simply advocates the Alberta viewpoint, it could swiftly cost him support in Ontario. Every Ontario seat he loses he must regain in Quebec, a very unpromising prospect."[18] Alberta Liberals faced essentially the same dilemma, although their position was more tenuous. Provincial Liberals were viewed as closely affiliated with the federal party and for that reason had little chance of success. Indeed, between 1971 and 1982 there were no Liberals in the provincial parliament, and, as one study of Alberta's party system explained, "in order to improve their showing in provincial elections, the Alberta Liberals would have to develop an organization, leaders, and policies independent of the federal party" (Long and Quo 1978: 14).[19]

[17] Of the seven of eight federal elections that the Liberals won between 1921 and 1957, Quebec's representatives formed either a majority or the largest group of the Liberal caucus even though Quebec's quota of parliamentary seats was approximately 27 percent. The western provinces, in contrast, were always "underrepresented" in the Liberal governing caucus.

[18] *Alberta Report*, June 1, 1979, available at <http://report.ca/classics/06011979/p11i790601f1.html>.

[19] Alberta's Liberal provincial leader, Nick Taylor, advocated not just official separation but abandonment of the partisan label. The party became organizationally independent but

Ultimately, this pattern of "punishing" the federal incumbent party in provincial contests created strong incentives for provincial politicians to distance themselves from their federal counterparts. Even when sharing labels, local political organizations separated themselves from their federal counterparts.

The next step in the evolution of Canada's party system was the emergence of parties that competed only in federal elections. After the failure of the Meech Lake Accord (1987) to recognize Quebec's special status as a "distinctive society," a number of Conservative members of the House of Commons (joined by a few Liberal MPs) formed the Bloc Québécois. The bloc became an independent party to compete in federal elections, leaving provincial politics to the provincially dominant party, the Parti Québécois. On the opposite flank the Reform Party emerged during the debate over Meech Lake and attracted support by opposing yet another unsuccessful attempt at constitutional revision – the Charlottetown Accord of 1992. The party's basic electoral appeal is the claim that neither major national party represents western interests, and its first leader, Preston Manning, presented a plan of constitutional change that included a directly elected federal Senate with equal provincial representation and effective powers to block legislation, along with a denial of any special status for Quebec (Manning 1992). As a clear signal that redistributive bargaining had fully infected bargaining over Canada's fundamental institutional parameters, the party evolved into the Canadian Alliance and in 2000 became Canada's second largest, winning 21.9 percent of the seats in the 2000 elections with all but one seat coming from the western provinces.

Canada versus Australia and India

We see here, then, the institutional sources of the disintegration of the Canadian party system. When its centralized federal structure confronted the challenge of constitutional revision, the western provinces, chafing under the strictures of institutionally sanctioned political underrepresentation, expanded the domain of federal renegotiation to include essentially all issues, substantive and institutional. But renegotiation could not occur within institutions in which provincial interests are represented unequally and inadequately. Although Canada's two main parties at the time may have together satisfied the definition of an integrated system, that system together with federal asymmetry and its consequences was not in equilibrium and the resulting renegotiation resulted in the full mutation of Canada's party system.

kept the name and experienced a reversal of its electoral misfortunes in 1986 when the Conservatives controlled the federal government. By the end of the Conservative incumbency in 1993, Liberals controlled thirty-two out of the total eighty-three provincial parliamentary seats. Yet their fortune was reversed again after the Liberal Party regained federal control in October 1993. They won eighteen seats in March 1997 and only seven seats in March 2001.

This record gives us some leverage in understanding the differences in federal relations and party systems between Canada and Australia despite their institutional similarities. Briefly, the search for an institutionally based explanation for why Canadian parties are nonintegrated leads us to the fact that Canada lacked a venue for federal bargaining of a "within" sort. Absent a meaningful Senate as well as national competition for a chief executive, bargaining occurred outside of established federal institutional structures, including the parties designed to compete for federal office. In contrast, though also parliamentary, Australia has a legislatively meaningful directly elected Senate. Moreover, because its Senate has been filled by a proportional representation electoral mechanism since 1949 and thereby offers the threat of small regionally based parties, established parties that seek to control the federal government cannot forsake regional interests. Federal-provincial bargaining of the "without" type was stimulated in Canada also by the need to implement constitutional reform, but in this case identifiable regions or even individual provinces in effect possessed a veto over any proposal, thereby allowing those regions or provinces to bargain unilaterally with the federal center. In Australia, in contrast, the constitutional amendment process was well institutionalized. And although New South Wales and Victoria may have possessed a veto in federal bargaining no less than Ottawa and Quebec, Australia enjoyed the luxury of no long-standing disputes over the exploitation of natural resources (and enjoyed as well, perhaps, the fact that there were no compelling reasons to incorporate New Zealand into its federation), thereby freeing parties to compete nationally.

In a comparison between Canada and India, Canada, of course, seems the greater success when measured by economic performance, its peaceful accommodation of Quebec's linguistic demands, and its ability to integrate an ethnically, linguistically, and culturally diverse population. India, in contrast, has seen a sharp disruption of its federal system under Indira Gandhi, lackluster economic performance, and continued linguistic and religious strife. If, on the other hand, we consider India's liabilities at the outset of self-rule – a historically entrenched caste system, linguistic and religious divides that correlate with geography, and a mass electorate with little experience with Western democratic practice – India must be deemed a great success. More interesting, although both India and Canada are, like Australia and Germany, parliamentary, and although both, like the United States, rely exclusively on single-member plurality districts for parliamentary representation, Canada's parties are anything but integrated whereas India's Congress Party, at least up until Gandhi's rule, seemed to exemplify what we mean by integration.

Almost certainly we could enter into an endless debate as to why one country's parties fail to integrate vertically whereas its less democratically endowed counterpart began with a party that pursued a strategy of integration as a seemingly inevitable course. Once again, we would not argue that any one or two institutional parameters dictate this difference – and, indeed, we cannot preclude the path dependence of history and Congress's role in securing India's independence. But again we should not forget that, although their core (Level 2) institutional structures are similar, Canada and India differ in several key electorally relevant provisions. First, until they were disconnected by Gandhi in 1971, India's state and federal elections were simultaneous, which allowed for coattails of the sort we see in the United States and which muted the incentive to vote for divided government by splitting one's vote between region and center. One might argue that the Congress's dominant position gave simultaneity a minimal role in this respect, but that dominance combined with one other fact arguably to give simultaneity a particularly important role in promoting integration – a pluralistic and competitive elite structure within each state. As a consequence, Congress's national leadership was less susceptible to demands for bilateral negotiation since the loss of any one local cadre from its ranks would not have damaged the party nationally, other cadres stood ready to take the place of any defection.[20]

There is a second factor – a Level 2 consideration – of potential significance. In contrast to the Canadian Senate's irrelevance, the role of India's upper legislative chamber, the Council of States or Raiya Sabha, is more ambiguous. On the one hand, although all but 12 of the 250 members of this chamber are appointed by the states' legislatures directly from their ranks, the constitution makes the council's approval unnecessary for the passage of any money bill. The additional provision that the Speaker of the House of the People (Lok Sabha) is decisive as to whether a bill is or is not a money bill would seem to make the council as impotent as the Canadian Senate. However, "the Raiya Sabha is not without importance. While [it] does not normally obstruct legislation passed by the Lok Sabha, it has occasionally done so, particularly on constitutional amendments which require a two-thirds vote in both houses. The second important power... is its coequal role with the Lok Sabha as an electoral college, which includes also the state legislative assemblies, for the election of the President of India. The significance of these two powers taken together is that the Rajya Sabha must also be controlled before a government can consolidate its power in Delhi" (Brass 1994: 50–1).

It would be foolhardy to assert that a not altogether impotent upper chamber and simultaneity combined with an otherwise fragmented political infrastructure to preordain an integrated Congress Party. Certainly there were other background conditions, including even the ideological commitment of

[20] Smiley (1972: 78) notes the importance of simultaneity for pre-1972 India and suggests that it can contribute to the integration of the Canadian political parties as well: "[I]t does indeed seem remarkable to a Canadian student of federalism that scholars of American politics give so little attention to the contrary circumstance in which a complex of intra-party dependencies must surely arise when voters make their choices at the same ballot for candidates for elective office at two or more levels."

the party's elite to a united, democratic, and independent India. But the core of our argument is not that these two items are necessary or by themselves sufficient, but rather that, if the Rajya Sabha and simultaneity did impact the calculations of political elites and voters, then we have an example of how a set of provisions intended to serve a purpose other than federal stability contributed nonetheless to party integration and India's position as a relatively unique success as a democratic federation drawn from the sample of economically underdeveloped postcolonial states.

7.5 Local and Regional Design Parameters

What emerges from the preceding discussion, including that of Chapter6, is the implication that the institutional determinants of political motives with respect to party integration are complex and interactive. No single institutional variable is decisive. Moreover, and somewhat problematical from the perspective of design, is that many of the parameters that we can reasonably suppose impact party integration and stable and coherent federal process are of a type that is not always addressed at the national level. Many, such as the number and character of the public offices filled by direct election at the local and regional level, can be treated only within federal subjects – by their constitutions, charters, administrative acts, and laws. Certainly, some of these institutions, rules, and provisions are what Voigt (1999) refers to as "spontaneous." They arise in part from the game a constitution establishes and then in turn interactively define a more complex game in which the popular support of a coordinating constitution is itself an equilibrium outcome – in which a constitution achieves legitimacy. But they and the motives they engender in combination with Level 1 and Level 2 choices are frequently overlooked when designing a federal state. And more often than not they are left to emerge only after a federal state comes into existence as a product of motives and institutions that may or may not be in equilibrium.[21]

It may be true that "the U.S. Constitution is a perfect example ... [of the] quintessential social contract [in which] ... many important details of that

[21] Here again we perhaps see one of the advantages of American federal development. The subnational institutional parameters that we believe encouraged integrated party development there – most notably, those institutions that framed a competitive political structure within states – were a part of the background conditions that confronted the founders of American federalism. There was little need, then, for the Framers of the U.S. Constitution to concern themselves with implementing these institutional choices. But if Stepan (1999: 12) is correct in suggesting that most modern federations have been designed primarily to hold together states threatened with disintegration or civil war, absent the decentralization implicit in federal forms, these subnational institutions need to be a conscious part of the plan and cannot be assumed to exist as prior background conditions. Thus, instead of interpreting the American experience as irrelevant to contemporary federal design, an argument can be made that the lesson is precisely the opposite – the American experience needs to be replicated, although not necessarily in the order in which events unfolded there.

institution have been worked out on the fly through presidential interpretation, court decisions, and public opinion" (Calvert 1995: 82). Unfortunately, there is little reason to assume that the rather fortuitous history of constitutional governance in the United States (with the obvious exception of 1860–5) can be repeated elsewhere absent careful and theoretically prescribed planning and design. Here, then, we offer a review of what appear to be the most conspicuous parameters and whose values there is no good reason to leave to chance or unplanned spontaneous development since they are subject to explicit institutional choice. Of course, we cannot proceed presuming that we know the correct values and choices in all circumstances. Our deductive analyses of institutional consequences are too underdeveloped, our comparative studies of states necessarily too few in number, and the opportunities for laboratory experimental study too little pursued for sustaining such a presumption. Aside from knowing general tendencies in terms of the relative number of parties and their ideological purity, we can only begin to guess, for example, at the implications for proportional representation schemes versus single-mandate elections when set in different institutional and social contexts. Only relatively recently, for example, have we come to understand the importance of simultaneous legislative and presidential elections in presidential systems (Shugart and Carey 1992; Mainwaring 1993; Jones 1995; Shugart 1995), the potential perversities of alternative schemes of representation (Schwartz 1995), or the interactive impact of election rules and social conditions on the number of parties in a political system (Ordeshook and Shvetsova 1994; Cox 1997). Nevertheless, proceeding as best we can, the first items on our list, which are suggested by the American experience, concern regional and local elections. There are three parameters in particular that interest us at the subnational level:

1. The number of meaningful local and regional offices filled by direct election.
2. The autonomy of regional governments with respect to the design and administration of regional election law.
3. The frequency of regional and local elections.

By "meaningful" here we do not mean simply that elections be fairly contested but that the offices filled have real authority – to tax, regulate, and reallocate resources. The economic advantage of allowing regional or local governments to make tax and spending decisions for goods and services that are best handled at the local level because of the limited domains of the externalities that concern them, because of the absence of any economies of scale in their production, or because of nonuniformity of taste across a polity, is self-evident. Ultimately, however, the political advantages are perhaps even more important. First, if elections to regional and local governments as well as to the national legislature have a strong local flavor, expertise at one level can be applied to the next, and those with political aspirations can position themselves to work up the ladder. Heads of city administrations, members of county councils, local judges, and so on can aspire not only to higher position within their region but also to national office, thus giving them a stake early on in a constituency greater than the one they currently represent and encouragement of the imperfect agency we believe desirable in federal states. Second, the opportunity (even necessity) to win local and regional office before embarking on a national political career removes the sharp distinction between regional and national elites. We suspect, in fact, that when local and regional elites can reasonably aspire to become a part of the national structure, it becomes far easier to maintain a consensus on the federal bargain, including the supremacy of federal law. Third, arguably the most important consequence of regional and local elections is their impact on the value political elites associate with integrated parties. The greater the number of offices filled by election, the greater is the informational load on voters and consequently the value of party labels, and, thereby, the greater is the incentive for politicians to develop and sustain integrated parties.

In assessing the consequences of local control of elections we should keep two facts in mind. First, local or regional control increases the value of regional and local office and thus the incentives to compete for those offices. Second, it affords relevant governments the opportunity and incentive to experiment with and find local solutions to local problems. This possibility is perhaps no better illustrated than in Russia's Republic of Dagestan, where an imaginative accommodation had been reached with respect to a society with a plentitude of ethnic divisions (Ware and Kisriev 2001). It might seem strange to look here for a solution to much of anything concerning democratic process, but building on a long tradition of accommodating ethnic diversity, the republic's executive power is shared by a fourteen-member council, with one member from each primary ethnic group. Additionally, the republic's 121-member legislature is designed to mirror the ethnic composition of the population but in an imaginative way. Using single-member districts, 65 seats are filled in multiethnic districts and 56 in districts drawn to be monoethnic. In the multiethnic districts, everyone is allowed to vote, but, with assignments made by an electoral commission for the purpose of achieving full proportionality, only persons of an assigned ethnicity are allowed to be candidates. This scheme yields what Horowitz (1991) seeks through preferential voting methods: candidates with an incentive to appeal outside of their ethnicity.[22]

[22] Interestingly, although these arrangements are deemed fair within the republic, they are being challenged in Russia's Constitutional Court and are further endangered by President Putin's recentralization of federal relations – in this case, in the form of a federal inspector as part of Putin's move to divide Russia into seven federal districts headed by persons answerable directly to the president. Unfortunately, then, Dagestan also illustrates how central control of regional elections (from Moscow) threatens to upset a somewhat imaginative if complex accommodation of ethnic diversity.

Local control of elections can, in addition, provide regional and local governments with some protection. Having been elected under rules chosen locally rather than by some distant national entity, politicians elected under them are likely to be awarded a degree of legitimacy by their electorates that a national government must, to some extent at least, respect. We are aware of the abuses to which this authority has sometimes been put. The opportunities for corruption and for infringing on individual rights are evident. But absent other institutional considerations, there is no guarantee that rights will be any better protected by a national entity, or that corruption is less likely to pervade a national government than a regional one.[23] In fact, corruption itself need not be an undesirable feature of democratic process, provided that there is some degree of competitiveness for control of its particularistic benefits. Much of the early organized activities of parties in the United States and much of the incentive to organize them at the local and regional level was directed at the manipulation of apportionment, suffrage, and the administration of election law for the purpose of advantaging one interest over another, and there is scant evidence that corruption was anything but a widely practiced normal feature of politics.[24] If anything, the access to corruption afforded by holding public office often served as a principle motive for contesting and winning office.

The issue of local control also brings to the fore another commonly overlooked design parameter – residency. Residency requirements can, of course, be part of a constitution, at least with respect to members of the national legislature, or they can be established within the region being represented. But whether constitutional or statutory, their impact can be consequential. Indeed, Riker (1995: 142) goes so far as to say "this requirement [Article I, section 2, clause 2] is probably today the most significantly federal feature of the whole [U.S.] Constitution and, without it, the central government might easily dominate the states completely.... The effect of these clauses is that they render nominations local. Unlike almost all unitary governments, the national leaders of political parties cannot impose nominees on states and districts. Congressmen thus owe their offices to local figures. This fact undoubtedly gives rise to a high degree of localism and state influence on national policy. It means that when state and local officials urge a member of Congress to support a particular measure, he or she is likely to comply, lest these officials cause trouble for him/her in the next nomination or election."

[23] For an assessment of the extent to which rights have been protected in the United States through state constitutional provision, see Finkelman and Gottleib (1991).

[24] For example, in describing voting in the early 1800s in Massachusetts, Goodman (1964: 140) offers the following description: "Selectman used a number of tricks to fool the opposition. They might not adequately publicize the time of the vote, and in one town they simply refused to accept certain voters' ballots; in another they delayed opening the polls until most of the voters had gone home except for the party faithful... but these devices were petty and local, and politicians developed more refined methods."

We are less certain than Riker of the critical nature of this provision or of his implicit argument that such a provision needs to be part of a federal constitution. One can imagine circumstances in which this and equivalent provisions arise spontaneously. For example, not every U.S. state constitution requires a governor to be a U.S. citizen, but to our knowledge, no elected or even appointed governor has ever failed to satisfy this requirement. Nevertheless, we do accept the argument insofar as it highlights a provision that encourages integration and local control.

The impact of the third item on our list – the frequency of elections – need not correspond to a critical parameter except insofar as it interacts with the next item, namely:

4. The timing of local, regional, and national elections.[25]

Our earlier example of the symbiotic relationship between the candidate for judge and Roosevelt requires simultaneous campaigns and illustrates how simultaneity contributes importantly to integration. The absence of simultaneity, in contrast, opens the door to campaigns based not on partisan attachments but on personality and the specific characteristics of candidates. To some observers, this might seem desirable, and indeed, the argument for simultaneity runs counter to the purpose of elections in at least one conceptualization of democratic process – namely, in what we would call the naive model of democracy, a view that sees elections as a mechanism for learning the will of the voter. The objection to simultaneity here is that if people are required to vote for many offices at once, and if their vote for one office is influenced by their vote for some other, then how can we decipher their intent and that will? Notice that this conceptualization also rationalizes the requirement that a specific level of turnout be reached before an election contest is deemed decisive, again with the argument that, if too few people vote, the will of the people may be wholly inaccurately expressed. This model of democracy, however, flies in the face of several decades of research in social choice theory, which tells us that a coherent public need not exist, and that even if it does, elections are too crude an instrument for measuring it. Instead, democratic elections serve a simpler and more theoretically justifiable purpose; they afford citizens the opportunity to choose their leaders and, in the event of unsatisfactory performance, to remove them from office. Elections are not the means for learning the public will; instead, they are a mechanism for giving political elites an incentive to do what they can to decipher that

[25] Simultaneity is often an example of a procedure that arises spontaneously as a function of other institutional parameters – most notably, the number of offices filled at the local, regional, and national levels and the assignment of the cost of administering elections. Local governments especially are likely to seek ways to minimize such costs, and one way to accomplish this is to make elections simultaneous. The suggestion here, then, is that simultaneity can be encouraged by the mere expedient of requiring that local and regional governments fund local and regional elections out of their own revenues.

will and to place before the electorate alternative versions of it for approval or disapproval. And although it may be true that the necessity for competing under partisan labels in a complex array of elections affords candidates some protection against their own foibles and incompetence, this is often a small price to pay in exchange, in a federal state, for establishing an incentive among political elites to cooperate, coordinate, and monitor each other – the essence of party integration.

Thus far the items we cite with respect to regional and local matters focus on elections and electoral mandates. What needs to be emphasized is that many of these matters, such as which public offices are to be filled by election versus appointment and the timing of elections, are not normally addressed in a federal constitution or even by federal law. Instead, they are treated by federal subject constitutions and charters (or even local statute). Hence, the next item on our list:

5. The content of federal subject constitutions.

This item can be as important to the functioning of a federal party system as any national Level 2 provision. In addition to whatever guarantees they can provide for regional democratic governance and whatever additional sources of protection they can provide with respect to individual rights, the other features of these documents that should be viewed as variables in federal design include:

- *Term limits and term lengths for local and regional offices.* If terms are limited, to what extent will local and unit-level politicians be encouraged, in anticipation of being compelled to move up the political ladder, to appeal to a larger constituency than they currently represent?
- *Oaths of office.* Because we and others argue that symbolic acts and bills of rights can coordinate beliefs and expectations, might an oath of allegiance to the constitutional order facilitate stability?[26]
- *Advisory referenda on federal matters.* Even if regional referenda have no legal status, can such expressions of opinion influence the political process affecting the ability of elected politicians to act as imperfect agents of their voters?
- *Provision for the selection of state and local judges and whether or not such elections are held on a partisan or a nonpartisan basis.* Direct election of judges, even if nonpartisan, can only add to the information value of partisan labels.

[26] Prior to the Civil War few American state constitutions acknowledged the supremacy of the federal Constitution, whereas the inclusion of such a provision became a uniform feature of the oaths prescribed for state officials in every state constitution written after 1865 (the remaining exception being that of the constitution of Massachusetts, adopted in 1780 and now the oldest operating written constitution in the world).

TABLE 7.3. *Term Lengths of State Officers*

	Representatives	Senators	Governors	Councillors
New Hampshire	1	1	1	–
Massachusetts	1	1	1	1
Connecticut	1	–	1	1
Rhode Island	1	–	1	1
New York	1	4	3	–
New Jersey	1	1	1	–
Pennsylvania	1	–	1	3
Delaware	1	3	3	2
Maryland	1	5	1	1
Virginia	1	4	1	3
North Carolina	1	1	1	1
South Carolina	2	2	2	2
Georgia	1	–	1	–

And although frequently overlooked as a component of federal design, the content of regional charters and constitutions is an integral part of the rules of the federal game, if only because they are likely to or can be made to contain provisions that affect political action at higher, and not just lower, levels of government. As an example of the ripple effect possibly produced by one item from this list, we note that the frequency of elections in the United States has, as its genesis, state and local election law in which, in the republic's early years, it was believed that a one-year term was optimal for public control of elected officials.[27] Adams (1973: 245) has summarized the term lengths of various statewide offices in the original thirteen states (see Table 7.3).

Frequent elections in the new federal state, then, were inherited directly from state (and local) charters – which, as we note earlier, ultimately yields simultaneity as a way to minimize the cost of administering elections.

[27] A controversial feature of the U.S. Constitution during ratification was the "excessive" term of the president without a term limit, and Noah Webster acknowledged objections to even the two-year congressional term: "Some may object to their continuance in power two years. But I cannot see any danger arising from this quarter (cited in Bailyn 1993: 1:143). John Stevens's attitude (*New York Daily Advertiser,* December 12, 1787) is typical of the opposition: "The Constitution directs that the members of the House of Representatives be elected biennially. This departure from good Democratic rule . . ." (Bailyn 1993: 1:490). And Edmund Randolph, in citing his reasons for not signing the document had, as the second item on his list, ". . . rendering the President ineligible after a given number of years" (Bailyn 1993: 1:610).

8

Institutional Sources of Federal Stability II

In all governments, whatever their form, however they may be constituted, there must be a power established from which there is no appeal, and which is therefore called absolute, supreme, and uncontrollable. The only question is where that power is to be lodged.

James Wilson, Pennsylvania Ratifying Convention, 1787

If a confederation should take place, one great question is how shall we vote? Whether each colony shall count one? Or whether each shall have a weight in proportion to its numbers, or wealth, or exports or imports, or a compound ratio of all? Another is whether Congress shall have the authority to limit the dimensions of each colony, to prevent those which claim, by charter or proclamation, or commission to the south sea [the Pacific Ocean] from growing too great and powerful, so as to be dangerous to the rest?

John Adams, 1776[1]

The general adoption of the popular, state-wide voting procedure [for president] gave a popular dimension to the presidential contest, created or enhanced the need for state party machinery, weakened the political authority of legislative caucuses, occasioned the development of national party conventions, and made the presidential election the dramatic focal point of American politics.

McCormick 1966: 29

Wilson was quick to supply the answer to his question concerning the ultimate source of state power: "[I]t remains and flourishes with the people." Of course, we might suppose that this answer was tinged with more than a pinch of hyperbole designed to turn back opponents of the document he was defending. Even if we take such sentiments at face value, however, we must

[1] In a letter to Abigail Adams concerning the Articles of Confederation, from McCullough (2001: 146–7).

still travel a distance to see how supremacy and power can and ought to be formally lodged, via the specifics of institutional design, in the people. The previous chapter details a few institutional choices that encourage federal-friendly parties – the critical intermediary between "the people" and those who act with the authority and resources of the state. Here we continue that discussion by focusing on the relation of those with authority to each other, including Adams's specifically practical question and McCormick's somewhat bold assertion – an assertion we must evaluate to learn how to erect a viable federal state if it chooses not to even have a president. This much is clear: to assess the incentives of political agents to uphold federal institutional stability, we must return to Level 2 and to the principles upon which the Framers rested their design and defense of the U.S. Constitution.

8.1 Electoral Mechanisms and Societal Structures

Representation

Of the various questions the Framers confronted, none it seems commanded more attention than the form of the new national legislature. Here two issues resided that needed to be dealt with simultaneously – representation of the diverse and conflicting interests of the states and the avoidance of legislative tyranny or at least a tyranny of the majority with the legislature as its agent. The concern of the Framers, of course, was not finding ways to encourage federal-friendly parties. But representation schemes are consequential for party development as well as for structuring the federal political process generally, and it is only reasonable that a critical element of any list of design parameters be the following:

1. The mode of federal subject representation and the principle of electing representatives to the national legislature.

Volumes can and have been filled addressing the issues raised by this one item – issues such as the definition and defense of the concept of fair representation (Young 1994), the advantages and disadvantages of parliamentary versus presidential systems (Lijphart 1992b), the rationale for a bicameral versus unicameral structure (Tsebelis and Money 1997), the logic of alternative schemes of proportional representation (Cox 1997; Lijphart 1994; Lijphart and Grofman 1984), the right of recall among those being represented (Riker 1982), term limits and terms of office (Carey 1998), and so on. Clearly, we can address only a few dimensions of design as they pertain to federalism and parties, especially since the literature on which we must rely only infrequently looks at these dimensions from the perspective of federal design and performance. The notable exception is Riker's (1955) discussion, summarized earlier, of the evolutionary development of the U.S. Senate as a product of the U.S. Constitution's failure to grant states the authority to recall their representatives and the consequences of the divergence between Senate terms and the terms of office of those who, prior to the Seventeenth Amendment, appointed them.

Insofar as other tools of design that pertain to representation and legislative selection are concerned, we can begin by noting that, despite their constitutional importance, it is common to specify by statute rather than in the body of a national constitution the electoral rules whereby seats in one or both chambers of the national legislature are filled. The United States, moreover, may be unique in the freedom it gives states to decide methods and modes of election (although that freedom has been seriously circumscribed by court interpretation with respect to the House and by constitutional amendment with respect to the Senate). There is at least one important implication of a decentralized arrangement of this sort in the case of single-member constituencies – namely, the decentralization of conflict over redistricting. Redistricting is clearly a redistributive game among parties and/or legislators, and authorizing federal subjects to draw district boundaries without interference from the national government keeps an important source of conflict from bubbling up to disrupt national politics or to become a contentious issue in bargaining among federal subjects. This problem is necessarily less evident in systems that apportion seats by proportional representation, provided that proportional representation districts correspond to federal subjects, and a well-established rule exists for allocating fractional seats among those subjects.

The usual comparison the literature offers between proportional representation and single-mandate districts, however, centers on the relationship between district magnitude and party fractionalization – the number of parties (somehow measured) that compete for legislative seats (for the seminal essays, see Rae 1967; Lijphart 1994; Taagapera and Shugart 1989).[2] In much of that literature the presumption is that the thing to be maximized is "the diversity of parties that win representation" and that the primary evaluative criteria are "the extent to which the distribution of seats among parties

[2] The most widely cited empirical generalization is that the greater the number of seats allocated on average in a legislative district, the greater is the number of parties contesting for seats. Such generalizations, though, hide a wealth of detail. Clearly, Germany's two-tier parliamentary electoral system, which gives rise to a calculation of two seats per district (with half the Bundestag elected in single-mandate districts and half by national party-list proportional representation) cannot be equivalent to a system in which all legislators are elected from two-member districts. And even the calculation of a dependent variable is subject to dispute. To discount for small parties and accommodate systems with a large dominant party, that variable is normally taken to be a creature called "the effective number of parties" – a calculation that weights parties by their vote share so that a system with two parties of approximately equal strength is equated with one in which four parties compete, but one generally dominates the remaining three with something more than a majority of the vote. An analysis based on effective number then is equivalent to requiring the researcher to gather data on market share before counting the number of cereals or brands of soup one finds in a supermarket.

accurately reflects the distribution of votes cast" (Carey 1997: 67). But as Carey correctly goes on to note, "[d]ata on party system fragmentation, proportionality, and majorities do not shed much light on the motivation of politicians, the types of public policies they value, and the ability of parties to act collectively in pursuit of partisan goals" (p. 88)[3] – and here, we would add, on the extent to which a party system works to sustain a federation. Although we can formulate good arguments against extreme party fractionalization such as we find in Israel, Belgium, or Russia, the relative success of German and American federalism demonstrates that there is no unique preferred election system or number of parties.[4] Although an electoral system based on single-mandate districts necessarily gives federal subjects representation in the national government via the representation afforded constituencies within them, Germany accomplishes the same thing even under the umbrella of a national proportional representation system by giving its separate states control of the party lists and by providing incentives for state party organizations to maximize their party's share of the vote. In this way deputies to the Bundestag, at least in principle, are no less representatives of their states than are deputies to the Bundesrat. Thus, what is relevant to federalism here is not that Germany uses a split system, both single-mandate and proportional representation, or a 5 percent threshold for representation, or even that its system is designed to correct for any disproportionate allocation of seats across parties occasioned by its single-mandate contests. Rather, what is relevant is that these provisions are contained in a system that sustains an integrated relationship between local, regional, and national party organizations.

Ethnicity

The United States and Germany are two polar and relatively easy-to-treat cases insofar as electoral design is concerned, because a common issue that belies any simple scheme of representation is the existence of ethnic (or linguistic or religious) divisions that may or may not correlate with geography. The United States is sufficiently heterogeneous and Germany homogeneous that special provision for ethnicity is either impractical or need not be considered as a symbolic trigger for a renegotiation of federal terms.[5] Either extreme is fortuitous, since the reward for attempting to base coalition building in federal bargaining on group identities pays the least in such circumstances.

[3] A list of contributions directly addressing the connection between electoral rules and electoral campaign strategies includes Enelow and Hinich (1984); Cain, Ferejohn, and Fiorina (1987); Ames (1994); Carey and Shugart (1995); Cox (1990); Powell (2000).

[4] For more specific details on this point and a comparative analysis of electoral systems in selected federations, see Weaver (1992).

[5] The obvious exception here is that of race in the United States, although owing to the geographic dispersion of African Americans, this issue no longer impacts politics in a way that so unambiguously pits the interests of one region against another.

But there are more problematic intermediate cases where special provision for minority or proportional representation becomes practically unavoidable, be it an advanced industrial country such as Belgium or one torn by ethnic strife like Bosnia. Here federalism in some form is seen as essential – the "essential nuisance" – short of establishing separate states and forgoing whatever economies of scale might exist from an united entity.

Here as much as anywhere we want representatives to be less than perfect agents of the ethnicities that describe their constituencies, lest they become entrepreneurial agents of ethnic strife a la Milošević in Yugoslavia. Unfortunately, ethnicity occasions special difficulties with encouraging the desired imperfection because it impacts directly the parameters of the distributive game. Recall that the solution we offer to inducing agency imperfection requires integrated parties, which in turn requires appeasing one's own constituency without alienating constituencies elsewhere. But in deeply divided polities, almost by definition, forging alliances across federal subjects or districts can require prohibitive vote losses locally, in which case political concessions for the sake of party or forward-looking career aspirations might not be justified by any rational calculus (Hechter 2000). We can speculate as to the reasons why ethnicity plays the role it does in our species.[6] But as far as the political agency is concerned, the most evident hypothesis is that, although a constituency acting as a collective principal in a heterogeneous (pluralist) polity may have difficulty informing itself about how well its agent has served its interest, or even determining what its self-interest is, that task is eased considerably when a unit is homogeneous – and even more so when it is homogeneous in a way that differentiates it from other constituencies.[7] Thus, acting as an imperfect agent becomes more problematical, perhaps even impossible. To see the problem in a more formal way, consider again the game we use in Chapter 5 to show how imperfect agency can be rewarded by voters if representatives have an unavoidable probability of being imperfect (Figures 5.1 and 5.2). Suppose we modify the payoffs there in a simple way; namely, suppose that whenever two constituencies direct their representatives to ignore a constitutional restriction against renegotiation and their representatives act as directed, the payoffs to those two constituencies increase by the amount g, whereas the payoff to the third hapless abiding constituency decreases by a compensating $2g$. The game in Figure 5.1, then, becomes the one shown in Figure 8.1.

[6] For models explaining how individuals come to identify with an ethnic group and why such alignments can be rational, see Hardin (1995); Laitin (1998); de Figueiredo and Weingast (1999); Snyder (2000); Fearon and Laitin (2000).

[7] This argument is consistent with the observation that nationalism seeks to homogenize constituencies by excluding all other groups (Wimmer 2002). According to Hechter (2000: 7, 9) nationalism is "collective action designed to render the boundaries of the nation congruent with those of its governance unit," where the governance unit is a "territorial unit which is responsible for providing the bulk of social order and other collective goods."

	Unit 3				
	abide			ignore	
	Unit 2			Unit 2	
Unit 1	abide	ignore		abide	ignore
abide	1, 1, 1	.9, .5, .9	abide	.9, .9, .5	0-2g, 1.2+g, 1.2+g
ignore	.5, .9, .9	1.2+g, 1.2+g, 0-2g	ignore	1.2+g, 0-2g, 1.2+g	0, 0, 0

FIGURE 8.1. Constitutional legitimacy problem when some federal benefits to groups are popularly perceived as mutually exclusive.

Recall that, absent g, it is possible to sustain an equilibrium in which all three constituencies vote to abide by the constitution and for that equilibrium to be coalition-proof if a representative instructed to "ignore" nevertheless chose "abide" with probability p greater than .25. Now, however, with the addition of g, this threshold necessarily rises: for $g = .2$, the probability of politician's defection from a constituency mandate to ignore must be at least .4 in order for (abide, abide, abide) to be a coalition-proof equilibrium among constituencies; for $g = .4$, the minimal probability must be .5; and for $g = 1$, this minimum probability is approximately .7. The magnitude of these numbers, of course, has no precise substantive meaning, but our example does illustrate that, as the stakes in federal bargaining increase, the "imperfection" required of elected officials becomes greater.[8]

There is, however, an even more vexing reason as to why ethnicity causes special problems. If constitutions and constitutional provisions are mere coordination devices that exist in an environment of countless other sources of social coordination, then, as we note in Chapter 5 when describing some simple rules of constitutional design, its objective of coordinating society to a stable nexus of political institutions and rules is more readily achieved if its provisions do not conflict with these other sources. To the extent that ethnicity coordinates people in any way, however, it is likely to operate in opposition to at least some constitutional objectives. Thus, attempting to control ethnic conflict by political institutional means – by a constitution – necessarily pits two coordinating mechanisms against each other and unavoidably runs afoul of at least one rule of design. And unfortunately, constitutions – especially those newly adopted – are in a strategically inferior position since ethnicity and all that concept implies is a ready and historically rooted mechanism of social and political coordination. Indeed, we can quite easily imagine circumstances in which no constitution, however well crafted, can have much chance of success.

[8] Notice also that the concave relationship between g and $p_{\min}$ implies that the fully cooperative equilibrium is not coalition proof for more than half the space over which p and g range.

We are not completely helpless here. First, if a decision has been made, for whatever reason, to form a federation that consists of two of more otherwise antagonistic or potentially antagonistic groups, the most obvious advice we can offer is – in accordance with our discussion of the dimensionality of the federal government's responsibilities – to provide for a national government with minimal scope.[9] Here, of course, the idea is to allow the domain of the national government to develop incrementally and slowly so that whatever coordination a constitution can provide develops its own roots – so that, as Ferejohn et al. (2001) might say, a spirit of constitutionalism is allowed to mature without requiring that it resolve problems that otherwise seem unresolvable. This, it seems, is part of the logic behind allowing the European Union to expand its authority only incrementally.

With respect to other institutional devices, more often than not design focuses on special provisions that in some purely mechanistic way are intended as barriers to conflict, including giving one or all groups a veto over the federal government's actions (Czechoslovakia), introducing a collegial executive (Switzerland, Dagestan, Bosnia), gerrymandering legislative districts and erecting quotas so that minorities are assured representation (the United States, Dagestan, India, Belgium), and, as often seems to be the policy of the World Bank and the International Monetary Fund, trying to buy out ethnic leaders with side payments (or society as a whole with the promise of lavish economic aid that is contingent on its cooperation). None of these alternatives, however, is likely to prove decisive or even useful. An unappealable legislative veto is a recipe for immobilization and legislative impotence. Collegial presidencies will fracture or be rendered irrelevant to the political process if the motives of their members remain defined strictly in terms of ethnic identities. If a gerrymander does nothing more than guarantee representation, then the incentive to eliminate its effects within the legislature will be a constant source of friction and resentment. And promises of aid and special payments can sometimes only raise the stakes of conflict, both across the ethnic divide and within ethnic leadership cadres without the promise that the "right side" will always prevail (Esman and Herring 2001).[10] More important, such devices and policies do little by themselves to modify the coordinating influence of ethnicity and, by institutionalizing it, may even magnify that influence. They can be of some use, if only for the reason that no institutional mechanism should be discarded a priori as wholly useless in any context. But, to restate once again the argument of this and the preceding

[9] In ethnically divided societies, the higher the scope of the public sector, the higher is the potential for conflict among groups over the distribution of public benefits. For example, in the Second Nigerian Republic, the introduction of free education at all levels in some Nigerian states eventually provoked the adoption of discriminatory measures to prevent nonlocal ethnic groups from "overstretching" the states' resources (Osaghae 1994).

[10] As Esman and Herring (2001: 166) point out, in dealing with divided societies "the carrots of foreign assistance may be as disruptive as the sticks."

chapter, they will serve their intended purpose only if they are fashioned with an eye to facilitating broad elite coalitions such as those that characterize a system of integrated parties.

Integration here necessarily implies both vertical (federal) and horizontal (social) integration, although the two are commonly the same whenever ethnic identities correlate with geography. And although we appreciate the possibility that there may be problems for which there are no solutions – at least no federal solution – there are opportunities for imaginative electoral design directed at the alleviation of conflict via a modification of political elite incentives. Horowitz (1985, 1991), for example, argues persuasively that electoral systems based on a preferential ballot are an important mechanism for mitigating such ethnic conflict. In his scheme the goal is not some naive mechanical formula for ensuring strict proportionality of representation or for even ensuring that all relevant potentially hostile social groups are somehow represented. Instead, Horowitz looks at the opportunities for using electoral institutional design as a means to create incentives on the part of parties and candidates not merely to refrain from becoming entrepreneurs of ethnic conflict but actually to prefer conflict-avoiding cross-ethnic appeals. Briefly, the argument here is that if ballots allow voters to express an ordinal preference, and if each candidate's likelihood of winning a seat is positively related to their average rank across all ballots, then candidates should be less motivated to make or base their campaign on divisive appeals and incumbents less likely to support policies that pit the interests of one identifiable group against another. The logic of this argument is simple: even if I know you will not rank me as highly as those candidates who share your ethnicity, I still might attempt to formulate a campaign that appeals to you – or at least not pursue a campaign in which I attempt to incite conflict – in the hope that you will respond by ranking me higher on your ballot than the other candidates who do not share your genetic roots. Integrated parties, in turn, become more viable because one of the barriers to integration across federal subjects – ethnic conflicts that correlate with geography – is removed.

There are alternatives to preferential voting, such as the previously discussed Dagestani scheme. It may be true that it, unlike Horowitz's scheme, seeks to impose a specific allocation of seats among its ethnic groups and thus, owing to the need to establish an agency that will determine the ultimate allocation across ethnicities, runs counter to our advice that every effort be made to decentralize such conflict. But, at the same time, notice that the mechanism in question here is more than a mere attempt to resolve conflict by a mechanical formula for fair representation.[11] Like Horowitz's,

11 Proponents of consociational power sharing argue that proportional representation electoral systems are most likely to give ethnic minorities a voice within legislatures and coalition governments, thereby promoting cooperation between groups in societies divided by ethnic conflict. However, as Norris (2002) notes, there is at best only limited evidence that such

it too seeks to impact elite motives. By allowing only members of a specific ethnicity to represent particular mixed districts, the ethnic appeal of candidates is muted by virtue of the fact that, ceteris paribus, a candidate's margin of victory is likely to be supplied by a minority ethnic group. And to the extent that all or nearly all candidates for office share similar motives, at least one obstacle to the development of integrated parties of the sort we deem essential for stable federal relations is removed.

This discussion should not be taken as an argument that such schemes are a universal solution to ethnic conflict for democracy generally or federal systems in particular. One danger, as we have already noted, is that absent other institutional safeguards, there is no reason to suppose that there is an entity that can guarantee fairness, however defined, when authorized to establish districts and ensure proportionality. And perhaps even more important is the fact that our understanding of such systems is incomplete. For example, a potential flaw in Horowitz's scheme is that not only are the motives of candidates affected by an electoral system's design, but the motives of voters are impacted as well. Thus, although preferential voting might, ceteris paribus, act to moderate campaigns, that ceteris paribus condition might not be met. Preferential voting can also help sustain parties or candidacies that are purely ethnically based, because voters have a reduced incentive to cast strategic ballots so as to avoid "throwing their vote away" on candidates who would otherwise have little likelihood of winning under a nonpreferential scheme. Voters might believe that they now have the freedom to give a high rank to candidates who appeal directly to their narrow ethnic interest, reasoning that, even if such candidates are uncompetitive, these choices will be discarded, and the preferences they reveal further down the list with respect to candidates making more muted ethnic appeals will be the ones that count. There is, therefore, a trade-off here, but not one that, to our knowledge, has been rigorously studied in order to ascertain the full equilibrium of candidate and voter strategies.[12]

There is one other reason for approaching electoral engineering cautiously. As Carey (1997: 88) states the matter, "party systems are largely the product of institutional rules [but] the most obvious challenge to [assessing the impact of a particular rule] is the straightforward observation that institutional design is not simply imposed on a political system exogenously. The rules of political contestation are themselves the products of political processes,

a voice makes any difference in mitigating the conflict, and one can suppose that proportional representation can exacerbate conflict by giving parties a disincentive to negotiate ethnic conflict within their structures. Once again, then, we can see that any unidimensional proposal for treating society's cleavages is necessarily incomplete and naive absent a more comprehensive assessment of the full institutional context of that proposal.

12 For a review of evidence from countries with preferential electoral systems, see Reilly (2002). For a more general analysis of the effect of electoral systems on conflict in divided societies, see Reilly and Reynolds (1999).

and are subject to ongoing dispute and negotiation." It may be that in some circumstances, electoral rules have a natural inertia born of the fact that the winners under them are hesitant to substitute different rules for fear of losing whatever advantage they currently enjoy – and this property of election laws is often essential for their ultimate preservation.[13] In other words, election laws may become immutable as soon as they are established (Shamir 1985; Moe 1990; Shugart 1992; Weaver and Rockman 1993; Norris 1995; Pierson 1996). But if their design contains an explicit bias or otherwise promotes the sort of political mobilization that would lead to calls for global renegotiation of federal terms, it may not be possible to alter that design in any meaningful way, which can then impact the legitimacy of the entire federal edifice. Thus, lack of attention to electoral design with respect to the ultimate legitimacy of federal institutional structures can preclude an otherwise good design from reaching a desired institutional equilibrium or any equilibrium at all.

8.2 Level 2 Again and a Proper Federal Structure

Defining Federal Subjects

Whatever the ultimate consequence of electoral design efforts might be, the Dagestani scheme – indeed, any scheme of representation – highlights another parameter of design that, although it seemingly moves us even further away from Level 3 and deeper into Level 2, reveals the close interaction of institutions and rules at these two levels.

2. The geographic definition of federal subjects.

The matter of defining federal subjects is intimately connected to that of defining the rules of representation, although only rarely are federations afforded the luxury that was given to the United States when it carved its western territories up into neat rectangles or in accordance with natural geography. More often than not, federal subjects are defined a priori; as a consequence, a tension arises as to whether, as Adams noted in 1776, they should be represented equally, proportionate to their populations, something in between, or by some other criterion entirely. In attempting to achieve a compromise among the varied criteria of representation here, unsurprisingly we find some of the widest variations in design. For example, while all citizens of Austria are nearly equally represented in their national legislature, the ratio of the best to worst represented federal unit on the basis of population equals 10-to-1 in Spain, 13-to-1 in Australia and Germany, 21-to-1

[13] Among the studies that address the issue of institutional endogeneity are, to list a few, Quintal (1970), Levi (1988), Shamir (1985), Przeworski (1991), Brady and Mo (1992), Lijphart (1992a), Bawn (1993), Geddes (1995, 1996), Remington and Smith (1996), Shugart (1998), Boix (1999), Grofman and Reynolds (2001), Shvetsova (2003b), and of course Voigt's (1999) discussion of spontaneous institutions in a constitutional context.

in Canada, 40-to-1 in Switzerland, 66-to-1 in the United States, 144-to-1 in Brazil, and 370-to-1 in Russia (Stepan 1999: table 1).

We can only guess at the implications of this variability for party development. However, to the extent that differences in population, wealth, and natural resources threaten federal center capture by one or more federal subjects – the reaction to which acts as a deterrent to integrated party development – avoidance of an oversized subject and a multiplicity of subjects seem to be reasonable design recommendations. As evidence to that conclusion, Lemco (1991: 49), after sorting states into the categories "stable," "partly stable," and "not stable or ended," presents his and Riker's data on the thirty-two federations formed since 1945, in which the impact of the presence of an oversized federal subject (keeping in mind that the analysis here was conducted prior to the dissolution of the USSR) is apparent and is illustrated by Figure 8.2. Similarly, with respect to the parameter "number of federal subjects," Lemco reports the data containing the relationship illustrated by Figure 8.3. Although merely suggestive owing to the great many variables that are not considered, these data are consistent with the hypothesis that the number of federal subjects and the existence of an oversized subject are important parameters.

The danger posed by the presence of an oversized federal subject seems clear, so consider the difference between a federation with "few" versus one

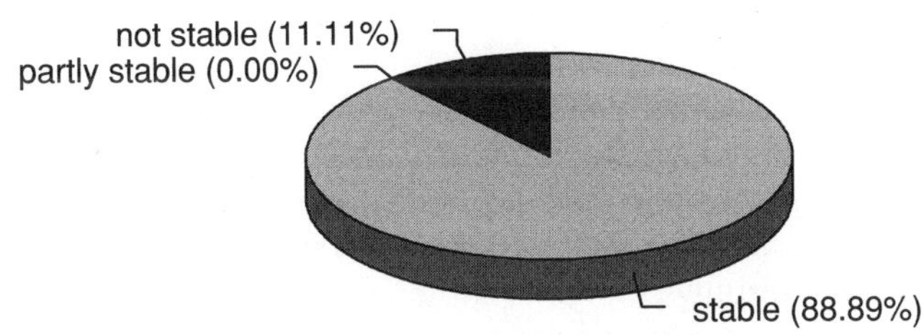

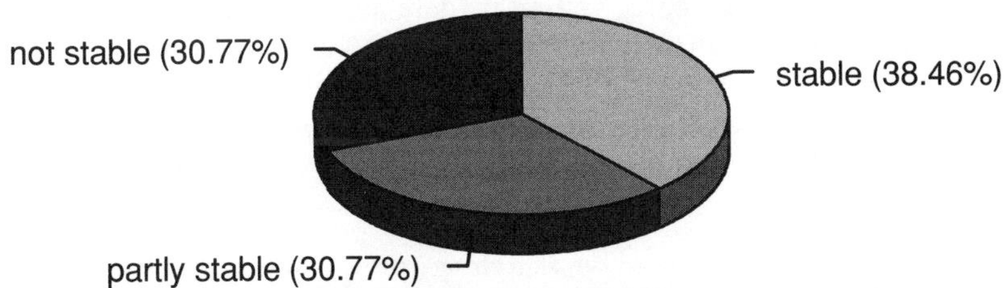

FIGURE 8.2. Relationship between the presence of an oversized federal subject and stability, in federations created between 1945 and 1990 (n = 32). Source: Lemco 1991.

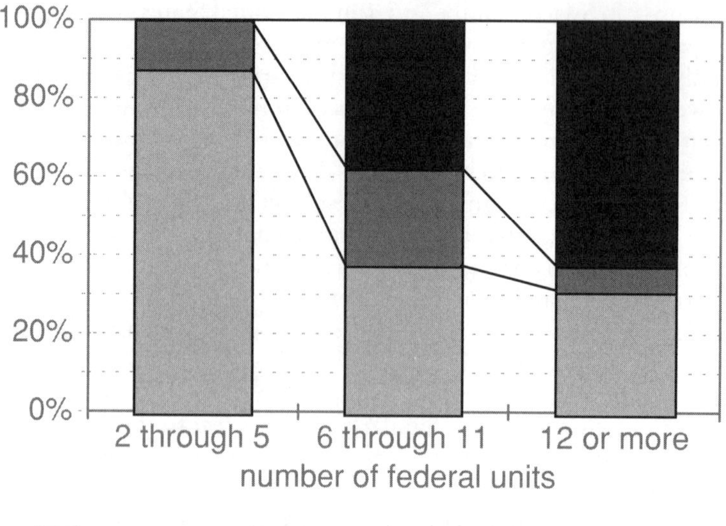

FIGURE 8.3. Relationship between the number of federal units and stability, in federations created between 1945 and 1990 (n = 32). Source: Lemco 1991.

with "many" subjects. If there are few subjects, then each is more likely to imagine itself as a viable independent state that can compete directly with the center, using if necessary credible threats of secession (explicitly or merely via the policy of withholding tax revenues from the center) as a ploy in federal bargaining. Conversely, if there are many small federal subjects, then we might reasonably anticipate a corresponding decrease in power relative to the center and a decrease in the likelihood of a federal subject seeing itself as a viable independent entity. At this point it seems valid to speculate that, absent any sense that one can fruitfully survive as an independent entity, political elites there will feel greater motivation to integrate their fates with those who hold or compete for national office. Put differently, all other things being equal, regional political elites should feel more comfortable with linking their fates in an integrated party system if there are many federal subjects, with none predominant, than if there are only a few such subjects and a danger that each might choose to be an independent player.

Although there are evident counterexamples (redrawing Länder boundaries in postwar Germany, dividing states in India and Nigeria),[14] the

[14] In western Germany, the Allies created new states from parts of Prussia and combinations of old states. In fact, only Bavaria and two small city-states, Hamburg and Bremen, had existed before World War II. Nigeria began as a three-state federation in 1960, with the number of states gradually expanding to four, twelve, nineteen, twenty-one, thirty, and most recently to thirty-six in 1997. The Indian Constitution created twenty-seven states. In 1956 the number

opportunities for geographic redefinition are not always used in full. We are reminded, for example, of Czechoslovakia's ill-fated attempts to accommodate its ethnic divide by various schemes for weighting voting and special provisions for the passage of legislation in its national parliament that gave each group a near veto over legislation. The danger here, of course, was a general paralysis of the state. An alternative approach, and one that to our knowledge was not considered, would have been to establish ethnically heterogeneous federal subjects by drawing horizontal lines on the map instead of the vertical one that corresponded to the Czech-Slovak cleavage. Moreover, in accordance with Lemco's (1991) findings, it also seems reasonable to suggest that more than one such line should have been considered. Russia, too, in 1990 bypassed an opportunity for geographic redesign that might have proved beneficial. The first concerned the existence of several federal subjects (autonomous regions) that fell wholly within other regions (e.g., Tumen) and which, because both were presumed to rule the same territory, confused the very definition of a federal subject and meaning of political equality among them. The second opportunity concerned the possibility of redefining regions so as to establish a more equitable distribution of the country's resources. In both cases, of course, redesign was politically infeasible, given the turbulent politics of that period and Yeltsin's dependence on regional leaders in thwarting his parliamentary opposition. Circumstances were somewhat different when the next president, Putin, came to power, and he did indeed launch a scheme of redesigning that country's federal geography. The steps taken, however, were contrary to Lemco's conclusions. Putin's scheme consolidated Russia's eighty-nine federal subjects into seven enlarged federal districts and introduced a new district administrative structure. Of course, rather than being a part of a policy of encouraging a coherent federal system in accord with some model of federal design, this scheme was implemented instead simply to erode the independent power bases of the governors and presidents of federal subjects in accord with Russia's centuries-old solution to its problems – concentrating as much power as possible in the hands of the center.

In the abstract and even in practical terms, a "best" geographic design need not exist, and any attempted change in a status quo may itself precipitate a crisis. It does not seem practical, for example, to suggest that the European Union redefine its component parts to offset the predominance of Franco-German coalition or even Germany alone, that Bosnia consider mixed Serb-Croat districts, or that the conflict between Hindus and Muslims and the partition of India and Pakistan could have been averted by a redefinition of federal subject boundaries. We also appreciate that Belgium's problems of representation and language in Brussels demonstrate that the

of states was reduced to fourteen. Currently, there are twenty-eight states and nine union territories in India.

creation of linguistically mixed regions can occasion other seemingly unresolvable issues (Fitzmaurice 1996). Nevertheless, we do want to draw attention to the fact that the parameter of federal subject definition is more than a means of empowering specific groups and more than a means of effecting a compromise between hostile or potentially hostile ethnic, linguistic, or religious groups. It is a parameter that impacts the motives of political elites and thus it can be used to manipulate their incentive to form and sustain parties that make cross-ethnic appeals. Indeed, the vertical integration of parties is not always sufficient for stable federal relations; federal friendly parties should also be horizontally integrated. For example, in Czechoslovakia vertically integrated parties – those competing solely for the Czech vote and those competing only in Slovakia – dominated the political system prior to the federal breakup, and their efforts in orchestrating the dissolution are easy to rationalize, since ultimately political elites would still owe their allegiance to one group or the other. On the other hand, if federal subjects are themselves heterogeneous, then parties that are integrated vertically have a greater chance, with the appropriate selection of voting schemes, of becoming integrated horizontally.[15]

Nothing we say here should be interpreted to mean that we believe that federal subject definition is an underappreciated parameter or that it is not foremost in the minds of those who would form a federation. However, when choices can be made, more often than not they are made to address purely redistributive issues via the autonomy granted to specific subpopulations and less with an eye to the party system that a design is likely to engender. Of course, if it is true that "there [are]... concrete circumstances in which individuals cannot develop or exercise their full rights unless they are active members of a group that struggles for some collective goods common to most of its members" (Stepan 1999: 12), and if such groups have a natural geographic definition, then the redistributive consequences of federal subject definition cannot and should not be ignored. Our argument here, though, is simply a restatement of the one Horowitz (1985, 1991) offers – namely, that if there is flexibility in federal subject definition, attention also ought to be paid to the implications that lines on a map have for the types of parties likely to arise in the competition for federal office. Can those lines be drawn so that they, in combination with the method for translating votes into seats, encourage integrated national parties with candidates preferring to share their labels across federal subjects? Or, as would have almost certainly been the case under any of Czechoslovakia's schemes of representation and legislative voting, will parties at best be vertically integrated but nevertheless largely regional?

[15] Dikshit (1975: 234) argues that the success of the Swiss federation is due to the fact that in cantons "the overlapping boundaries of language and religion... have weakened language and religion as divisive forces, for each linguistic group contains representatives of both faiths and... vice versa."

We suspect, in fact, that there is a commonly overlooked trade-off here between vertical and horizontal integration. If the geographic identities of federal subjects are set, as in Belgium, Switzerland, Bosnia, and Czechoslovakia, so as to isolate potentially hostile ethnic groups from each other behind the wall of federal subject definition, then vertical integration is made easier since political elites will see themselves as united in defense of their ethnic constituencies. Ethnicity, then, will be the primary integrating mechanism but in such a way as to make horizontal integration more difficult or impossible. On the other hand, if geographic identities are set to encourage horizontal integration, such as when we establish federal subjects that mix ethnic groups, then special care must be made in the setting of other parameters (e.g., those we consider in the previous chapter) so as to encourage vertical integration as well.[16] The general import of what we have just said, then, is that federalism, in the form of decentralized decision making and regional (read: ethnic) autonomy, need not be a solution to much of anything unless it is accompanied by institutional mechanisms that facilitate cross-ethnic (and, therefore, cross-federal subject) cooperation and coordination. Thus, a Bosnian federation based on strictly separate political representation of constituent ethnicities seems little more than a political and diplomatic cover for those who encouraged intervention with the assertion that only poor governmental design precluded political stability and interethnic cooperation.

Number of Local Jurisdictions

Even when it is infeasible to manipulate the number and geographic definition of federal units, there remains the surrogate tool of manipulating the number of subunits (local governments). Specifically,

3. The number of local jurisdictions.

In evaluating this design parameter, it is useful to proceed with a closer examination of contemporary Switzerland with the data in Table 8.1 in mind. We offer these data and this focus here because Switzerland stands out in terms of the average number of local governments with electoral offices and because, as discussed in Chapter 7, there are numerous reasons for believing that a large number of local governments encourages federal-friendly parties, including the fact that it at least opens the door to filling a large number of official positions by direct election and thereby promotes the rise of local

16 The interplay of ethnicity and electoral rules as a determinant of party systems is documented by Cox (1997) and Ordeshook and Shvetsova (1994), who show that the impact of such parameters as district magnitude and heterogeneity is multiplicative and not additive. That is, district magnitude has a greater impact on the number of parties when ethnic heterogeneity is high than when it is low. And the impact of heterogeneity is most clearly felt when district magnitude is high – when the formal institutional barriers to party fragmentation are low. Of course, this research merely serves to emphasize that the background conditions cannot be ignored when evaluating any institution.

TABLE 8.1. *Number of Electoral Jurisdictions at Subnational and Local Levels in Selected Federations, 1998*

Country	Population (million)	Federal Unit Governments (2002)	Elected Local Governments	Local Governments/ 10,000
Switzerland	7	23 cantons 3 half-cantons	3,000	4.3
Austria	8	9 states	2,353	2.9
United States	270	50 states 1 federal district	70,500	2.6
India	980	28 states 7 union territories	237,687	2.4
Spain	39	17 autonomous communities	8,082	2.1
Germany	82	13 states 3 city-states	16,121	2.0
Canada	31	10 provinces 2 territories	4,507	1.5
Belgium	10	3 communities 3 territories	589	0.6
Australia	19	6 states 2 territories	900	0.5
Pakistan	132	4 provinces	5,195	0.4
Argentina	36	23 provinces	1,617	0.4
Mexico	96	31 states 1 federal district	2,418	0.3
Brazil	166	26 states 1 federal district	5,581	0.3
Bosnia	4	2 states	137	0.3
Ethiopia	61	9 regions 2 special cities	910	0.1
Russia	147	89 units	2,000	0.1
Malaysia	22	13 states	143	0.1
Nigeria	121	36 states	589	0.05

Source: World Bank (1999).

politicians and local political organizations. Even if local politics focuses on technical and ideologically empty issues in the context of elections that are formally nonpartisan, the American and Swiss experiences show that party organizations can be especially active there. Correspondingly, it becomes more difficult for a fragmented federal subject to speak with a single voice, since at least some local politicians will prefer not to agitate on behalf of purely regional interests, however defined. Instead of being an entity capable of placing unified demands on the federal center, a region becomes an aggregation of distinctive communities, each focused on issues whose salience need not be shared uniformly across a region. Finally, when national parties operate locally, an electoral coalition across units becomes a coalition of local organizations, which, in turn, diminishes the ability of the new parties to challenge the status quo nationally since they are unlikely to be able to match a national party's network of local supporters. As Ladner (1999: 238) explains matters with respect to Switzerland, "[t]he tight network of local parties and the remarkable integration of the four main federal parties at the communal level is another, often forgotten, reason for the famous stability of the Swiss political system. Although new political groups have succeeded on several occasions in gaining an important share of the vote, most have never been able to develop a similar organizational structure at the communal level. Most were thus bound to disappear as the importance of their claims on the political agenda decreased."

Of course, the data Table 8.1 summarizes hold implications beyond any one country. For example, they help us understand some of the reasons for India's success as a federation. With 60 percent more elected local governments per capita than Canada, four times that of Belgium, and eight times that of Brazil, we should not be surprised at the Congress Party's dependence on local political elites and local political organizations when maintaining its national position. The Swiss experience, however, is especially instructive in teaching us how developed local governments promote integrated parties. Local governments there are not only numerous on a per capita basis – 45 percent greater than its closest competitor, Austria, and 65 percent greater than the United States – their number is remarkably stable. In its first century (from 1848 to 1950) the number of municipalities decreased only from 3,203 to 3,097; and since the 1950s, as most European countries hugely reduced the number of local governments, there was only a 7 percent decline in their number in Switzerland (from 3,097 to 2,903 by 2000).[17] When the Swiss federation was formed in 1848 it was, in fact, an agglomerate of 3,000 tiny communities, often practicing local democracy and self-government, many minting their own coin, and all eager to protect their economic and political independence from federal and canton governments.[18] Even after 150 years, many Swiss have greater loyalty and attachment to their communes than to the confederation or cantons. Especially in the mountainous areas, most

[17] For an interesting comparison, we note that local governments are much fewer in number in Russia. For example, in the European "North-West Administrative Region," with a considerably larger population and almost five times the territory of Switzerland, we find only 190 local governments.

[18] Most recently, political independence of communes from canton governments was demonstrated when a new Jura canton was created in 1979. While originally a number of communes were instrumental in the split, some subsequently shifted their loyalties and moved to other cantons – for example, in 1989 Laufenthal voted to leave Bern and join Basel-Land, and in 1995 tiny Vellerat (population of seventy) voted to join Jura.

still view themselves first and foremost as the citizens of their individual communes, with commune citizenship limited either to direct descendants of citizens or to those who are admitted by the old members. All other persons are merely residents, be they citizens of other communes or foreigners, and a foreigner must obtain both canton and commune citizenship before he or she can become a Swiss citizen.[19] In addition, communes maintain a high level of economic and political autonomy, with all government activities not explicitly assigned to federal and canton levels falling under communal authority.[20]

Unsurprisingly, when parties first emerged in the mid-nineteenth century, they originated not at the national but at canton and local levels: "The foundation of local parties was not restricted to towns, canton capitals, and rural centers but also took place in smaller communities . . . independent local parties emerged according to the structure of the local population and its political preferences and eventually joined one of the larger parties" (Ladner 1999: 221).[21] Today, only the smallest communes have no operating political groups and parties, and about three-fourths of all communal executive seats are held by members of some party – almost exclusively by parties that are active at the national level. Altogether there are about 180 cantonal and 5,000 local parties, but almost 90 percent of local parties are units of parties active at the canton and federal levels (Ladner 1999, 2001). The reasons for the continuance of such intense local-party activity are not hard to find. In addition to seemingly voting all the time on every local policy issue one can imagine,[22] elections are used as well to fill a large number of local offices. Each commune has a collective executive consisting of at least three elected officials, and, as in the United States, elections are used to fill technical positions as well. Table 8.2 gives the average numbers of executive and councillor seats across communes of different sizes and the average number of parties competing for these seats.[23] The intense local

[19] Noncitizens constitute almost 20 percent of the population of Switzerland.

[20] Thus, they independently levy taxes to a degree that most taxes paid can be communal – for example, the tax bill of an average member of Zurich's middle class was 4 percent federal, 44 percent cantonal, and 52 percent communal (Kubler 2001).

[21] The process was similar to the American experience, where "the national party system was initially formed out of extant state and local parties, factions, and cliques" (Aldrich 1995: 109).

[22] For example, between 1934 and 1996, the citizens of Zurich voted on more than eighteen hundred issues, 42 percent of which were local, 40 percent cantonal, and 18 percent national (Ladner 1998).

[23] Insofar as attempting to discern an impact of election laws, two-thirds of all communes use majority rule to elect collective executives, whereas proportional representation is used mostly in larger communes. However, Ladner and Milner (1999) find that the relationship between the number of parties and the electoral system holds only in the smallest communities and vanishes completely in communities with more than two thousand members. That is, in relatively large communes, four national party labels appear on the ballot in almost all local elections, regardless of the electoral system.

TABLE 8.2. *Average Number of Elected Local Offices and Number of Represented Parties by Size and Linguistic Type of a Commune*

	Inhabitants				
	<500 (34.8%)	501–2,000 (37.9%)	2,001–5,000 (17.3%)	5,001–10,000 (5.9%)	>10,000 (4.2%)
German cantons					
Executive	5.1	6.1	7.2	8.2	8.0
Council	10.0	16.8	24.1	36.0	43.7
Parties	0.7	2.1	3.6	4.9	7.0
French cantons					
Executive	5.1	6.0	6.9	7.0	7.2
Council	19.3	33.4	49.4	53.6	72.7
Parties	0.4	1.6	3.3	3.8	5.5
Italian cantons					
Executive	4.3	5.6	6.7	6.8	7.0
Council	22.1	23.8	26.4	35.6	46.7
Parties	1.4	3.4	4.1	4.3	5.0

Source: Geser (1997).

organization and activities of parties suggested by this table has its impact on national parties – something that is perhaps most clearly demonstrated by the fact that almost all politicians at the cantonal or federal level are recruited from local parties. Indeed, at least one comparative study of political careers in nine federal countries (Stolz 2000) shows that Switzerland has the highest proportion of federal politicians recruited from regional assemblies – 68 percent in 2000 (followed by the U.S. Congress with 38 percent).[24] Swiss national parties, then, are essentially federations or alliances of local entities, all sharing common labels during elections.

Repeating the story offered by the United States, Germany, and India, the loose coalitional nature of Switzerland's national parties is credited with playing a critical role in maintaining Swiss federal stability: "Given the highly heterogeneous nature of Swiss society, party networks help overcome the many centrifugal forces stemming from different local and regional traditions. These networks are mutually reinforcing, with central-level parties providing resources and ideological guidance and local levels providing substantial organizational support during elections" (Saiz and Geser 1999: 213). This situation contrasts sharply with Canada, which a recent comparative study of local governments singles out as the country with almost no local penetration by national-level parties: "The case of Canada contrasts with our other studies in that mostly independent parties and candidates,

[24] As Hughes (1962: 42) observed: "There is also regularly a personal union of federal and cantonal political office."

unaffiliated with national parties, vie for control of local politics. As a result, the Canadian local political system appears to be more volatile.... Canada experienced an upsurge of local party activity during the 1970s like most other Western countries, but these developments were not channeled by national party organizations and did not result in stable change. The lack of national party involvement, together with Canada's federal system of government, appears to reinforce political regionalism" (Saiz and Geser 1999: 323; see also Filion 1999).

The limited scope of the national party involvement in local politics would seem to be the logical consequence of Canada's highly centralized system of municipal governance. The Canadian Constitutional Act assigned responsibility for "municipal institutions" to the provinces, encouraging them to subordinate local governments. Thus, the complaint can be lodged that Toronto requires provincial permission to install a traffic light (Stein 2001). More generally, the well-being of cities and municipalities depends more on who controls provincial and federal governments rather than the local administration, in which case "the benefits a municipal presence would bring to a senior-level [national] party were not perceived as sufficient to offset expenses associated with entering the local scene and the risks this involves. There were few anticipated rewards from a successful municipal performance but rather fears that a poor local record would tarnish provincial and federal branches" (Filion 1999: 97).

Although Canada looks much like Germany in this respect – signaling once again the fact that no single design parameter explains differences in federal performance – Table 8.3 shows that Canada does contrast sharply with other federal democracies, especially Switzerland, the United States, and India, in terms of the overall average numbers of government positions filled by direct election. (No aggregate data on the number of elected offices are available for Switzerland, but even a conservative estimate would put the number of its elected officials per 10,000 of the population above that of the United States. With 4.2 local governments per 10,000 inhabitants, and at least 3 elected officers of the collective executive per local government, that alone gives 12.6 officials per 10,000; but there are also local legislatures, elected local technical offices, approximately 3,000 people in elected cantonal positions, and federal-level officeholders.) Of course, one can reasonably ask whether and to what extent the number and nature of municipal governments is a manipulable design parameter, and here we can refer to the fact that in the 1990s several Canadian provincial legislatures proceeded with municipal "restructuring." However, rationalized doubtlessly by some purely economic as opposed to political view of federalism, Ontario's "reform" yielded a *reduction* in the number of local governments and elected local politicians. Thus, the Ministry of Municipal Affairs and Housing (with the staff of 1,065) in 2001 could proudly report significant progress in reforming local governments. The Minister of Municipal Affairs

TABLE 8.3. *Number of Elected Officials in Canada and Selected Federal Countries in 1998*

		Number of Politicians Elected at		
	Number Elected per 10,000	Federal Parliament	Provincial Parliaments	Local Governments
Canada	3.26	301	742	9,070
Germany	3.73	669	1,972	27,933
Brazil	4.07	594	1,066	65,893
Pakistan	5.35	217	552	69,900
Belgium	14.06	230	1,131	12,697
Spain	17.21	353	1,181	65,589
United States (1992)	20.18	535	7,461	493,830
Switzerland	na	246	2,979	na
India	30.66	543	4,120	3,000,000
Austria	49.98	247	463	39,270

Sources: U.S. Census, *Popular Elected Officials* (Washington, D.C.: Government Printing Office, 1995); Council of European Municipalities and Regions, "Men and Women in European Municipalities in Figures" (Paris, 1999), available at <http:www.ccre.org/women/pub_an_html>; Council of Europe, *Women in Politics: in the Council of Europe Member States* (Strasbourg, September 2001); India Election Commission, 2002, available at <http://www.eci.gov.in>; Brazilian Superior Electoral Court, 2002, available at <http://www.tse.gov.br/eleicoes/index.html>.

and Housing signed restructuring orders that further reduced the number of municipalities [in Ontario] from 815 in 1996 to 447 by March 31, 2001. There are now 2,804 local politicians – a 39 per cent reduction in just five years."[25]

We appreciate that local democracy with active local party organizations is only one variable that contributes to federal-friendly party development. But it can be of special significance in the formative stages of party system evolution. We cannot say that an established party system requires the proliferation of local party organizations such as the one maintained in Switzerland, although it seems evident that such proliferation doesn't hurt. One thing is clear: the use of rationalization, agglomeration, consolidation, and other efforts at cost reduction driven by a purely economic view of federalism is not an example for new federations to follow without a careful assessment of political consequences. Moreover, even though the comparison of states such as Switzerland and Canada, or Canada and India, is illuminating and moves us in the direction of understanding the differences in the relative performance of these federations, contemporary descriptions give an inaccurate picture of what was in place at the time of party system development. After World War II especially, local governments almost everywhere, under

[25] Business Plan, Ontario Municipal Affairs and Housing, 2001–2002, available at <http://www.publications.gov.on.ca>.

the pressure of fiscal competition with central and regional authorities, faced a lack of financial resources and were forced to merge so that despite significant population growth, the number of local governments in Europe, the United States, Canada, and Australia is considerably lower than it was one hundred or even fifty years ago.[26] It is a mistake, then, for those who would design a new federation to view the current state of local governments there as models; instead, designers can benefit by analyzing the path of local government development and its effect on party system integration. To emphasize the critical point here, local government design – both in terms of their numbers, political autonomy, and use of elections within them – is an important federal design parameter that can, perhaps, substitute for manipulations in the number and character of federal subjects when such manipulations are politically infeasible.

Of course, party systems are the consequence of a complex interaction of a multitude of institutional choices – witness the fact that Canada and Germany, despite the considerable differences in party systems, seem comparable in the data offered in Table 8.3. Thus, we continue with the discussion of those provisions relevant for party development that are properly a part of the national constitution, that largely belong to the Level 2 institutional superstructure, and that include those parameters Madison and Hamilton would have included in any description of a proper design. Without claiming that our list is exhaustive or sufficient to make the federal government sustainable for the long run, even a minimal list of such provisions would include the following:

4. The authority of the national versus regional governments over local governments (e.g., a supremacy clause, the right of the federal government to enforce contracts, prohibitions of restraints of trade).
5. Bicameralism and the relative legislative strength of the upper chamber.
6. Special provisions for the passage of legislation in the national legislature or special provisions for representation in order to accommodate national, ethnic, linguistic, and similar issues, or other asymmetries in design.
7. In presidential systems, the constitutional authority of the president relative to that of the legislature; in parliamentary or quasi-presidential systems, rules of government dissolution and votes of no confidence.
8. In the case of presidential systems, the method of electing the president.
9. For presidential systems, the timing of national legislative and presidential elections.

[26] The exceptions to this trend can be found in some postcommunist democracies and Italy. On the other hand, between 1965 and 1977 the number of local governments in (West) Germany was reduced from approximately 24,000 to 8,500.

Authority over Local Governments

The first item on the preceding list, number 4, is addressed almost universally in any discussion of federalism. However, such discussions commonly occur with an eye to such matters as minority rights, efficient markets, and the general notion of subsidiarity – that of allocating responsibilities among governments in accordance with their fiscal capacity and the extent of externalities involved in the production and distribution of goods and services. Here we want to note one additional criterion – that of allowing governments at different levels a degree of fiscal and decision-making autonomy so as to encourage electoral competition for political office at each level. It seems evident that we would encourage political competition at the local level by affording local governments some control over local services. What warrants emphasis here, though, is that giving regional governments, as opposed to the federal center, some authority over local governments encourages political competition at the regional level and the integration of local and regional party organizations. That is, just as we want to encourage a symbiotic relationship between national and regional political elites, we want to encourage the same thing between regional and local politicians as well.

Bicameralism

The next item on this list, number 5, bicameralism, is also extensively discussed in the literature – largely in two contexts: as a partial resolution of the need to decide whether the "thing" to be represented is people or federal subjects, and as a means for making the federal legislature more conservative by raising the effective quota for the passage of legislation (Lijphart 1987; Riker 1992; Tsebelis and Money 1997; Patterson and Mughan 1999). In achieving these objectives, however, bicameralism meets another related need: differences in the structure of representation between two chambers that are both veto players further encourages an increase in the size of electoral coalitions required to enact policy. In addition to those instances in which a president comes from a party other than the one that controls the legislature, the word deadlock can be appended to those instances in which different parties or coalitions control each legislative chamber. Deadlock, however, is more often than not a pejorative word applied by those who prefer an activist state, and although bicameralism may act as a brake in one way by making it more difficult formally to pass legislation, it is an accelerant in another to the extent that it adds to the incentives to expand electoral coalitions through legislative compromise. By permanently fixing the incentives for oversized electoral coalitions, it also fixes the incentives to maintain those coalitions as permanent (read: political party) formations.

Of course, bicameralism comes in many forms, and differences in form, like the preceding item, are intimately related to the matter of representation (Baldwin and Shell 2001). For example, an upper legislative chamber can be coequal with the lower chamber (e.g., in the United States and Australia), subject to a veto override by its sister chamber (e.g., in Russia), or be essentially impotent (e.g., in Canada). Representatives can be directly elected, can consist of regional chief executives themselves (e.g., in Russia prior to Putin's "reforms"), or be appointees of those executives and regional legislatures; they can serve terms that coincide with those of regional authorities (again in Russia after Putin) or be wholly disjointed from them; and they can serve their terms with or without the threat of recall by whatever authority appoints or elects them (e.g., in the Iroquois Confederation).[27] Finally, in a manner made wholly explicit in Germany, when an upper chamber is formed in a delegated fashion, that is, by the governments of federation members, that chamber can be made an essential actor in enforcing and administering federal legislation. There are no well-defined or easily discerned rules for how various combinations of these parameters encourage or inhibit a smoothly functioning federal institutional equilibrium. Indeed, as with essentially all the institutional parameters discussed in this volume, the impact of any one arrangement will be determined by other parameter choices. Nevertheless, when designing a federal state, the parameters that describe bicameralism need to be examined according to criteria that include their impact on encouraging symbiotic relationships among political elites that operate principally at different levels of government and not merely as a way to achieve a compromise over representation.

Symmetry

The sixth item on our list refers to the treatment of federal subjects that formally and even constitutionally gives explicit advantage to one region over others beyond any asymmetries in formal representation and asymmetries of size. Admittedly, asymmetry is a fact of life since no federation operates with units that are identical in all respects, including levels of economic development and the advantages of nature's endowments (Tarlton 1965; Keating 1999; Agranoff 1999; Congleton, Kyriacou, and Bacaria 2002). For example, the United States, upon Texas's annexation in 1845, became an explicitly asymmetric federation since that state, by the terms of the treaty upon which it was admitted, was authorized to divide itself into as many as five states once its territory had achieved sufficient population.[28] The sizable

[27] The Iroquois Confederation of upstate New York began initially as an alliance of five nations – Mohawk, Seneca, Cayeuga, Oneida, and Onondaga (in 1715 the confederation admitted the Tuscarora). As a matriarchal society, not only were women alone allowed to elect (male) members to the alliance's governing body, the Confederation Council, and fill vacancies, but the women of the clan whom a member represented also possessed the right of recall. For the full translated and generally accepted text of the confederation's constitution ("the great binding law"), which arguably dates to the fifteenth century, see Parker (1916).

[28] A different asymmetry, size, was allowed when Nevada achieved statehood in 1864 to offset potential southern dominance in a reformed Union despite the fact that its virtually nonexistent population did not meet the constitutional quota required for it to be a state.

and unequal distribution of federal land in the separate American states is yet another asymmetry, since it directly links the federal government to development policies in some states but not in others. Such asymmetries in the American federal system, however, have been the exception and not the rule, thereby contributing to America's success in avoiding disruptive federal bilateral bargaining.[29]

In practice, there may be a felt need to introduce asymmetries of various types in the quest for balance along other dimensions, such as when there is an apparent need to compensate a geographically concentrated ethnic minority with inflated representation in the national legislature or with various voting schemes that give that minority a veto or effective veto over legislation (as was attempted in Czechoslovakia). However, as attractive or as imperative as such schemes might seem as a tool of design in the initial stages of federal formation – especially when attempting to secure the consent of one group or another – asymmetric "rights" can also serve as a provocation for others to demand "equality." Here we are not concerned so much with the degree of fairness or distributive equality that might characterize specific federal arrangements, but rather with whether such adjustments are best described as statutory or as fundamental contractual provisions in which the rules of membership are differently defined for different members. If statutory, then calls for their revision or augmentation can be treated without necessarily disrupting fundamental institutional arrangements. But if formulated as contractual obligations, then in obvious ways those calls can open the door to a wholesale revision of federal institutional arrangements. This, of course, was the danger Czechoslovakia confronted but failed to overcome.

Presidential Authority

Perhaps no set of design parameters is more important than those that pertain to the constitutional authority of presidents in presidential systems relative to that of the legislature – item 7 in our list. We appreciate, of course, that no single constitutional provision can account fully for the actual allocation of authority between these two branches. Shugart and Carey (1992), for example, offer a comparative assessment of presidential powers by cataloging that office's veto powers (i.e., legislative requirements for a veto override, the opportunity for a line-item veto), decree powers (the ability of the president

[29] In addition to the structure of its party system, when searching for those things that discourage bilateralism, we should perhaps also give some credit to the physical mobility of the population, which allows people to vote with their feet and move from disadvantaged states to advantaged ones, as well as the mobility of capital, which allows states to compete for investment and encourages them to make good use of whatever advantages they possess in terms of attracting investment, or, if need be, in inventing advantages (e.g., noncorrupt politics, efficient bureaucracies, low corporate taxes, relaxed regulation).

to make law or merely administer the law), the authority to call for national referenda, the exclusive authority to introduce legislation, the president's authority to form cabinets and dismiss ministers, and the ease with which the legislature can censure the state's chief executive. There is no straightforward way for determining the proper constellation of parameter values here, and the task of choosing these values is made more difficult by the fact that they determine more than some simple balance of legislative-executive power. For example, it is reasonable to argue that a combination of provisions giving elected presidents broad legislative prerogatives would serve to weaken the prestige and policy value of parliamentary seats, thereby mitigating the stimuli to integrated party formation that bicameralism and various schemes of representation might otherwise engender. To avoid this, we might want to encourage not only balanced bicameralism but also parliaments that are legislatively strong – parliaments with a ready means of overriding executive vetoes, with the authority to direct the executive to specific actions through statute, and with the authority to oversee executive action.[30] The fact remains, however, that the parameters of formal presidential power reverberate through a political system.

We appreciate that the authority of a chief executive relative to that of the legislature is, more often than not, the product of an internal power struggle, and even when that authority is established with clear and considered deliberation, the issues discussed are likely to be addressed with foreknowledge of the identities of the leading candidates for that office. The formal dimensions of presidential power, however, need to be treated carefully not simply because of their impact on other institutions; in order to facilitate party integration, we also want whoever holds that office to be motivated to operate within the structure of the country's party system and for presidential electoral campaigns to be an integral and integrating part of that system. Put simply, it is not possible to assess the role and relative authority of a presidency without, at the same time, considering the occupant of that office's extraconstitutional role in the state's party system.[31]

[30] The same is not necessarily true for the no-confidence votes and rules for parliament dismissals in parliamentary systems. In those systems such tools, though they may seem to work against the parliament, do not work against parties. While they might serve to strengthen the hand of the executive (meaning the cabinet), since that executive itself is the creature of a partisan parliamentary majority, it therefore should strengthen the cohesiveness of a party or coalition behind it (Huber 1996).

[31] Indeed we find constitutional or statutory provisions such as those that preclude a president's association with a party not merely silly but potentially dysfunctional. They derive largely from a nineteenth-century European conceptualization of democracy not far removed from autocracy, and those who argue that a political figure can somehow be above party politics are fooling themselves, are attempting to fool someone else, or are simply uninformed about the role of parties in a democracy.

It is, of course, Neustadt's (1960: 23) famous dictum, when referring to the American presidency, that "Presidential *power* is the power to persuade." And that power, which Neustadt saw as requiring personal skill as much as formal authority, resides for the most part in a president's position, in the United States at least, as head of a political party. That an American president's ultimate authority derives as much from the informal powers his position in the state's party system affords as from explicit constitutional allocations of power is well illustrated by the comparison in Chapter 6 between the fortunes of Lincoln and his counterpart in the Confederacy, Jefferson Davis. Indeed, absent the levers of power often available to presidents elsewhere, an American president has little choice but to operate within a party system, since it is the critical basis upon which he must sustain any hope of implementing whatever legislative agenda he might establish for himself.[32] A Russian president, in contrast, armed with the authority to dismiss regional governors and assemblies, to vacate regional legislation, and to issue decrees with the force of law, has far less need for a party except insofar as he chooses to influence the coalitions within the lower legislative chamber. In either case, it is not the specifics of formal (institutionally defined) presidential power versus the legislature that dictates the power of that office, but rather the overall constellation of authority and the extent to which a president can lead via the exercise of leadership – via appropriate opportunities to persuade.

Presidential Selection

If presidential power requires skills at persuasion and if the exercise of those skills both requires an integrated party system and contributes to the development of such a system, then there is one additional and critically important parameter that needs to be considered – item 8 on our list, the method of presidential selection. Of course, if that method is legislative appointment, then we can safely assume that the object of analysis is essentially a parliamentary system, and the question then is what role, if any, the president plays in the operation of the state and the nature of its party system. The fact, however, that we might raise this question points to the critical role played by popular, direct election of chief executives and heads of state. There is little need here to review the nature of the legitimacy that direct election affords, and the role a directly elected president can play as a coordinating agent for public policy and action. Nor do we want to argue for the superiority of any particular scheme of election. Simple plurality rule has the

[32] In comparing the legislative powers of forty-four directly elected presidential regimes in thirty-five countries, Shugart and Carey (1992: 155) offer an index in which twenty-four regimes achieve a presidential power rank greater than the U.S. presidency as compared to only fourteen with a lesser score, where those with lesser scores include the wholly impotent presidents of Haiti, Bulgaria, and Ireland.

ostensible advantage of encouraging only a few nationally integrated parties and avoiding what appears to be a poor institutional fit – presidentialism and multipartism (Taagapera and Shugart 1989; Mainwaring 1993). But it holds the disadvantage of allowing for the election of someone with a barely discernible mandate to lead in newly formed democracies if the consolidating imperatives of plurality rule require decades to have full effect. Majority rule with a runoff ensures that the eventual winner secures a majority over his or her chief competitor, and thus appears to provide a surer guarantee of legitimacy than does plurality rule. But runoffs can also encourage a multiparty system that lessens pressure for integration and party consolidation.[33] An electoral college as implemented in the United States discourages purely regional parties, since, under a winner-take-all format within each federal subject, winning more than a plurality in a subject adds nothing to a candidate's electoral vote. But it can yield reversals in which the winner of the electoral vote is someone other than the winner of the popular vote, thereby undermining the winner's legitimacy, and it can raise anew, in a different context, debates over the weight that ought to be given to each federal subject.

Electoral Connections

It is difficult, however, to discuss the implications of alternative constitutional schemes of presidential power as well as alternative selection mechanisms without also considering the electoral connection between presidents and legislatures – item 9 on our list. With respect to presidential selection, we note earlier that the timing of executive elections has only recently been identified as a critical determinant of political stability in presidential regimes. In an otherwise vacuous debate over the relative advantages of presidential versus parliamentary government – a debate devoid of theoretical content but replete with empirical and methodological fallacies – a convincing case can be made that presidential systems with simultaneous presidential and legislative elections as opposed to sequential elections is the better choice (Shugart and Carey 1992; Mainwaring 1993; Jones 1995). Jones (1995: 160–1) states the matter boldly: "If the goal of a presidential system is to provide for an

[33] As for the choice between plurality and majority rule with runoffs, here we concur with Jones (1995) that plurality rule is preferable. Most recently, constitutional drafters have tended to shy away from simple plurality rule (Taiwan is an exception) owing to the fear that presidents might lack legitimacy and the authority to lead if they are elected with, say, 30 or 35 percent of the vote. Majority rule with a runoff provision, however, postpones the incentives to form permanent broad-based coalitions and is more likely to yield a majority coalition that survives only past a second ballot. One alternative is to require a runoff if no one receives, say, 40 percent of the vote. This rule, we suspect, would greatly diminish the incentive to form blocking parties or candidacies that exist only to force a second round in the balloting. In other words, the most direct route to securing a majority president may be to not formally require it.

effective, stable, and democratic form of government . . . then the system must typically provide the president with a legislative majority or near-majority," where the route to this end is "[e]mploying the plurality formula to elect the president [as opposed to a majority with runoff] and concurrent timing [of presidential and legislative contests]." Jones may not apply his argument to federal systems in particular, but on theoretical grounds it is as applicable there as anywhere. This argument's logic and its applicability to party integration is straightforward. First, its initial premises – namely, that "two related effects of the electoral cycle are important to the shape of party systems: first is the effect, in conjunction with the presidential election formula, on party-system fragmentation; second is the effect on partisan support in the legislature for the president" (Carey 1997: 74) – are by now well-established empirical facts (Shugart 1995). To apply these facts to federal systems all we need do is supply the seemingly reasonable inference that to the extent that legislators are representatives of constituencies within federal subjects and the president a representative of a national constituency, concurrent elections link the fate of legislative parties to that of the president, which, both in support and opposition to his program, encourages party integration of the sort we argue is most compatible with a stable and effective federal system.

It is, of course, inappropriate to limit our discussion here to presidential systems. Not only are there many more parliamentary systems than presidential ones, regardless of definitions, but Germany's contemporary success and the assumption that the United States has enjoyed special and unique historical circumstances probably prejudices designers in the direction of parliamentary forms. However, "presidential" and "parliamentary" are themselves merely labels that seek to categorize and summarize the motives of political elites as a product of institutional structure, and as a summary of these motives it is useful to consider a classification of systems according to their connection to the ultimate sovereign, the people. If we are to judge by the content of research, the institutional incentives for party formation are commonly assumed to derive primarily from the rules by which national legislators are elected; it is, after all, those rules that researchers commonly look to when they try to explain party fragmentation or the number of parties in a system. Executive selection rules in presidential systems affect parties as well, but the analysis of their impact – generally limited to a comparison of plurality versus majority with runoff procedures – is clouded by the variability across political systems in presidential authority relative to the legislature. Our objective of finding the mechanism to motivate the establishment and maintenance of integrated parties leads us to look at these institutional parameters in a somewhat different way. Rather than concern ourselves uniquely with such variables as the number of parties, we are interested in the motives for vertical and horizontal cooperation and coordination, and here the effects of parliamentary and executive selection mechanisms may differ substantially.

First, the winner-take-all approach to electing legislators – essentially the single-member district systems of the United States, Canada, Britain, and India – facilitates national party formation, if it facilitates it at all, on the basis of combining into one entity something akin to simple majorities across districts (ignoring the complications of plurality rule versus runoff systems). Arguably, this encourages parties to become more inclusive across a federation's territory, at least in those constituencies in which it is competitive. Ceteris paribus, then, single-mandate contests are at least consistent with (though not necessarily decisive for) a small number of broad-based parties (although the comparison of the United States and Canada should alert us to the relevance and even decisiveness of other parameters). Proportional representation schemes, in contrast, generally fail to impose meaningful size requirements for party support (aside from representational thresholds, which are of little consequence to the issues we address). There are two forces in operation here. First, because a party can exist comfortably in a district with many seats, it is less in need of forming partisan alliances across districts. Second, marginal seat returns within a district do not drop to zero once a party achieves 50 percent of the vote. Proportional representation, then, as opposed to single-member district systems, tends to relieve the pressure on parties to become broad alliances that aggregate rather than articulate diverse preferences across district electorates. Put simply, proportional representation in combination with parliamentary government is little more than an excuse to postpone political compromise so that it occurs, if it occurs at all, in parliament rather than within parties (Herring 1940).

A somewhat different logic applies to executive selection. The executive equivalent of single-member district winner-take-all corresponds to a situation in which one candidate captures control of the executive branch without the need to construct an electoral coalition that appeals to a diverse set of interests – from more federal subjects than is minimally required to form a redistributive coalition. Examples of such winner-takes-all mechanisms are majority party cabinets in parliamentary systems of the Westminster type or direct plurality rule or majority rule presidential elections. The alternative is when a parliamentary coalition must support the cabinet or when the presidency is collective, as in Switzerland, the European Union, and now also in Bosnia. Yet another version of this alternative is the current form of the U.S. Electoral College, whereas with the single-member district system for legislators, winning any votes beyond a simple plurality in a state contributes nothing to one's electoral success. It is true that the Electoral College opens the door to presidents without a popular vote plurality (e.g., Adams in 1824, Hayes in 1876, Kennedy in 1960, and Bush in 2000) and that it tends to magnify the winning candidate's margin of victory (as measured by electoral votes as compared with popular votes). But there are reasonable arguments for supposing that in polities that offer a relatively uniform distribution in the socioeconomic characteristics of states, candidates will find it more efficient to campaign broadly rather than sectionally (Hinich and Ordeshook 1974). Finally, we can look to Germany for yet another way of encouraging executive-level campaigns based on a broad electoral consensus among those parties that hope to control selection of a prime minister. Here, of course, we are referring to regional control of the federal government's administrative apparatus. Merely being a member of a majority coalition in the Bundestag, while hardly unimportant, is likely to yield an impotent administration unless that administration also has strong support across a range of federal subjects. But again, this alternative encourages consensus or at least centrist agendas only to the extent that federal subjects themselves are similar – and here the viability of Germany's institutional structure is in the process of being tested.

We should not, of course, exclude the possibility that appropriate combinations of Level 2 and Level 3 provisions will encourage integrated parties in each of the four pure types that correspond to these variations in executive-legislative selection and authority. On the other hand, if the evidence is that presidentialism, for instance, is best served by simultaneous presidential and legislative elections, then we also cannot exclude the necessity for carefully avoiding inappropriate combinations of Level 2 and Level 3 provisions. For example, a winner-take-all scheme of executive selection, combined with a proportionally elected legislature might be difficult to fit into a federal framework, especially if proportional representation is implemented in a way that encourages a highly fragmented party system. Indeed, it is possible that the best way to avoid such a system may be to move in the direction of the winner-takes-all parliamentary electoral design by reducing the size of the proportional representation districts to a few seats (e.g., <10) or by moving in the direction of the consensus-presidential category by imposing explicit distributional requirements on presidential selection. That both the United States and Germany could be described as using a consensus-building approach in executive selection and winner-takes-all as a dominant seat-getting mechanism for the legislature, moreover, is not evidence of the inherent compatibility of federalism to this arrangement. The historical roots of Germany's institutional structure in particular can be readily traced back to the nineteenth century and to considerable refinement, experimentation, and evolutionary change. In that sense at least, Germany is no less special than the United States.

8.3 Level 1 and the Scope of the Federal Mandate

Thus far in our discussion of ways to encourage integrated parties, we have left behind those Level 1 rules and constraints we commonly associate with allocations of jurisdictional authority. Our decision to do so is predicated on the argument that by themselves, such allocations are without substance unless enforced by at least two higher levels of institutional structure – a Level 2 constitutional structure and those Level 3 provisions that, along with Level 2, structure the political game, and party competition in particular. At this point, however, we need to return to this first level and to some general guidelines for its content, if only because this content is commonly seen as not only critical to federal design but even as a measure of the degree to which a state is best described as federal or unitary.

Fully appreciating the fact that federal states function with considerable variation in the detail provided by a constitution with respect to jurisdictional authority, with Brazil at one end of the spectrum and Switzerland and the United States at the other, our discussion is predicated on the assumption that the fewer is the number of constraints, the lower is the dimensionality of the issue space that the constitution addresses, and the more room is given to parties to shape and retain an internal consensus against constitutional renegotiation. If, as Kramer (1994, 2000) and we argue with respect to the United States, policy negotiation and renegotiation occurs largely within parties, where, presumably, integrated parties are more successful at this negotiation than nonintegrated ones, once an initial federal agreement is reached and further bargaining is institutionalized, subsequent partial renegotiations and adjustments of particular issues are less dangerous. Still, the more issues one allocates to the authority of a federal government and the greater the magnitude of its activities, the more there is to argue about and the greater are the dangers of bargaining disequilibrium infecting basic institutional structures.

Arguably, the increased scope of the public sector helps explain why federal institutional design has been less successful in the twentieth century as compared with the eighteenth and nineteenth centuries, when the government, especially national governments, played a more limited economic and social role. Federations in the twentieth century had the disadvantage of being established at a time when the importance of an active public sector as a stimulus to economic development was widely accepted. Thus, whereas older federations were designed for a presupposed limited governmental role (which could be expanded incrementally), newer federations have from the outset incorporated constitutional provisions intended to facilitate the financing, coordinating, and implementing of a significant state role in economic and social life. One of the great issues of the day in early nineteenth-century America was the role, if any, of a national bank, whereas today it is not exceptional to find the structure of such a bank outlined in a constitution. We also need to recall that the United States lacked even a national currency until its Civil War, preferring instead to leave the issuance of currencies (essentially promissory notes redeemable, to a greater or lesser degree, in gold) to state-chartered banks. This reminds us once again about the limits of borrowing successful institutional solutions. The institutional forms sufficient to stabilize bargaining when the scope of federal government activities was less than 2 or 3 percent of GDP (as was the case in nineteenth-century

America) may not work in a new federation where the government is involved in a great number of social and economic activities from its inception, before a constitution fully coordinates beliefs and expectations, and before the appropriate subsidiary institutions have arisen to fill in the gaps of a government's structure. Put simply, the scope of issues constitutionally assigned to a federal government may not be inconsequential for that document's ultimate survival.

Insofar as scope is concerned, Level 1 constraints generally take two forms: (1) a delineation of jurisdictions between the national government and federal subjects along with empowerments of the federal government; and (2) constraints such as a prohibition of secession, a comity clause, and procedures for amending the boundaries of federal subjects. Our discussion here applies especially to the first category since, other things being equal, the more functions the federal government performs, the more consequential is any tinkering with federal institutions and the greater are the stakes of reopening constitutional renegotiation (e.g., in the direction of strengthening the hand of the "center"). Although it is impractical to advocate the same limited scope of government as prevailed at the time of the writing of *The Federalist Papers*, a successful modern federal design can at least attempt to moderate the speed with which a federal government extends its functions. Not only do we want to lower the dimensionality of change during the initial bargaining period, but, because constitutional amendments and modifications in constitutional interpretation can be implemented only though and within corresponding federal institutions, bargaining over a change in the status quo along only one dimension can produce an "institutionally induced" stability. Indeed, one can argue that this is the theory underlying the European Union's gradualist approach to its own development and the limited authority formally given to Bosnia's "national government" in the constitution imposed there by the Dayton Accords.

There are, of course, problems in trying to be ambitious in constitutionally regulating the pace of federal government expansion. Nevertheless, our argument brings to the fore three more specific issues: (1) constitutional provisions that direct the government to specific actions (i.e., social welfare guarantees), (2) constitutionally mandated formulas for redistribution, and (3) establishing the federal government as a residual property owner. The first matter has received considerable attention recently with the collapse of the Soviet Union and the spate of constitutional designs emanating from its territory and the territories of its satellite states in Central Europe. Here the argument concerns whether the federal state should be directed to policies that address housing, wages, employment, health care, and retirement – the provision of things commonly termed "positive rights." The argument against such clauses is twofold. The first is that constitutions ought to be limited to a description of the state and to restrictions on its actions (e.g., bills of individual rights). Second, governments should not be directed by constitutions to achieve infeasible ends (e.g., housing for all), since, to the extent that they fall short of meeting those obligations, the legitimacy (coordinating authority) of that constitution is undermined (Sunstein 1991). The counter to this argument has been the assertion that the societies to which these provisions are directed would not deem a constitution legitimate if it did not direct the state to policies that appear to fall under the purview of governments elsewhere or of those governments, however imperfect, under which they existed until democratic reform. Unfortunately, the theoretical paradigm upon which the arguments we offer in this volume rest provide no ready resolution of this debate, since that debate sets in conflict two competing objectives – avoiding opportunities for redistributional conflict and assuring the legitimacy, or equivalently, the coordinating authority of a constitution. The assignment of positive rights increases the redistributional role of the state, whereas excluding those rights from a constitution may impair its coordinating authority. Thus, all we can do here is note the potential relevance of these provisions to federal design.

With respect to that conflict and explicit constitutional allowances (even encouragement) for redistribution, we appreciate that governments necessarily redistribute and that it is perhaps unavoidable that their authority to do so be formally recognized. A number of governments either constitutionally mandate redistribution (e.g., Germany) or raise redistributive mechanisms to near constitutional status (e.g., Australia). We also appreciate those theoretical results which argue that federal stability not only requires economic efficiency but redistribution (Le Breton and Weber 2000; Haimanko et al. 2001). But those results assume that the domain of redistributive possibilities is one-dimensional, in which case there necessarily exists a stable bargaining point (a core) and no opportunity for renegotiation. In this way it may have been possible for a homogeneous state like West Germany to reach a consensus on equity, but that consensus appears to be threatened by the fiscal strains of incorporating the economically underdeveloped East into its constitutional structure, with interests that do not parallel those of the western states (Benz 1999). Similarly, although Australia appears to have successfully regulated the redistributive role of its national government by assigning that task to independent commissions that look much like a central bank or court in terms of their political independence, the fact that a commission is structured as it is stands as testimony to the recognized dangers of granting redistribution full legislative play in an otherwise wholly endogenously regulated political arena. Hence, the question here, given the near certainty that redistribution in some form is unavoidable, is whether a constitution ought to enshrine explicit guidance and authority to that purpose or whether it is best to settle for vague clauses such as "the legislature shall provide for the general welfare," as in the American case.

Although our prejudice is for the latter alternative, neither existing theory nor empirical research provides definitive guidance. We are sympathetic to the now amended clause in the U.S. Constitution prohibiting redistribution through direct taxation: "No...direct tax shall be laid, unless in proportion to the census" (Article 1.9, now superceded by the Sixteenth Amendment: "The Congress shall have the power to lay and collect taxes on incomes, from whatever source derived, without apportionment among the several states and without regard to any census or enumeration"). There are, nevertheless, ways to mitigate against the redistributive role of the state without explicit constitutional prohibitions, the most evident of which is private ownership of resources. For example, federal involvement in energy politics in the United States has not had the same redistributive dimension as in Canada, largely because mineral rights in the United States are primarily in private hands whereas in Canada they are the property of provincial governments. Thus, energy and mineral-related revenues can be captured by the federal government in the United States through corporate and personal income taxes, without explicit interference in state functions, whereas in Canada such revenues can be captured only from provincial governments in a process that has provoked intense intergovernmental and regional conflict (Gibbins 1987: 19–20). Similarly, although the politics and attendant corruption of land policy with respect to federal lands in nineteenth-century America are legendary, we can only guess at what those politics might have been had the territories involved been perceived as anything more than agricultural or points of passage for railroads. Thus, we can appreciate the destructive tensions inherent in an evolving federalism such as Russia, where property rights with respect to its vast natural resources of oil, gas, coal, metallurgy, and diamonds have yet to be firmly established both between the individual and the state and between the central government and its constituent parts, and where the definition of those property rights is the focus of ongoing intergovernmental negotiations and evolving traditions (Hedlund 2001).

The Russian experience and its problems of federal stabilization directs us to the fact that the size of nonpublic sectors of the economy is critical in determining the redistributive importance of government. In the American, Canadian, Australian, and European federations, the private sector was already well developed before their federal governments became significant economic actors. But in Africa, Asia, and even Latin America, governments have inherited a proportionately more decisive economic role (Watts 1970: 98). As a consequence, the relative redistributive impact of federal policy is more pronounced there. Similarly, the weakness (or rather absence) of the private sector in the Soviet and Czechoslovak federations arguably was critical to their dissolution since even minor adjustments in political structure held profound redistributive consequences. Once economic reform began, federal economic policy not only became the focus of a democratic (as opposed to autocratic) redistributive conflict, but with the state in control of nearly all social assets, privatization policies created incentives for the subnational governments to resist those reforms in the attempt to capture whatever resources were within their reach.

8.4 Level 0 – Things beyond Design

To this point our discussion identifies three levels of rules and institutional structure that impact the stability and general functioning of a federation. Those levels are summarized in Table 8.4, but earlier, in Chapter 5, we note that if constitutions are best conceptualized as coordination devices, then they must also be conceptualized as a part of some larger game. The elements of that game certainly include all other dimensions of political institutional design: federal subject constitutions and charters, the structure of local

TABLE 8.4. *The Three Levels of Institutional Design*

Level 1: *Constitutional constraints on federal bargaining*	These provisions empower the state, limit its incursions into private affairs (bills of rights), and restrict the dimensionality of constitutional negotiation – the scope of the federal government. But as such these provisions are not self-enforcing and can prove meaningless without an appropriate Level 2 and Level 3 design.
Level 2: *General principles of government structure*	Aside from defining the general structure of the state – its presidential or parliamentary form, federal or unitary, bicameral or unicameral, etc. – this level largely determines whether bargaining among federal units occurs within the institutional structure of the federal government or directly between federal and regional officials. Although designed to ensure the enforcement of Level 1, provisions here are not of themselves fully enforceable except insofar as they define an equilibrium to a game defined in part by Level 3.
Level 3: *Institutional devices to encourage political party integration*	These parameters impact the motives of politicians to cooperate and coordinate across levels of government. Although no single factor is effective to this end, various combinations of them (e.g., simultaneous elections, the pervasive use of elections, local control of local elections) facilitate integration. To the extent, moreover, that the parameters at this level serve as the background conditions to the operation of Level 2 institutions and Level 1 constraints, they impact the enforceability of Level 2 and Level 1

governments and their relation to all other governmental levels, the attendant federal administrative apparatus (ministries, regulatory agencies), independent commissions, the central bank, and so on. Of necessity, we have tried to highlight only those dimensions which impact parties and party integration most directly and which are susceptible to design. But even the game of democracy is itself played in a larger context that encompasses society and all its rules, norms, definitions of justice, political traditions, and so on, where this game and that context influence each other in a complex and evolutionary way. It is only natural, then, that the discussion in the preceding section draws our attention to several background conditions that we do not include in our list of federal design parameters, including the structure of property rights and patterns of expectations as to the legitimate role of the state. It is at the designer's peril to assume that the operation and impact of any formal institutional structure is unaffected by such things, that these things are irrelevant to the institutional choices that have to be made, and that the consequences of these choices can be understood without understanding this broader context: "The main driving force behind institutional change . . . lies in the interplay between formal rules, which may be changed overnight, and informal norms, which change only gradually if at all" (Hedlund 2001: 51).

Clearly, we cannot discuss all of society, and it is perhaps even impossible at this stage of our theoretical understanding of institutions and the mechanisms of their enforcement to be certain we can identify the most important things. But one clear background condition relevant to enforcement and political party type is the weight political elites and citizens place on the future. It is by now well known, of course, that cooperation in general, and the avoidance of mutually distasteful outcomes in such games as the repeated prisoner's dilemma in particular, can be sustained if (1) the games people play are in some sense repeated;[34] (2) there is monitoring of defections so as to allow for targeted punishment of those defections; and (3) relevant decision makers give the future sufficient weight so that the short-term gains of defection can be offset by the long-term loss of inflicted punishment. However, rather than simply appeal to this argument as a justification for asserting the importance of time discounts, let us consider how it applies in particular to the career paths of political elites and the overall impact of political party integration.

[34] By "in some sense repeated" we allow for the possibility that no two people ever "play" against each other more than once. But the threat of sanctions in the future for a defection today is made possible by the general observability of actions and the opportunity of others to sanction those who defect. This is not to say that such third-party enforcement is likely, but only that we do not require strict repetition to sustain cooperation in ongoing social processes. For a discussion of repetition, norms, the law, and the issue of endogenous enforcement, see Sened and Knight (1995).

Briefly, our argument here is that since the system of incentives we associate with integrated parties appends the immediate office-seeking goals of political elites with the promise of medium- to long-term career opportunities that are incompatible with extreme forms of particularistic behavior, much will depend on how heavily those elites discount the future. The extent to which they prefer to preserve their ability to reach agreements on federal issues and build a reputation that positions them to compete for national office depends on how much those objectives weigh against their immediate unit-level reelection concerns. However, two institutionally induced possibilities exist as far as career prospects are concerned. Either local (regional) and national careers are mutually exclusive or they lie along the same path. In both cases the greater the value given to the future, the more likely are we to see cooperation and stable federal relations emerge. But the impact of that value is likely to be greater in the second instance. Of course, even if a politician's long-term career goals do not include federal office, if the future is not discounted too heavily, then we cannot exclude the possibility that norms of reciprocity across levels of government can be sustained. However, insofar as those who would represent federal subjects in federal bargaining anticipate future constituencies not much different than the ones they currently represent, those norms will generally apply only to other political elites within their respective regions or to whatever coalitions serve the immediate interests of their constituencies. On the other hand, if party integration implies a reasonable chance of pursuing federal office as a long-term career goal, then greater attention must be paid to a broader constituency. In this case valuing the future highly increases the weight a candidate should give to the party's general interests and, thereby, the greater should be his willingness to be an imperfect agent of his constituency and to seek an accommodation between those interests and the interests of his immediate constituency. Similarly, to the extent that voters themselves value the future, we might reasonably speculate that their demands for immediate reward from the public sector will be lessened and that they will be more likely to accede to imperfect agency in the form of voting on the basis of party identities rather than on the basis of narrow short-term benefits.

What then are the circumstances that raise or lower the value political elites and the electorate are likely to give to the future? Here we can only speculate, but perhaps the most important is the belief that the democratic process will continue. We appreciate that such expectations have a variety of sources, ranging from a prolonged history of the current democratic regime, perhaps as in Germany, from the determination of the international democratic community that stability *will* prevail, to a desire on the part of the population in general to recover a lost past, imagined or real, as in Poland and Hungary. The future will be discounted heavily, on the other hand, to the extent that circumstances are reversed. Thus, when explaining the failures in Russia's transition to democracy and its imperfect adjustment to the rule of law, Hedlund (2001: 49) cites two path-dependent causes: "One is the . . . absence in the Russian tradition of a state that is willing, ready, and able to shoulder its role as a legitimate guarantor of the basic rules of the game. The other is the equally path-dependent evolution of organizational responses and mental models that push economic actors in the direction of exploiting the opportunities for gain offered by the weak state."

Also, we should not overlook economic circumstances. If the economy is weak or in decline, then the rational course would seem to be to "get while the getting is good," whereas if an economy is prosperous or at least promises to be so, then immediate gains are more likely to be given less weight than future prospects. Evaluations here are monetary, but they can impact the degree to which a state is susceptible to corruption generally – the degree to which the state is seen merely as a source of immediate private gain (rent seeking) and its institutions illegitimate or at best transitory (Klochko and Ordeshook forthcoming). Notice, by the way, that if the domain of the state is sufficiently large, then the gains from rent seeking are correspondingly increased, in which case the avoidance of corruption as an equilibrium will require that an even greater weight be given to the future. Finally, if a federal constitution is perceived as a high-stakes distributive arrangement, as when there are historically deep ethnic divides, then the domain of stable constitutional arrangements may be limited or even empty. Absent any belief that political institutions will operate to alleviate long-standing ethnic hostilities, stability as a form of cooperation becomes increasingly elusive.

Notice now that in this view, discount rates are not wholly exogenous. They are not, as in virtually all economic models, parameters that fall from the sky. To the extent that either low or high discounts can become self-fulfilling prophecies, we see here how the parameters of the game of politics and what we might label general social background conditions are in fact interdependent. The stability of the state depends on the weight people give to the future; but the weight given to the future depends on perceptions of that stability. Thus, those who would design a federal state must at least be cognizant of this interdependence, and to that end we can cite some of the things we believe heighten the weight politicians and citizens generally give to the future, several of which are in turn impacted by that weight: (1) prolonged experience with stable democratic federalism; (2) the prestige of holding public office; (3) few rent-seeking opportunities in public office; (4) a civic culture that monitors the public sector and gives citizens some access, however indirect, to that sector; and (5) the absence of ethnic, linguistic, religious, or racial cleavages with a history of redistributive conflict.

The difficulty here, of course, is that few if any of the items on this list can be manufactured or simply set to the "correct" values. We are not, however, wholly at the mercy of circumstance and history, because the institutional parameters that encourage integrated parties can also encourage a view of the future more compatible with stability. Simultaneity applies here as well: not only is integration encouraged by a polity that values the future, but such valuations are themselves encouraged by integration (or, less directly, by those institutions that encourage integration). First, integrated parties, virtually by definition, provide an important monitoring and punishment function by allowing those candidates to advance who do not damage the party's overall purpose, which is to win votes generally by resolving disputes internally. Second, by offering rungs on the ladder of political advancement, such parties provide a specific reason for valuing the future. Finally, by virtue of the other functions they perform, such as sustaining the electoral process and being generally conservative with respect to institutional change, their dominance of the electoral landscape gives evidence of the stability that is essential to any long-term planning horizon.

9

Designing Federalism

> We thought that the utmost which the discontented colonists could do was disturb authority; we never dreamt that they could of themselves supply it, knowing in general what an operose business it is to establish a government absolutely new.
>
> Edmund Burke as cited in Beer 1993: 205

> The citizens of Europe are entitled to expect two things that their governments have thus far denied them. The first is a vigorous debate, starting from first principles and with the widest possible participation, about what the future of the European Union should be. The second is an intelligible account, capable of commanding popular agreement, of the rules by which the future of the Union will be shaped. The right way to meet both needs is to discuss and then frame a written constitution for the EU.
>
> *Economist*, October 28, 2000, p. 11

> And as to those mortal feuds, which in certain conjunctures, spread a conflagration through a whole nation . . . proceeding either from weighty causes of discontent given by government, or from the contagion of some violent popular paroxysm, they do not fall within the ordinary rules of calculation. When they happen, they commonly amount to revolutions and dismemberments of empire. No form of government can always either avoid or controul them. It is in vain to hope to guard against events too mighty for human foresight and precaution, and it would be idle to object to a government because it could not perform impossibilities.
>
> Hamilton, *Federalist* 16

9.1 Introduction

Our book does not – indeed, it cannot – provide a wholly comprehensive guide to federal design. Given the diverse circumstances of geography, history, economic condition, and political tradition that all potential and existing federations confront, no mechanical guide can suffice any more than we can build an aircraft or span a river according to some fixed formula. Solutions must adapt to circumstances because the choices that encourage stability and a well-functioning state in one case need not work in another. We should also consider the possibility, as Hamilton warns, that there may not be a solution to every problem. A federal Bosnian state, for instance, may be more a fiction than a viable entity, a fabrication implemented merely as a temporizing solution to a problem that has no solution, whereas other states may function in a wholly satisfactory manner under a wide variety of institutional alternatives. Nevertheless, when confronted with a set of circumstances and institutions that describe a federation, we must be theoretically equipped to diagnose whether there are fundamental flaws in its design relative to the circumstances it must accommodate. We must be able to assess an overall design from the point of view of incentives it creates for players in the political game to sustain the rules and institutions that seek to constrain that game. In this chapter, then, we consider two developing federations – Russia and the European Union – and consider the impact on incentives of the multiplicity of institutional choices that underlie each of these designs.

We emphasize that any institutional recommendations we might offer must take the form of a mechanism whose parts are not only consistent with the circumstances in question – with preexisting social norms, preexisting political-economic interests, preexisting political structures, and with prior democratic experience – insofar as that is possible. They must also be complete and internally consistent. Here, though, we need to be both cautious and perhaps even somewhat circumspect. Certainly, a federal constitution without a guarantee of comity must be deemed incomplete, since such a guarantee is an essential component of a unified state – of a state that is something more than a mere alliance or confederation. Similarly, one that proclaims a president the "defender of the constitutional order" but also authorizes a constitutional court to adjudicate disputes between the national and federal subject governments or among the separate branches of the national government will most likely prove to be inconsistent. Nevertheless, we can imagine circumstances in which such degrees of incompleteness and inconsistency can be resolved by evolving tradition and constitutional amendment if all other incentives encourage people to that end. It may be true, of course, that our science of institutional design is far too primitive to allow us to discern or even measure acceptable degrees of inconsistency and incompleteness. However, in trying to direct incentives in ways that allow for the gradual improvement of an imperfect design, we also need to understand that since we are looking for a *combination* of rules capable of becoming an equilibrium in a larger, societal game, it is futile to look for one right electoral system, the right design of an executive, or the right allocation of jurisdictional responsibilities. For this reason we suspect that an isolated debate over the advantages of presidentialism versus parliamentary forms is not only theoretically vacuous but fruitless as well. Instead, we must endeavor to design a *system* of rules and institutions at different levels that, when put together, promise a nexus of individual beliefs and incentives consistent with an institutional equilibrium of a democratic and efficient sort.

In mapping these things out in the specific instances of Russia and the European Union, the preceding chapters, although not offering a definitive template of design, tell us to proceed with three levels of institutional complexity in mind: explicit constraints on state action (Level 1), constitutional institutions (Level 2), and a more general encompassing institutional infrastructure that operates directly on individual incentives (Level 3). We also identify as consequential those Level 0 preconditions we associate with a society's legal and political culture and those economic and demographic characteristics that help identify the problem at hand – problems that can range from merely encouraging coherent environmental policy, to accommodating the interests of regional political elites who resist any abrogation of their authority, to finding ways to accommodate a society's ethnic, linguistic, and religious cleavages.

These four levels taken as a whole can be broadly understood as the complete federal constitution. But in assessing the completeness and consistency of a design, we must also take cognizance of the law of unintended consequences. Societies are complex – certainly more so than any aircraft or bridge – and even if we allow for stable evolutionary development, political institutional systems are mankind's most involved creation. To suppose that even the most comprehensive theory would allow us to anticipate fully the consequences of any specific design requires a degree of hubris that was not shared even by arguably the most successful corps of political engineers, the Framers of the U.S. Constitution. Academics find it difficult, for example, to trace the implications of the concept of rationality in strategic situations with even a modicum of complexity. To believe that we can describe or predict with precision the full play of individual self-interest in a political system of even moderate complexity is a belief unsupported either by experience or logic. Nevertheless, we must proceed as best we can. Instead of assuming either that constitutional prescriptions will be followed or that the law of unintended consequences leaves matters wholly to chance, we must instead endeavor to assess the interplay of self-interest and institutional design with the hope that our political engineering project will at least contribute ultimately to a more refined theory.

9.2 Russia

Prescriptions for encouraging federal stability in Russia are typical of the advice offered political leaders elsewhere: "[T]he future of the Russian Federation [RF] depends on a well-designed intergovernmental system that matches expenditures and revenues . . . the fiscal system is at the heart of any solution" (Wallich 1994: 249) and "until markets integrate Russian regions and hence locally based political interests, the country will fail to develop . . . a federal system which stimulates economic growth and imposes self-enforcing restrictions on counterproductive discretion of public officials" (Polishchuk 1996).[1] We are not surprised that, for an economist, "political structures are of less importance: what is crucial for him is simply that different levels of decision-making do exist, each of which determines levels of provision of particular public services in response largely to the interests of its geographic constituency" (Oates 1972), or that when attempting to treat the political-economic transformation of the Soviet Union and Central Europe, "economic reform theorists discounted politics. They focused on inflation, deficit spending, and exchange rates, and considered political issues a distraction" (McFaul 1995: 87). The explanation for this focus is not that economists easily succumb to disciplinary blindness. Political elites also give special emphasis to economic matters, if only because the issues they confront that require immediate attention are typically economic in character – balancing a budget, ensuring the collection of taxes, privatizing industries, sorting responsibilities for social welfare programs, and controlling inflation. In contrast, the problems that require a political institutional resolution often appear either as intractable redistributive matters or as things susceptible only to speculative long-term solutions.[2]

Bolstering this emphasis on economic parameters is the fact that economic issues more often than not are, as we saw in Chapter 1, the basis for justifying federal governmental forms in the first place. Having thus rationalized federalism with economic arguments about the efficient regulation of externalities and optimal production of public goods, it is only natural that advice on political-economic reform will focus on those things that appear most directly to thwart market efficiency – a tax system that penalizes productive regional development; allocations of jurisdictional authority that empower the central government to regulate things best handled by local authorities and curb regional initiative and innovation; regional governments that thwart rational macroeconomic monetary policy; a central monetary policy

[1] Hanson (2001), however, stresses as essential for Russia's institutional stability the creation of an environment where political elites would generally find it in their interest to back those institutions.

[2] It is not unreasonable to argue that economic matters are emphasized in the Russian case because the most difficult to massage Level 0 parameters – deep ethnic divisions and historical animosities – are largely absent. But where those divisions and animosities are found (e.g., Chechnya) Russian federalism seems ill-equipped to offer practical and theoretically prescribed remedies. Indeed, as Ware and Kisriev's (2001) assessment of Russian policy toward Dagestan suggests, even when those remedies exist in the form of imaginative electoral arrangements, they are rejected because of the failure to appreciate the ultimate import of electoral processes in mitigating ethnic conflict.

that stifles regional investment; a legal infrastructure that precludes coherent contract, antitrust, and labor law; an incoherent or nonexistent legislation governing foreign ownership and partnerships; faulty bank regulation; and an income redistribution policy that makes regions wholly subservient to central directive or that encourages disruptive competition among regions.

In part because Russia's federal problems seem at times to be of such monumental proportions, because the efforts at solving its problems with purely economic instruments have run their course without the intended or hoped for results, and because of its self-evident political incoherence, there are those who did see a political dimension to reform: "Whoever is looking out from the Kremlin in the year 2000 ... [w]inning at the 'game' of reform ... will require a perceptive and nuanced grasp of political tactics" (Shleifer and Treisman 2000: 184). Still, mere tactics are insufficient – a fact noticed by Russia's newest president, who has taken such advice a step further by pursuing a number of structural solutions, chief among them being the attempt to rein in the independence of Russia's regional bosses and imposing an intermediate bureaucratic structure in the hope that it can make federal processes both more coherent and more to the Kremlin's liking. But neither tactics nor these institutional "reforms" – reforms limited to Level 1 and Level 2 – will suffice, in our estimation, because Russia has otherwise adopted a configuration at all three institutional levels that is sharply at odds with theoretically justified prescriptions for successful federal design.

Electoral Arrangements

We can begin our assessment of that configuration by noting that despite a succession of elections at both the regional and national level, little in the way of a coherent party systems has yet emerged: not only has "the development and institutionalization of national parties ... been sporadic, at best" (Slider 2001: 224), but, with the exception of the Communist Party, the parties that do exist possess "little presence outside Moscow, and almost no ties to 'civil society'" (Whitefield 2001: 235). One potential explanation for this state of affairs is simply that Russia's democratic institutions have not yet had the time to exert their influence on motives, perceptions, and strategies. The view here is the assumption that one can hardly expect a society with essentially no democratic tradition to move effortlessly to a system that exhibits all the characteristics of a constitutional democracy, including a party system that integrates and regulates political competition. Why would we suppose that a state whose political traditions encompass literally centuries of totalitarian rule, exhibit in a few years political processes that took decades to develop in other less historically challenged states?

As compelling as this argument might be, we contend here that Russian federalism is, in addition, based on a fundamentally flawed conceptualization of democracy and democratic practice. First, with respect to the underlying philosophy dictating the choice of Level 2 and Level 3 institutional parameters that pertain to elections – such things as the timing of elections, turnout requirements, and the number and scope of offices filled by direct election – we find a view more consonant with the naive perspectives of civics textbooks that see elections as a means for measuring the will of the people than with any theoretically justifiable assessment of their role in a democratic state, federal or otherwise. With the presumption that holding elections for more than one office and allowing people to vote for a multitude of things simultaneously can only confuse that measurement, Russia's electoral arrangements eschew the idea that, in terms of immediate instrumental value, voters rarely view an election as anything more than an opportunity to throw the bums out. It is certainly true that the casting of a ballot is a terribly imprecise way of communicating details about one's policy predispositions, assessments of candidates, and recent life experiences, but what appears to be even less well understood in Russia is the role played in encouraging or discouraging a coherent and integrated party system by the full panoply of electoral arrangements, from local to national contests. Insofar as a stable federal system is most readily established through the agency of a decentralized yet vertically integrated party system, it seems clear that Russia requires electoral institutional arrangements that are wholly different from what it has thus far adopted. Specifically,

- As we described earlier, simultaneous national, regional, and local elections encourage party development by encouraging party leaders to organize voters by presenting them with slates of candidates across levels of government. This, in turn, encourages "coattails" and symbiosis – the national candidate whose popularity helps elect local and regional candidates and the local and regional candidate who finds it in his or her interest for the national candidate on the same slate to do well. Russia abides by an institutional configuration inimical to this end. There, elections to the State Duma are held in December whereas elections to the presidency were initially held six months later in June, and now are held in March. Rather than encouraging symbiosis and presidential coattails, this nonsimultaneity fragments the Duma contest much like an American presidential primary is more fragmented than the final race (Ordeshook 1996; Ordeshook and Shvetsova 1997). When combined with party-list proportional representation organized at the national level, "parties" in Duma elections become little more than campaign vehicles for presidential aspirants, as was boldly demonstrated in the 1999–2000 round of elections (Myagkov and Ordeshook 2001; Shvetsova 2003a).
- Reflecting either a distrust of the electorate or the view, outlined earlier, that allowing voters to cast ballots for too many offices obscures the reading of the tea leaves presumed to exist in election returns, most new democracies allow few regional public offices to be filled by direct election – usually only a governor, a regional legislature, and the

corresponding offices at the local level. Russia follows this pattern. With the exception of regional legislatures, the only regionwide office filled by election in any of Russia's regions is that of governor (or president in the case of the republics). There are only 3,709 seats in all 89 regional legislatures, compared with the 2,979 canton-level representatives elected in tiny Switzerland. Out of a total of 177,600 local government officials (as of January 1, 2000), 94.5 percent are not elected but appointed (Kourliandskaia, Nikolayenko, and Golovanova 2002). Unfortunately, by thus discouraging the development of ladders of career advancement (a design error that, interestingly, was not committed by the USSR's Communist Party) and the corresponding symbiotic relationship among political elites within a region that exist when compelled to compete using partisan labels, such arrangements are more likely to occasion forms of boss rule in which regional elections focus on candidate personalities rather than partisan attachments. And with weak partisan attachments, the interests of local and regional candidates are typically best served by campaigns that set regions in opposition to any national authority, or at least campaigns that encourage bilateral bargaining. Following a pattern that has already emerged, regionally secure or powerful bosses will pursue federal policies that consolidate their positions, whatever the direction of such policies might be, while less secure bosses will seek to negotiate with the center to improve their status, often at the expense of other regions.

- It is by now well understood that election laws have an important influence on the number of parties (e.g., Taagepera and Shugart 1989; Lijphart 1999). Less well understood is the influence of election systems when one method is used to elect the national legislature and another to elect regional assemblies. One reasonable hypothesis, though, is that similar systems, such as we find in the United States, Germany, and Spain, encourage parallel party systems that are more readily vertically integrated. Once again, Russia abides by a model that chooses inconsistency of forms – a mixture of proportional representation and single-mandate constituencies at the national level, but single-mandate districts at the federal subject one.
- More generally, a national party-list proportional representation system such as Russia's seems inimical to the development of a decentralized party system, or at least to a decentralized vertically integrated one, because, for any number of contemporaneous and historical reasons, a national list will most likely be controlled by political elites at the federal center (Moscow). In contrast, the German system, in which party lists are organized and seats allocated at the state level, encourages decentralization and vertical integration.[3]

[3] Like Germany, half of the State Duma's 450 deputies are elected in single-mandate constituencies and half by party-list proportional representation with a 5 percent threshold. And

Regional Autonomy

To this point our assessment of Russia's problems are not necessarily at odds with President Putin's early initiatives, which seem aimed more at a consolidation of the Kremlin's position in the face of otherwise seemingly anarchic federal relations. What seems not to be understood, however, is how democracies function and how bureaucratic centralization as opposed to the cooperation encouraged by an integrated party system can undermine that integration and exacerbate the anarchic relations it is designed to resolve. Admittedly, the temptation is great, especially in disruptive political-economic circumstances, to try to implement change through central directive – a temptation that seems irresistible, given Russia's political traditions. However, without entering into a discussion of the legitimate policy domains of federal subjects versus the national government, we notice that this view has at least two spillovers into the arena of political institutional design:

- A common assumption is that regional and local politics are more readily corrupted than are national politics; hence the argument for federal regulation if not outright federal control of regional and local elections. On paper at least Russia, once again, abides by this assumption. Ideally oversight of those elections should lay in the hands of a politically independent court, which can rely on constitutional guarantees of republican or democratic regional governance. But even if the judiciary is poorly formed, central regulation and control have distinct disadvantages. First, as we note earlier with respect to regional elections in Dagestan, innovation and creative adaptation to local circumstances is stifled. Second, with respect to the development of meaningful regional parties, such parties can develop only when the offices being filled control real resources. And from the perspective of political elites one of the most important resources is control of the methods of election. Third, as with inefficient markets, there is only one long-term solution to the elimination of political corruption – competition – which can arise at the regional level only if there is something worth competing for, including the right to regulate (or manipulate) regional elections. There is, moreover, no good theoretical or empirical reason for supposing that central directive will be any less subject to corrupt manipulation than some decentralized process. Finally, in countries such as Russia that use single-member districts, a critically

although current Russian election law requires that national parties use regional lists, parties are free to define the regions as they choose, and the first eighteen Duma seats filled by a party through proportional representation are reserved for its national list, which is not truly national at all but is Moscow-centered. Thus, although some degree of party decentralization is encouraged, there is no reason to suppose that true regional representation or decentralized and vertically integrated parties will arise out of this system. Interestingly and somewhat inexplicably, Ukraine has chosen to copy Russia's lead for its national parliament, except to use a 4 percent threshold.

important process is that of drawing district boundaries, which is laden with political meaning since boundaries can be drawn to favor one party or candidate over others. This gerrymandering process is, of course, very much like a constant-sum game among parties (the constant being the number of seats in the legislature), which, if played at the national level, can disrupt all other political processes. Decentralizing this game, then, keeps conflict from bubbling up to the federal center so as to encourage institutional renegotiation at the national level.

- Giving the national government direct authority over local governments establishes a system whereby the national government can attempt to play off local authorities against regional ones in its contest with regional governments for supremacy. This strategic situation, though, wholly disrupts the development of an integrated party since it often makes it impossible for regional and local members of the same party to coordinate their election campaigns. Instead, we are likely to see the same conflicts within regions that characterize the conflicts of Canada's "without" bargaining arrangements – local politicians who campaign primarily on the basis of their opposition to the regional government.

We hasten to add that the design of regional charters and constitutions has proceeded without a full appreciation of the fact that such documents are as much a part of federal design as anything else. Certainly people understand that many of those charters and constitutions contradict federal law or the federal constitution itself (as when Tartarstan, in violation of the Russian Federation Constitution's supremacy clause [Article 4] proclaimed its constitution and laws to be equal in status to federal law and the federal constitution), but what seems unappreciated again is the impact of those documents on local and regional party systems and the opportunities of regional political bosses to lead and govern through their position as head of a party organization as opposed to the direct exercise of constitutional authority.

Constitutional Matters

A number of other Level 2 institutional features may foreshadow ongoing problems of federal stability and efficient performance. First, one might interpret President Putin's "reform" of the Federation Council whereby it no longer consists of governors and heads of regional legislators but rather of their appointees, as an attempt to move that chamber in the direction of the original plan for the U.S. Senate (although as we know it was a part of Putin's attack on the power of governors relative to his own).[4] Unfortunately,

[4] Putin's authority to change the basis of federal subject representation with the consent of parliament but without constitutional amendment derives from the constitutional provision that "The Federation Council shall be composed of two representatives from each member of the RF – one from its representative and one from its executive body of state authority"

Russia's constitution also includes the provision that the lower legislative chamber, the State Duma, can override a Federation Council veto with a two-thirds vote (Article 105), which, in effect, moves Russia in the direction of a "without" bargaining format. Specifically, to the extent that the Federation Council is an ineffective legislative chamber as in Canada, relations of regional authorities to the center will be determined largely by bilateral and often informal mechanisms – especially when the Duma is itself a poor representative of regional interests (owing in part to the national proportional representation election format for one-half of its deputies). A third factor, which compounds the second and which we have discussed in the context of Russia's apparent institutional bias toward bilateralism, is the implicit constitutional sanction given to the negotiation of bilateral agreements between regions and the center.[5] Further encouraging this bias, moreover, is Russia's reliance on an extensive constitutional list of exclusive and joint jurisdictional authority (Articles 71 and 72) that are taken largely from Germany's Basic Law, but without Germany's other constitutional safeguards.[6] Rather than act as barriers to federal bargaining, such provisions can actually encourage renegotiation when the different sides to a dispute find it in their self-interest to interpret each list differently. We are not surprised, then, to find such observations as the one Solnick (2002: 237) offers: "[T]he *de facto* and *de jure* asymmetries produced by territorial bargaining extended well beyond traditional protection of cultural autonomy for ethnic enclaves. They affected the core functions of the national state in domains such as commerce, national defense, regulation of the media and revenue collection. Concessions made to individual regions have undermined the legitimacy of federal law and the federal constitution, weakened the protection of civil rights and undercut any potential economic benefits federalism might be expected to deliver."

In a traditional contractual conceptualization of federalism, the objective is to ensure that contracts are honored, including the contract to maintain fundamental institutions. In Russia, on the other had, we not only see a continual renegotiation of terms vis-à-vis policy, but now institutional instability as well – an instance of Level 2 institutions inheriting the properties of the

(Article 95) and that "the procedure for forming the Federation Council . . . shall be determined by federal legislation" (Article 96).

5 See Article 66, Section 5, which reads "The status of a member of the RF may be altered by the mutual consent of the RF and the member of the RF in accordance with federal constitutional law." Constitutional law here refers to a law that requires a three-fourths vote in the Federation Council, a two-thirds vote in the State Duma, and the president's signature. We also note that part 2 of the constitution's transitional provisions allows the asymmetries of earlier bilateral negotiations to remain in place: "All laws and *other legal acts* enforced throughout the RF before this Constitution became effective shall remain valid as long as they do not contravene the Constitution of the RF" (emphasis added).

6 Curiously, Article 73 constitutes a residual powers clause that parallels the Tenth Amendment to the U.S. Constitution. In light of the extensive and often vague content of Articles 71 and 72, however, its behooves us to imagine to what Article 73 might apply.

base bargaining game. Following the Putin regime's ascension to power after the 2000 presidential election, the characteristic feature of the regime was a revisionist attitude with respect to federal relations, with special attention being paid to those governors and public figures (financial and media oligarchs) with influence in federal affairs (including even those who supported Putin's election). And although most regional governors and republic presidents fell into line following Putin's suggestion for revisions in local laws on privatization, governmental structure, and citizenship, Russia's president saw fit to establish a new quasi-constitutional institution at the federal center – a new layer of federal control consisting of a seven-member council of presidential envoys to oversee Russia's regions. Putin attempted to play down the import of this reform, arguing that his supergovernors would be concerned solely with the administration of *federal* policy, although in Articles 71 and 72 of the Russian Constitution a search for any clear demarcation between federal and regional is futile. However, even if we take such assurances at face value, the reform amounted to an overhaul of core federal institutional relations at a constitutional level.[7] Regional governors will no longer be members of the Federation Council. Instead, their seats will be taken by appointees of the governors (subject to a two-thirds veto of the regional legislature), who, along with those assigned to the Federation Council by regional legislatures, will serve terms that are coincident with those who appoint them. This change and an additional provision that grants regional governments the right of recall over their Federation Council representatives seem a welcome means of ending Russia's bilateral bargaining and making the Federation Council a more authoritative and effective legislative branch for a "within" system of federal relations. Unfortunately, Putin's "reforms" did not end here. Through a not entirely cumbersome process involving decisions of the court, the Duma, and the Federation Council, the Russian president now has the power to dismiss regional assemblies and call new elections (which, in effect, would also require the recall of the representative in the Federation Council appointed by any dismissed assembly). Second, that office has the authority, without the consent of the national legislature, to remove a regional governor if the general procurator asserts evidence of a crime, or in the event that the president deems acts of the governor to be contrary to federal or constitutional law, with the concurrence (if appealed) of Russia's Supreme Court.

Precisely what this new presidential authority ultimately implies in terms of federal relations remains to be seen. If one could make clear distinctions, it would be tempting to assert that the current trend is an end to federalism and a return to a Soviet-style bureaucratic decentralization. But projections are foolhardy. The early implementation of a bilateral bargaining format clearly encouraged this institutional instability, but many of the critical institutional

[7] For a more detailed description of these "reforms," see Solnick (2002).

sources of the motives behind such bargaining remain in place and sustain the foundations of continued instability. Thus, we should not suppose that Putin's initial success at imposing his will constitutes a permanent realignment of authority between the Kremlin and the regions. Insofar as there is no constitutional (Level 2) impediment to bilateralism, the remaining rules seem ill-equipped to coordinate or constrain bargaining, including bargaining over institutions. Hence, absent any evidence of an institutional equilibrium, we would not be surprised to see another swing of the pendulum in which regional leaders once again incrementally extract concessions from the center as the Kremlin maneuvers to maintain its position.

Any survey of Putin's overhaul of federal structures highlights the Level 2 design matter of greatest concern in terms of its specific impact on party systems and on the overall style of Russia's politics – the package of constitutional provisions that preclude the application of democratic leadership. Too often, not only in Russia but in a great many new democracies, those who hold national office attempt to rule by the direct application of their constitutionally sanctioned powers (or beyond those) and insist on constitutional provisions that award them the greatest authority feasible. As we note earlier, however, the American presidency is constitutionally weak, and any person holding it cannot govern through the simple expedient of manipulating the formal levers of power. Rather, an American president must govern informally – through leadership. Leadership, of course, is difficult to define, aside from noting that it commonly proceeds through positive rather than negative incentives. But certainly a part of the practical meaning of this word in a democratic state is using one's position as head of a party to encourage its candidates for lesser office to coordinate and comply with presidential actions. Leadership, then, not only requires a vertically integrated party system, its exercise also helps develop that system by giving all participants an interest in that development. In contrast, political systems that give excessive powers to a president or prime minister, or which even preclude these office holders from being associated with any party, undermine the essential integrating function of parties.

The constitutional authority of a chief of state (president) and head of government (president or prime minister) needs to be prescribed carefully. Too little authority renders competition for that office irrelevant to the operation of a state's party system; too much threatens the absence of leadership. Russia, largely as a consequence of Boris Yeltsin's victory in 1993 over a recalcitrant parliament and the authority he assumed subsequently over drafting a new constitution, opted for this second alternative.[8] In addition to proclaiming the Russian Federation president "the guarantor of the

[8] However, given the Duma's authority to vote no confidence in the president's administration, we are presented with a governmental form that is neither fully presidential nor parliamentary. Instead, it is something else – something left to evolutionary development.

Constitution" (Article 80) without providing for simultaneous elections so as to encourage a symbiotic relationship with candidates for lesser offices, Russia's constitution puts in the president's hands the authority to announce states of emergency (Articles 88 and 102c), to veto constitutional amendments (Article 136),[9] to block wholly the introduction of legislation pertaining to "taxes, tax exemption, the issue of state loans and changes in the financial obligations of the state" (Article 104, Section 3), and to "suspend the acts of executive bodies of RF members [federal subjects] if they contradict the Constitution of the RF, federal laws or . . . international obligations" (Article 85, Section 2). This later provision, of course, merely elaborates on the meaning of yet another federal-unfriendly clause, which proclaims that "federal executive bodies and bodies of executive authority of the members of the RF [federal subjects] shall form a single system of executive authority in the RF" (Article 77, Section 2). But perhaps the most troubling provision is one that concerns presidential decrees. Here Article 90 pertains: "(1) The President of the RF shall issue decrees and directives; (2) Decrees and directives . . . shall be binding for execution throughout the territory of the RF; (3) Decrees and directives . . . shall not contradict the Constitution of the RF or federal laws." This provision allows a president to issue decrees with full legal status insofar as the law is otherwise silent, so that, in contrast to an American president who, in principle at least, can act only as authorized by Congress, a president of the Russian Federation has first move and can, in effect, make law until and unless his acts are thwarted by legislation that either he approves or is passed over his veto. Together, Articles 85 and 90 give the president not only executive but judicial and legislative authority as well.

Parties and the Current Status Quo

One might well argue that Russia's constitution merely follows a tradition of the strong central hand. However, we can attribute many of the document's flaws not only to Yeltsin's desire to provide himself with as much authority as possible but also to the manner in which it was written and the theoretical perspective that surrounded its preparation. After its broad outlines were established by Kremlin insiders, Yeltsin in the summer of 1993 called

[9] Curiously, in a somewhat convoluted set of provisions, the Russian Federation Constitution appears to make it easier to replace the entire document than to amend any one provision. Article 136 states that any proposed amendment to chapters 3–8 requires approval of *three-quarters* of the Federation Council, *two-thirds* of the State Duma, and *two-thirds* of all regional legislatures. But chapters 1, 2, and 9 (Principles, Rights, and Amendment provisions) can be amended by a wholly new document if *three-fifths* of each legislative chamber votes to convene a Constitutional Assembly. In the event the assembly drafts a new constitution, that document will go into effect if two-thirds of its members approves *or* if the assembly's proposal is ratified in a national referendum by half of those voting (provided that turnout exceeds 50 percent). What appears to have escaped notice in this country of world-class mathematicians is the fact that three-fifths is less than both two-thirds and three-fourths.

for a more than four-hundred-member constitutional conference to iron out details and develop an elite consensus around his design.[10] That convention, owing to its size, divided itself into five task groups: (1) representation, (2) federalism (regional government relations), (3) local governments, (4) parties and elections, and (5) business interests. Although each group could consider any issue, all but the last (which was designed primarily to co-opt Moscow's economic elite) reflected the view that a constitution is something other than a unified whole. Indeed, throughout most of its development, federal provisions were, with the exception of the structure of representation in the national legislature, treated in an isolated manner – as a part of the Kremlin's negotiations with regional leaders as it sought to thwart the authority of the Congress of People's Deputies. Even though the Kremlin had effective unilateral control over the selection of the election law and there was some understanding that a coherent party system should be encouraged (Remington and Smith 1996), little thought was given to how other institutional provisions (e.g., the timing of elections, electoral provisions pertaining to the presidency, presidential authority, and the nature of representation in the Federation Council) would impact party development and, ultimately, federal performance. Thus, Russia's parliamentary electoral law has the appearance of copying the German system but without those parts that encourage integrated parties. Needless to say, as federal-level constitutional provisions were ironed out, no thought was given to the design of regional governments, to the impact of federal elections on regional political systems, and to the impact of regional elections on national party development.

Unsurprisingly, one influential governor, Eduard Rossel of Sverdlovsk, has complained that there is not one party with an interest in preserving federalism. In fact, it is not an overstatement to claim that all of Russia's parties view federalism as at best an unavoidable nuisance. The Duma, ostensibly the home of those parties, has consistently sustained the most extreme procentralization positions,[11] all of which is consistent with the fact that those parties are Moscow-based with weak or nonexistent regional ties (the communists are an exception, as always). At the same time, with federal bargaining the exclusive domain of executive interactions – between the administration and regional bosses – and with ties to political parties of little value to regional bosses, the Federation Council has largely remained a

[10] The choice of the label "conference" rather than "convention" allowed Yeltsin to proceed without the involvement of Russia's Supreme Soviet.

[11] Ideological differences among parties led to some marginal differentiation of positions. The nationalist party of Vladimir Zhirinovsky insisted on the unitary form of government; communists, characterizing the power-sharing treaties between regions and Moscow as "unacceptable," advocated greater redistribution of resources by Moscow; and democrats argued against giving too much power to nondemocratic regional "barons" (whom they could not defeat in elections) while supporting the Kremlin's authority to remove regional elected officials if needed (Mitrokhin 1996).

party-free zone, with most regional executives unaffiliated with any party.[12] The only way for a party to win the attention and support of regional bosses was to assume the role of lobbyist with regard to redistribution of federal money. Correspondingly, all parties – from communists to nationalists to democrats – insisted on greater centralization of fiscal resources, hoping for an increase in the Duma's opportunities to regulate as many issues as possible. In the Yeltsin era, the attitudes of parties toward federalism provoked constant conflict between the Duma and Federation Council, and when the time came, all parties within the Duma supported Putin's attacks on the Federation Council and regional executives.[13]

In the absence of parties that would support the status quo of federal arrangements, one can assume that regional executives would at least try to resist some forms of adverse institutional change. However, governors as politicians whose careers are wholly independent from each other absent an integrated party system have few incentives to coordinate to oppose federal intrusion. They prefer instead to bargain with the center to maintain their official positions, with only a few able to risk opposition to Putin's "reforms." Indeed, although most regional leaders voted against Putin in the Federation Council in a secret ballot, there was virtually no public debate in opposition. Perhaps the best illustration of their unwillingness to assume the political risk of defending regional rights against the Kremlin are the debates on whether regional executives should continue to be directly elected or appointed by the president. Since 2000, Unity and later the so-called centrist bloc of progovernment parties in the Duma proposed various schemes for replacing elected governors with presidential appointees.[14] These proposals were widely discussed in media and, in the opinion of observers, would complete the transition to a unitary governmental system if implemented.[15] But not only were most governors unwilling to voice opposition; a number

[12] After Putin "reformed" the Federation Council in 2000 there was an attempt to create a pro-Putin parliamentary faction (party) among senators, "the Federation." However, the faction was dissolved in January 2002. See "Political Affiliations of Russia's Governors: A List," *EWI Russian Regional Report* (April 29, 1999, p. 4).

[13] On May 31, 2000, 362 Duma deputies voted to support the Senate reform. The only real criticism of the reform there came from the then independent deputy, financial oligarch Boris Berezovsky.

[14] Arguably, such a reform would require a constitutional amendment. Instead, in February 2002 the "centrist bloc" proposed changes to the election law that would preserve elections but allow Putin to nominate governors. The amendment requires successful candidates to win support of more than 50 percent of *all* registered voters (*NG*, February 5, 2002). Currently most winners are selected by less than 20 percent of the voters, therefore most elections are likely to be invalid. In case of invalid elections, however, as the head of the Central Election Commission suggested, the Russian president should select a two-year interim appointee to fill the office (*Izvestia*, March 13, 2002).

[15] Notice that in Russia governors are the regional executives, whereas in India, for example, though state governors are appointed, they are not regional executives. State prime ministers are the heads of state governments and normally are selected by state parliaments.

of them publicly supported Putin's right to nominate and dismiss them.[16] Some governors, of course, expected to lose the next election whereas others faced term limits that might be annulled by the change. But as Stroev, then chairman of the Federation Council, explained, most governors would accept the shift from direct election to appointment if it provided some guarantee of their ability to maintain their positions without subjecting themselves to the vagaries of electoral politics.[17] It would seem, then, that the only office in Russia that might have an electoral interest in federalism is the presidency. Of course, Putin's most serious opponents in the 2000 presidential election – the communist Zuganov and former prime minister Primakov – were strong antifederalists,[18] but it is also true that the support of regional elites, and regional bosses in particular, has been crucial for all successful presidential campaigns (Shvetsova 2000; Myagkov and Ordeshook 2001; Solnick 2002). However, once elections pass, regional bosses are more a hindrance than anything else, and the balance of bargaining power changes. In fact, there was a rehearsal of Putin's attack on the regions in 1997–8. Following Yeltsin's reelection in 1996 the Kremlin attempted to squeeze regional and ethnic republic positions but failed to capitalize on Yeltsin's victory following his illness and a growing financial crisis.[19] In contrast, as long as Putin's popularity remains high there seems to be no reason to expect he would lose the support of regional leaders in any bid for reelection. And perhaps not by accident, Putin's reforms put under his control any group that could form or finance a political opposition – regional leaders, corporate businesses, and the media.

In evaluating the staying power of current arrangements, we can reasonably speculate that the administrative devices on which the post-Yeltsin government relies, will, in the long run, thwart the realization of the goal

[16] Among those who supported the proposals were such well-known governors as Lebed (Alexander), Tuleev, Ayatskov, Prusak.

[17] Interview in *RIA Novosti*, March 28, 2000, available at <http://www.polit.ru/news.html>.

[18] The regional elites' choice of Putin over Primakov is easily rationalized as the choice of a lesser evil. While Putin's view of federalism remained largely undefined, Primakov's campaign repeatedly promised to restore "the vertical model of state power" and to reduce sharply the number of regions, with the remaining being ruled by Moscow appointees.

[19] By the end of 1996, the president instructed his chief of administration (Chubais), the justice minister, and the prosecutor-general to prepare proposals on the responsibility of regional officials and unification of regional laws. Chubais proposed to increase the powers of presidential representatives, unite regions into several economic groups, and centralize tax collection while leaving the regions with the receipts of taxes that were difficult to collect (e.g., on corporate profits). At the same time, Chubais proposed to use federal transfers as a method of economic pressure on the regional executives and to weaken the regional bosses from the inside – by supporting local (mostly municipal) governments in their struggle with the regional authorities. As part of this approach, local governments were given a larger share of tax revenues and some political representation through the Council of Local Governments (created by presidential decree in May 1997, with Yeltsin serving as head of the council).

to which they are directed. By adding yet another lever of power to the president's arsenal, even less reliance will be placed on leadership and, in particular, on developing a more formidable instrument for the exercise of democratic leadership – the integrated party. Indeed, although written in 1994, the following observation is as valid today as it was then: "Economic interest groups are now the key players in Russian politics; political parties, by contrast, have been and remain weak and unstable. In the corridors of power, they wield much less influence than associations of managers and entrepreneurs" (Mau 1994: 32).[20] Absent institutional reforms aimed at encouraging the development of federal-friendly parties – simultaneous elections, the more widespread use of elections in regional governmental administration, greater regional autonomy in electoral regulation, and a revision of its national proportional representation format – Mau's observation will continue to apply and Putin's reforms will most likely be little more than another phase of an endless cycle of expansion and contraction in the authority of the Kremlin relative to Russia's regions, and no solution whatsoever for the incessant jockeying for political-economic advantage that has thus far characterized Russia's federal politics.

9.3 The European Union

In one respect at least Russia in the early 1990s presented constitutional architects with a nearly ideal circumstance – a state with little democratic infrastructure that would otherwise constrain their efforts. Many of the parameters of a federal state, including electoral laws, electoral incentives, the governing structures of federal subjects, and the relationship of local governments to regional and national authorities, either awaited definition or were subject to manipulation and modification. Thus, constitutional architects could proceed with proposals that consisted almost exclusively of "essential components," with an understanding that many of the critical Level 1 and Level 3 details could be supplied subsequently. Even the various bilateral federal treaties signed between the Kremlin and Russia's republics failed to constrain significantly Yeltsin's freedom to fashion a document to his liking. In this respect, then, Russia stands in sharp contrast to the European Union, which must shape its political institutions subject to the constraints imposed not only by federal subjects with the ability to defect from any agreement and sustain themselves as ongoing political entities, but also by a cadre of political elites with well-articulated preferences and interests. As such, then, the EU presents not only an interesting contrast to the Russian Federation but also a challenge to those who prefer to move the union in the direction of a more traditional federal state.

[20] For a more recent assessment of the business influence on Russian politics, see Rutland (2001).

Surprisingly, despite the substantial literature devoted to the EU, one can find only a few studies that attempt to apply any coherent theory of federal design to the analysis of integration.[21] Instead, discussion focuses on goals – on whether the EU should be viewed ultimately as a federal union or some other form of international organization. A popular position, at least among American students of international relations, is that the EU is a regime that is not substantively different from other types of international organizations, whereas their European counterparts seem more inclined to accept the view that the EU is a core political system verging on being a classical nation-state (Hix 1998). And there are those who argue that the EU is something different entirely – "more than a regime, but less than a federation" (Wallace 1983: 409), an entity that "has been transformed from a bargained agreement among nation-states, to a quasi-federal polity" (Stone Sweet and Sandholtz 1998: 1).

Such debates merely provoke endless discussion of definitions, and we have no intention of contributing to them. Instead, abiding by the general format of this volume, we assume, correctly or incorrectly in this instance, that the decision to be federal is made and thereby limit our analysis to those institutional traits that seem best able to encourage the EU's evolution to a more traditional federal form.[22] We hasten to add, however, that in doing so, we assume that it is premature to offer commentary in the form of yet another draft "Federal Constitution for Europe," if only because, as we note earlier, the constraints that operate within the union are of such complexity as to render the ultimate implications of any institutional change we might consider here as anything but simple.[23] Nor is it clear that the major constraints that must be accounted for in a successful European federal design are matters can be treated wholly within a constitutional document.

Background

The evolution of EU institutions began with the Treaty of Rome (March 1957), when Belgium, France, the former West Germany, Italy, Luxembourg,

[21] But see McKay (1996, 2000, 2001).

[22] It is certainly the case that some European officials not only advocate federalism but see institutional reform and constitutional development as the route to that end. As German president Johannes Rau argued (*Le Monde,* November 4, 1999), "we already have the essential stones to build a European federation of nation-states. All that is needed is to supplement them, to assemble them, and to make an architecture of it.... To constitute such a federation, we need an European constitution." More generally, a recent survey (Hooghe 1999) reports that whether a European official came from a federal or federalizing country was the most powerful predictor of his stand on European governance. Austrian, Belgian, German, and Spanish officials are significantly more likely to support federal principles (measured as support of "supranationalism") than officials from unitary states like Denmark, France, Ireland, the Netherlands, or Portugal.

[23] For debates on the concept and principles of European constitutionalism, see Joerges, Mény, and Weiler (2000); Piris (2000).

and the Netherlands formed the European Economic Community (EEC) in order to provide a reasonably transparent institutional framework for cooperation on a number of economic matters. However, it took nearly thirty years of negotiations and amended treaties to move from this limited free-trade alliance to the supranational organization of the European Community (EC). The Single European Act of 1986, which created the EC was itself but a step toward a common monetary system and still greater political unification. In 1992 the Maastricht Treaty (or the Treaty on European Union, as it is officially called) reiterated the open-ended goal of moving toward an "ever-closer union among the Peoples of Europe" and, as some argue, initiated the formation of at least a nascent federal system.

Only through this incremental and sometimes contentious process has the EU's formal jurisdiction grown. And tensions persist, as symbolized perhaps by the fact that the EU remains small by the traditional measure of budgetary authority (accounting for a bit less that 1.3 percent of domestic GNP), although it now exercises significant influence through an enormous volume of policy regulations.[24] The literature, in attempting to understand and justify this process, offers two primary "theories" of integration. The first, the liberal intergovernmental approach, identifies national governments as the decisive players in bargaining over integration, where those governments are agents of their respective states or, more precisely, of relevant political constituencies within those states. Here, then, the process of integration and bargaining is modeled as a game with two stages. First, there is a domestic game among political and economic groups to determine national interest.[25] In the second stage national leaders, as representatives of those interests, bargain with an eye to maximizing a specific set of corresponding benefits. The alternative to this view, neofunctionalism, argues that the key players are relatively autonomous politicians, bureaucrats, transnational businesses, and other supranational entrepreneurs, where the identities, loyalties, expectations, and preferences of these players change as the process of integration proceeds (see, e.g., Haas 1958; Pierson 1996).[26]

Our perspective, especially our approach to political agency in federal maintenance as outlined in Chapter 5, differs somewhat from both views. The intergovernmental theory models the players of the integration game as perfect agents of national constituencies. This is not to say that politicians are seen necessarily as perfect representatives of domestic interests, but only

[24] According to some estimates the EU has set over 80 percent of all rules governing the market activities in the member states (Hix 1999), where those rules enjoy supremacy over national laws.

[25] Correspondingly, as Rometsch and Wessels (1996) argue, member states have incentives to reorganize their domestic institutions so as best to present national concerns into EU institutions and decision making.

[26] For a critique of neofunctionalism, see Keohane and Hoffmann (1991); Moravcsik (1991); Milward (1992); Hix (1994).

that the argument here stresses the importance of domestic connections and institutional parameters that contribute to perfection.[27] Neofunctionalism, on the other hand, focuses on factors that allow politicians and bureaucrats to play the game as imperfect agents of their immediate constituencies. Of course, there are always true masters of political preference, but while at the initial stages of integration those masters are transnational economic interests, the processes of integration in subsequent stages are driven largely by those with an interest in expanding the domain of the federal state and governmental apparatus (see, e.g., Haas 1968). Our approach is to see the content of the principal's mandate as itself modified by the electorate's awareness of the agents' imperfectness, and in this sense we are looking for elites who are told by their constituents to do what they would do anyway, while constituents are coordinated by the fact of imperfect agency to settle for something other than short-term goals. Furthermore, with an eye to the future of bargaining and the role elites are likely to assume, the constructs we offer are not specifically concerned with how the EU operates today except insofar as that description informs us about the need for and feasibility of institutional change.

Before we elaborate, we note that the approach taken to date to understand the role of representation in the politics of European integration commonly emphasizes the point that those engaged in bargaining over the terms of integration often benefit from being challenged by a domestic opposition. In this game, politicians and their constituencies may have incentives to sustain a level of domestic opposition on specific issues to gain leverage in bargaining. This is not to suggest that national elites intentionally mobilize opinion against integration (although one cannot exclude that strategy), but only that there are incentives not to disavow wholly public opposition to specific proposals. Thus, to understand fully the politics of integration one must consider a larger game in which national leaders not only bargain among themselves but also seek to influence the level of domestic opposition with which they must contend. Of course, this elite interest has been balanced somewhat by the fact that through most of the 1960s and 1970s the public was relatively unconcerned with integration – a degree of indifference, even ignorance, that was conveniently labeled a "permissive consensus" (Lindberg and Scheingold 1970), or passive support of national elites dealing with seemingly complex and remote issues.[28] "[F]ree to take steps favorable

[27] Notice that for intergovernmental theories, relevant "constituencies" are primary interest groups, not voters (see, e.g., Moravcsik 1998).

[28] Even the members of the European Parliament were not familiar with the details of negotiations. For example, as Jens-Peter Bonde, Danish MEP, noted: "I was greatly surprised when I read it through carefully and found important things, which had not been mentioned at the many press briefings in Nice, either by the French President or by others who had taken part in the meeting. The decision that, in future the whole Commission is to be appointed by majority voting, had been kept completely hidden!" (Bonde 2001: 1).

to integration if they wished" and possessed of a "wide liberty of choice" (Inglehart 1970: 773), national decision makers had little incentive to act against the institutional status quo. As long as only special interests paid attention to the issues, those interests could be satisfied through careful logrolling rather than institutional reformulation. Integration could thereby proceed with incremental success because different governments could, sequentially, place emphasis on different issues (Hix 1999a,b). Domestic political elites could "lose" on some issues in return for "winning" on those of greatest importance to their immediate domestic constituents, with the result that negotiated outcomes gravitated toward a lowest "common denominator" and special deals for particular countries.[29]

With poorly informed and indifferent voters, calls for renegotiation of previous agreements were rare, and even when made, politicians seemed more interested in quick "success" than in tough bargaining. For example, after the United Kingdom joined the EC in 1973 led by the Conservatives, Labour went to the polls in 1974 with a pledge to seek better terms or, if necessary, to pull out of the community altogether. Its list of demands included reform of the Common Agricultural Policy, monetary and trade regulation, and a smaller contribution to the EC budget. After elections, however "re-negotiation was a sham. No serious suggestion was made to undertake the impossible task of re-negotiating the Treaty of Rome, nor was the 1972 Treaty of Accession to be unraveled" (Greenwood 1992: 100). Nevertheless, the Labour government promptly declared that renegotiations had been successful and recommended that voters support European membership in the 1975 referendum. The mutability of public opinion generally throughout much of this period in Europe is reflected by the fact that domestic public support of the EU largely moved with government support, at least to the extent that the outcomes of referenda on proposed changes in European treaties were essentially determined by the position of the governments proposing those referendums (Franklin, Marsh, and McLaren 1994; Franklin, Marsh, and Wlezien 1994).[30] As a consequence, any number of scholars and commentators agree that the so-called democratic deficit in European decision making is a precondition for the success of intergovernmental bargaining.[31]

[29] During the negotiation of the Maastricht Treaty British prime minister Major explained to the leaders of European states: "[J]ust as for you, signing this treaty without the social provisions creates problems, for me it is the other way round. I would not get the support of the British parliament or business" (quoted in Gardner 1991). As a compromise solution, a special Social Protocol was added to the treaty, to be signed only by eleven European countries – without Britain.

[30] We should note however that Franklin and McGillivray (1999) offer a model that predicts a negative relation between domestic government popularity and mass support for an alternative government, the EU.

[31] Majone (1996) offers an extreme version of this argument wherein he asserts that integration must be protected from democratic political mechanisms, because democratic decision

There also appears to be a consensus, however, that the more federal in character the EU becomes, the more difficult it will be for politicians to insulate themselves from public opinion. Since Maastricht in 1991, elites have faced growing public pressure (Niedermayer and Sinnott 1995; Gabel 1998; Carrubba 2001), and, especially following monetary union, EU matters now often attract considerable media attention.

The Role of Parties

Even for those suspicious of the value of comparing the EU to "old" federations, it is difficult to avoid the conclusion that political parties will play an increasingly important role in integration not merely because of the increasing public salience of EU matters, but also because domestic politics within the EU's member states will continue to be organized by parties. On the other hand, students of integration have been and largely remain openly skeptical about the role of parties *at the European level*. For example, Katz and Wessels (1999: 14), in their review of prevailing trends in the development of the Pan-European party system, offer the pessimistic conclusion "it is not yet clear whether a real European party system can or will emerge," whereas Bartolini (2000: 30–1) asserts that "[t]he hypothesis that further European integration will institutionalize a supra-national party system, with all European parties having branches in each member state, may be regarded as either premature or simplistic, or both."

If we accept these observations, then in keeping with our arguments as to a necessary condition for a stable and well-functioning federation, the relative absence of any disruption of the process of integration suggests that national parties have acted as imperfect agents of their electoral constituencies and that parties within the EU's member states are playing an integrating role, although only at the domestic as opposed to both domestic and federal level. Thus, the question for Europe becomes, How resilient is this particular form of political integration to the future dynamic of EU development?

To answer this question we need to examine existing sources of integration in more detail. Earlier we argue that politicians must have individual-level (i.e., electoral) incentives to preserve the stability of institutions that regulate federal bargaining and to avoid competing over those issues that would lead to a global institutional renegotiation. In democracies, such incentives exist when, to win elections, politicians are motivated to form broad electoral coalitions that extend across constituencies and levels of government. And with respect to federalism in particular, the natural way to think about such coalitions is to conceptualize them as national or federal entities. This approach is the way U.S. and German parties operate and corresponds as well to the federal-preserving incentives of India's Congress Party until the late

making promotes purely redistributive policies as opposed to the implementation of "efficient" ones.

1960s and what we find lacking in many of the parties that compete for federal office in Canada.

Matters seem different in Europe. Note that generally the political incentive to redistribute will be limited if any proposed redistribution benefits one element of a party's constituency only at the expense of some other element. In this instance, the leaders of an electoral coalition contained wholly within a federal subject may have an incentive to avoid *some* forms of institutional redistribution that parallel the incentives of intersubject coalitions. Arguably, mainstream political parties in Europe confront incentives of this sort. However, that was almost certainly not the state of affairs envisioned originally. Although Haas's classic *The Uniting of Europe* (1958) offers two chapters on the role of political parties in which he argues that "[b]ecause of their appeal to an overlapping and diffuse group constituency political parties are far more crucial carriers of political integration or disintegration than even supranationally organized interest groups" (p. 437), Deutsch (1957: 51) merely suggests that "political parties might become a possible link across national borders." It certainly could not have escaped notice that without providing for meaningful Pan-European elections – something wholly absent until the 1987 European Parliament became a relevant institutional player – there would be few reasons for Pan-European parties to form. Put simply, there is not much hope for the development of the EU political parties "as long as European elections do not, in practice, designate a European government or at least an Assembly which has a real say in EC legislation" (Reif and Niedermayer 1993: 172).[32]

Quite possibly, an equally important obstacle to the development of a European party system is the systems of well-established national parties with which any European-level party would have to compete. Indeed, even now European parliamentary elections are controlled by domestic parties: "National political parties, consciously operating within the terms of reference of their national party systems, serve as the principal gatekeepers within the European electoral arena, and hence seek to monopolize access and to dominate the agenda" (Mair 2000: 38). Thus, European level electoral alliances and European Parliament party groups are disappointing "as mechanisms of electoral mobilization" (Lord 1998: 5), whereas "in European elections national voters vote for their national party and label and know little about European wide groupings.... All parties will continue to depend on national elections and on national representation systems for their competition and survival and all citizens will continue to be offered only national partisan alternatives" (Bartolini 2000: 28).

[32] However, as Taylor (1983: 48; see also Majone 1996; Weiler 1997; Scharpf 1999; Attina 2000) notes, the weakness of European parties may also correspond to a chicken-and-egg problem: European parties cannot develop until there are European institutions with real power, but real power is unlikely to be granted to elected institutions in the absence of a well-developed European party system and supportive electoral processes.

The development of a Pan-European party system, then, faces two obstacles: an institutional one and one that derives from the motives of domestic party leaders. Both obstacles may, of course, be two sides of the same coin, but it is useful to see how domestic parties operate in the EU arena. Briefly, party systems in most member states crystallized long before the process of integration was initiated. If, prior to integration, electoral competition between major domestic parties was based on some ideological and policy matter, we might have assumed that the introduction of the issue of integration would influence the pattern of electoral competition and result in internal splits among existing parties (Bogdanor 1989). But as Mair (2000: 28) notes, "of the many areas of domestic politics that may have experienced an impact from Europe, party systems have perhaps proved to be most impervious to change." Between 1960 and 1998 more than 250 parties contested domestic elections in the twelve traditional democracies of the EU (excluding the more recently democratized Greece, Portugal, and Spain). Among those, more than 140 were newly created during this period, and of these over half were rising parties presenting new issues to voters (Mair 1999; Meguid 2001). However, of these "only three appear to have been established with the explicit and primary intention of mobilizing support for or against the EU. Moreover, these three parties have proved among the least successful of any new parties to have emerged in the same period, polling an average of just 1.5 per cent of the votes in domestic elections to date... [so that] were the European issue to disappear in its entirety, this would be unlikely to have any significant impact on the overall structure of competition in these systems" (Mair 2000: 35).

As part of their avoidance of the issue of integration, centrist parties by the early 1990s, including most social democratic, Christian democratic, liberal, and conservative parties, converged to a largely pro-integration position, leaving extreme left and right parties to share in "Euro-skepticism" (Taggart 1998; Hix 1999b; Schmitt and Thomassen 2000; Mair 2000; Hooghe, Marks, and Wilson 2001). Consequently, antiintegration platforms account for few votes in domestic elections (Ray 1999). In 1996 anti-Europe parties accounted for only 8 percent of national vote totals as compared with the 66 percent enjoyed by explicitly pro-European parties, and support for anti-EU parties in Belgium, Ireland, the Netherlands, and Spain approached 0 percent. Taggart and Szczerbiak (2001) suggest further that we can distinguish between two forms of Euro-skepticism, hard and soft. "Hard" corresponds to a "principled opposition" to integration that emphasizes disagreement with the entire design, whereas in the case of soft skepticism opposition is qualified, focuses on specific policy matters, and includes parties that support the EU in its current form but oppose further integration. Predictably, hard skepticism is less common than its soft counterpart (see Table 9.1); seven member states have no parties in this category, whereas only two countries have no parties

TABLE 9.1. *Party Vote Shares as a Function of Position on European Integration*

Country	Estimate by Taggart and Szczerbiak (2001)			Estimate by Mair (2000) Based on Ray (1999)		
	Hard Skepticism (%)	Soft Skepticism (%)	Total (%)	% Votes for Strong Pro-integration Parties (N parties)	% Votes for Strong Antiintegration Parties (N parties)	% Votes for Parties That Are Neither Strong Pro- nor Antiintegration (N parties)
Austria	0	26.9	26.9	71.9 (3)	22.2 (2)	4.8 (1)
Belgium	9.2	0	9.2	72.8 (7)	0 (0)	21.0 (5)
Denmark	29.9	7.1	37.0	77.1 (5)	12.5 (3)	10.0 (2)
Finland	.8	5.2	6.0	49.0 (3)	6.0 (2)	40.6 (3)
France	26.7	3.7	30.4	49.3 (4)	16.1 (2)	20.2 (2)
Germany	3.3	5.1	8.4	75.5 (3)	1.8 (1)	18.5 (3)
Greece	5.5	2.7	8.3	92.0 (4)	5.6 (1)	0 (0)
Ireland	0	5.9	5.9	32.7 (2)	0 (0)	58.0 (6)
Italy	0	4.5	4.5	39.9 (4)	24.3 (2)	28.9 (3)
Luxembourg	0	13.0	13.0	75.0 (3)	2.6 (1)	19.9 (3)
Netherlands	0	15.9	15.9	56.4 (3)	0.6 (1)	37.1 (5)
Portugal	0	9.0	9.0	79.6 (3)	9.9 (3)	9.3 (2)
Spain	0	0	0	85.9 (10)	0 (0)	10.7 (1)
Sweden	16.4	5.1	21.5	75.8 (4)	16.5 (2)	5.1 (1)
United Kingdom	2.1	32.4	34.5	63.3 (5)	2.6 (1)	30.7 (1)
AVERAGE	6.3	9.1	15.4	66.4	8.0	21

TABLE 9.2. *Comparison of Elite and Mass Support for European Integration (%)*

	Membership a "Good Thing"			Membership "Beneficial"		
	Elite	Mass	Difference	Elite	Mass	Difference
Austria	86	31	55	73	34	39
Belgium	96	45	51	95	40	55
Denmark	84	44	40	91	55	36
Finland	88	39	49	70	37	33
France	93	46	47	91	44	47
Germany	98	39	59	98	33	65
Greece	92	57	35	92	66	26
Ireland	95	76	19	98	86	12
Italy	97	68	29	91	51	40
Luxembourg	93	73	20	97	64	33
Netherlands	96	74	22	97	69	28
Portugal	91	54	37	94	69	25
Spain	97	51	46	83	37	46
Sweden	84	27	57	63	18	45
United Kingdom	86	36	50	84	34	50
European Union	94	48	46	90	42	48

Source: Spence (1998).

expressing soft Euro-skepticism (with Spain having neither hard nor soft variants).

These numbers belie the fact that European voters appear to be consistently more skeptical about integration than are their elected representatives (see Table 9.2).[33] Thus, the most significant disagreements appear to be not among major parties but within them – between the leadership and rank and file (Ray 1999). That party elites are consistently more pro-Europe than voters is a reflection of another fact – namely, the electoral bases of mainstream parties are themselves divided in their attitudes. Put simply, most major parties draw support both from the individuals and groups supporting and opposing further integration.

The Puzzle of the Collusion

If we accept the preceding description, the following picture emerges: European political elites and government executives initiated a process in which governments were shielded from an ill-formed and even nonexistent

[33] Schmitt and Thomassen (1999) report similar conclusions based on data from the 1979 and 1994 *European Election Studies;* for analyses specific to the Nordic states, see Valen, Narud, and Hardarsson (2000).

public opinion but not necessarily from special interests. And although government actions were supported by governing parties, almost all mainstream parties chose not to attack incumbents on the issue of integration: "[T]he issue of Europe [has been] taken out of the national arena... and depoliticized" (Mair 2000: 47). As a consequence, most mainstream parties are electorally pro-European even though their electorates are now divided on the issue. These facts, as Franklin and McGillivray (1999: 2) argue, constitute a puzzle – a puzzle as to "why political elites... are so willing to support a process that has never been demanded by voters and which erodes their own freedom of action when they are (as most of them hope at some time to be) government leaders."

There is a ready supply of hypotheses that address this puzzle. One is that the elites support integration because it creates evident benefits for their respective countries. This hypothesis, of course, falls in the cooperative approach to explaining federal stability: even if the average citizen cannot see matters clearly, cooperation is socially beneficial and therefore politicians support it. But such an argument and the flavor of elite European arrogance it offers, ignores the electoral constraints politicians face. If there are benefits from integration, they are likely to be realized primarily in the long run, where long may be measured in decades. In the short run there are risks, immediate costs, and potentially unpopular measures requiring implementation that should, in principle at least, make politicians vulnerable to attack from opponents. Thus, one must assume not only that incumbent elites accept immediate sacrifice for the opportunity to claim credit for long-term successes but that their opponents will not (or cannot) exploit any temporary government vulnerability. This hypothesis, then, presupposes a degree of altruism (or impotence) among challengers that it seems safe to assume is lacking on all other dimensions of public policy.

A second hypothesis argues that the major parties in and out of government simply *collude* to avoid competition along the European dimension, because collusion is mutually electorally beneficial. Bartolini (2000), for example, notes that various domestic and international factors have contributed to a lessening of the capacity of domestic political elites to intervene on certain issues – notably economic redistribution, social policy, employment protection, and the protection of national industries. The purpose of the EU, then, is to deal with these issues in much the same way as the U.S. Congress often prefers to avoid potentially contentious specifics in favor of allowing administrative entities to fill in the details of legislation: parties and the elites within them "collude, resorting to gag rules to expel those issues from the political agenda whose solution are no longer under their control" (Bartolini 2000: 40). In examining this hypothesis in greater detail, Katz (1999: 27; see also Katz and Mair 1995) notes that collusion is not normally an optimal strategy, since it should be the case that opposition parties can exploit it without taking responsibility for outcomes: "[O]ne could envision national parties raising precisely the issues over which control has been lost in order to pursue a strategy of 'running against Brussels.' Rather than promising to produce results, they would promise to make demands. While some of these demands might concern the return of autonomy to the national level . . . many could concern the substance of European policy without challenging the idea that the policy should be decided at the European level. Thus, this electoral strategy would be perfectly compatible with acceptance of the inevitability, and indeed the desirability, of further European integration." As a slight variant of the collusion hypothesis, then, Katz argues that collusion can be explained by a more general cartel model, whereby established parties suppress the emergence of issues that might be used by new and smaller parties to gain a foothold in government formation. This argument parallels Riker's (1982) discussion of how politicians – especially those who are disadvantaged if competition is limited to an established menu of issues – can upset a coalitional status quo by raising new issues. In this instance, the status quo is not a specific government coalition but rather a well-orchestrated ballet among existing parties: "[O]ne could certainly interpret the actions of the leaders in many of Europe's governing parties in portraying further integration as both inevitable and unquestionably desirable in this light, as in effect a manifestation of the cartel party hypothesis that party elites will conspire to keep serious but threatening (to them) issues off the political agenda" (Katz 1999: 23).[34]

France versus Britain

Support for the view that, in one form or another, political party elites prefer to collude to suppress issues associated with European integration comes from a variety of sources, including Ross's (1998) arguments as to why France's Socialist leaders supported integration, and, as a counterexample to collusion being uniformly successful, the observations provided by any number of commentators (see, e.g., Greenwood 1992; Garry 1995; Evans 1998, 1999; Baker, Gamble, and Seawright 1999; Aspinwall 2001) about the shifting fortunes of Britain's Conservatives as a function of their stance

[34] The idea that competition on the issue of European integration is a shared danger is not Katz's alone. Hix (1994, 1996, 1999a, 1999b; Hix and Lord 1997), for example, notes that the proponents of both the intergovernmental and neofunctional views assume that EU integration is a one-dimensional game along which all EU institutions, member states, domestic social groups, and political parties can be located. Thus, any decision maker's strategy with respect to integration, including the design of EU institutions, the delegation of powers, and the support of particular EU policies, can be derived from his position on this integration dimension. Hix, however, contends that integration is better understood as a game along two orthogonal dimensions. The first corresponds to the usual more versus less integration, whereas the second is the traditional left-right continuum that represents alternatives on a libertarian versus authoritarian or state intervention versus free market issue. Existing parties prefer to compete only on the second of these dimensions, since competition on the first would produce divisions within these parties.

on integration and its competition with Labour, as well as the divisions that appeared within Labour as the salience of European integration increased in British politics. In fact, the comparison of the French and British experiences is instructive in terms of what it suggests about the role of electoral institutions in encouraging or discouraging inter- and intraparty disagreement.

Ross's (1998) explanation for the motives of France's Socialist leadership comes in two parts. The first emphasizes the role of the presidency under France's 1958 constitution and the fact that the Socialist Party organized itself explicitly to win control of that office by submerging divisive issues within it. Correspondingly, anyone securing that office was afforded a significant degree of autonomy from lower-level party leaders. This is not to say that the head of the party could wholly ignore opinions within his coalition, but only that subleaders also had to accommodate their positions. The second part of Ross's explanation concerns the motives of the president himself (specifically Mitterand). Put simply, to win the presidency, a successful candidate needs to build a coalition across several parties. Although there may have existed any number of geopolitical justifications for Mitterand's policies (including weaning Germany away from Britain), by pursuing the European option Mitterand could fashion an electoral appeal that extended beyond his own party: "The domestic side... was the hope that making European integration the centerpiece of Mitterandist policy could ensure the longevity of the Mitterand presidency (what counted most to Mitterand), provided a credible platform for reorienting domestic coalitions (away from the Communists and towards the pro-European Centrists, thereby isolating the right) and winning elections into the future" (Ross 1998: 9).[35]

Matters proceeded differently in Britain. First, both major parties, Labour and the Conservatives, were divided early on with respect to Britain's membership in the EC, although generally the Conservatives supported membership whereas Labour promised to pull Britain out if returned to power. There is, however, considerable evidence that both parties sought to suppress the issue in their electoral campaigns. For example, even though tensions over European policy played a major role in Thatcher's downfall within her party, the Maastricht Treaty was not an issue in the 1992 general election itself (Garry 1995). But when, a few years later, Labour moved to a more pro-European position, the Major government reacted

[35] Ross (1998) also suggests that one of the important reasons for Mitterand to call the constitutionally unnecessary 1992 referendum to approve France's membership in the European Monetary Union was the expectation that the referendum campaign would further divide the center-right. To some extent, however, Mitterand's strategy backfired. By placing European integration on the public agenda, he succeeded in not only deepening divisions within the center-right but also within the left itself. Nevertheless, "once the Maastricht referendum was over, new efforts were made to put the body back into the ground. This was because leading politicians of both Right and Left needed to do whatever they could to prevent divisions in their coalitions in the runup to the 1995 Presidential elections" (Ross 1998: 14).

in a way to provoke an even greater split within the Conservative Party that led in 1997 to the party's worst electoral defeat since 1832 (Baker, Gamble, and Seawright 1999). In searching for the reasons why the Conservatives failed to sustain their coalition, the most evident institutional parameter is Britain's first-past-the-post electoral system. Certainly this system establishes some incentive for candidates to be members of a major party, and thereby some disincentive to see intraparty tensions relieved by intraparty fractures. Those tensions, nevertheless, are likely to exist since competition in single-member districts compels candidates to pay some heed to the specifics of constituents. And absent competition for the presidency and the national symbiosis that competition encourages, candidates are more likely to be perfect agents of constituents. Thus, when some policy benefits and hurts different groups and creates antagonistic majorities in different districts, a successful electoral campaign requires that a party let its candidates choose independent positions. Even though party leaders may work to maintain party unity by avoiding taking a formal position on an issue such as European integration, MPs of the same party can be deeply divided over it (Aspinwall 2001). One consequence of this absence of intraparty consensus is that a party's leadership may be compelled to move from a pro- to an antiintegration stance and back again, depending on the parliamentary balance between as well as within parties. Indeed, "[a]mong all the member-countries the British case stands out. Nowhere else are party movements as pronounced as in Britain.... In 1979, the Conservatives took a clear integrationist position while Labour elites were still very skeptical of European integration. The reverse is found for 1994, when Labour took the lead towards further unification, while Conservatives opposed it. It is astounding how far these shifts in party elite positions go. Nowhere else do we find a similar phenomenon" (Schmitt and Thomassen 2000: 330–1).

EU Institutional Design

It may be true that Britain's institutional arrangements make elite collusion difficult; however, it also seems evident that party leaders in all member states will face increasing difficulties. First, there are those limits on them that stem from the current configuration of domestic party systems and their ability to deal with the growing scope of issues decided at the "federal" level. Certainly the expansion of the EU's regulatory domain can only increase opportunities for redistribution within member states and, thereby, the demand for inter- and intraparty bargaining that can disrupt any collusive understanding. It is important to remember that the EU's *direct* control of some important issues (e.g., social welfare, health care, education, and public order) has thus far been limited. So even if we consider only the current set of EU members, we need to ask what will happen to the incentives of domestic party elites when the scope of the EU increases up to that of a full-scale federation? And, second, even if collusion among the mainstream parties of existing members is sufficiently resilient to sustain a stable process of gradual expansion in the EU's scope, we cannot assume that this strategy will succeed in any new member state. It seems evident that at least during any negotiation over the terms of admission and in any subsequent transitional period, a new member will confront some form of discrimination. Thus, parties in countries applying for membership are sharply divided over the issue of European union (Taggart and Szczerbiak 2001). Add to this the fact that candidates for EU membership possess party systems that are far more fluid than are the systems of existing members, which, taking the form for instance of weaker partisan attachments among voters, allows for easier entry and disruption of cooperation among incumbent parties. Thus, even though there is a consensus among economic and political elites in Eastern Europe as to the desirability of joining the EU, they will be less willing to avoid competition on this issue to the same extent as their West European counterparts.

In an ideal world, of course, politicians will control the expansion of the EU in such a way as to block proposals for institutional renegotiations that threaten the electoral status quo. Indeed, because almost all important institutional actors in the EU are party politicians, there are sound reasons for supposing that institutional design and reform will remain endogenous to party politics.[36] On the other hand, the incumbents' ability to control institutional change is far from perfect. First, national executives may have incentives to support changes that do not lie entirely within the logic of domestic electoral competition. For example, a popular belief is that integration strengthens executives and makes them more independent from domestic control (Moravcsik 1994). Second, institutional change might be proposed simply because debate over the issue promises to split an opposition block. Third, a minority party, seeking to upset a cartel of major parties, might attempt to appeal directly to public opinion in a referendum. In this regard and somewhat paradoxically, a high level of public support for federal Europe as well as calls for a new constitution could pose the greatest challenge to long-term institutional stability. Public support for further integration can provoke demands for institutional change that mainstream domestic parties might find difficult to accommodate without engaging in a fight over institutional alternatives. And not only might a call to fashion and adopt a constitution open the door to potentially unstable bargaining over all issues; it would also force parties to confront issues they might prefer to avoid.

In speculating about the future it is reasonable nevertheless to suppose that calls for constitutional reform will increase, if only in response to

[36] Commissioners, who are formally required to be independent of their member states, are recruited primarily from major parties. Similarly, the heads of government and members of the Council of Ministers are at the same time members of national governments controlled by national parties, whereas deputies in the European Parliament are elected as representatives of these parties.

the EU's "democratic deficit." Over the past decade, scholars, pundits, and even a few politicians have become increasingly preoccupied with the idea that European institutions need to be reshaped to give voters a greater voice. While some see the failure of the major parties to compete over the issues of integration as unavoidable, such tactics are nevertheless deemed a regrettable "reduction in the range of policy alternatives available to voters" (Mair 2000: 49). Others go so far as to argue that the absence of institutional legitimacy has already resulted in a type of constitutional crisis: "Europe stands before a series of ongoing constitutional debates. The focus in the future will be on the construction of a legitimate constitutional order for policy-making responsive to the desires of national governments and their citizens" (Moravcsik and Nicolaidis 1998: 34; see also Cowles and Smith 2000). In the event of any formal constitutional reform, parties, at least theoretically, would feel some need to propose institutional packages that would benefit their core constituencies at the expense of others, and here it needs to be appreciated that such open constitutional bargaining is fundamentally different from negotiating a sequence of treaties that treat matters issue by issue. It is by no means clear that mainstream domestic parties are equipped to regulate this process. The incremental process of the past avoided the more general issue of negotiating an overall institutional blueprint and "offered actors the opportunity to legitimately neglect or postpone the definition of Europe and the objectives of political union" (Dom-Bedu and Smith 1999: 26). Open debate over a constitution for Europe would disallow the political cover afforded by ambiguity.

There seems no escape, then, from Bartolini's (2000: 33) conclusion that "for the time being we have to work in the interstices of the two radical conclusions: not much can be done to strengthen the European party system, and not much can be done to insulate the national party system from the consequences of Europeanization. As a matter of fact, *it is exactly the imbalance between the difficulties of party system structuration at the EU level and the potentially growing consequences at the national level that makes the analysis of the current situation extremely interesting*" (emphasis in original). Unfortunately, a more integrated Europe that approximates a classic federation requires a resolution of precisely this difficulty. We cannot say whether that resolution needs to be found in whole or is best approached, as in the past, incrementally. On the one hand it is difficult to see how the institutional prerequisites for an integrated Pan-European party system can be put in place incrementally, because any such process will, as we state earlier, most likely be subverted by existing domestic parties. On the other hand, a nonincremental process will only open the door to a potentially destabilizing wholesale renegotiation.

There is, of course, a danger in overstating this dilemma. If our analysis of federalism and the role of parties is correct, then it is a mistake to assume that any Pan-European party system should be wholly divorced from domestic party structures. A certain degree of domestic party co-optation is desirable if that system is to be both vertically and horizontally integrated. It is a mistake to implement institutional change in Brussels with the assumption that Pan-European parties will develop, as in Russia, from the top down rather than, as in Germany and the United States, from the bottom up, where the bottom here corresponds to existing domestic parties. Nevertheless, if institutional changes are to be made to encourage Pan-European party development, those changes must come from Brussels. And here, to begin, we are tempted to suggest that the EU consider a chief executive (president), indirectly elected via a mechanism that would forestall a campaign for that office from being successful if its appeal was directed exclusively at the three or four largest members of the EU. Such a proposal may simply be too radical and out of character for the members of the EU, but we suspect that merely augmenting the legislative authority of the European Parliament will do little in the way of encouraging parties of the form deemed most desirable. On the other hand, proposals such as the *Economist*'s (October 2000) suggested constitution for a federal Europe, which again makes no attempt at implementing an institutional structure that would encourage Pan-European party development but seems instead directed at making an otherwise increasingly overbureaucratized incoherent institutional system coherent, is itself more a model for a confederation than a federation. Absent other institutional changes, if Pan-European parties emerge in any form, they will at best be agents of domestic parties, with cross-national cooperation appearing only on a case-by-case basis. But one needs to be sanguine about the possibility that a European elite, even an elected one, would be willing to allow voters – especially voters who are more skeptical of the benefits of integration than those elites – direct access to an entity that addresses issues they feel are too complex for "ordinary" minds.

9.4 Conclusion

Regardless of whether one contemplates the prospects for a fully functioning democratic federal state in Russia or Europe, we must appreciate that there may be circumstances where a broad range of institutional solutions are sustainable, as well as situations in which federalism, if it exists at all, will do so only in a form that bears the weakest correspondence to any definition of the concept. We suspect that while Europe will correspond more to a confederation or alliance for the foreseeable future, Russia will be federal and democratic only by the loosest definitions of terms. Projections aside, this much is clear: Level 0 circumstances come in such varied combinations – from the near democratic *tabula rasa* of Russia to the seemingly entrenched democratic interests of Europe – that one should not assume that an endogenously sustainable institutional equilibrium within the federal format is even theoretically attainable in every contiguous part of the world. Moreover, even if we reject the supposition that there are contexts in which no democratic form will operate successfully, we cannot reject the argument that a given context can make federal design more or less sensitive to the specifics of institutional choices and mistakes with respect to the consistency of those choices with social norms and political tradition.

Does the proposed state exhibit a schism such as the one between slave and free that characterized the United States before 1860 and that rendered a constitution's otherwise unimportant ambiguity about the right of secession a basis for armed conflict? Or can federalism begin, as in Europe, as an incompletely specified administrative convenience born of the need to compete economically with Japan and the United States and with the hope that the inconsistencies or inadequacies of design will be resolved over time as a function of other processes? Does society possess norms and other institutions that can compensate for design deficiencies and even carry the polity over dangerous stretches of renegotiation, or will those deficiencies, as we argue is the case for Russia, allow and even encourage endless institutional revision? Design is more of a challenge and greater precision in that design may be required where markets are subverted or underdeveloped, civil society weak, legal norms primitive, the processes of democracy poorly understood, and cultural communities isolated and often at odds with each other across communal divides. Even if we were to deem a state such as Belgium poorly designed to accommodate its linguistic divide, its position within the European Union, its well-developed economy and civil infrastructure, and its political traditions make those design defects less than consequential. Those same defects in states such as Russia and Ukraine, where centuries of totalitarian rule yield populations that are arguably deficient in terms of respect for the law and ability to coordinate in accord with formally stated constitutional principles, may prove to be catastrophic for federal and democratic stability.

Despite these cautions, we proceed under the working hypothesis that undue pessimism is unwarranted. Even if we take Hamilton's warning to heart, we should also keep in mind that the Swiss cantons of the nineteenth century seemed especially inhospitable to a well-functioning federal state. Yet even there success was eventually realized – in this case through a process in which Level 0 conditions were found not to be set in concrete but were themselves susceptible to endogenous change. Two Level 0 characteristics in particular can greatly impact the sensitivity of design. The first is the degree of development of markets able to sustain the uninterrupted flow of goods and services across what would otherwise be the boundaries of sovereign states. Developed markets and prosperous populations occasion integrating incentives that can often be given political voice with minimal effort. Thus, in the nineteenth century, a series of corporate instigated court cases (brought by the Chicago meatpackers and Singer Sewing Machine) served to encourage a coherent commercial code across the United

States essential to a more perfect common market and a fuller realization of the U.S. Constitution's prohibition against restraint of trade. This code, although implicitly mandated by the constitutional requirement that states be precluded from erecting barriers to domestic commerce and trade, did not take full form until commercial interests that saw profit in exploiting the new technology of transcontinental transportation and communication developed.

Well-developed markets contribute to the ease with which federal design can proceed in another way – by encouraging the growth of an extensive framework of cross-cutting and often single-issue nonpolitical associations (something akin to a requirement of having a developed civil society). Such a framework erects a sort of a pluralist "defense perimeter" for federal institutions, ensuring their survival in interim periods when their disruption is temporarily threatened by some short-term circumstance. Prosperity may not be sufficient for federal stability nor is stability ensured by an "appropriate" redistribution of resources across federal subjects, but a degree of prosperity and the existence of efficient markets that sustain it do have an impact. At a minimum, to the extent that both political cooperation and adherence to the rules of the game are sustained by the threat of sanctions – especially third-party sanctions (as when members of a political party sanction someone who has tarnished the value of a partisan label) – a complex, well-developed political-economic infrastructure supplies most of the ingredients needed to make the threat of sanctions for defections viable: payoffs that defectors prefer not to lose, monitoring, and a free flow of information about who has defected, including those who defect by failing to implement punishments. Thus, although they are not always deemed to be political or even institutional variables, such things as a well-developed transportation and communications system, a banking system that assures the efficient flow of fungible resources including information, and entrepreneurs with an interest in a uniform and stable system of contract law across federal subjects have a contribution to make to federal stability. The variables that encourage such things ought not be forgotten in federal design if in fact we can identify them and discern even approximately the complex nexus of their interaction and causal relations.

Such admonitions, however, are of little practical value other than to note the obvious – that everything matters to some degree. If we turn then to the more limited subset of variables that concern us, which we label explicit federal parameters, we appreciate that it is far too late in this volume for any comprehensive review. Nevertheless, as a matter of final emphasis we note that if there is a part of federal design that approximates the contractual conceptualization of constitutional democracy and is likely to have an immediate impact on federal relations, that part is found in the institutional parameters and constraints we place in Level 1. Despite our argument that a constitution should not be conceptualized in its entirety as a contract, a good contract is, essentially, what a designer should pursue in this regard by laying down the fundamental constraints on what can and cannot be subject to renegotiation. If otherwise enforceable, its terms must create stable expectations of continued overall institutional stability as well as consistent beliefs with regard to who takes care of what. Moreover, those constraints, as with any contract, should be clear at least to the extent that there is a well-defined board of appeals for resolving ambiguities and differences of interpretation and should not be inconsistent with the existence of mechanisms for detecting violations of its terms and for the incremental adjustment, renegotiation, and redefinition of terms as circumstances change.

Concerning some specific provisions in this contract level of design, we have several well-defined opinions that derive from our view of the inherent danger of unregulated bargaining. Thus, we justify in earlier chapters the argument that secession is best explicitly disallowed, since otherwise it offers a ready means for reopening a global renegotiation in an uninstitutionalized or weakly institutionalized condition. We also see as essential the inclusion of things like unambiguous supremacy, residual powers, and comity clauses. And, of course, we include here a concise list of individual rights that can be used to coordinate people's views as to the permissible domain of the state and the legitimacy of court decisions. At the same time, it follows from the self-enforceability argument that, with the exception of rights, the set of such constraints should be minimal, and jurisdictional delineations, to the extent they are part of a constitution, need not be treated as the equal of the previously mentioned fundamentals since they can and most likely will be subject to renegotiation and reinterpretation. One constraint we prefer to see included (but which not all federations find feasible) are limits on the asymmetries allowed in the treatment of federal subjects, including restrictions on bilateral jurisdictional adjustments. With perhaps the exception only of those asymmetries deemed essential to a federation's formation (including schemes of representation), constitutionally sanctioned asymmetry is little more than an invitation to the wholesale renegotiation of federal terms. Even in the limited domains of revenue sharing, tax allocation, and representation in the national government – domains where asymmetry may be unavoidable – great care needs to be taken to isolate (via such devices as special commissions that are somehow inoculated from contemporaneous political forces) the issues that any renegotiation is likely to encompass.

If the provisions of Level 1 can be thought of as the terms of a contract, the legal environment within which those terms are enforced is described largely by Level 2, which is where we identify the core federal governmental structures and their relationship to each other. Here design must choose between a presidential and a parliamentary state (or some amalgam of the two), between within and without representation, between a federation that seeks explicitly to recognize and institutionalize its geographic heterogeneity and one that assumes a homogeneous state (including the very definition of federal subjects), and between a unitary and dual national court (supreme and constitutional, separate or one?). The parameters here that need to be set are seemingly endless and include such things as the requirements for override of an executive veto, the authority of the legislature over ministers, the methods of appointment of judges and members of a cabinet, impeachment provisions, the structure of federal subject representation on one or two legislative chambers, the legislative authority of a chief executive as well as that of each chamber, and so on and so forth. Moreover, if the history of the Swiss, German, Canadian, Indian, U.S., and Australian federations teaches us anything, it is that there is no uniquely best Level 2 configuration. Still, certain things are best avoided, such as a chief executive that is too strong relative to the other branches of the national government (e.g., Russia), a legislative chamber that serves little purpose (e.g., the Senate in Canada), and emergency provisions that open the door to a usurpation of power by one branch of government or the other and the loss of an integrating party's relevance (e.g., India).

Level 2, however, requires exogenous enforcement. Even if design succeeds in having ambition counter ambition so that the internal dynamics of the federal government maintain the balance we build into its design, a constitutional document needs a source of global enforcement so that it can resist the varied winds that tear at its fabric – the demands for regional advantage, the career aspirations of regional and local political elites, the arrogance of national political elites, and the policy imperatives visited upon it by extraconstitutional actors (e.g., interest groups, corporate lobbies, and the international community). Perhaps we should not be surprised, then, that constitutionalism does not have a stellar record and that it is not difficult to find states that have experienced literally dozens of constitutional regimes. Regardless of particulars, however, we need to understand a constitution for what it is; unlike some of its Level 2 components, it is a social coordination mechanism that works in tandem (or competes) with those other traditions and conventions that coordinate society.

Saying this, however, merely pushes the ball back (or up) to Level 3, which we identify as the *political* game in which a constitution is embedded. And here our argument is that federal design cannot end with the drafting of a constitution. It must also attend to those ancillary institutions that sometimes develop spontaneously and that are not always associated with federal design or even given the label constitutional, including the charters of federal subjects insofar as those documents impact the structure of political competition across the federation. In particular, design needs to pay special attention to the likely impact on party systems (or, more generally, on the individual level incentives to political agents) of any constellation of institutional parameters – especially the extent to which any proposed constellation is likely to encourage or discourage an integrated system. If there is, then, a single lesson of design to be gleaned from this volume, it lies not in specific institutional suggestions or the advocacy of specific parameters of design, but rather in the simple admonition that no *process* of federal design can be considered complete until and unless full consideration is given to those things that might encourage or discourage the development of a federally integrated political party system.

References

Abromeit, Heidrun. 2002. Contours of a European Federation. *Regional and Federal Studies* 12 (1): 1–20.

Ackerman, Bruce. 1992. *The Future of Liberal Revolution*. New Haven: Yale University Press.

Adams, William. 1973. *The First American Constitutions*. Chapel Hill: University of North Carolina Press.

Adelberger, Karen. 1999. Federalism and Its Discontents: Fiscal and Legislative Power-Sharing in Germany, 1948–1999. University of California at Berkeley Department of Political Science. WP 99-16.

Afanasyev, Yurii Nikolaevich. 1988. *Inogo Ne Dano*. Moscow: Progress.

Agranoff, Robert. 1996. Federal Evolution in Spain. *International Political Science Review* 17 (October): 585–401.

ed. 1999. *Accommodating Diversity: Asymmetry in Federal States*. Baden-Baden: Nomos.

Aldrich, John. 1995. *Why Parties?* Chicago: University of Chicago Press.

Alesina, Alberto, and Enrico Spolaore. 1997. On the Number and Size of Nations. *Quarterly Journal of Economics* 112 (November): 1027–56.

Alesina, Alberto, Enrico Spolaore, and Roman Wacziarg. 2000. Economic Integration and Political Disintegration. *American Economic Review* 90 (December): 1276–96.

Ambrose, Stephen. 2000. *Nothing Like It in the World: The Men Who Built the Transcontinental Railroad, 1863–1869*. New York: Simon and Schuster.

Ames, Barry. 1994. Electoral Strategy under Open List Proportional Representation. *American Journal of Political Science* 39 (2): 406–33.

Amoretti, Ugo. 2002. Italy Decentralizes. *Journal of Democracy* 13 (2): 126–40.

Anderson, William. 1955. *The Nation and the States, Rivals or Partners?* Minneapolis: University of Minnesota Press.

Aranson, Peter, and Peter Ordeshook. 1985. Public Interest, Private Interest, and the Democratic Polity. In *The Democratic State*, edited by R. Benjamin and S. Elkin, pp. 87–178. Lawrence: University Press of Kansas.

Arnim, Hans von Herbert. 1993. Campaign and Party Finance in Germany. In *Campaign and Party Finance in North America and Western Europe*, edited by A. B. Gunlicks, pp. 201–18. Boulder, Colo.: Westview Press.

Arrow, Kenneth Joseph. 1963. *Social Choice and Individual Values*. New York: Wiley.

Aspinwall, Mark. 2001. Institutionalized Europhobia: Britain and Monetary Policy Integration. Paper presented at the annual meeting of the American Political Science Association, San Francisco, August 30–September 2.

Attina, Fulvio. 2001. Strategies for Democratising Multi-State Systems and the European Union. *Current Politics and Economics of Europe* 10 (8): 227–43.

Axelrod, Robert. 1984. *The Evolution of Cooperation*. New York: Basic Books.

Bailyn, Bernard, ed. 1993. *The Debate on the Constitution: Federalist and Anti-Federalist Speeches, Articles and Letters during the Struggle over Ratification*. New York: Library of America.

Baker, David, Andrew Gamble, and David Seawright. 1999. The European Exceptionalism of the British Political Elite. Paper presented at the ECPR Joint Sessions, Mannheim, March 26–31.

Baker, David, and David Seawright, eds. 1998. *Britain for and against Europe: British Politics and the Question of European Integration*. Oxford: Oxford University Press.

Baldwin, Nicholas, and Donald Shell, eds. 2001. *Second Chambers*. London: Frank Cass.

Baron, David, and John Ferejohn. 1989. Bargaining in Legislatures. *American Political Science Review* 83 (4): 1181–1206.

Barro, R. 1991. Economic Growth in a Cross-Section of Countries. *Quarterly Journal of Economics* 106 (2): 407–43.

Bartolini, Stefano. 2000. Political Representation in Loosely Bounded Territories: Between Europe and the Nation-State. European University Institute 1999–2000 European Forum, conference on Multi-level Party Systems: Europeanization and the Reshaping of National Political Representation Conference paper, EUR/10.

Bartolini, Stefano, and Peter Mair. 1990. *Identity, Competition, and Electoral Availability: The Stabilisation of European Electorates, 1885–1985*. Cambridge: Cambridge University Press.

Batt, Judy. 1993. Czecho-Slovakia in Transition: From Federation to Separation. Royal Institute of International Affairs Discussion Paper 46. London.

Bawn, Kathleen. 1993. The Logic of Institutional Preferences: German Electoral Law as a Social Choice Outcome. *American Journal of Political Science* 37: 965–89.

Baybeck, Brady, and William R. Lowry. 2000. Federalism Outcomes and Ideological Preferences: The U.S. Supreme Court and Preemption Cases. *Publius: The Journal of Federalism* 30 (3): 73–97.

Beach, Walter G. 1899. The Australian Federal Constitution. *Political Science Quarterly* 14 (4): 663–80.

Bednar, Jenna, Jr., William N. Eskridge, and John Ferejohn. 2001. A Political Theory of Federalism. In *Constitutional Culture and Democratic Rule*, edited by John Ferejohn, Jack Rakove, and Jonathon Riley, pp. 223–70. Cambridge: Cambridge University Press.

Beer, Samuel. 1993. *To Make a Nation: The Rediscovery of American Federalism*. Cambridge, Mass.: Harvard University Press.

Benz, Arthur. 1999. From Unitary to Asymmetric Federalism in Germany: Taking Stock after 50 Years. *Publius: The Journal of Federalism* 29 (4): 55–78.

Bianco, W., and R. Bates. 1990. Cooperation by Design: Leadership, Structure and Collective Decisions. *American Political Science Review* 84: 133–47.

Black, Duncan. 1958. *The Theory of Committees and Elections*. Cambridge: Cambridge University Press.

Bogdanor, Venon. 1989. Direct Elections, Representative Democracy and European Integration. *Electoral Studies* 8 (3): 205–16.

Boix, Carles. 1999. Setting the Rules of the Game: The Choice of Electoral Systems in Advanced Democracies. *American Political Science Review* 93 (3): 609–24.

Bolton, Patrick, and Gerard Roland. 1997. The Breakup of Nations: A Political Economy Analysis. *Quarterly Journal of Economics* 112 (November): 1057–90.

Bonde, Jens-Peter. 2001. *The Nice Treaty Explained*. Copenhagen: Vindrose.

Bookman, Milica. 1992. *The Economics of Secession*. New York: St. Martin's Press.

Boorstin, Daniel. 1953. *The Genius of American Politics*. Chicago: University of Chicago Press.

Borchert, Jens. 2000. The Political Class and Its Self-Interested Theory of Democracy: Historical Developments and Institutional Consequences. Paper presented at the European Consortium for Political Research Joint Sessions of Workshops, Copenhagen, April 14–19.

Brady, Alexander. 1938. The Critical Problems of Canadian Federalism. *American Political Science Review* 32 (5): 957–65.

Brady, David, and Jongryn Mo. 1992. Strategy and Choice in the 1988 National Assembly Election of Korea. *Comparative Political Studies* 24: 405–29.

Braid, Don, and Sydney Sharpe. 1990. *Breakup: Why the West Feels Left Out of Canada*. Toronto: Key Porter Books.

Brams, Steven. 1994. *Theory of Moves*. Cambridge: Cambridge University Press.

Brass, Paul R. 1994. *The Politics of India since Independence*. Cambridge: Cambridge University Press.

Brennan, Geoffrey, and James Buchanan. 1985. *The Reason of Rule*. Cambridge: Cambridge University Press.

Breton, A. 2000. Federalism and Decentralization: Ownership Rights and the Superiority of Federalism. *Publius: The Journal of Federalism* 30 (2): 1–16.

Brown, Gordon. 1994. Canadian Federal-Provincial Overlap and Presumed Government Inefficiency. *Publius: The Journal of Federalism* 24 (Winter): 21–37.

Brown-John, C. Lloyd, ed. 1995. *Federal-Type Solutions and European Integration*. Lanham, Md.: University Press of America.

Buchanan, Allen. 1991. *Secession: The Morality of Political Divorce from Fort Sumter to Lithuania and Quebec*. Boulder, Colo.: Westview Press.

1998. Democracy and Secession. In *National Self-Determination and Secession*, edited by M. Moore, pp. 14–33. Oxford: Oxford University Press.

Buchanan, James M. 1995. Federalism as an Ideal Political Order and an Objective for Constitutional Reform. *Publius: The Journal of Federalism* 25 (2): 19–28.

Buchanan, James M., and Roger L. Faith. 1987. Secession and the Limits of Taxation: Toward a Theory of Internal Exit. *American Economic Review* 77 (December): 1023–31.

Buchanan, James M., and Gordon Tullock. 1962. *The Calculus of Consent, Logical Foundations of Constitutional Democracy*. Ann Arbor: University of Michigan Press.

Bunce, Valerie. 1999. *Subversive Institutions: The Design and the Destruction of Socialism and the State*. Cambridge: Cambridge University Press.

Burgess, Michael. 1995. *The British Tradition of Federalism*. Madison, N.J.: Fairleigh Dickinson University Press.

Burgess, Michael, and Alain G. Gagnon, eds. 1993. *Comparative Federalism and Federation: Competing Traditions and Future Directions*. London: Harvester Wheatsheaf.

Cain, Bruce, John Ferejohn, and Morris Fiorina. 1987. *The Personal Vote*. Cambridge: Cambridge University Press.

Cairns, Robert D. 1992. Natural Resources and Canadian Federalism: Decentralization, Recurring Conflict, and Resolution. *Publius: The Journal of Federalism* 22 (1): 55–71.

Calvert, Randall L. 1995. The Rational Choice Theory of Social Institutions: Cooperation, Coordination and Communication. In *Modern Political Economy*, edited by J. S. Banks and E. A. Hanushek, pp. 216–67. Cambridge: Cambridge University Press.

Cammisa, Anne. 1995. *Governments as Interest Groups: Intergovernmental Lobbying and the Federal System*. Westport, Conn.: Praeger.

Carey, John. 1997. Institutional Design and Party Systems. In *Consolidating the Third Wave Democracies*, edited by L. Diamond, M. Plattner, Y.-H. Chu, and H.-M. Tien, pp. 67–92. Baltimore: Johns Hopkins University Press.

1998. *Term Limits and Legislative Representation*. Cambridge: Cambridge University Press.

Carey, John, and Matthew S. Shugart. 1995. Incentives to Cultivate a Personal Vote: A Rank Ordering of Electoral Systems. *Electoral Studies* 14 (4): 417–39.

1998. *Executive Decree Authority*. Cambridge: Cambridge University Press.

Carrubba, C. 1997. Net Financial Transfers in the European Union: Who Gets What and Why? *Journal of Politics* 59 (2): 469.

2001. The Electoral Connection in European Union Politics. *Journal of Politics* 63 (1): 141–58.

Carty, Ken. 1988. Three Canadian Party Systems: An Interpretation of the Development of National Politics. In *Party Democracy in Canada: The Politics of National Party Conventions*, edited by G. Perlin, pp. 15–30. Scarborough: Prentice-Hall of Canada.

Casella, Alessandra, and Bruno S. Frey. 1992. Federalism and Clubs: Towards an Economic Theory of Overlapping Political Jurisdictions. *European Economic Review* 36 (2–3): 639–46.

Chandler, William. 1987. Federalism and Political Parties. In *Federalism and the Role of the State*, edited by H. Bakvis and W. M. Chandler, pp. 149–70. Toronto: University of Toronto Press.

Chen, Yan, and Peter C. Ordeshook. 1994. Constitutional Secession Clauses. *Constitutional Political Economy* 5 (1): 45–60.

Chibber, Pradeep. 1999. *Democracy without Associations*. Ann Arbor: University of Michigan Press.

Chibber, Pradeep, and Ken Kollman. 1998. Party Aggregation and the Number of Parties in India and the United States. *American Political Science Review* 92 (2): 329–42.
Choper, Jesse. 1980. *Judicial Review and the National Political Process*. Chicago: University of Chicago Press.
Clark, S. 1954. Foreword. In *Social Credit and the Federal Power in Canada*, edited by J. R. Mallory, pp. VII–IX. Toronto: University of Toronto Press.
Clemens, Walter. 2000. Could More Force Have Saved the Soviet System? *Journal of Cold War Studies* 2 (1): 116–23.
Coleman, James. 1986. Norms as Social Capital. In *Economic Imperialism*, edited by G. Radnitzky and P. Bernholz. New York: Paragon House.
Congleton, Roger D., Andreas Kyriacou, and Jordi Bacaria. 2003. Political and Economic Origins of Asymmetric Federalism: A Model of Endogenous Centralization. Unpublished manuscript.
Conquest, Robert. 1967. *Soviet Nationalities Policy in Practice*. London: Bodley Head.
Conradt, David. 1999. *The German Polity*. London: Longman.
Corry, J. A. 1969. *Law and Policy*. Toronto: Irwin.
Cowles, M., and M. Smith. 2000. Risks, Reform, Resistance, and Revival. In *The State of the European Union: Risks, Reform, Resistance, and Revival*, edited by M. Cowles and M. Smith, pp. 3–16. Oxford: Oxford University Press.
Cox, Gary. 1990. Centripetal and Centrifugal Incentives in Electoral Systems. *American Journal of Political Science* 34 (4): 903–35.
1997. *Making Votes Count: Strategic Coordination in the World's Electoral Systems*. Cambridge: Cambridge University Press.
Cross, Frank B., and Emerson H. Tiller. 2000. The Three Faces of Federalism: An Empirical Assessment of Supreme Court Federalism Jurisprudence. *Southern California Law Review* 73 (4): 741–72.
Dafflon, Bernard. 1999. Fiscal Federalism in Switzerland: A Survey of Constitutional Issues, Budget Responsibility and Equalization. In *Fiscal Federalism in the European Union*, edited by A. Fossati and G. Panella, pp. 255–94. London: Routledge.
Dahl, Robert Alan. 1956. *A Preface to Democratic Theory*. Chicago: University of Chicago Press.
Daniels, Robert. 1976. The Dynamics of Soviet Politics. In *The Dynamics of Soviet Politics*, edited by P. Cocks, R. Daniels, and N. Heer, pp. 77–95. Cambridge, Mass.: Harvard University Press.
Dashkevych, Iaroslav. 1991. Maibutnia Ukraina: Federatsiia? *Slovo* 12 (June): 6.
Davis, S. Rufus. 1978. *The Federal Principle: A Journey through Time in Quest of a Meaning*. Berkeley: University of California Press.
de Figueiredo, Rui, and Barry R. Weingast. 1999. The Rationality of Fear: Political Opportunism and Ethnic Conflict. In *Civil Wars, Insecurity, and Intervention*, edited by B. F. Walter and J. Snyder, pp. 261–302. New York: Columbia University Press.
Dedek, Oldrich, ed. 1996. *The Break-Up of Czechoslovakia: An In-Depth Economic Analysis*. Aldershot: Avebury.
d'Encausse, Helene Carrere. 1993. *The End of the Soviet Empire: The Triumph of the Nations*. New York: Basic Books.

Dent, Martin. 1989. Federalism in Africa, with Special Reference to Nigeria. In *Federalism and Nationalism*, edited by M. Forsyth. New York: St. Martin's Press.

Deschouwer, Kris. 2001. Multilevel Systems and Political Careers: The Pleasures of Getting Lost. Paper presented at the workshop on Political Careers in a Multi-level Europe, ECPR Joint Sessions, Grenoble, April 6–11.

Deutsch, Karl, ed. 1957. *Political Community in the North Atlantic Area*. Princeton: Princeton University Press.

Diamond, Larry. 1988. *Class, Ethnicity, and Democracy in Nigeria: The Failure of the First Republic*. London: Macmillan.

Dicey, Albert Venn. 1889. *Introduction to the Study of the Law of the Constitution*. London: Macmillan.

Dikshit, Ramesh Dutta. 1975. *The Political Geography of Federalism: An Inquiry into Origins and Stability*. New York: Wiley.

Dolive, Linda L. 1976. *Electoral Politics at the Local Level in the German Federal Republic*. Gainesville: University Presses of Florida.

Dom-Bedu, Anne-Laure, and Andy Smith. 1999. Enlarging or Deepening: The Framing of a European Problem. Paper presented at the ECPR Joint Sessions, Mannheim, March 26.

Dowley, K. M. 1998. Striking the Federal Bargain in Russia: Comparative Regional Government Strategies. *Communist and Post-Communist Studies* 31 (4): 359–80.

Dunlop, John B. 1993. *The Rise of Russia and the Fall of the Soviet Empire*. Princeton: Princeton University Press.

Dyck, Rand. 1991. Links between Federal and Provincial Parties and Party Systems. In *Representation, Integration and Political Parties in Canada*, edited by H. Bakvis, pp. 129–77. Toronto: Dundurn Press.

Earle, Valerie, and George Carey. 1968. *Federalism: Infinite Variety in Theory and Practice*. Ithaca: F. E. Peacock.

Eavey, Cheryl, and Gary. Miller. 1989. Constitutional Conflict in State and Nation. In *The Federalist Papers and the New Institutionalism*, edited by B. Grofman and D. Wittman, pp. 205–15. New York: Agathon Press.

Ehrmann, Winston W. 1947. Post-War Government and Politics of India. *Journal of Politics* 9 (4): 653–91.

Elazar, Daniel. 1962. *The American Partnership: Intergovernmental Co-operation in the Nineteenth-Century United States*. Chicago: University of Chicago Press.

ed. 1979. *Federalism and Political Integration*. Ramat Gan: Turtledove.

ed. 1991. *Constitutional Design and Power Sharing in the Post Modern Epoch*. Lanham, Md.: University Press of America.

1994. *Federal Systems of the World: A Handbook of Federal, Confederal and Autonomy Arrangements*. London: Longman.

1995. From Statism to Federalism: A Paradigm Shift. *Publius: The Journal of Federalism* 25 (2): 5–18.

Elkins, Stanley, and Eric McKitrick. 1993. *The Age of Federalism: The Early American Republic, 1788–1800*. New York: Oxford University Press.

Ellis, Joseph J. 2000. *Founding Brothers: The Revolutionary Generation*. New York: Knopf.

Ellman, Michael, and Vladimir Kontorovich. 1997. The Collapse of the Soviet System and the Memoir Literature. *Europe-Asia Studies* 49 (2): 259–79.

1998. *The Destruction of the Soviet Economic System: An Insiders' History*. Armonk, N.Y.: M. E. Sharpe.

Elster, Jon. 1995. Transition, Constitution-Making and Separation in Czechoslovakia. *European Journal of Sociology/Archives Europennes de Sociologie* 36 (1): 105–34.

Elster, Jon, and Rune Slagstad, eds. 1988. *Constitutionalism and Democracy.* Cambridge: Cambridge University Press.

Endersby, James, and Michael Towle. 1997. Effects of Constitutional and Political Controls on State Expenditures. *Publius: The Journal of Federalism* 27 (1): 83–99.

Enelow, James M., and Melvin J. Hinich. 1984. *The Spatial Theory of Voting: An Introduction.* Cambridge: Cambridge University Press.

Epstein, David, and Sharyn O'Halloran. 1999. *Delegating Powers: A Transaction Cost Politics Approach to Policy Making under Separate Powers.* Cambridge: Cambridge University Press.

Epstein, Lee, and Gary King. 2002. The Rules of Inference. *University of Chicago Law Review* 69 (1): 1–133.

Epstein, Lee, Jack Knight, and Olga Shvetsova. 2001. The Role of Constitutional Courts in the Establishment and Maintenance of Democratic Systems of Government. *Law and Society Review* 35 (1): 117–64.

Erikson, Robert, and Mikhail Filippov. 2001. Electoral Balancing in Federal and Sub-national Elections: The Case of Canada. *Constitutional Political Economy* 12 (4): 313–31.

Eskridge, William. 1991. Overriding Supreme Court Statutory Interpretation Decisions. *Yale Law Journal* 101 (2): 331–455.

Esman, Milton J., and Ronald J. Herring. 2001. *Carrots, Sticks and Ethnic Conflict: Rethinking Development Assistance.* Ann Arbor: University of Michigan Press.

Evans, Geoffrey. 1998. Euroscepticism and Conservative Electoral Support: How an Asset Became a Liability. *British Journal of Political Science* 28: 573–90.

1999. Europe: A New Electoral Cleavage? In *Critical Elections*, edited by G. Evans and P. Norris, pp. 207–22. London: Sage Publications.

Evatt, Herbert. 1940. *Australian Labour Leader: The Story of W. A. Holman and the Labour Movement.* Sydney: Angus and Robertson.

Fearon, James, and David Laitin. 2000. Violence and the Social Construction of Ethnic Identity. *International Organization* 54 (4): 845–77.

Ferejohn, John, Jack Rakove, and Jonathan Riley. 2001. *Constitutional Culture and Democratic Rule.* Cambridge: Cambridge University Press.

Fidrmuc, Jan, Julius Horvath, and Jarko Fidrmuc. 1999. The Stability of Monetary Unions: Lessons from the Breakup of Czechoslovakia. *Journal of Comparative Economics* 27 (4): 753–81.

Filion, Pierre. 1999. Civic Parties in Canada: Their Diversity and Evolution. In *Local Parties in Political and Organizational Perspective*, edited by M. Saiz and H. Geser, pp. 77–100. Boulder, Colo.: Westview Press.

Filippov, Mikhail, Peter C. Ordeshook, and Olga Shvetsova. 1999. Party Fragmentation and Presidential Elections in Post-Communist Democracies. *Constitutional Political Economy* 10 (1): 3–26.

2001. Ensuring a Stable Federal State: Economics or Political Institutional Design. In *Rules and Reason: Perspectives on Constitutional Political Economy*, edited by R. Mudambi, P. Navarra, and G. Sobbrio, pp. 207–36. Cambridge: Cambridge University Press.

Filippov, Mikhail, and Olga Shvetsova. 1999. Asymmetric Bilateral Bargaining in the New Russian Federation: A Path-Dependence Explanation. *Communist and Post-Communist Studies* 32: 61–76.

Finkelman, Paul, and Stephen E. Gottlieb, eds. 1991. *Toward a Usable Past: Liberty under Sate Constitutions*. Athens: University of Georgia Press.

Fish, Steven M. 1995. *Democracy from Scratch: Opposition and Regime in the New Russian Revolution*. Princeton: Princeton University Press.

Fitzmaurice, John. 1996. *The Politics of Belgium: A Unique Federalism*. Boulder, Colo.: Westview Press.

Flanz, Gisbert H. 1968. West Indian Federation. In *Why Federations Fail*, edited by T. M. Franck, pp. 91–123. New York: New York University Press.

Formisano, Ronald P. 1981. Federalists and Republicans: Parties, Yes – System, No. In *The Evolution of American Electoral Systems*, edited by P. Kleppner, pp. 33–76. Westport, Conn.: Greenwood Press.

Forsyth, Murray Greensmith. 1981. *Unions of States: The Theory and Practice of Confederation*. New York: Leicester University Press.

Fowke, Vernon C. 1947. *Canadian Agricultural Policy*. Toronto: University of Toronto Press.

Franck, Thomas M. 1968. *Why Federations Fail: An Inquiry into the Requisites for Successful Federalism*. New York: New York University Press.

Franda, Marcus. 1962. The Organizational Development of India's Congress Party. *Pacific Affairs* 35 (3): 248–60.

Franklin, Mark, Michael Marsh, and Lauren McLaren. 1994. Uncorking the Bottle: Popular Opposition to European Unification in the Wake of Maastricht. *Journal of Common Market Studies* 32 (4): 455–72.

Franklin, Mark, Michael Marsh, and Christopher Wlezien. 1994. Attitudes toward Europe and Referendum Votes: A Response to Siune and Svenson. *Electoral Studies* 13 (2): 117–21.

Franklin, Mark, and Fiona McGillivray. 1999. European Union Politics as a Multi-Level Game against Voters. Paper presented at the annual meeting of the American Political Science Association. Boston, September.

Frey, Bruno, and Reiner Eichenberger. 2001. A Proposal for Dynamic European Federalism: FOCJ. In *Rules and Reason: Perspectives on Constitutional Political Economy*, edited by R. Mudambi, P. Navarra, and G. Sobbrio, pp. 237–57. Cambridge: Cambridge University Press.

Friedman, Milton. 1953. *Essays in Positive Economics*. Chicago: University of Chicago Press.

1977. *The Nobel Prize in Economics, 1976: A Talk*. Stanford: Hoover Institution, Stanford University.

Friedrich, Carl Joachim. 1968. *Trends of Federalism in Theory and Practice*. New York: Praeger.

Frohlich, Norman, and Joe Oppenheimer. 1970. I Get By with a Little Help from My Friends. *World Politics* 23: 104–20.

Gabel, M. 1998. Public Support for European Integration: An Empirical Test of Five Theories. *Journal of Politics* 60: 333–54.

Galligan, Brian. 1987. *Politics of the High Court*. St. Lucia: University of Queensland Press.

2001. Parliament's Development of Federalism. In *Parliament: The Vision in Hindsight*, edited by G. Lindell and R. Bennett, pp. 1–36. Sydney: Federation Press.

Gardner, David. 1991. EC Leaders Find Social Chapter Hard to Read. *Financial Times*, December 11.
Garry, John. 1995. The British Conservative Party: Divisions over European Policy. *West European Politics* 18 (4): 170–90.
Geddes, Barbara. 1995. A Comparative Perspective on the Leninist Legacy in Eastern Europe. *Comparative Political Studies* 28 (2): 239–74.
1996. Initiation of New Democratic Institutions in Eastern Europe and Latin America. In *Institutional Design in New Democracies: Eastern Europe and Latin America*, edited by A. Lijphart and C. Waisman, pp. 15–42. Boulder, Colo.: Westview Press.
Geser, Hans. 1997. *Die Politisch-Administrative Organisation der Schweizer Gemeinden*. Zurich: Soziologisches Institut der Universität Zürich.
Gibbard, Allan. 1973. Manipulation of Voting Schemes: A General Result. *Econometrica* 41 (4): 587–601.
Gibbins, Roger. 1980. *Prairie Politics and Society: Regionalism in Decline*. Toronto: Butterworths.
1982. *Regionalism: Territorial Politics in Canada and the United States*. Toronto: Butterworths.
1987. Federal Societies, Institutions, and Politics. In *Federalism and the Role of the State*, edited by H. Bakvis and W. Chandler. Toronto: University of Toronto Press.
Gibson, James L., John P. Frendreis, and Laura L. Vertz. 1989. Party Dynamics in the 1980s: Change in County Party Organizational Strength, 1980–1984. *American Journal of Political Science* 33 (1): 67–90.
Gill, Graeme. 1994. *The Collapse of a Single Party System: The Disintegration of the CPSU*. Cambridge: Cambridge University Press.
Gill, Graeme, and Roderic Pitty. 1997. *Power in the Party: The Organization of Power and Central-Republican Relations in the CPSU*. New York: St. Martin's Press.
Gleason, Gregory. 1990. *Federalism and Nationalism: The Struggle for Republican Rights in the USSR*. Boulder, Colo.: Westview Press.
Goldman, Marshall I. 1991. *What Went Wrong with Perestroika*. New York: W. W. Norton.
Goldman, Minton. 1999. *Slovakia since Independence: A Struggle for Democracy*. Westport, Conn.: Praeger.
Goldsworthy, Jeffrey. 1997. A Role for the States in Initiating Referendums. In *Upholding the Australian Constitution*, vol. 8 of *Proceedings of the Eighth Conference of the Samuel Griffith Society*, pp. 48–54. Melbourne: Samuel Griffith Society.
Golsch, Lutz. 1995. Careers and Political Professionalization: German and American Perspectives on Backbenchers in the Bundestag. Paper presented at the annual meeting of the American Political Science Association, Chicago, August.
Goodman, Paul. 1964. *The Democratic Republicans of Massachusetts*. Cambridge, Mass.: Harvard University Press.
Gorbachev, Mikhail Sergeevich. 1988. *Perestroika: New Thinking for Our Country and the World*. New York: Perennial Library.
Green, Fletcher Melvin. 1930. Constitutional Development in the South Atlantic States, 1776–1860: A Study in the Evolution of Democracy. Chapel Hill: University of North Carolina Press.
Greenwood, Sean. 1992. *Britain and European Cooperation since 1945*. Cambridge: Blackwell.

Grodzins, Morton. 1966. *The American System: A New View of Government in the United States*. Chicago: Rand McNally.

Grofman, Bernard. 1996. Arend Lijphart and the New Institutionalism. Paper presented at the annual meeting of the American Political Science Association, San Francisco, August 29–September 1.

Grofman, Bernard, and Andrew Reynolds. 2001. Electoral Systems and the Art of Constitutional Engineering: An Inventory of the Main Findings. In *Rules and Reason: Perspectives on Constitutional Political Economy*, edited by R. Mudambi, P. Navarra, and G. Sobbrio, pp. 125–64. Cambridge: Cambridge University Press.

Gruner, Erich, and Kenneth Pitterle. 1983. Switzerland's Political Parties. In *Switzerland at the Polls*, edited by H. Penniman, pp. 30–59. Washington, D.C.: American Enterprise Institute for Public Policy Research.

Gunlicks, Arthur B. 1988. Campaign and Party Finance in West Germany. *Review of Politics* 50 (Winter): 30–48.

Gunther, Richard, and Anthony Mughan. 1993. Political Institutions and Cleavage Management. In *Do Institutions Matter? Government Capabilities in the United States and Abroad*, edited by R. K. Weaver and B. A. Rockman, pp. 272–301. Washington, D.C.: Brookings Institution.

Gupta, A. 2000. India: Democracy and Dissent. *Parliamentary Affairs* 53 (1): 181–88.

Haas, E. B. 1958. *The Uniting of Europe: Political, Social and Economic Forces, 1950–1957*. London: Stevens & Sons.

1968. *Beyond the Nation-State; Functionalism and International Organization*. Stanford: Stanford University Press.

Habek, Rudolf. 1987. The Political Dynamics of Regionalism. In *Regionalism in European Politics*, edited by R. Morgan, pp. 29–64. London: Policy Studies Institute.

Hadley, Charles D., Michael Morass, and Rainer Nick. 1989. Federalism and Party Interaction in West Germany, Switzerland and Austria. *Publius: The Journal of Federalism* 19 (4): 81–97.

Hahn, Gordon M. 2001. Putin's "Federal Revolution": The Administrative and Judicial Reform of Russian Federalism. *East European Constitutional Review* 10 (1): 60–7.

Haider, Donald H. 1974. *When Governments Come to Washington: Governors, Mayors, and Intergovernmental Lobbying*. New York: Free Press.

Haimanko, Ori, Michel Le Breton, and Shlomo Weber. 2001. Transfers in a Polarized Country: Bridging the Gap between Efficiency and Stability. Unpublished manuscript.

Hamilton, Marci. 2001. The Elusive Safeguards of Federalism. *Annals – American Academy of Political and Social Science* 574 (March): 93–103.

Hanson, Stephen. 2001. Defining Democratic Consolidation. In *Postcommunism and the Theory of Democracy*, edited by R. D. Anderson, S. Fish, S. Hanson, and P. Roeder, pp. 126–51. Princeton: Princeton University Press.

Hardin, Russell. 1989. Why a Constitution? In *The Federalist Papers and the New Institutionalism*, edited by B. Grofman and D. Wittman, pp. 100–20. New York: Agathon Press.

1995. *One for All: The Logic of Group Conflict*. Princeton: Princeton University Press.

Harrison, Selig S. 1960. *India: The Most Dangerous Decades*. Princeton: Princeton University Press.

Hayden, Robert. 1992. The Beginning of the End of Federal Yugoslavia: The Slovenian Amendment Crisis of 1989. *The Carl Beck Papers,* no. 1001. Center for Russian and East European Studies, University of Pittsburgh.

Hayek, Friedrich A. von 1945. *The Road to Serfdom*. Chicago: University of Chicago Press.

1973. *Law, Legislation and Liberty*. Vol. 1: *Rules and Order*. Chicago: University of Chicago Press.

1976. *Law, Legislation and Liberty*. Vol. 2: *The Mirage of Social Justice*. Chicago: University of Chicago Press.

1979. *Law, Legislation and Liberty*. Vol. 3: *The Political Order of a Free People*. Chicago: University of Chicago Press.

Hazan, Barukh. 1990. *Gorbachev's Gamble: The 19th All-Union Party Conference*. Boulder, Colo.: Westview Press.

Hechter, Michael. 2000. *Containing Nationalism*. Oxford: Oxford University Press.

Hedlund, Stefan. 2001. Can Property Rights Be Protected by Law? *East European Constitutional Review* 10 (1): 48–52.

Heidenheimer, Arnold J. 1963. Comparative Party Finance: Notes on Practices and toward a Theory. *Journal of Politics* 25: 790–811.

Hennessy, Alistair. 1989. The Renaissance of Federal Ideas in Contemporary Spain. In *Federalism and Nationalism*, edited by M. Forsyth, pp. 11–23. Leicester: Leicester University Press.

Herring, Edward Pendleton. 1940. *Presidential Leadership: The Political Relations of Congress and the Chief Executive*. New York: Farrar and Rinehart.

Hesse, Joachim Jens, and Vincent Wright. 1996. *Federalizing Europe? The Costs, Benefits, and Preconditions of Federal Political Systems*. Nuffield European Studies. Oxford: Oxford University Press.

Hicks, Ursula K. 1978. *Federalism: Failure and Success, a Comparative Study*. New York: Oxford University Press.

Hinich, Melvin, and Michael Munger. 1994. *Ideology and the Theory of Political Choice*. Ann Arbor: University of Michigan Press.

Hinich, Melvin, and Peter C. Ordeshook. 1974. The Electoral College: A Spatial Analysis. *Political Methodology* 1 (3): 1–29.

Hix, Simon. 1994. The Study of the European Community: The Challenge to Comparative Politics. *West European Politics* 17 (1): 1–30.

1996. The Transnational Party Federations. In *Political Parties and the European Union*, edited by J. Gaffney, pp. 308–31. London: Routledge.

1998. Elections, Parties and Institutional Design: A Comparative Perspective on European Union Democracy. *West European Politics* 21 (3): 19–53.

1999a. Dimensions and Alignments in European Union Politics: Cognitive Constraints and Partisan Responses. *European Journal of Political Research* 35: 69–106.

1999b. *The Political System of the European Union*. London: Macmillan.

Hix, Simon, and C. Lord. 1997. *Political Parties in the European Union*. London: Macmillan.

Hoadley, John F. 1986. *The Origins of American Political Parties, 1789–1803*. Lexington: University Press of Kentucky.

Hoag, Clarence Gilbert, and George Hervey Hallett. 1926. *Proportional Representation*. New York: Macmillan.

Hofstadter, Richard. 1969. *The Idea of a Party System*. Berkeley: University of California Press.

Holmes, Jean, and Campbell Sharman. 1977. *The Australian Federal System*. Boston: George Allen & Unwin.

Hooghe, Liesbet. 1999. Supranational Activists or Inter-governmental Agents: Explaining the Orientations of Senior Commission Officials towards European Integration. *Comparative Political Studies* 32 (4): 435–63.

Hooghe, Liesbet, Gary Marks, and Carole J. Wilson. 2002. Does Left-Right Structure Party Positions on European Integration? *Comparative Political Studies* 35 (8): 965–89.

Horowitz, Donald L. 1985. *Ethnic Groups in Conflict*. Berkeley: University of California Press.

1991. *A Democratic South Africa? Constitutional Engineering in a Divided Society*. Berkeley: University of California Press.

Hough, Jerry F. 1997. *Democratization and Revolution in the USSR, 1985–1991*. Washington, D.C.: Brookings Institution.

Howlett, Michael. 1991. The Politics of Constitutional Change in a Federal System: Negotiating Section 92A of the Canadian Constitution Act (1982). *Publius: The Journal of Federalism* 21 (Winter): 121–42.

Huber, John. 1996. *Rationalizing Parliament*. Cambridge: Cambridge University Press.

Huber, Max. 1909. The Intercantonal Law of Switzerland (Swiss Interstate Law). *American Journal of International Law* 3 (1): 62–98.

Hughes, Christopher. 1962. *The Parliament of Switzerland*. London: Published for the Hansard Society by Cassell.

Hughes, James. 1994. Regionalism in Russia: The Rise and Fall of the Siberian Agreement. *Europe-Asia Studies* 46 (7): 1133–61.

Hyde, Matthew. 2001. Putin's Federal Reforms and Their Implications for Presidential Power in Russia. *Europe-Asia Studies* 53 (5): 245–74.

Iarycrower, Matias, Sebastian Saiegh, and Mariano Tommasi. 2002. Coming Together: The Industrial Organization of Federalism. Unpublished manuscript.

Inglehart, Ronald. 1970. Public Opinion and Regional Integration (in Elaboration of Conceptual and Causal Paradigms). *International Organization* 24 (4): 764–95.

Inman, Robert P., and Daniel L. Rubinfeld. 1996. The Political Economy of Federalism. In *Perspectives on Public Choice: A Handbook*, edited by D. C. Mueller, pp. 106–23. Cambridge: Cambridge University Press.

Irving, Helen. 1997. *To Constitute a Nation: A Cultural History of Australia's Constitution*. Studies in Australian History. Cambridge: Cambridge University Press.

Jaensch, Dean. 1994. *Power Politics: Australia's Party System*. Sydney: Allen & Unwin.

Jahn, D., and A. S. Storsved. 1995. Legitimacy through Referendum? The Nearly Successful Domino-Strategy of the EU-Referendums in Austria, Finland, Sweden and Norway. *West European Politics* 18 (4): 18–37.

Jeffery, Charlie. 1999. Party Politics and Territorial Representation in the Federal Republic of Germany. *West European Politics* 22 (April): 130–66.

Jeffery, Charlie, and Hans Mackenstein. 1999. Financial Equalization in the 1990s. In *Recasting German Federalism*, edited by Charlie Jeffery. New York: Printer.

Joerges, C., Y. Mény, and J. Weiler, eds. 2000. *What Kind of Constitution for What Kind of Polity? Responses to Joschka Fischer*: San Domenico di Fiesole: European University Institute Press.
Johns, Gary. 2000. Party Democracy: An Audit of Australian Parties (Candidate Selection Procedures). *Australian Journal of Political Science* 35 (3): 401–25.
Jones, Mark P. 1995. *Electoral Laws and the Survival of Presidential Democracies*. Notre Dame: University of Notre Dame Press.
Joyner, Conrad. 1958. Australian Politics and Constitution Alteration Referenda. *Midwest Journal of Political Science* 2 (2): 191–99.
Kahn, Jeffrey. 2002. *Federalism, Democratization and the Rule of Law in Russia*. Oxford: Oxford University Press.
Kammen, Michael. 1986. *A Machine That Would Go of Itself: The Constitution in American Culture*. New York: Knopf.
Katz, Richard. 1999. Parties in Europe and Parties of Europe. Paper presented at the conference on Multi-level Party Systems: Europeanisation and the Reshaping of National Political Representation, European University Institute, Florence, December.
Katz, Richard, and Peter Mair. 1995. Changing Models of Party Organization and Party Democracy. The Emergence of the Cartel Party. *Party Politics* 1: 5–28.
Katz, Richard, and Bernhard Wessels, eds. 1999. *European Parliament and European Integration*. Oxford: Oxford University Press.
Keating, M. 1998. What's Wrong with Asymmetrical Government? *Regional and Federal Studies* 8 (1): 195–218.
1999. Asymmetrical Government: Multinational States in an Integrating Europe. *Publius: The Journal of Federalism* 29 (1): 71–86.
Kenyon, Daphne, and John Kincaid, eds. 1991. *Competition among States and Local Governments: Efficiency and Equity in American Federalism*. Washington, D.C.: Urban Institute Press.
Keohane, Robert, and Stanley Hoffmann, eds. 1991. *The New Community of Europe: Decision Making and Institutional Change*. Boulder, Colo.: Westview Press.
Key, Valdimer Orlando. 1964. *Politics, Parties and Pressure Groups*. 5th ed. New York: Crowell.
Keyssar, Alexander. 2000. *The Right to Vote: The Contested History of Democracy in the United States*. New York: Basic Books.
Khadduri, Majid. 1963. *Modern Libya: A Study in Political Development*. Baltimore: Johns Hopkins University Press.
Kiewiet, D. Roderick, and Mathew D. McCubbins. 1991. *The Logic of Delegation: Congressional Parties and the Appropriation Process*. Chicago: University of Chicago Press.
Kiewiet, D. Roderick, and Kristin Szakaly. 1996. Constitutional Limitations on Borrowing: An Analysis of State Bonded Indebtedness. *Journal of Law, Economics, and Organization* 12 (1): 62–97.
Kincaid, John. 2001. Economic Policy-Making: Advantages and Disadvantages of the Federal Model. *International Social Science Journal* 167 (March): 85–92.
King, Preston. 1982. *Federalism and Federation*. Baltimore: Johns Hopkins University Press.

Kirschbaum, Stanislav. 1995. *A History of Slovakia: The Struggle for Survival.* New York: St. Martin's Press.

Klingemann, Hans-Dieter, and Bernhard Wessels. 2001. Political Consequences of Germany's Mixed-Member System: Personalization at the Grass-Roots? In *Mixed Member Electoral Systems: The Best of Both Worlds?*, edited by M. Shugart and M. Wattenberg, pp. 279–96. Oxford: Oxford University Press.

Klochko, Marianna A., and Peter C. Ordeshook. Forthcoming. Corruption, Cooperation and Endogenous Time Discounts. *Public Choice.*

Knight, J. 1992. *Institutions and Social Conflict.* Cambridge: Cambridge University Press.

Knight, J., and I. Sened, eds. 1995. *Explaining Social Institutions.* Ann Arbor: University of Michigan Press.

Kochanek, Stanley A. 1966. The Indian National Congress: The Distribution of Power between Party and Government. *Journal of Asian Studies* 25 (4): 681–97.

1968. *The Congress Party of India; the Dynamics of One-Party Democracy.* Princeton: Princeton University Press.

Kohli, Atul. 1990. *Democracy and Discontent: India's Growing Crisis of Governability.* Cambridge: Cambridge University Press.

Kolmar, Martin. 2000. Constitutions as Commitment or Coordination Device? *Constitutional Political Economy* 11 (4): 371–74.

Kourliandskaia, Galina, Yelena Nikolayenko, and Natalia Golovanova. 2002. Local Government in the Russian Federation. In *Developing New Rules in the Old Environment: Local Governments in Eastern Europe and Central Asia*, edited by V. Popa and I. Munteanu, pp. 163–264. Budapest: Local Government and Public Reform Initiative.

Kramer, Larry. 1994. Understanding Federalism. *Vanderbilt Law Review* 47 (5): 1485–1561.

1998. But When Exactly Was Judicially-Enforced Federalism "Born" in the First Place? *Harvard Journal of Law and Public Policy* 22 (Fall): 123–37.

2000. Putting the Politics Back into the Political Safeguards of Federalism. *Columbia Law Review* 100: 215–93.

Krejci, Oskar. 1996. *Czechoslovak National Interests.* Boulder, Colo.: East European Monographs.

Krishna, Gopal. 1966. The Development of the Indian National Congress as a Mass Organization, 1918–1923. *Journal of Asian Studies* 25 (3): 413–30.

1967. One Party Dominance – Development and Trends. In *Party System and Election Studies*, edited by R. Kothari, pp. 19–98. Bombay: Allied Publishers.

Kubler, Daniel. 2001. Undoing the Link between Local Autonomy and Local Democracy: Recent Tendencies of Metropolitan Governance in Switzerland. Paper presented at the workshop on Local Autonomy and Local Democracy: Exploring the Link, ECPR Joint Sessions, Grenoble, April 6–11.

Kuras, I. 1993. Federatsiia Chy Unitarna Derzhava? *Polityka i Chas* 6 (June): 8.

Kux, Stephan. 1990. *Soviet Federalism: A Comparative Perspective.* Boulder, Colo.: Institute for East-West Security Studies.

Laba, Roman. 1996. How Yeltsin's Exploitation of Ethnic Nationalism Brought Down an Empire. *Transition* 2 (1): 5–13.

Ladner, Andreas. 1998. Direct Democracy on the Local Level: Some Experiences from the City of Zurich. Paper presented at the international seminar on Citizens and City Government: The Role of Municipal Referendum Forms and Experiences in Italy, the United States and Switzerland, Bologna, January 23–24.

1999. Local Parties in Switzerland: An Active Pillar of the Swiss Political System. In *Local Parties in Political and Organizational Perspective*, edited by M. Saiz and H. Geser, pp. 213–41. Boulder, Colo.: Westview Press.

2001. Swiss Political Parties – Between Persistence and Change. *West European Politics* 24 (2): 123–44.

Ladner, Andreas, and Henry Milner. 1999. Do Voters Turn Out More under Proportional Than Majoritarian Systems? The Evidence from Swiss Communal Elections. *Electoral Studies* 18 (2): 235–50.

Laitin, David. 1998. *Identity in Formation: The Russian-Speaking Populations in the Near Abroad*. Ithaca: Cornell University Press.

Lapidus, Gail. 1999. Asymmetrical Federalism and State Breakdown in Russia. *Post-Soviet Affairs* 15 (1): 74–82.

Lapidus, Gail, and Edward W. Walker. 1995. Nationalism, Regionalism, and Federalism: Center-Periphery Relations in Post-Communist Russia. In *The New Russia: Troubled Transformation*, edited by G. W. Lapidus, pp. 79–114. Boulder, Colo.: Westview Press.

Laponce, Jean. 1995. The Institutional Options of the Multi-Ethnic State. Presidential or Parliamentary Regimes? PR or Majority Systems? Referendum or No Referendum? Consensual or Adversary Politics? Federal or Unitary Structures? *Journal of Behavioral and Social Sciences* 2: 51–65.

Lasswell, H. D. 1950. *Who Gets What When How*. New York: Peter Smith.

Latouche, Daniel. 1986. *Canada and Quebec, Past and Future: An Essay*. Toronto: University of Toronto Press.

Le Breton, Michel, and Shlomo Weber. 2000. The Art of Making Everybody Happy: How to Prevent a Secession. Unpublished manuscript.

Leff, Carol. 1988. *National Conflict in Czechoslovakia: The Making and Remaking of a State, 1918–1987*. Princeton: Princeton University Press.

1999. Democratization and Disintegration in Multinational States: The Breakup of the Communist Federations. *World Politics* 51 (2): 205–35.

Lehmbruch, Gerhard. 1976. *Parteienwettbewerb in Bundesstaat*. Stuttgart: Kohlhammer.

1978. Party and Federation in Germany: A Developmental Dilemma. *Government and Opposition* 13 (2): 151–77.

2000. The Institutional Framework: Federalism and Decentralisation in Germany. In *Comparing Public Sector Reform in Britain and Germany: Key Traditions and Trends of Modernisation*, edited by H. Wollmann and E. Schroter, pp. 85–106. Aldershot: Ashgate.

Leigh, Andrew. 2000. Factions and Fractions: A Case Study of Power Politics in the Australian Labor Party. *Australian Journal of Political Science* 35 (3): 427–48.

Lemco, Jonathan. 1991. *Political Stability in Federal Governments*. New York: Praeger.

Lemieux, Vincent. 1978. Quebec: Heaven Is Blue and Hell Is Red. In *Canadian Provincial Politics: The Party Systems of the Ten Provinces*, edited by R. Martin, pp. 248–82. Scarborough: Prentice-Hall of Canada.

Leonard, T. J. 1963. Federalism in India. In *Federalism in the Commonwealth, a Bibliographical Commentary*, edited by W. Livingston, pp. 87–144. London: Published for the Hansard Society by Cassell.

Leonardy, Uwe. 1991. The Working Relationships between Bund and Länder in the Federal Republic of Germany. In *German Federalism Today*, edited by C. Jeffery and P. Savigear, pp. 40–62. London: Leicester University Press.

Leslie, Peter. 1987. *Federal State, National Economy*. Toronto: University of Toronto Press.

Levi, Margaret. 1988. *Of Rule and Revenue*. Berkeley: University of California Press.

Ligachev, Yegor. 1993. *Inside Gorbachev's Kremlin*. New York: Pantheon.

Lijphart, Arendt. 1984. *Democracies: Patterns of Majoritarian and Consensus Government in Twenty-one Countries*. New Haven: Yale University Press.

1987. Bicameralism: Canadian Senate Reform in Comparative Perspective. In *Federalism and the Role of the State*, edited by H. Bakvis and W. M. Chandler, pp. 101–12. Toronto: University of Toronto Press.

1992a. Democratization and Constitutional Choices in Czechoslovakia, Hungary and Poland, 1989–91. *Journal of Theoretical Politics* 4: 207–23.

ed. 1992b. *Parliamentary versus Presidential Government*. Oxford: Oxford University Press.

1994. *Electoral Systems and Party Systems: A Study of Twenty-seven Democracies, 1945–1990*. Oxford: Oxford University Press.

1996. The Puzzle of Indian Democracy: A Consociational Interpretation. *American Political Science Review* 90 (2): 258–68.

1999. *Patterns of Democracy: Government Forms and Performance in Thirty-six Countries*. New Haven: Yale University Press.

Lijphart, Arend, and Bernard Grofman. 1984. *Choosing an Electoral System: Issues and Alternatives*. New York: Praeger.

Lindberg, Leon N., and Stuart A. Scheingold. 1970. *Europe's Would-be Polity: Patterns of Change in the European Community*. Cambridge, Mass.: Harvard University Press.

Linder, W. 1998. *Swiss Democracy: Possible Solutions to Conflict in Multicultural Societies*. New York: Macmillan.

Linder, W., and A. Vatter. 2001. Institutions and Outcomes of Swiss Federalism: The Role of the Cantons in Swiss Politics. *West European Politics* 24 (2): 95–122.

Lipset, Seymour, and Gary Marks. 2000. *It Didn't Happen Here: Why Socialism Failed in the United States*. New York: W. W. Norton.

Livingston, William S. 1952. A Note on the Nature of Federalism. *Political Science Quarterly* 67 (1): 81–95.

Loewenstein, Karl. 1965. *Political Power and the Governmental Process*. Chicago: University of Chicago Press.

Long, Anthony, and F. Quo. 1978. Alberta: Politics of Consensus. In *Canadian Provincial Politics: The Party Systems of the Ten Provinces*, edited by R. Martin, pp. 1–27. Scarborough: Prentice-Hall of Canada.

Lord, Christopher. 1998. Introduction. In *Transnational Parties in the European Union*, edited by C. Lord and D. Bell, pp. 1–9. Aldershot: Ashgate.

Low, Alfred D. 1958. *Lenin on the Question of Nationality*. New York: Bookman Associates.

Lubell, Samuel. 1952. *The Future of American Politics*. New York: Harper.

Lupia, Arthur. 2003. Delegation and Its Perils. In *Delegation and Accountability in Parliamentary Democracies*, edited by K. Strom, W. C. Muller, and T. Bergman. Oxford: Oxford University Press.

Lustick, Ian. 1979. Stability in Deeply Divided Societies: Consociationalism versus Control. *World Politics* 31 (3): 325–44.

Lutz, Donald S. 1988. *The Origins of American Constitutionalism*. Baton Rouge: Louisiana State University Press.

Lynn, Nicholas, and Alexei Novikov. 1997. Re-federalizing Russia: Debates on the Idea of Federalism in Russia. *Publius: The Journal of Federalism* 27 (2): 187–203.

Macmahon, Arthur, ed. 1955. *Federalism, Mature and Emergent*. Garden City, N.Y.: Doubleday.

Maddox, William. 1941. The Political Basis of Federation. *American Political Science Review* 35 (6): 1120–27.

Mainwaring, S. 1993. Presidentialism, Multipartism, and Democracy: The Difficult Combination. *Comparative Political Studies* 26 (2): 198–228.

Mair, Peter. 1999. New Political Parties in Long-Established Party Systems: How Successful Are They? In *Elites, Parties and Democracy: Festschrift for Mogens N. Pedersen*, edited by E. Beukel, K. K. Klausen, and P. E. Mouritzen, pp. 207–24. Odense: Odense University Press.

2000. The Limited Impact of Europe on National Party Systems. *West European Politics* 23 (4): 27–51.

Majone, Giandomenico, ed. 1996. *Regulating Europe*. London: Routledge.

Mallory, J. R. 1954. *Social Credit and the Federal Power in Canada*. Toronto: University of Toronto Press.

Manning, Preston. 1992. *The New Canada*. Toronto: Macmillan Canada.

Manor, James. 1995. Regional Parties in Federal Systems: India in Comparative Perspective. In *Multiple Identities in a Single State*, edited by B. Arora and D. Verney, pp. 105–35. New Delhi: Konarak Publishers.

Marthe, Narud Hanne, and Henry Valen. 2000. Does Background Matter? Social Representation and Political Attitudes. In *Beyond Westminister and Congress: The Nordic Experience*, edited by P. Esaiasson and K. Heidar, pp. 83–106. Columbus: Ohio State University Press.

Mau, Vladimir. 1994. The Ascent of the Inflationists. *Journal of Democracy* 5 (April): 32–35.

McAuley, Alistair. 1997. The Determinants of Russian Federal-Regional Fiscal Relations: Equity or Political Influence? *Europe-Asia Studies* 49 (3): 431–44.

McChesney, Fred S. 1997. *Money for Nothing: Politicians, Rent Extraction, and Political Extortion*. Cambridge, Mass.: Harvard University Press.

McCloskey, Robert G. 1960. *The American Supreme Court*. Chicago: University of Chicago Press.

McCormick, Richard P. 1966. *The Second American Party System*. Chapel Hill: University of North Carolina Press.

McCullough, David. 2001. *John Adams*. New York: Simon and Schuster.

McFaul, Michael. 1995. Why Russia's Politics Matter. *Foreign Affairs* 74 (1): 87–99.

2001. *Russia's Unfinished Revolution: Political Change from Gorbachev to Putin*. Ithaca: Cornell University Press.

McKay, David H. 1996. *Rush to Union: Understanding the European Federal Bargain*. Oxford: Oxford University Press.

1999a. *Federalism and European Union: A Political Economy Perspective*. Oxford: Oxford University Press.

1999b. The Political Sustainability of the European Monetary Union. *British Journal of Political Science* 29: 463–85.

2000. Policy Legitimacy and Institutional Design: Comparative Lessons for the European Union. *Journal of Common Market Studies* 38: 25–44.

2001. *Designing Europe: Comparative Lessons from the Federal Experience*. Oxford: Oxford University Press.

McKelvey, Richard D. 1976. Intransitivities in Multidimensional Voting Models and Some Implications for Agenda Control. *Journal of Economic Theory* 12: 472–82.

McKelvey, Richard, D. and Norman Schofield. 1986. Structural Instability of the Core. *Journal of Mathematical Economics* 15 (December): 179–98.

McKitrick, Eric. 1967. Party Politics and the Union and Confederate War Efforts. In *The American Party System: Stages of Political Development*, edited by W. Chambers and W. Burnham, pp. 35–68. New York: Oxford University Press.

McWhinney, Edward. 1962. *Comparative Federalism: States' Rights and National Power*. Toronto: University of Toronto Press.

1966. *Federal Constitution-Making for a Multi-National World*. Leyden: A. W. Sijthoff.

Meguid, Bonnie. 2001. Competing with the Neophyte: The Role of Mainstream Party Strategy in Rising Party Success. Paper presented at the annual meeting of the American Political Science Association, San Francisco, August 30–September 2.

Meny, Ives, and J. H. H. Weiler, eds. 2000. *What Kind of Constitution for What Kind of Polity? Responses to Joschka Fischer*. Cambridge: European University Institute.

Miller, Gary J., and Thomas Hammond. 1989. Stability and Efficiency in a Separation of Powers Constitutional System. In *The Federalist Papers and the New Institutionalism*, edited by B. Grofman and D. Wittman, pp. 85–99. New York: Agathon Press.

Milward, A. 1992. *The European Rescue of the Nation State*. London: Routledge.

Mitrokhin, Sergei. 1996. Tendency: It's a Rare Governor Who Doesn't Dream of Becoming a Khan. *Obshchaya Gazeta*, no. 44, November 6–13, p. 8.

Moe, Terry M. 1990. Political Institutions: The Neglected Side of the Story. *Journal of Law, Economics and Organization* 6 (2): 213–53.

Moravcsik, Andrew. 1991. Negotiating the Single European Act: National Interests and Conventional Statecraft in the European Community. *International Organization* 45: 17–56.

1994. Why the European Community Strengthens the State: Domestic Politics and International Cooperation. Center for European Studies Working Paper Series, no. 52. Harvard University, Cambridge, Mass.

1998. *The Choice for Europe*. Ithaca: Cornell University Press.

Moravcsik, Andrew, and Kalypso Nicolaidis. 1998. Keynote Article: Federal Ideals and Constitutional Realities in the Treaty of Amsterdam. *Journal of Common Market Studies* 36 (Annual Review Issue): 13–38.

Mudambi, Ram, Pietro Navarra, and Giuseppe Sobbrio, eds. 2001a. *Rules and Reason: Perspectives on Constitutional Political Economy*. Cambridge: Cambridge University Press.

2001b. *Rules, Choice, and Strategy: The Political Economy of Italian Electoral Reform*. Cheltenham: Edward Elgar.

Murray, Don. 1995. *A Democracy of Despots*. Montreal: McGill-Queen's University Press.

Musgrave, Richard. 1959. *The Theory of Public Finance*. New York: McGraw-Hill.

Musil, Jir, ed. 1995. *The End of Czechoslovakia*. Budapest: Central European University Press.

Myagkov, M., and P. C. Ordeshook. 2001. The Trail of Votes in Russia's 1999 Duma and 2000 Presidential Elections. *Communist and Postcommunist Studies* 34 (3): 353–70.

Nardulli, Peter F. 1992. The Constitution in American Politics. In *The Constitution and American Political Development*, edited by Peter F. Nardulli, pp. 3–34. Urbana: University of Illinois Press.

Neustadt, Richard E. 1960. *Presidential Power, the Politics of Leadership*. New York: Wiley.

Newell, James. 1998. At the Start of a Journey: Steps on the Road to Decentralization. In *Italian Politics: Mapping the Future*, edited by L. Bardi and M. Rhodes, pp. 149–67. Boulder, Colo.: Westview Press.

Nichols, Roy. 1967. *The Invention of the American Political Parties*. New York: Macmillan.

Niedermayer, Oskar, and Richard Sinnott, eds. 1995. *Public Opinion and Internationalized Governance*. Oxford: Oxford University Press.

Nikonov, V. 1996. Presidential Election and State Power (in Russian). *NG*, February 21, 1996.

Niou, Emerson, and Peter C. Ordeshook. 1985. Universalism in Congress. *American Journal of Political Science* 29 (2): 246–58.

1998. Alliances versus Federations: An Extension of Riker's Analysis of Federal Formation. *Constitutional Political Economy* 9 (4): 271.

Norris, Pippa. 1995. The Politics of Electoral Reform. *International Political Science Review* 16 (1): 65–78.

2002. Ballots Not Bullets: Testing Consociational Theories of Ethnic Conflict, Electoral Systems, and Democratization. In *The Architecture of Democracy: Institutional Design, Conflict Management, and Democracy in the Late Twentieth Century*, edited by Andrew Reynolds, pp. 206–47. Oxford: Oxford University Press.

North, Douglass. 1990. *Institutions, Institutional Change, and Economic Performance: Political Economy of Institutions and Decisions*. Cambridge: Cambridge University Press.

Oates, Wallace E. 1972. *Fiscal Federalism*. New York: Harcourt Brace Jovanovich.

Olson, M., and R. Zeckhauser. 1966. An Economic Theory of Alliances. *Review of Economics and Statistics* 48 (3): 266–79.

Ordeshook, Peter C. 1992. Constitutional Stability. *Constitutional Political Economy* 3 (2): 137–75.

1993. Some Rules of Constitutional Design. In *Liberalism and the Economic Order*, edited by E. F. Paul, F. D. Miller, and J. Paul, pp. 198–232. Cambridge: Cambridge University Press.

1995. Institutions and Incentives. *Journal of Democracy* 6 (2): 46–60.

1996. Russia's Party System: Is Russian Federalism Viable? *Post-Soviet Affairs* 12 (3): 145–217.

2002. Are "Western" Constitutions Relevant to Anything Other Than the Countries They Serve? *Constitutional Political Economy* 13 (1): 3–24.

Ordeshook, Peter C., and Olga Shvetsova. 1994. Ethnic Heterogeneity, District Magnitude, and the Number of Parties. *American Journal of Political Science* 38 (1): 100–23.

1997. Federalism and Constitutional Design. *Journal of Democracy* 8 (1): 27–42.

Ordeshook, Peter C., and L. Zeng. 1994. Some Properties of Hare Voting with Strategic Voters. *Public Choice* 78 (1): 87.

Orttung, Robert. 2001. Putin's Federal Reform Package: A Recipe for Unchecked Kremlin Power. *Demokratizatsiya* 9 (3): 341–9.

Osaghae, Eghosa. 1994. Interstate Relations in Nigeria. *Publius: The Journal of Federalism* 24 (4): 83–99.

Ostrom, Vincent. 1991. *The Meaning of American Federalism: Constituting a Self-Governing Society*. San Francisco: ICS Press.

Overacker, Louise. 1949. The Australian Labor Party. *American Political Science Review* 43 (4): 677–703.

1952. *The Australian Party System*. New Haven: Yale University Press.

Pai, Sudha. 1998. The Indian Party System under Transformation: Lok Sabha Elections, 1998. *Asian Survey* 38 (9): 836–52.

Palmer, Norman. 1973. Elections and the Political System in India: The 1972 State Assembly Elections and After. *Pacific Affairs* 45 (4): 535–55.

Paltiel, K. 1970. *Political Party Financing in Canada*. Toronto: McGraw-Hill.

Paretskaya, Anna. 1996. Regional Governors Could Offset the "Red Duma." *Transition* 2 (4): 34–35, 64.

Parikh, Sunita, and Barry Weingast. 1997. A Comparative Theory of Federalism: India. *Virginia Law Review* 83 (7): 1593–1615.

Parker, Arthur C. 1916. *The Constitution of the Five Nations*. Ontario, Canada: Iroqrafts.

Patapan, Haig. 2000. Politics of Interpretation. *Sydney Law Review* 22 (4): 247–72.

Patterson, S. C., and Anthony Mughan, eds. 1999. *Senates: Bicameralism in the Contemporary World*. Columbus: Ohio State University Press.

Perlman, Selig. 1928. *A Theory of the Labor Movement*. New York: Macmillan.

Persson, Torsten, and Guido Tabellini. 1996a. Federal Fiscal Constitutions: Risk Sharing and Moral Hazard. *Econometrica* 64 (May): 623–46.

1996b. Federal Fiscal Constitutions: Risk Sharing and Redistribution. *Journal of Political Economy* 104 (5): 979–1009.

Pierson, Paul. 1996. The Path to European Integration: A Historical Institutionalist Analysis. *Comparative Political Studies* 29 (2): 123–63.

Piris, Jean-Claude. 2000. Does the European Union Have a Constitution? Does It Need One? Harvard Jean Monnet Working Paper 5/00. Cambridge, Mass.

Polishchuk, Leonid. 1996. Russian Federalism: Economic Reform and Political Behavior. Social Science Working Paper, no. 972. California Institute of Technology, Division of Humanities and Social Sciences, Pasadena, California.

1998. The Russian Model of Negotiated Federalism (Political-Economic Analysis). *Problems of Economic Transition* 41 (7–8): 3–29.

Porter, David M. 1960. Jefferson Davis and the Political Factors in Confederate Defeat. In *Why the North Won the Civil War*, edited by D. Donald, pp. 79–90. Baton Rouge: Louisiana State University Press.

Posner, Eric A. 2000. *Law and Social Norms*. Cambridge, Mass.: Harvard University Press.

Posner, Richard A. 1971. Taxation by Regulation. *Bell Journal of Economics and Management Science* 2 (1): 22–50.

Powell, Bingham. 2000. *Elections as Instruments of Democracy*. New Haven: Yale University Press.

Prakash, S., and J. Yoo. 2001. The Puzzling Persistence of Process-Based Federalism Theories. *Texas Law Review* 79 (6): 1459–1524.

Proctor, Jesse Harris. 1963. Federalism in the West Indies. In *Federalism in the Commonwealth, a Bibliographical Commentary*, edited by W. S. Livingston. London: Published for the Hansard Society by Cassell.

Proudhon, P. J., and Richard Vernon. 1979. *The Principle of Federation*. Toronto: University of Toronto Press.

Przeworski, Adam. 1991. *Democracy and the Market*. Cambridge: Cambridge University Press.

Qian, Yingyi, and Barry R. Weingast. 1997. Federalism as a Commitment to Preserving Market Incentives. *Journal of Economic Perspectives* 11 (4): 83–92.

Quintal, David. 1970. The Theory of Electoral Systems. *Western Political Quarterly* 73: 752–53.

Ra'anan, Uri. 1990. The Nation-State Fallacy. In *Conflict and Peacemaking in Multiethnic Societies*, edited by J. V. Montville, pp. 5–19. New York: Lexington.

Ra'anan, Uri, and John Pearson Roche. 1980. *Ethnic Resurgence in Modern Democratic States: A Multi-Disciplinary Approach to Human Resources and Conflict*. New York: Pergamon Press.

Rabushka, Alvin, and Kenneth A. Shepsle. 1972. *Politics in Plural Societies: A Theory of Democratic Instability*. Columbus: Merrill.

Rae, Douglas W. 1967. *The Political Consequences of Electoral Laws*. New Haven: Yale University Press.

Ray, Leonard. 1999. Measuring Party Orientations towards European Integration: Results from an Expert Survey. *European Journal of Political Research* 36: 283–306.

Rector, Chad. 2001. The Australian Transition from International Organization to Federal Union: Some Implications for the Study of the European Union. Paper presented at the annual meeting of the American Political Science Association, San Francisco, August 30–September 2.

Reid, G. S., and Martyn Forrest. 1989. *Australia's Commonwealth Parliament, 1901–1988: Ten Perspectives*. Carlton: Melbourne University Press.

Reif, K., and O. Niedermayer. 1987. The European Parliament and Political Parties. *Journal of European Integration* 10 (2): 157–72.

Reilly, Benjamin. 2002. Electoral Systems for Divided Societies. *Journal of Democracy* 13 (2): 156–70.

Reilly, Benjamin, and Andrew Reynolds. 1999. Electoral Systems and Conflict in Divided Societies. Papers on International Conflict Resolution No. 2. Committee on International Conflict Resolution Commission on Behavioral and Social Sciences and Education. National Research Council. Washington, D.C.: National Academy Press.

Remington, Thomas, and Steven Smith. 1996. Political Goals, Institutional Context, and the Choice of an Electoral System: The Russian Parliamentary Election Law. *American Journal of Political Science* 40: 1253–79.

Remington, Thomas, Steven Smith, and Moshe Haspel. 1998. Decrees, Laws, and Inter-Branch Relations in the Russian Federation. *Post-Soviet Affairs* 14: 287–322.

Renzsch, Wolfgang. 2001. Bifurcated and Integrated Parties in Parliamentary Federations: The Canadian and German Cases. IIGR Queen's University Working Paper 4.

Resnick, Philip. 2000. *The Politics of Resentment: British Columbia Regionalism and Canadian Unity*. Vancouver: University of British Columbia Press.

Riker, William H. 1955. The Senate and American Federalism. *American Political Science Review* 49 (2): 452–69.

1962. *The Theory of Political Coalitions*. New Haven: Yale University Press.

1964. *Federalism: Origin, Operation, Significance*. Boston: Little Brown.

1980. Implications from the Disequilibrium of Majority Rule for the Study of Institutions. *American Political Science Review* 74 (2): 432–46.

1982. *Liberalism against Populism: A Confrontation between the Theory of Democracy and the Theory of Social Choice*. San Francisco: W. H. Freeman.

1986. *The Art of Political Manipulation*. New Haven: Yale University Press.

1992. The Merits of Bicameralism. *International Review of Law and Economics* 12 (2): 166–68.

1995. The Experience of Creating Constitutions: The Framing of the United States Constitution. In *Explaining Social Institutions*, edited by J. Knight and I. Sened. Ann Arbor: University of Michigan Press.

1996. *The Strategy of Rhetoric: Campaigning for the Ratification of the Constitution*. New Haven: Yale University Press.

Riker, William H., and Jonathan Lemco. 1987. The Relations between Structure and Stability. In *The Development of American Federalism*, edited by W. Riker, pp. 113–34. Boston: Kluwer Academic Publishers.

Riker, William H., and Peter C. Ordeshook. 1973. *An Introduction to Positive Political Theory*. Englewood-Cliffs, N.J.: Prentice-Hall.

Rodden, Jonathan. 2001. Creating a More Perfect Union: Electoral Incentives and the Reform of Federal Systems. Unpublished manuscript.

Rodden, Jonathan, and Susan Rose-Ackerman. 1997. Does Federalism Preserve Markets? *Virginia Law Review* 83 (7): 1521–72.

Roeder, Philip. 1991. Soviet Federalism and Ethnic Mobilization. *World Politics* 43 (2): 196–232.

1993. *Red Sunset: The Failure of Soviet Politics*. Princeton: Princeton University Press.

2000. The Robustness of Institutions in Ethnically Plural Societies. Presented at the annual meeting of the American Political Science Association, Washington, D.C., August–September.

Romanow, Roy, John Whyte, and Howard Leeson, 1984. *Canada, Notwithstanding: The Making of the Constitution, 1976–1982*. Toronto: Carswell and Methuen.

Rometsch, D., and W. Wessels. 1996. *The European Union and Member States: Towards Institutional Fusion?* Manchester: Manchester University Press.

Rose Ackerman, Susan. 1981. Does Federalism Matter? Political Choice in a Federal Republic. *Journal of Political Economy* 89 (1): 152–65.

Ross, George. 1998 French Social Democracy and the EMU. ARENA Working Papers 19. Oslo.

Ross, George. 2001. French Social Democracy and EMU: Presidential Prose and Its Pitfalls. In *Social Democracy and Monetary Union*, edited by T. Notermans, pp. 21–46. New York: Berghahn Books.

Rossiter, Clinton. 1960. *Parties and Politics in America*. Ithaca: Cornell University Press.

Rowe, Nicholas. 1989. *Rules and Institutions*. Ann Arbor: University of Michigan Press.

Rowley, Charles K., Robert D. Tollison, and Gordon Tullock. 1988. *The Political Economy of Rent Seeking*. Boston: Kluwer Academic Publishers.

Roy, Ramashray. 1967. Congress Defeat in Farrukhabad: A Failure of Party Organization. In *Party System and Election Studies*, edited by R. Kothari, pp. 119–216. Bombay: Allied Publishers.

Rudolph, Susanne Hoeber, and Lloyd I. Rudolph. 2002. New Dimensions of Indian Democracy. *Journal of Democracy* 13 (1): 52–66.

Rutland, Peter, ed. 2001. *Business and State in Contemporary Russia*. Boulder, Colo.: Westview Press.

Rychlik, Jan. 1995. National Consciousness and the Common State: A Historical-Ethnological Analysis. In *The End of Czechoslovakia*, edited by J. Musil, pp. 97–105. Budapest: Central European University Press.

Saiz, Martin, and Hans Geser, eds. 1999. *Local Parties in Political and Organizational Perspective*. Boulder: Colo.: Westview Press.

Sandholtz, W., and J. Zysman. 1989. 1992: Recasting the European Bargain. *World Politics* 42 (1): 95–126.

Satterthwaite, Mark A. 1975. Strategyproofness and Arrow's Conditions: Existence and Correspondence Theorems for Voting Procedures and Social Welfare Functions. *Journal of Economic Theory* 10 (2): 187–217.

Saunders, Cheryl. 2001. The Parliament as Partner: A Century of Constitutional Review. In *Parliament: The Vision and Hindsight*, edited by G. Lindell and R. Bennett, pp. 454–85. Sidney: Federation Press.

Sawer, Geoffrey. 1967. *Australian Federalism in the Courts*. Melbourne: Melbourne University Press.

Sbragia, Alberta M. 1993. The European Community: A Balancing Act. *Publius: The Journal of Federalism* 23 (3): 23–38.

Scharpf, Fritz. 1988. The Joint-Decision Trap: Lessons from German Federalism and European Integration. *Public Administration* 66: 239–78.

1995. Federal Arrangements and Multi-Party System. *Australian Journal of Political Science* 30: 27–39.

1999. *Governing in Europe: Effective and Democratic?* Oxford: Oxford University Press.

Schattschneider, E. E. 1942. *Party Government*. New York: Farrar and Rinehart.

Schmitt, Hermann, and Jacques Thomassen, eds. 1999. *Political Representation and Legitimacy in the European Union*. Oxford: Oxford University Press.

2000. Dynamic Representation: The Case of European Integration. *European Union Politics* 1: 319–40.

Schofield, Norman. 2000. Constitutional Quandaries and Critical Elections. Center in Political Economy, Washington University, St. Louis. WP 212.

2002. Evolution of the Constitution. *British Journal of Political Science* 32 (1): 1–20.

Schuttemeyer, Suzanne. 2001. Parliamentary Parties in the German Bundestag. *German Issues* 24: 1–54.

Schwartz, Thomas. 1977. Collective Choice, Separation of Issues, and Vote Trading. *American Political Science Review* 71: 999–1010.

1995. The Paradox of Representation. *Journal of Politics* 57 (2): 309–23.

1999. The Executive Veto: Purpose, Procedure, and Paradox. *Constitutional Political Economy* 10 (1): 89–106.

Sened, Itai. 1995. A Political Theory of the Evolution of Rights: A Game Theoretic Approach. In *Explaining Social Institutions*, edited by Jack Knight and Itai Sened. Ann Arbor: University of Michigan Press.

Shamir, Michael. 1985. Changes in Electoral Systems as "Interventions": Another Test of Duverger's Hypothesis. *European Journal of Political Research* 13: 1–10.

Sharlet, Robert. 1992. *Soviet Constitutional Crisis from De-Stalinization to Disintegration*. Armonk, N.Y.: M. E. Sharpe.

1994. The Prospects for Federalism in Russian Constitutional Politics. *Publius: The Journal of Federalism* 24 (2): 115–28.

Sharma, Brij Mohan. 1953. *Federalism in Theory and Practice*. Chandausi: Bhargava.

Sharman. 1990. The Party Systems of the Australian States. *Publius: The Journal of Federalism* 20 (4): 84–104.

Sharp, James. 1993. *American Politics in the Early Republic: The New Nation in Crisis*. New Haven: Yale University Press.

Shaw, Denis. 1992. Russian Federation Treaty Signed. *Post-Soviet Geography* 6 (June): 414–17.

Sheehy, Ann. 1993. Russia's Republics: A Threat to Its Territorial Integrity? *RFE/RL Research Report* 2 (20): 34–40.

Shleifer, Andrei, and Daniel Treisman. 2000. *Without a Map: Political Tactics and Economic Reform in Russia*. Cambridge, Mass.: MIT Press.

Shugart, Matthew. 1992. Electoral Reform in Systems of Proportional Representation. *European Journal of Political Research* 21: 207–224.

1995. The Electoral Cycle and Institutional Sources of Divided Government. *American Political Science Review* 89 (June): 327–43.

1998. The Inverse Relationship between Party Strength and Executive Strength: A Theory of Politicians' Constitutional Choices. *British Journal of Political Science* 28 (1): 1–29.

Shugart, Matthew, and John M. Carey. 1992. *Presidents and Assemblies: Constitutional Design and Electoral Dynamics*. Cambridge: Cambridge University Press.

Shvetsova, Olga. 2003a. Resolving the Problem of Pre-Election Coordination: The Parliamentary Election as an Elite Presidential Primary. In *Elections, Parties and the Future of Russia*, edited by V. Hesli and W. Reisinger. Cambridge: Cambridge University Press.

2003b. Endogenous Selection of Institutions and Their Exogenous Effects. *Constitutional Political Economy*.

Simeon, Richard. 1972. *Federal-Provincial Diplomacy: The Making of Recent Policy in Canada*. Toronto: University of Toronto Press.

Simon, Yves. 1973. A Note on Proudhon's Federalism. *Publius: The Journal of Federalism* 3 (1): 19–30.

Skilling, H. Gordon. 1976. *Czechoslovakia's Interrupted Revolution*. Princeton: Princeton University Press.

Slider, Darrell. 2001. Russia's Governors and Party Formation. In *Contemporary Russian Politics – A Reader*, edited by A. Brown, pp. 224–34. Oxford: Oxford University Press.

Smiley, Donald. 1962. The Rowell-Sirois Report, Provincial Autonomy, and Post-War Canadian Federalism. *Canadian Journal of Economics and Political Science* 28: 54–69.

1972. *Canada in Question: Federalism in the Seventies*. Toronto: McGraw-Hill Ryerson.

Smith, Graham, ed. 1990. *The Nationalities Question in the Soviet Union*. New York: Longman.

ed. 1995. *Federalism: The Multiethnic Challenge*. London: Longman.

Snyder, Jack. 2000. *From Voting to Violence: Democratization and Nationalist Conflict*. New York: W. W. Norton.

Snyder, James M., and Michael M. Ting. 2002. An Informational Rationale for Political Parties. *American Journal of Political Science* 46 (1): 90–110.

Solchanyk, Roman. 1994. The Politics of State Building: Center-Periphery Relations in Post-Soviet Ukraine. *Europe-Asia Studies* 46 (1): 47–68.

Solnick, Steven. 1995. Federal Bargaining in Russia. *East European Constitutional Review* 4 (4): 52–58.

1998. *Stealing the State*. Cambridge, Mass.: Harvard University Press.

2002. Big Deals: Territorial Politics and the Fate of the Russian Federation. Unpublished manuscript.

Solozabal, Juan Jose. 1996. Spain: A Federation in the Making? In *Federalizing Europe? The Costs, Benefits, and Preconditions of Federal Political Systems*, edited by J. Hesse and V. Wright, pp. 260–3. Oxford: Oxford University Press.

Spence, Jacqueline. 1998. The European Union: A View from the Top. Top Decision Makers and the European Union. Report prepared for EOS Gallup Europe. Available at <http:www.europa.eu.int/comm/public_opinion/archives/top/top.pdf>.

Springer, Hugh W. 1962. Federation in the Caribbean: An Attempt That Failed. *International Organization* 16 (4): 758–75.

Stanley, G. 1969. *A Short History of the Canadian Constitution*. Toronto: Ryerson Press.

Stein, David. 2001. Canada: The Cities Look for More Power. *Federations* 2 (1): 7–8.

Stein, Eric. 1997. *Czecho-Slovakia: Ethnic Conflict, Constitutional Fissure, Negotiated Breakup*. Ann Arbor: University of Michigan Press.

Stepan, Alfred. 1999. Federalism and Democracy: Beyond the U.S. Model. *Journal of Democracy* 10 (4): 19–34.

2000. Russian Federalism in Comparative Perspective. *Post-Soviet Affairs* 16 (2): 133–76.

Stevens, Bron, and Patrick Weller. 1976. *The Australian Labor Party and Federal Politics: A Documentary Survey*. Carlton: Melbourne University Press.

Stigler, George J. 1971. The Theory of Economic Regulation. *Bell Journal of Economics and Management Science* 2 (1): 3–21.

Stokes, Susan. 1999. Political Parties and Democracy. *Annual Reviews of Political Science* 2: 243–67.

Stolz, Klaus. 2000. The Regional Political Class in Comparative Perspective: Career Patterns in Western Democracies. Paper presented at the triennial congress of the IPSA, Quebec City, August 1–5.

Stone Sweet, A., and W. Sandholtz. 1998. Integration, Supranational Governance and the Institutionalization of the European Polity. In *European Integration and Supranational Governance*, edited by W. Sandholtz and A. Stone Sweet, pp. 1–26. Oxford: Oxford University Press.

Stoner-Weiss, Kathryn. 1999. Central Weakness and Provincial Autonomy: Observations on the Devolution Process in Russia. *Post-Soviet Affairs* 15 (1): 87–106.

Stranger, Allison K. 1996. Czechoslovakia's Dissolution as an Unintended Consequence of the Velvet Constitutional Revolution. *East European Constitutional Review* 5 (Fall): 40–46.

Strom, Kaare. 2003. Parliamentary Democracy and Delegation. In *Delegation and Accountability in Parliamentary Democracies*, edited by K. Strom, W. C. Muller, and T. Bergman. Oxford: Oxford University Press.

Sunstein, Cass. 1991. Constitutionalism and Secession. *University of Chicago Law Review* 58: 633–70.

Suny, Ronald. 1994. *The Revenge of the Past: Nationalism, Revolution, and the Collapse of the Soviet Union*. Stanford: Stanford University Press.

Taagepera, Rein, and Matthew Shugart. 1989. *Seats and Votes: The Effects and Determinants of Electoral Systems*. New Haven: Yale University Press.

Taggart, Paul. 1998. A Touchstone of Dissent: Euroscepticism in Contemporary Western European Party Systems. *European Journal of Political Research* 33: 363–88.

Taggart, Paul, and Aleks Szczerbiak. 2001. Crossing Europe: Patterns of Contemporary Party-Based Euroscepticism in EU Member States and the Candidate States of Central and Eastern Europe. Paper presented at the annual meeting of the American Political Science Association, San Francisco, August 29–September 2.

Tarlton, Charles. 1965. Symmetry and Asymmetry as Elements of Federalism: A Theoretical Speculations. *Journal of Politics* 27 (4): 861–74.

Taylor, Michael. 1976. *Anarchy and Cooperation*. New York: Wiley.

1987. *The Possibility of Cooperation*. Cambridge: Cambridge University Press.

Taylor, Paul. 1983. *The Limits of European Integration*. New York: Columbia University Press.

Thomas, Schwartz. 1986. *The Logic of Collective Choice*. New York: Columbia University Press.

Thorburn, Hugh, and Alan Whitehorn, eds. 2001. *Party Politics in Canada*. Toronto: Prentice-Hall.

Tiebout, Charles. 1956. A Pure Theory of Local Expenditures. *Journal of Political Economy* 64 (5): 416–24.

Tocqueville, Alexis de. 1955. *The Old Regime and the French Revolution*. Garden City, N.Y.: Doubleday.

Todd, Emmanuel. 1979. *The Final Fall: An Essay on the Decomposition of the Soviet Sphere*. New York: Karz Publishers.

Tolz, Vera, and Irina Basygina. 1997. Regional Governors and the Kremlin. *Communist and Post-Communist Studies* 30 (4): 401–26.

Treisman, Daniel. 1997. Russia's "Ethnic Revival": The Separatist Activism of Regional Leaders in a Post Communist Order. *World Politics* 49 (2): 212–49.

1999. Political Decentralization and Economic Reform: A Game-Theoretic Analysis. *American Journal of Political Science* 43 (2): 488–517.

Truman, David. 1955. Federalism and the Party System. In *Federalism, Mature and Emergent*, edited by A. Macmahon, pp. 115–36. Garden City, N.Y.: Doubleday.

Tsebelis, George. 1991. *Nested Games: Rational Choice in Comparative Politics.* Berkeley: University of California Press.

2002. *Veto Players: How Political Institutions Work.* Princeton: Princeton University Press.

Tsebelis, George, and Jeannette Money. 1997. *Bicameralism.* Cambridge: Cambridge University Press.

Tullock, Gordon. 1987. The Calculus: Postscript after 25 Years. *Cato Journal* 7 (2): 313–21.

Uslaner, Eric. 2000. Strong Institutions, Weak Parties: The Paradox of Canadian Political Parties. Unpublished manuscript.

Valen, Henry, Hanne Marthe Narud, and Olafur Hardarsson. 2000. Geographical Representation. In *Beyond Westminister and Congress: The Nordic Experience*, edited by P. Esaiasson and K. Heidar, pp. 107–31. Columbus: Ohio State University Press.

Van der Eijk, Cees, and Mark Franklin, eds. 1996. *Choosing Europe? The European Electorate and National Politics in the Face of Union.* Ann Arbor: University of Michigan Press.

Varshney, Ashutosh. 2000. Is India Becoming More Democratic? *Journal of Asian Studies* 59 (1): 3–25.

Verney, Douglas. 1995. Federalism, Federative Systems, and Federations. *Publius: The Journal of Federalism* 25 (2): 81–97.

Vile, John. 1991. *Rewriting the United States Constitution: An Examination of Proposals from Reconstruction to the Present.* New York: Praeger.

Vile, M. 1957. Judicial Review and Politics in Australia. *American Political Science Review* 51 (2): 386–91.

Voigt, Stefan. 1999. *Explaining Constitutional Change: A Positive Economics Approach.* Cheltenham: Edward Elgar.

Walker, Edward W. 1996. The Dog That Didn't Bark: Tatarstan and Asymmetrical Federalism in Russia. *Harriman Review* 9: 41–35.

Wallace, William. 1983. Less Than a Federation, More Than a Regime: The Community as a Political System. In *Policy-Making in the European Communities*, edited by H. Wallace and W. Wallace, pp. 401–22. Chichester: Wiley.

Wallich, Christine, ed. 1994. *Russia and the Challenge of Fiscal Federalism.* Washington, D.C.: World Bank.

Ware, R. B., and Enver Kisriev. 2001. Ethnic Parity and Democratic Pluralism in Dagestan: A Consociational Approach. *Europe-Asia Studies* 53 (1): 105–31.

Warleigh, Alexander. 1998. Better the Devil You Know? Synthetic and Confederal Understandings of European Unification. *West European Politics* 21 (3): 1–19.

Wattenberg, Martin. 1991. *The Rise of Candidate Centered Politics.* Cambridge, Mass.: Harvard University Press.

Watts, Ronald L. 1966. *New Federations: Experiments in the Commonwealth*. Oxford: Clarendon.
1970. *Administration in Federal Systems*. London: Hutchinson Educational.
Weaver, R. K. 1992. *The Collapse of Canada?* Washington, D.C.: Brookings Institution.
2002. Electoral Rules and the Governability of Federations. *Journal of Democracy* 13 (2): 111–25.
Weaver, R. K., and B. A. Rockman. 1993. Assessing the Effects of Institutions. In *Do Institutions Matter? Government Capabilities in the United States and Abroad*, edited by R. K. Weaver and B. A. Rockman, pp. 1–41. Washington, D.C.: Brookings Institution.
Wechsler, Herbert. 1954. The Political Safeguards of Federalism: The Role of the States in the Composition and Selection of the National Government. *Columbia Law Review* 54: 543–60.
Weeks, A. L. 1989. *The Soviet Nomenklatura: A Comprehensive Roster of Soviet Civilian and Military Officials*. Washington, D.C.: Washington Institute Press.
Weiler, John. 1997. The Reformation of European Constitutionalism. *Journal of Common Market Studies* 35 (1): 97–131.
Weiner, Myron. 1956. Struggle against Power: Notes on Indian Political Behavior. *World Politics* 8 (3): 392–403.
1967. *Party Building in a New Nation: The Indian National Congress*. Chicago: University of Chicago Press.
Weingast, Barry R. 1995. A Rational Choice Perspective on the Role of Ideas: Shared Belief Systems and State Sovereignty in International Cooperation. *Politics and Society* 23 (December): 449–64.
Weisskirchen, Gert. 1994. The Ukraine at the Crossroads. *Aussenpolitik* 4: 331.
Wheare, K. C. 1946. *Federal Government*. London: Oxford University Press.
1953. *Federal Government*. London: Oxford University Press.
White, Randall. 1990. *Voice of Regions: The Long Journey to Senate Reform in Canada*. Toronto: Dundurn Press Limited.
Whitefield, Stephen. 2001. Partisan and Party Divisions in Post-Communist Russia. In *Contemporary Russian Politics – A Reader*, edited by A. Brown, pp. 235–46. Oxford: Oxford University Press.
Wibbels, Eric. 2000. Federalism and the Politics of Macroeconomic Policy and Performance. *American Journal of Political Science* 44 (4): 687–702.
Wilson, James. 1993. Speech before the Pennsylvania Ratifying Convention, November 24, 1787. In *The Debate on the Constitution*, edited by Bernard Bailyn, 1: 791–803. New York: Library of America.
Wilson, Woodrow. 1911. *Constitutional Government in the United States*. New York: Columbia University Press.
Wimmer, Andreas. 2002. *Nationalist Exclusion and Ethnic Conflict: Shadows of Modernity*. Cambridge: Cambridge University Press.
Wincott, Daniel. 1996. Federalism and the European Union: The Scope and Limits of the Treaty of Maastricht. *International Political Science Review* 17 (October): 403–15.
Wolchik, Sharon. 1994. The Politics of Ethnicity in Post-Communist Czechoslovakia. *East European Politics and Societies* 8 (1): 153–88.

1995. The Politics of Transition and the Break-Up of Czechoslovakia. In *The End of Czechoslovakia*, edited by J. Musil, pp. 225–44. Budapest: Central European University Press.

Wolczuk, Kasia. 2002. Catching up with "Europe"? Constitutional Debates on the Territorial-Administrative Model in Independent Ukraine. *Regional and Federal Studies* 12 (2): 65–88.

Wood, G. 1969. *The Creation of the American Republic.* Chapel Hill: University of North Carolina Press.

Woods, Dwayne. 1992. The Center No Longer Holds: The Rise of Regional Leagues in Italian Politics. *West European Politics* 15 (2): 56–76.

World Bank. 1999. *Entering the 21st Century: World Development Report.* Oxford: Oxford University Press.

Yeltsin, Boris Nikolayevich, and Catherine Fitzpatrick. 1994. *The Struggle for Russia.* New York: Belka Publications Corp. and Times Books.

Young, Ernest. 1999. State Sovereign Immunity and the Future of Federalism. *Supreme Court Review* 1: 1–79.

Young, Peyton. 1994. *Equity in Theory and Practice.* Princeton: Princeton University Press.

Ziblatt, Daniel. 2001. Just How Powerful Are Ideas? The Failed Push for Fiscal Decentralization and the Persistence of Germany's Federal System. Paper presented at the annual meeting of the American Political Science Association, San Francisco, August 30–September 2.

Zimmerman, Joseph F. 1996. *Interstate Relations: The Neglected Dimension of Federalism.* Westport, Conn.: Praeger.

Zines, Leslie. 1997. *The High Court and the Constitution.* Sydney: Butterworths.

Name Index

Subject Index